SUPERVISION IN ACTION
The Art of Managing Others

Fourth Edition

SUPERVISION IN ACTION
The Art of Managing Others

Fourth Edition

Claude S. George, Jr.

University of North Carolina at Chapel Hill

Reston Publishing Company, Inc.
A Prentice-Hall Company
Reston, Virginia

Library of Congress Cataloging in Publication Data

George, Claude S.
    Supervision in action.

    1. Supervision of employees.   I. Title.
HF5549.G427   1985   658.3'02   84-13397
ISBN 0-8359-7160-0

Cartoons by Bruce Bolinger

10   9   8   7   6   5   4   3   2   1

PRINTED IN THE UNITED STATES OF AMERICA

CONTENTS

Preface, vii

Part I   **THE CHALLENGE OF SUPERVISION**
Chapter **1**   What a Supervisor Does, 3
Chapter **2**   Leading and Supervising Others, 25
Chapter **3**   Using Time Wisely, 41
Chapter **4**   The Big Job: Communications, 63

Part II   **PEOPLE PROBLEMS**
Chapter **5**   Getting Your Employees Motivated, 91
Chapter **6**   Putting Human Relations to Work, 109
Chapter **7**   The Supervisor and Morale, 129
Chapter **8**   You, Unions, and Public Policy, 143
Chapter **9**   How to Handle Discipline and Settle Grievances, 161

Part III   **SUPERVISORY SKILLS**
Chapter **10**   How to Solve Problems and Make Decisions, 181
Chapter **11**   How to Plan and Lead a Meeting, 199
Chapter **12**   How to Supervise Special Employees, 217
Chapter **13**   How to Use Planning Tools for Better Management, 237
Chapter **14**   How to Use Management by Objectives, 257

Part IV   **GETTING THE JOB DONE**
Chapter **15**   How Organization Helps You Supervise, 269
Chapter **16**   How Your Personnel Department Helps, 297
Chapter **17**   Interviewing, Orienting, and Training Employees, 311
Chapter **18**   How to Use Performance Evaluation, 333
Chapter **19**   How to Simplify Work and Increase Production, 353
Chapter **20**   How to Measure Work, 379
Chapter **21**   How to Convince Management to Buy New Equipment, 397

Glossary, 411
Index, 417

PREFACE

This book deals with what a supervisor is and does. Whether you are a manager involved in the challenging process of supervising others, or a potential supervisor who will someday be responsible for the work of others, this text is written to help you.

As a potential supervisor, you will be acquainted with the overall scope of your job, introduced to some of the many problems you will face, and offered practical advice on how to solve these problems. Written in a direct, easy-to-read and easy-to-understand manner, this text assumes no prior training or knowledge of the subject.

In today's complex business world, practicing supervisors recognize the need to gain new insights into directing the efforts of others. This book will help them achieve this objective by providing them a clear and effective approach to understanding and dealing with such areas as motivating employees, using time wisely, management by objectives, communicating ideas, unions and public policy, making decisions, handling discipline, and supervising special employees. Covering these and other areas, the text takes the supervisor step by step through the rough spots of supervision, giving helpful hints and positive actions to take.

Ideas and materials for this text came from many sources—from my own personal supervisory experience in industry, from the experiences of practicing supervisors and administrators, from the stimulating discussions that emerged from the supervisory development programs I have been involved in at the University of North Carolina at Chapel Hill, and from the research and publications of numerous scholars. To attempt to acknowledge each one here would be impractical. I would, however, like to express my appreciation to Art Asbury, James W. Bishop, Rick Bradstreet, Dick Brigham, Vincent G. Bush, Paul de Benedictis, Jack Graham, James L. Hyck, W. J. Jacobs, Joseph L. Massie, Susan D. Neal, Karl F. Simpson, William N. Smith, Dan R. Turner, and Theodore Zaner. Their ideas have made this a better book, and to each I am grateful.

Finally, I am indebted to my wife, who encouraged me in this endeavor and shielded me from distractions as this volume took shape.

Claude S. George, Jr.

PART ONE
THE CHALLENGE OF SUPERVISION

1

WHAT A
SUPERVISOR DOES

This chapter explains—

- What you will do as a supervisor
- The skills and qualities you will need
- What your functions and responsibilities will be

The key to success for any business is good supervision. On the national scene, it is the single most important factor in the success of our American economy. In fact, good supervision has enabled us to more than double our national output during the past twenty years. It has helped us produce a staggering array of new products every year—new homes, new automobiles, new drugs, new clothing, new tools, new TVs, and so on. And how have good supervisors done all this through good supervision? By wisely directing the efforts of others, by wisely using the manpower available to them, and by wisely putting the right combination of men and materials together to get the work done most efficiently. For any firm to be successful, be it the corner grocer or the largest corporate giant, it must have a first-rate supervisory team.

Truly, *good supervision is America's most valuable resource.*

HOW COMPLEX IS A SUPERVISOR'S JOB?

Supervisor's jobs vary widely in their complexities. For example, as a supervisor, you may be responsible for supervising a moving gang whose duty is to load and unload trucks at the loading dock. You may do little more than tell the crew what to load into a truck and where to put material being taken out. Basically, you see what needs to be done and tell your employees what to do. Notice that we said, "tell your employees what to do." That is what supervision is all about. You decide what needs to be done (set goals) and then *get these things done through the efforts of other people.* Supervisors, then, accomplish the objectives of the organization by directing the efforts of others.

"Supervisors get things done
through the efforts of other people."

Some supervisory jobs, of course, are much more complex than the *working through others* loading and unloading job described above. A complex supervisory position may require a full knowledge of word processing and computer operation and application, a full knowledge of health services, a vast comprehension of consumer needs and wants, and the ability to issue directives to skilled employees who have advanced educations. But, even though these jobs are more complex than the loading job, the supervisor's part is still the same: *determining objectives and getting them accomplished through the efforts of others.*

HOW MANY SUPERVISORY LEVELS ARE THERE?

Basically, there are three levels of supervision. Most of the time you hear people speak of them as (1) top-level supervisors (or managers), (2) middle-level supervisors, and (3) first-line supervisors.

Top-level supervisors are the big bosses in charge of the whole operation. The president of a corporation is a top-level supervisor. A person in charge of a textile mill is a top-level supervisor, as is the owner-manager of a small firm. In each instance, the person holding down the top job is the top-level supervisor.

Middle-level supervisors are higher up than first-line supervisors but are below the top-level supervisor. A department manager in a retail store who has several supervisors working for him would be a middle-level supervisor. A person in charge of purchasing or production for a business would be a middle-level supervisor, with a title such as Director of Purchasing or Production Manager.

three levels

First-line supervisors are the key employees in the managerial family who carry out the policies and directives of middle and top management through face-to-face contact with the workers. Middle management's directives are carried out by first-line supervisors through the efforts of the nonsupervisory employees. Figure 1–1 indicates the typical supervisory groups by level and rank above the nonsupervisory workers.

WHAT IS A SUPERVISOR CALLED?

Supervisors are known by different names in different companies. A supervisor might be called either a foreman or forelady, a leadman, a section chief, a front-line supervisor, a floor chief, a section head, or a department head. Whatever he or she is called, a supervisor must be able to understand people, be able to motivate them, be an energetic leader, be a good planner and allocator of work, be wise and just in making decisions, be knowledgeable about technical aspects of the work, and finally, be able to serve as an effective liaison between top management and the workers. All this sounds like a description of a superman—and it is! Most of us are not born with all

many names

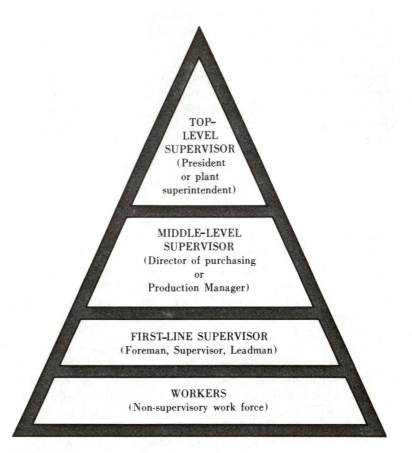

FIGURE 1-1.
The pyramid of different supervisory levels in a firm.

these attributes and capacities; therefore, we need to study what the supervisor does and how he does it so that we can grow in that direction—so that we can develop our capacities to the point where we can be effective supervisors.

WHAT DOES A SUPERVISOR DO?

If you were to follow a supervisor about all day and list everything he or she does *as a supervisor*, the list would probably look something like the following:

- Talks to employees.
- Gives directions to employees.
- Dictates letters.
- Sets production or sales goals.

- Hires new employees.
- Reads mail, reports, etc.
- Attends meetings.
- Makes decisions about new projects.
- Decides who will be promoted.

Note that this is a list of activities performed by a *supervisor*. Every supervisor, of course, may also perform *nonsupervisory* activities such as running a machine, looking up a letter in a file, or stapling sheets of a report together. A manager's job may be 10% nonsupervisory and 90% supervisory, or it may be 20% nonsupervisory and 80% supervisory, etc. What is of interest to us is the supervisory activities that are listed. You will note that these activities, along with others you can think of, are one of two types:

thinking and communicating

1. Physical, or
2. Mental

The *physical* activities usually involve some form of communication. The supervisor is *telling* someone something face to face, *telling an employee something over the telephone*, *writing* to an employee, or *communicating* to someone by gestures. When a supervisor is not talking and sending communications to others, he or she is frequently receiving communications by listening or reading.

The *mental* activities, on the other hand, cannot be seen by us, but we know from what supervisors say that they have been thinking and have made a decision—a mental activity. We can say, therefore, that all the acts performed by supervisors are either physical (involving some form of communication) or mental (involving mental activity and decision making). The ultimate objective of both these acts, of course, is to determine objectives and get them accomplished through the efforts of others.

DOES A SUPERVISOR NEED SKILLS?

To be a good supervisor, you will need to possess at least these three skills:

1. Technical skills.
2. Human skills.
3. Conceptual skills.

Take a look at each of these.

Technical Skills.   You will need *technical* skills so that you can understand the technical aspects of the work done in your department. As a supervisor in a machine shop, for example, you will need to understand the operation of lathes, drill presses, punch presses, etc., in order to supervise the men running them. As an accounting supervisor, you will need to understand the operation of accounting machines, bookkeeping machines, and the techniques of double-entry bookkeeping. As a foreman in an electric firm, on the other hand, you will need to know how to make a good solder connection, how to lace cable, and so on. As a nursing supervisor, you will need to know how to give shots, take blood pressure, change bandages, etc. In fact, it's difficult to supervise people who are doing jobs or working with equipment if you yourself do not understand how it works. For example, could you be a good foreman in a service garage if you do not understand what a dwell meter is and how it is used to set the points on a gasoline engine? Of course not! To be a good supervisor, therefore, you must have the *technical* skills necessary to understand the processes as well as the equipment used. In many instances, these technical skills can be acquired through on-the-job training, through vocational programs, or through evening schools.

Human Skills. As a supervisor, you will also need *human* skills. Human skills are those skills that primarily concern working with *people,* whereas technical skills primarily concern working with *things.* Human skills involve being aware of your own feelings, beliefs, and attitudes about others. By being aware of yourself, you can *understand* and *accept* the beliefs and attitudes of others and can *recognize* that these may differ from your own. By understanding and accepting different beliefs and viewpoints, you will be more skillful in understanding what others mean by their statements and actions. By recognizing these differences, you can do a better job of communicating ideas to others. As a supervisor, for example, you may not be in favor of having a union in the company. Most of your employees, however, may be in favor of having a union represent them. By knowing and understanding your employee's feelings about unions and why they want to be represented by a union, you can create an atmosphere of understanding in which employees can freely discuss unionism—an atmosphere in which they feel free to express their ideas without fear of ridicule. With human skills, you as a supervisor can be sensitive to the motivations and needs of others and can judge the probable effects various courses of action may have on your employees. You can, therefore, take steps that will tend to promote harmony and good effort within your group.

Human skills should be so much a part of you as a supervisor that you apply them continuously. Even when you are not directly supervising your employees, everything you say or do will have some effect on them because what you do will reflect your true self to your employees. Human skills, therefore, should not be thought of as techniques you can apply or use at will. On the contrary, as a good supervisor you should develop and make human skills so much a part of you, that they cannot be separated from yourself.

Most of us know people who have poor human skills. They are the ones who always seem to open their mouths and put both feet in. They rub others the wrong way. The supervisor who tells an employee, "I don't want to know why you are late. If this happens again, you'll be fired!" doesn't have good human skills.

Conceptual Skills.   Finally, as a supervisor you will need *conceptual* skills. Conceptual skills are those that enable you to visualize something in its entirety. With good conceptual skills, you can "see" and understand all parts of a business and how each part contributes to the whole organization. You understand the role that accounting plays; how purchasing, sales, and finance relate to accounting; how personnel is a part of the total concern; how personnel functions in relation to each of the other divisions or parts of a firm; and so on. A supervisor with conceptual skills can visualize the part that the organization plays in the social, economic, and political forces in the community, state, or region. As a supervisor, you will need these conceptual skills so that you can make wise decisions. With good conceptual skills, you can make wiser decisions because you will have the capacity to consider the impact that a certain decision will have on all parts and functions of a firm. You will understand, for example, how a wage increase would affect the whole business. You can see that a 10% wage increase might raise employee morale; but you can see that it would also increase the selling price of the product, which in turn might hurt consumer acceptance, and hence damage the long-run chances of success of the firm in the community.

the big picture

With good *conceptual and human* skills, you will be able to visualize the effect that would result from giving a relatively new employee a choice job on a new machine. You could see, for example, that such action might cause discontent among other employees, promote a possible labor slow-down or stoppage, lower product quality, and so on. You can easily think of other possible consequences.

As a good supervisor, then, you will need these three skills: *technical* skills so that you can understand and perform the technical activities required, *human* skills so that you can both motivate others and understand individual (and group) feelings and actions, and *conceptual* skills so that you can clearly understand and coordinate all the activities of the firm through wise decision making.

Technical skills are probably in greatest need in the lower levels of a firm. Human skills, on the other hand, are in real need throughout every level of the firm. Conceptual skills are more critical at the higher levels of the firm.

WHAT FUNCTIONS DOES A SUPERVISOR PERFORM?

Supervision deals with getting things done through others. A supervisor tells other employees what to do. As previously indicated, a supervisor can also perform some job—such as running a machine. While you are running a machine, of course, you are not supervising. You are performing a job.

On the other hand, when you are getting things done through the efforts of others, you are supervising and will engage in a variety of functions:

1. You must plan your work and establish objectives. This is called the *planning* function.
2. You must organize people and materials in order to coordinate activities and actions. This is the *organizing* function.
3. You must secure qualified personnel to do the work—the *staffing* function.
4. You must direct the efforts of your employees—the *directing* function.
5. You must control the activities of your employees—the *controlling* function.

Let's look at each of these functions and see why a supervisor needs to perform them.

Planning. The first thing you'll need to do as a supervisor is set forth clearly what you want to achieve—your objective. Once this is done, you establish a plan to achieve the objective. This plan is a course of action to accomplish your goal. Planning, therefore, is the process involved in developing and formulating the course of action needed to accomplish your objective. Planning is not a function reserved just for top and middle management alone. On the contrary, first-line supervisors are actively engaged every day in planning—although their planning may not be as complex or extend as far into the future as that performed by top-level managers. A good supervisor must plan what needs to be done, who will do it, when it will be done, how it will be done, and so on. Without this planning by the supervisor, a department's activities may well become disorganized, confused, and ineffective. In fact, thoughtful and careful planning can change you from a mediocre supervisor to an outstanding one, ready for promotion to a bigger job. In Chapter 13 we will cover this point in more detail.

Organizing. Organizing consists of:

1. Determining what activities need to be accomplished to get the job done.
2. Assigning these activities to employees.
3. Giving the employees the necessary authority to carry out the activities in a coordinated manner.

All supervisors perform the function of organizing. Those at the top level are usually interested in organizing the broader aspects of the firm, whereas the first-line supervisor is primarily interested in organizing a department so that work can be accomplished in the best way possible. Whenever you establish objectives, fix authority relationships, or group activities, you are organizing. When you bring order to your department through organizing, you thereby create a workplace which will be conducive to achieving the activities you might list in item one above. Organization is one of your important activities and will be covered in greater detail in Chapter 15.

Staffing.   The staffing function covers all activities needed to recruit, hire, and retain individuals in the firm. In some companies this is done by a personnel department, in some it is a joint responsibility shared by the supervisor and the personnel department, and in other companies it is the sole responsibility of the supervisor. Staffing means putting people with skills and growth potential in spots where their skills are needed and growth is possible.

Directing.   Directing deals with influencing, guiding, or supervising subordinates in their jobs. It consists not only of telling employees what to do, but more importantly, of explaining *why* the job needs to be done. It involves a great deal of cummunication and, in most supervisory positions, consumes the greater part of a supervisor's workday. This is a complex function which will be explored more fully in Chapters 4 and 12.

Controlling.   In its simplest sense, controlling consists of monitoring and taking corrective action when necessary. This keeps you on track. From a supervisory standpoint, the essence of control is, simply, that a supervisor must control people. If people are controlled properly, then actions and events will conform to plans. Control is the check-up part of managing.

TO WHOM IS A SUPERVISOR RESPONSIBLE?

In the past, many people felt that a supervisor was responsible only to management. In fact, they said that a supervisor had only one responsibility—making money for the business. Today, however, smart managers are developing a new sense of supervisory responsibility. Some people call it *business statesmanship.* Others call it *enlightened leadership.* Whatever its name, it refers to the fact that supervisors are beginning to realize that they have responsibilities not just to the owners but to many other groups both inside and outside the firm. Today, good supervisors recognize a sense of responsibility to the community as well as to the people inside the plant. They recognize their responsibility to their *owners,* their *employees,* their *customers,* the *general public,* and the *government.* Let's look at each of these briefly.

Responsibility to Owners.   An owner (or stockholder) invests in a firm to make money. Perhaps more than anything else, the owner wants a good return from his investment, along with some security. He will, of course, agree that his company should treat its employees fairly and that it should be honest with the public and its customers; but primarily he wants dividends, and dividends can only come from profits.

A supervisor's responsibility to the owner of the business, then, is to operate his department so as to give him (the owner) the highest *long-run* return on investment. Working for the highest long-run profit will never conflict with obligations that a supervisor has to other individuals and groups. For example, an extensive program to construct new buildings and purchase new equipment may materially reduce profits for several years, but in the long run, profits would be greater than if the new programs were not undertaken. In fact, without the new building program, the business might lose its competitive advantage and fail.

Responsibility to Employees.   An enlightened supervisor also recognizes a very definite responsibility to employees. As stockholders have invested their money, so have employees invested their time, their energies, and their efforts with a firm. Having thus cast their lot, employees are entitled to have a farsighted supervisor who recognizes their contributions as well as his specific responsibilities to them.

A supervisor is responsible for giving employees a courteous reception when they start on the job, and for placing them in positions for which they are both qualified and interested. Inasmuch as employees spend about 50% of their waking time at work, supervisors are also responsible for providing physical facilities that meet accepted standards of cleanliness, light, heat, ventilation, and safety. In addition, supervisors are responsible for providing leadership that will inspire employee cooperation and will allow the employees to work in a relaxed manner, confident that their best interests will be served.

Supervisors are also responsible to their employees for planning the work of the department so that a *steady* job will be provided. This may call for intricate planning even of seasonal work, but the benefit to the employee and the community is obvious.

Supervisors have an obligation to stand up for their employees, to support and defend them when they rightly stick their necks out, and to tell them how they are getting along on the job.

Finally, supervisors are responsible for increasing the day-by-day satisfaction and well-being of their employees in relation to their work, their fellow employees, and the company. This responsibility includes the obligation to provide the opportunity for advancement and promotion within the limits established by the size and nature of the organization. It incorporates a moral responsibility to train employees so that they can attain the highest level of responsibility of which they are capable. And it includes the responsibility to recognize and respect the individual dignity of people—to treat each worker as an entity and not as an impersonal part of a group of humans.

Although the above list is not all-inclusive, it will give you some idea of the many responsibilities that enlightened supervisors should feel toward their employees.

Responsibility to Customers.   A supervisor's basic responsibility to the customer is to help the company provide a quality product or service that the customer wants, produce it when the customer wants it, and provide it at a price the customer is willing and able to pay—and all at a fair profit. In addition, the supervisor is responsible to the customer for building integrity into the company's goods and services—for striving to improve them so that they represent better buys for the customers and uphold the company's reputation for quality products.

Responsibility to the Public and Government.   Business exists because the public and the government *allow* it to exist. Corporations come into being and are allowed to operate because the citizens and the government of a particular state *agreed* through their laws that they (the corporations) could do so. Business owns property and locates buildings in accordance with the rights *granted* by local governments. Inasmuch as a business exists and operates through the consent of the public and government, it has a very definite responsibility to each of them.

To help meet these responsibilities, a supervisor should first of all obey the operating laws set forth by the local, state, and federal governments. This supervisory responsibility includes obeying not only the letter of the law, but the spirit of the law as well. Where a law is vague and loopholes exist, the supervisor is responsible for operating within the total meaning of the law, considering the best interests of his employees and the community.

Many of the supervisory responsibilities discussed here were not recognized twenty years ago. Today, however, enlightened supervisors are developing an awareness and a philosophy of their multiple obligations and responsibilities. Supervisors are recognizing as never before that a firm will not prosper for any considerable time if its sole objective is to make as much money as quickly as possible.[1]

ARE SUPERVISORS LOOKED UP TO?

Like it or not, as a supervisor you will always be in the forefront of your employees. The way you do things, what you say, and what your thoughts are will have a profound influence on those who work for you. They will naturally look to you as their guide and leader. You, therefore, should serve as a good example in all your actions.

If you always get to work ahead of time, this action will have a posi-

[1] Adapted with permission from Claude S. George, Jr., *Management in Industry* (Englewood Cliffs, N.J.: Prentice-Hall, Inc., 1959), pp. 564–69.

*supervisor as a
role model*

tive influence on your employees to be punctual. If you are habitually late, your employees will not be as concerned about getting started on time. Likewise, leaving early sends a similar signal to your employees. If you are neat in your dress as well as your work habits, your employees will naturally tend to emulate your work style. Sloppiness and slovenliness likewise will be emulated. The same is true about how well you are organized, how carefully you plan ahead, and how precisely you explain the plan to your employees. If you possess these positive attributes, your employees will strive to "be like the boss"—to organize themselves well, to think and plan ahead.

Likewise, if you approach your supervisory job with enthusiasm and drive, this, too, will be contagious. Enthusiastic, energetic supervisors make for enthusiastic, energetic workers. Remember, you are your employees' leader. What you do and how you do it will have an impact on what they do and how they do it. Whether you like it or not, you will serve as a role model for everyone who works for you. It behooves you, therefore, as a supervisor to always lead and supervise through example. Don't tell employees to perform a job in a manner different from the way you would do it. If you ask an employee to do something, you should be willing to do it too. "Do as I say, not as I do" is a poor motto for a supervisor.

DO YOU HAVE TO BE LIKED TO BE A SUPERVISOR?

*getting along
with others*

Being liked by your employees, your peers, and your bosses is becoming more and more important these days. This is not to say that you have to be a "hail fellow well met" to be a good supervisor. However, with business becoming more democratic, you do need to know how to get along with others. If you are well liked as a supervisor, you will be willingly followed—not feared. Your employees will work harder for you. Remember, however, that in a supervisory position your employees follow your directives because they want to—because they like and respect you. *Your true supervisory powers come from those you supervise.* As a supervisor, therefore, you need to understand the feelings of those working for you. In other words, you should be able to put yourself in your employees' shoes. Finally, to be liked as a supervisor, you will need to go the extra mile—go to bat for your employees, even go out of your way for them. When you understand your employees and respect their dignity and feelings, then you are well on the road to being liked.

WHAT SPECIAL QUALITIES DOES A SUCCESSFUL SUPERVISOR NEED?

The characteristics or qualities that will make you a successful supervisor are difficult to pinpoint precisely. Some qualities are more important than others, and some are difficult to describe. However, we do know that as a successful supervisor you must be able to inspire your employees, to motivate them, and to direct their work. As previously indicated, you will need to possess technical, human, and conceptual skills. In addition to these qualities, you will also need to have an open mind. You must learn to search outside the everyday rut for a better method, a new policy, an improved way of doing things. You must, in other words, always be open to suggestions for a better way of performing any task.

A good supervisor needs to be able to discover what the problem is in times of trouble. Few people have this ability; they simply cannot see what is wrong when trouble erupts. They see and treat the symptoms of the problem rather than the causes of the problem. They may give aspirin for a stomach-ache (the symptom), when the real problem or cause of the stomach-ache is no breakfast. The cure, therefore, is food—not aspirin. Thus, a good supervisor needs to have the ability to get to the heart of the problem, to discover its real cause, and to take action to *cure* the trouble.

*desirable
qualities*

To do a good job, supervisors also need most of the following qualities. See how many you have, and make plans to develop those in which you are weak.

1. *A good supervisor should possess the desire to be a top-notch manager and to grow.* You should always be willing to learn, to develop new skills, to broaden your job. You should not be afraid to take a chance, but instead should possess the confidence that you will succeed.

2. *A supervisor should be able to formulate a clear picture of what he or she wishes to accomplish.* Knowing the objective, knowing the end result, and knowing what is desired are necessary in any successful undertaking.

3. *A supervisor should be a self-starter.* You should think and move on your own initiative and not wait to be told by others to do something. To be a self-starter, you will need self-confidence and courage to move ahead.

4. *A supervisor should be able to think.* This is perhaps the hardest task you will face. Most of us find it easy *to do, to act, to perform.* We have difficulty, however, in thinking clearly about a problem—our minds wander, we are distracted by noises or other problems, or we prefer to *do things* rather than *think* about how to solve problems.

5. *A supervisor should be able to express thoughts clearly.* The best idea in the world is worthless unless it is communicated well. As you know, supervisors spend most of their time communicating; therefore, they need to do it well. We aren't talking about great speaking or great writing. What we are talking about instead is the basic ability to get your ideas across clearly to your employees so that they can understand what you want them to do.

6. *A supervisor should be a salesman.* Any idea that you think up and communicate to others needs to be "sold." Selling your idea—con-

vincing others of its worth—is one of your prime tasks. Selling a plan of action is a vital part of a supervisor's job of communicating to employees.

7. *A supervisor should possess moral integrity.* Truthfulness, honesty, and integrity should be so much a part of you that your subordinates will have total confidence in you and your actions.

8. *A supervisor should be able to organize.* This is another very important attribute, because as a supervisor you will be constantly called on to organize your own work as well as the work of your employees in order to maximize output.

9. *A supervisor should have the ability to work with and through other people.* You must be able to get along with others and to get them to do what needs to be done for the organization.

10. *A supervisor should be willing to tackle hard problems and make tough decisions.* Anyone can make an easy decision, but as a good supervisor you must be willing to tackle the hard problems and make tough or unpopular decisions.

11. *A supervisor should be dynamic and have the ability to inspire others.* This is that special quality, which you can't put your finger on, that makes others want to follow your directions and work with you as their leader.

12. *A supervisor should have the ability to evaluate others and to recognize individual strengths and weaknesses.* This is a critical ability needed by supervisors in order to get the right person in the right job, as well as to reject the unqualified applicant.

13. *A supervisor should like people.* You should like to be with people and work with people. In fact, it is hard to visualize a supervisor who doesn't like employees—who doesn't have a sense of loyalty and feeling for them.

14. *A supervisor should be a balanced person.* This means that you should be levelheaded, understanding, firm, able to laugh, and fair.

15. *A supervisor should have the ability to delegate authority to others.* You should get satisfaction from seeing things done through the independent efforts of your employees.

16. *A good supervisor should have a willingness to subordinate personal desires and wishes.* You'll have to realize that you cannot have your own way in every matter, but must instead submit to your bosses' wishes.

17. *A supervisor should be fair and wise.* Despite all that can be done by you and others, disputes, grievances, and problems will sometimes arise among your employees. In each instance, you will need to call on all the wisdom you possess to mediate these situations and render fair and impartial answers to the petitions.

18. *A supervisor should understand what each employee's job is.* Knowing

the technical aspects of the job will give you confidence and assurance in dealing with problems and in talking with employees.

19. *A supervisor should be able to win the friendship, loyalty, and support of employees and associates.* In addition to this, you will need to possess and show a spirit of willing cooperation with other supervisors in your division as well as in other areas of the firm. You live and work with others, and to succeed as a supervisor you will need all the help you can get from your associates.

20. *A supervisor should have a good mind and a good education.* A good mind is reflected in an open and willing-to-learn attitude; that is, you don't mind tackling problems. A good education is reflected not in the number of years spent in school, but in the quality and amount of information you absorbed. Experience in many instances can more than compensate for formal education. For example, getting along well with your associates and employees is learned from experience rather than from books.

21. *A supervisor should try to see the whole picture.* Use your conceptual skill in order to understand what top and middle management want done and why. To be a successful supervisor, you will need to understand the whole picture and communicate this in an understandable way to your fellow employees.

22. *A supervisor needs patience.* You will need patience to be successful—patience to listen to and understand employees, patience to spend whatever time is needed to understand and improve work situations and worker relations, and patience to take the time necessary to plan the total work flow and organize it in such a way that employees will feel comfortable in doing their jobs.

23. *A supervisor needs to be flexible.* You must be able to adjust to new procedures, new and changing conditions, and new ways of solving problems. Resisting change is one of the surest ways to slow down progress. Successful supervisors are the ones with open and receptive minds, who do not resist change. They welcome new ideas, new ways of performing old jobs, and new concepts about how things can be improved.

24. *A supervisor should be self-confident.* Therefore, you will need to have faith and confidence in your abilities and in your capacity to plan, organize, and direct the efforts of others.

25. *A supervisor must be able to take criticism.* If you are thin-skinned or supersensitive, your supervisory career will be short lived. No one is perfect, and good criticism will help sharpen your supervisory skills.

26. *A supervisor must possess initiative and the desire to succeed.* This may be the most important quality because if your desire to be a successful supervisor is strong enough, you can overcome shortcomings that you see in yourself. Determination, willingness, and the strong

desire to be a successful supervisor will put you well on the way to achieving your goal.

27. *A supervisor should have the ability to learn from failure.* Good leaders don't consider a failure as terminal. Instead, they learn from their mistakes and move forward.

28. *A supervisor should be accessible.* Your employees need to know that you are available when they need you. This means you should be *mentally* as well as physically available. You need to listen with understanding and empathy. Curt or noninterested replies tend to choke communications, and your employees will stop turning to you for advice and help.

WHAT MAJOR TRAITS DETERMINE POTENTIAL FOR SUPERVISION?

traits for success

According to a *Wall Street Journal/Gallup* survey[1] of 782 top executives in 282 of our largest corporations, the three most important traits are integrity, industriousness, and the ability to get along with people. Also high on the list are dedication to work (doing it better and caring about it) and having the ability to work well with and through people.

The survey showed that in medium and small firms, the ability to get along with others ranked first, followed by integrity, industriousness, business knowledge, intelligence, leadership abilities, and education. In commenting on these traits or capacities, many of the top executives mentioned in particular honesty, sound judgment, self-reliance, and hard work. Other items high on the list included the ability to communicate, desire to move ahead, flexibility, willingness to sacrifice time, ability to plan and set objectives, and total or nearly total dedication to the job.

WHAT TRAITS WILL PROBABLY MEAN FAILURE AS A SUPERVISOR?

traits leading to failure

According to the same survey,[2] a lack of concern for people as human beings was a major shortcoming of potential supervisors. In addition, lack of team play (that is, being a self-centered prima donna) was a strong detriment. The seven traits that most often caused failure as a supervisor were: (1) having a limited point of view, (2) not being able to understand others, (3) not being able to work with others, (4) being indecisive, (5) not having initiative, (6) not assuming responsibility, and (7) lacking integrity. In addition to these seven traits, many executives found that failure to manage well was caused by lack of aggressiveness, lack of commitment to a job and employees, being content with things as they are (not innovative), reluctance

[1] *Wall Street Journal*, p. 33, Nov. 14, 1980.
[2] *Ibid.*

to think independently, inability to solve problems, and/or wanting to be popular.

HOW CAN YOU DEVELOP THE NEEDED QUALITIES?

The answer to how to develop the needed supervisory qualities lies in hard work, motivation on your part, and formal and informal education. Managerial or supervisory courses will help in many instances. Experience can also teach you if you will allow yourself to profit from it. Another learning method that has been used by many successful people is to watch good supervisors at work: observe what they do, see how they handle difficult employees, and watch how they solve tough problems; learn from their good as well as from their poor habits; accept and model your actions after their good habits, but reject their poor behavior patterns.

One of the most successful supervisors I ever worked for had no formal education in the area of human relations and supervision. He didn't know what anthropology or sociology was. He finished high school and immediately started working and learning from the school of hard knocks. He worked hard and possessed many of the characteristics talked about above. A few years after starting work, he was promoted to a supervisory position. He was well liked by those he supervised; they could always count on his going to bat for them and getting a fair decision. He got along well with other managers and earned their respect and admiration. His employees could always be sure that he would recognize and reward hard work and talent. They could always count on his being available to hear out a problem or mediate a tough decision. He was no patsy or easy pushover, but he did welcome the discussion of ideas that were at variance with his own. He was, in fact, one of the smartest, hardest-working managers I have ever known. And he developed into this position through extra effort and desire. But some managers don't always succeed as easily. For example, a leader that you would know failed miserably at first. He failed in business. He failed in his bid for a seat in his state legislature. He tried business again and failed again. He finally won a seat in the legislature, but was defeated for Speaker of the House and defeated for Congress on his first and third tries. He was defeated for the Senate. He was defeated in his bid for the Vice Presidency. He was defeated on his second try for the Senate. Finally he was elected President. His name was Abraham Lincoln.

work, experience, and education

Lincoln succeeded because he had the drive and ambition to be a leader. He didn't quit because he failed once or twice. And you, too, can become a supervisory leader if you are willing to apply yourself, work hard, and not give up with the first few defeats! Successful supervisors have a purpose or drive strong enough to make them do the things necessary to get a job done effectively and efficiently. They strive, they work hard, and they don't give up trying to improve themselves and to develop the qualities needed to be a good supervisor.

IS IT EASY FOR A SUPERVISOR TO GET PROMOTED?

If you want to get promoted, the most important thing is to do a good job—do it well, do it on time, and do it right. In other words, you have to do what your superior expects and wants to be done. Don't ever forget that you work for your boss. This means that, as a supervisor, you should always meet your boss's needs if you are to be recognized, praised, and promoted for doing a good job. In other words, your boss has to be convinced that you are doing a good job and deserve a promotion before he will even consider it.

When you work for someone else, be sure you know what is expected of you—what your job is and what your boss wants you to do. If you have a question about priorities, tell your boss, "I have several projects under way and I'd like your advice on which is the most important." Then follow his advice. You'll be doing what is most important in your superior's opinion—and you'll be recognized and remembered.

know your job—don't hide your accomplishments
Don't be afraid of putting your accomplishments in a good light. When you've completed a report or a project that your boss gave priority to, give him or her a follow-up report several weeks later, pointing out changes or recent developments that you think your boss would be interested in or should be aware of. If you are in a conference or meeting with your superior, don't hesitate to speak out about any expertise or insights that you might have concerning one of his or her special projects. Obviously, you should not do this in a know-it-all or boasting way, but neither should you hide your light under a bushel.

Finally, have periodic one-on-one reviews of your work with your boss so that the two of you can discuss what you have done, how you did it, and what you could have done to do a better job. If you know what your boss wants, if you do it well, and if you strive to improve your performance—and your boss knows all this—you'll be steps ahead of others in the promotion line.

ARE THERE OPPORTUNITIES IN SUPERVISION?

The opportunities in supervision are innumerable. Virtually every business enterprise, every governmental office, and every institution present possibilities for the application of supervisory skills. Every business is a potential source of employment for a supervisor. Young men and women who qualify as potential supervisors are being sought by business today as never before because their worth and contributions to a going concern are recognized.

As indicated throughout this chapter, you cannot be a supervisor by simply deciding to be one. Instead, the road to supervision involves a lot of study, hard work, and on-the-job training. Making yourself successful and earning promotions as a supervisor, therefore, is a long but rewarding process. The field offers abundant opportunities for self-expression and financial reward if you are willing to work at it.

1. Who is the critical person in the management pyramid? Why?
2. Explain what a supervisor does.
3. What is a top-level supervisor? A middle-level supervisor? A first-line supervisor?
4. When a supervisor is waiting on a customer, is he or she managing? Why?
5. To be a good supervisor, what skills do you need? Explain.
6. List and explain the functions that supervisors perform.
7. What general qualities do you need to be a good supervisor? Which ones do you think are most important?
8. Are there any special qualities needed to be a supervisor? Explain each one.
9. Explain the responsibilities that supervisors have to owners, employees, customers, and the public.
10. What opportunities do you see in supervision?
11. Explain how supervisors are looked up to.
12. Can you be a good supervisor and not be liked? Explain.
13. What major traits determine potential for supervisors?
14. What can supervisors do to get promoted?

A Case Study
BILL WILDER'S OPPORTUNITY

For three years, Bill Wilder had worked as a clerk in the men's department of a large department store. He liked his job, the people he worked with, and his boss Bob Teal. The men's department was one of the largest and best-run departments in the store. The fourteen clerks in the department consistently sold more merchandise than any others in the entire operation, and customer complaints and returns were at a minimum. In Bill Wilder's eyes, it was an "ideal department with a staff of dedicated, hard-working employees."

Because of the success of the men's department, Bob Teal had earned a reputation in the store as being the best supervisor in the business and was generally regarded as being groomed for higher-level positions.

Last week, Teal was called into the manager's office to talk about the poor showing that the home furnishings department had made during the past six years. Despite the fact that the store carried nationally advertised brands of quality merchandise, sales in home furnishings seemed to lag. Harry Vaughan, the department supervisor, planned to retire in two months, and the store manager offered the job to Bob Teal. For Teal, it would mean managing a larger department made up of four separate sections employing twenty-seven clerks. In addition to the challenge it would offer him to improve sales, Bob Teal recognized the new position as a step up the managerial ladder with a generous increase in salary. He was eager to make the move, but his first job was to recommend someone to succeed him as manager in the men's department.

Bill Wilder seemed a likely candidate, so he asked Wilder to meet him in his office at 10:30 A.M. to discuss the opening. As he waited for Wilder to come, Bob Teal wondered what he should tell Wilder—how he should describe his supervisory role and what "sales" approach he should take.

1. If you were Bob Teal, what would you tell Wilder? How would you describe the job of supervising the men's department?
2. Would you try to "sell" Wilder on the job or simply let him make his decision without a sales pitch? Why?
3. What managerial abilities would you stress as being most important when you describe the job to Bill Wilder?

A Case Study
SUPERVISOR HARRIS

"It looks like everything is going wrong," Bob Harris thought. "I come to work and what do I find? Nothing right!

"Four employees didn't show up today, leaving me short-handed. I have problems enough with this old equipment without having the added problems of workers who goof off, don't show up, or come in late. And they ought to know better. Yesterday I got them all together and read them the riot act. Chewed them out properly. A supervisor's got to show them who's boss; let them know from the beginning that they can't get by with anything.

"Every time they have a problem—no matter how small—they call me. And I have to get in the middle of it all and do the job for them. It looks like I'm always repairing a machine, or adjusting a feeder, or taking an employee's place in the assembly line when he's absent. I'm always on the run. Always trying to catch up on a job. Always behind in production. If I didn't understand our production process as well as I do, I don't know how the company would get along. I know these machines and products inside out. I could run any one of them in my sleep. But my workers couldn't care less about the whole darn works!

"And these idiots don't seem to appreciate all I do for them. Every time I start to tell them something for their own good, they bristle and 'get their dander up.' If they want me to treat them like babies, they've got another thought coming! If a man can't take it and dish it out, he shouldn't be working for me."

About this time, Bob was interrupted in his thoughts by one of his men saying, "Hey Bobbie, we've run out of lag bolts."

"Well, what do you expect?" Bob shouted at him. "If you don't order material you won't have any!" The employee shrugged his shoulders and said, "Ordering ain't my job."

Bob immediately picked up the phone and called a local supplier to see if he could let him have three gross of the bolts.

Bob just didn't understand why things like this were always happening. He had told every one of his employees that they should watch out for things like this. He made it clear whenever a new man came on the job that his job was to "keep the machines going—to keep production rolling." He felt that his employees ought to have enough "get up and go" to look after things like this and not have production always being held up because they were out of materials, or a machine needed to be repaired, or for some other darn reason.

Lately, Bob's boss, Mr. Nelson, had been on Bob's back because he was behind in his orders. Customers were calling for parts, and Bob's department was holding up the works. In fact, Mr. Nelson was always telling Bob about how his work affected other parts of the company. "Hell," Bob thought, "all I'm interested in is the work in my own department. If I can keep it going, the rest of the plant can take care of itself. I can only do so much. Haven't got time to look after everybody else's job. A man shouldn't have someone on his back all the time, and I'm fed up with Mr. Nelson always telling me something. This is the second time this year he has jumped on me."

1. What kind of supervisor do you think Bob Harris is?
2. What are his good points? His weaknesses? Cite evidence in the case study to support your conclusions.
3. If you were Mr. Nelson, what would you do about Bob Harris?

A Case Study
EDITH GATES' PROBLEM

Edith Gates was recently promoted to supervise the twenty-two women in the sewing department. All of the employees were on piece work—that is, each employee's pay was determined by the amount of work she performed. Everything went well for about the first month or so. Then it seemed that things began to fall apart.

On Tuesday a group complaining about poor light at the machines came to see Edith and threatened to slow down their work if the lights weren't fixed. Edith thought about the problem and decided to write a memo to her boss about it.

Wednesday morning another group complaining about the machine adjustments approached her. Thread tangled and frequently broke, they complained, making it hard to meet their sewing quota. Then, at noon two employees indicated that the lavatories in the restrooms were stopped up. She added these two items to her memo to her boss.

Later in the day two employees gave notice that they were quitting to go to work for a competing company where pay and working conditions were better.

After the employees left at 5:00 P.M., Edith sat at her desk and pondered her problems and possible solutions.

1. What kind of supervisor do you think Edith is?
2. How would you have handled each of her problems?
3. What should Edith do to arrive at long-run solutions to her problems?

A Personal Case Problem

As Personnel Manager for the General Services Company employing 860 employees, you have been asked by the supervisor of the Accounting Department to screen a group of applicants for a supervisory opening in the Posting Section. The job consists of supervising 17 employees who post accounts receivable and accounts payable using computers. The applicants for the position are from inside as well as outside the company. The accounting supervisor wants your recommendations in rank order—from the best qualified to the least qualified. You made the following notes after the interviews with the applicants.

1. Janice Carter, 34 years old, high school education plus two courses at night school in community college. Worked 2 yrs. as typist; 2 yrs. as clerk in candy shop; 8 yrs. in the company's billing department; 4 yrs. in company's typing pool. Comments: attractive, pleasant, talkative, said little about her work with company.

2. Edna Raymond, 38 years old, high school education plus completion of one year business course at local college. Worked 3 yrs. as office employee of local railroad company; 18 yrs. at the Builders Lumber Company as office manager in charge of customer billings. Comments: rather quiet but articulate, nice looking, neat, likes her work.

3. Alice Morning, 27 years old, high school education plus one year business course. Worked 2 yrs. selling cosmetics door to door; 7 yrs. as teller in local savings and loan. Comments: alert, attractive, enjoys new experiences.

4. Harold Jones, 36 years old, high school education plus two years of college. Served 2 yrs. in Army; worked 3 yrs. in sales; 1 yr. in collection service; 7 yrs. as teller in a bank; 3 yrs. in Company's customer service department. Comments: mature, settled, neat, quiet, asked a lot of questions, interested in the job.

1. How would you rank the applicants? Why?
2. Why do you think your number one choice is the best?
3. How much better is your number one choice than your number two and three.
4. Why did you pick the person you did for your last choice?

2

LEADING AND SUPERVISING OTHERS

This chapter explains—

- The qualities you need to be a good leader
- How leadership is important in supervision
- The four types of leaders

Good leaders know where they are going and can persuade others to join them. They are out front *leading*, rather than staying behind *pushing*. They are the most valued people in any organization today. Most of us recognize a good leader but can't define precisely what makes one.

Leadership is the elusive quality that inspires others to perform. It is a quality that enables a supervisor to influence others to accept directions freely and willingly. Good leaders seem to have a special knack of getting others to follow them and do what they want done.

Although you might be a good leader, you may not necessarily be a good supervisor. You might, for example, be a good leader of a rowdy mob. You might have the capacity to excite the mob and get them to break windows and follow your directions. Under calmer conditions, however, you might be a poor supervisor. You may well lack the qualities we talked about in the previous chapter—qualities of supervision dealing with technical skills, human skills, and conceptual skills. You may not be able to plan, organize, and perform the other functions that supervisors are expected to perform. A good leader, therefore, does not have to be a good supervisor. On the other hand, if you want to be a good supervisor, you will need to possess many of the qualities of a good leader. Let's take a look at some of these qualities and see what they are.

"Most of us recognize a good leader,
but can't discover precisely what makes one."

Believe it or not, it is almost impossible to find the correct answer to this question. Although you and I can recognize a good leader, we cannot say with certainty that if you possess certain traits or characteristics, you will be a good leader.

By observing outstanding leaders, however, we can list a few qualities that most of them possess. We can say, therefore, that if you want to be a good leader, you will probably need to possess the following characteristics:

1. *You will need a desire to excel.* Leaders are never content with being second; they always want to be out front. Leaders are self-starting individuals who are willing to exert themselves to achieve success.

2. *You will need a sense of responsibility.* Leaders are never afraid to seek and accept obligations, and always willingly discharge any responsibilities assumed.

3. *You will need a capacity for work.* Good leaders are always willing to accept the demands of leadership success—long hours and hard work.

4. *You will need a feel for good human relations.* Leaders are always involved with their fellow workers, studying them, analyzing their needs and demands, and trying to understand their problems. This interest and ability to discover what their fellow workers need is probably the single most important characteristic of a good leader.

5. *You will need a contagious enthusiasm.* No one wants to follow a dull, uninspired leader. Enthusiasm is something like mob appeal—once we are caught up in it, we move along with it. And once workers are caught up in the web of enthusiasm for their jobs and their work, they take on a new sense of commitment to the jobs they are asked to do.

6. *You will need a high sense of integrity.* Leaders who succeed have to be honest with themselves and with their followers. You may fool some of the people for a while, but sooner or later a lack of trustworthiness will force you out of a position of leadership. Individuals who are insecure and undependable seldom succeed as leaders. To be a good supervisor, however, you have to earn this trust by being fair and square with all employees regardless of their abilities, status, friendliness, or stubbornness. In other words, don't play favorites. Employees like to work for a leader who can be trusted to say precisely what he or she means, without pussyfooting about the facts, squirming to get out of an unpleasant situation, or using double talk. You should, therefore, strive to be a straight shooter, always open, fair, and above board. If you earn this reputation, then most of your employees will respond in like manner: they, too, will be fair and square with you, above board in all their dealings.

*needed
characteristics*

Obviously, these are not the only qualities you will need. Many of the prerequisites of a supervisor previously discussed also apply here. Such qualities as intelligence, character, and loyalty are important too.

WHAT TRAITS INDICATE POOR LEADERSHIP?

Poor leaders send out signals that indicate that they are doing a poor job. You can probably recognize many of these traits in leaders you have known. Make every effort to observe the following nine rules if you want to be an effective leader.

1. *Don't pass the blame.* If something goes wrong and it is your responsibility, don't blame someone else. Be willing to accept blame as well as praise.
2. *Don't be self-centered.* Leaders who think mostly of themselves lose the support and help of their employees. Show interest in the group, not in yourself. Encourage others to participate.

signals of a poor supervisor

3. *Don't ask an employee to do something that you wouldn't do.* And, likewise, don't do something (like break a rule) that you wouldn't want your employees to do.
4. *Don't be aloof, cool, or unfriendly. Don't talk down to your employees.* These tactics only serve to isolate you and lower employee morale. Instead, be easy to see and talk to.
5. *Don't be a "Big I."* Don't lord your position of authority over your employees.
6. *Don't drag your feet.* When something needs doing—do it!
7. *Don't say "yes" and not mean it.* Always be truthful, honest, and fair.
8. *Don't agonize over decisions.* Look at the facts, use your best judgment, then commit yourself. Don't be a procrastinator.
9. *Don't jump to conclusions.* Too quick a decision can frequently cause more harm than good. Get the facts, use your best judgment, then make your decision.

WHAT IS THE CONNECTION BETWEEN LEADERSHIP AND SUPERVISION?

Although most people recognize that leadership is a part of supervision, they sometimes fail to see that supervision isn't the same thing as leadership. Supervisors must make plans, establish a satisfactory organization, hire people to staff the organization, tell them what to do, and set up controls. A leader doesn't necessarily do these same things. All a leader needs to do is to get other people to follow him. A supervisor, however, is asked to perform all of the functions associated with supervision in addition to being a leader. Therefore, although a strong leader may be a weak supervisor, a strong supervisor must be a good leader too.

The leader of a group is not always the foreman appointed by management. In other words, the leader of a group isn't necessarily the supervisor of the group. Leadership roles are often assumed by members of a work group. For example, a nonappointed leader of a work group would be the member who could get the group to, say, reduce or hold their output to a certain level. Leadership, therefore, is something that is an active process and not necessarily something that grows out of a position of authority, such as a supervisory position.

*leaders vs.
supervisors*

Before leadership can exist, you have to have—

1. Leaders and followers who agree on a common cause or goal.
2. Leaders and followers who agree on what needs to be done to reach that goal.

To illustrate this story, consider a work group that follows one of its own members and restricts output. Here you have a leader and followers who agree on their goal (restrict output) as well as on what they need to do (reduce production) to reach their objective. Although a leader needs only to get his or her associates to follow him, the appointed supervisor of the group must perform all the other functions (planning, organizing, etc.) associated with supervision.

WHAT IS AN INFORMAL LEADER?

Every work group has a leader. This leader may be officially *appointed* by the management of the firm and be thus accepted by the group, or an employee may be an *informal* leader unofficially selected by the group itself.

Informal leaders chosen by a group may be selected because they are taller and can be seen, because they have loud booming voices and can be heard, because they have work seniority and are thus the most respected, or because they say funny things and can relieve group tension. Whatever the reason, an informal leader's reign is a precarious thing. An informal leader might be the leader today and be replaced tomorrow. This is particularly true where the composition of the work group changes rather frequently or where the work location or product worked on changes.

Who leads a group depends on what the group's objective is. If the group centers its attention on getting work done, like producing 400 units per hour, then the leader will probably be the person who can generate the most enthusiasm for reaching this goal. On the other hand, if the work group needs to have tension relieved because of the stress and critical na-

*source of
leadership
authority*

ture of the job, the leader may well be one who can reduce tension through his humor. A work group may, however, have both of these objectives (400 units per hour and relief of tension), in which case it may choose two leaders—if it can't find one person possessing both attributes.

WHAT ARE THE DIFFERENCES BETWEEN JOB-CENTERED AND EMPLOYEE-CENTERED SUPERVISORS?

Some supervisors are *job-centered* in their approach to leadership. They spend most of their time initiating and directing their employees' actions toward solving production or job-related problems. Job-centered supervisors are more interested in the things of production than in their employees. They arrange working conditions so that the human element—the worker—interferes to a minimum degree. They keep employees at their jobs and insist that the work be accomplished in accordance with directions. They force their employees to think "job," to think "achieving production."

Other supervisors are *employee-centered*. They spend a great deal of their time helping employees and satisfying needs of the work group. These supervisors are more interested in people than in things. They want to eliminate frustration on the part of their employees. They want their employees' personal needs satisfied. They want to develop a comfortable, friendly atmosphere or environment in which their employees work. They want to boost their employees' morale, reduce their tensions, and help them realize their personal needs for social sanction and work satisfaction.

Good leaders manage to combine both qualities in their leadership style. They know that if they emphasize the job only, they will be considered drivers and hard taskmasters, thereby risking the loss of group cooperation and support. On the other hand, if they emphasize only the employee or social aspect, they will be regarded as popularity seekers. Employees may even use the efforts of such a leader for their personal advantage, and productive output will suffer.

approach to job

To be a good leader, therefore, you should strive to combine both qualities. Try to provide a balanced approach, giving emphasis to maintaining morale and at the same time getting an adequate work performance. In other words, you should be thoughtful and help promote employee satisfaction, but at the same time you should recognize the role that productive output plays.

WHAT ARE THE FOUR TYPES OF LEADERS?

Some leaders are very bossy, some are very strict, others try to get their employees involved in making decisions, and still others just leave their employees alone. These four types of leaders are:

1. Dictatorial.
2. Authoritarian.
3. Democratic.
4. Permissive.

You will easily recognize these types when you see them.

Dictatorial leaders are exactly what the name implies. They are negative leaders and hold threats of punishment, discharge, and fear over the heads of their employees to get them to perform. Although this type of leader gets results in some work situations, most managers doubt that the quality and quantity of his results can long remain at a high level. This type of leader almost invariably promotes unrest and dissatisfaction. Sooner or later the employees "revolt" by implementing a work slowdown or by simply transferring to other jobs. Dictatorial leadership seldom lasts over long periods of time.

Authoritarian leaders exercise strong control over their subordinates. You have probably seen this type—leaders who always resist help from others and play their cards close to their chests, withholding information from their employees, making them dependent on the leader for decisions. The authoritarian leader is the strong "captain of the ship" and controls all coordination and interface between workers in achieving the group's goal. Because of this leader's strong control and the group's dependence on precise directions, the group is virtually lost in the leader's absence.

Democratic leaders, on the other hand, solicit aid and advice from employees, trying to get them involved in work problems and their solutions. This is the type of leader whose group can function effectively even during the leader's prolonged absences. The reason, of course, is because the employees are used to working with problems and their solutions and are aware of the group's situation and progress. In the leader's absence, therefore, they can take over and move ahead.

*supervisory
styles*

Permissive leaders are not very effective leaders at all. Inasmuch as their positions of leadership are decreed by upper management, they are leaders in name only. They are sometimes the boss's kids, or they may have married into the "old man's" family to get the position. Permissive leaders are more or less figureheads with little or no power and are virtually never listened to or respected by the employees. They are so eager to appease the requests of their employees, that they gradually lose all their power. In situations like this, where the appointed leader is really a leader in name only, the true position of leadership is usually assumed by some other individual (perhaps the leader's assistant) or by some senior person in the work group whom the workers like and respect.

Which Type Is Best?   We can't say that one particular type of leadership is best in every case. What is best in one situation may be worst in another. It depends on you, the work, and the employees you are working with. In general, the democratic form is probably the all-around best. In situations where close control must be maintained, your group might well prefer an authoritarian type of leader. For example, if you are supervising a rescue effort, then an authoritarian type might be best. But if you are supervising a group of highly skilled self-starters (such as research scientists), then the permissive or let-them-alone type of leadership may be best. In most work situations you will have to judge which type would be best suited to or which combination would be best for your particular operation and the employees involved.

DO BEHAVIOR PATTERNS AFFECT TEAMWORK?

Both experience and studies have shown that the one factor that affects a group's behavior and motivation most is the behavior pattern of the leader.

If your behavior shows that you are the *dependent* (vs. *independent*) type of leader, then you are probably afraid to make decisions—to take chances. You are primarily concerned with saving your own hide; therefore, you follow rules and regulations to a "T." You communicate with your employees only when absolutely necessary. As a result of all this, your employees have no spirit and lack incentive. A general atmosphere of apathy and doing nothing prevails. Teamwork suffers.

If your behavior pattern is *commanding* in nature, then your actions may promote anger and antagonism. You exercise close control and generally limit your communications with your employees to giving them orders or directions. You may get work done by being dictatorial, but your employees are unhappy, antagonistic, and rebellious. Poor teamwork results.

If you want to concentrate on your own personal advancement, then your behavior pattern may be *diplomatic* in its approach. If you are this type, you know how to handle people and get along reasonably well with both your employees and your superiors. You have frequent contacts with your employees, but largely on a superficial basis. You tend to manipulate people, and your employees are not team-oriented. Instead, they are interested in their own selfish ends.

If you want to promote an air of cooperation and teamwork, your behavior pattern should be that of a *coach* or *team* leader. Using this pattern of behavior, you aim at building a team, at coaching the individual members. The group as a whole, instead of the individual, is dominant in your thinking. You have free and easy communications with your employees, and a sincere two-way exchange of ideas takes place. Your entire team seeks to achieve productive goals *as a team*, and thereby the whole team wins advancement as well as security in the organization. Using the coaching style, you emphasize the "we" versus the "I" or "you" approach. You discuss problems and solutions rather than give orders. You decide on action by mutual agreement instead of by rules and direct orders. You promote an atmosphere where two-way communications can easily take place between

effect of leader's behavior pattern

you and your employees. And, finally, you promote teamwork and loyalt instead of apathy.

The team approach is probably the ideal behavior pattern fc leader. Such individuals are concerned both with their employees and production. They are successful at motivating people to achieve Their employees are committed to doing the job that needs to be done. They see the relationship between their personal job satisfaction and work achievement. A leader possessing the coach or team behavior pattern thus successfully shows the employees the need for the existence of a mutual relationship of trust and respect both among themselves and between themselves and the leader. Thus, the team leader promotes respect among employees for their individual jobs and accomplishments.

WHAT CHARACTERISTICS OF LEADERSHIP DO EMPLOYEES LOOK FOR?

No two leaders are exactly alike, and no one type can be singled out as the ideal leader that employees are looking for. One person might look for one aspect of leadership, whereas another employee might emphasize another aspect. Despite these differences, surveys show that there are specific qualities that most employees look for in a leader. A majority of employees want a leader who gives recognition and credit for doing a job. They like to be patted on the back. They also want to work for leaders who are friendly and who keep them informed about what is going on in the department—not leaders who rarely communicate and who play their cards close to their chests.

Employees like to work for a leader who lets them know where they stand, how they are doing, and what their chances for promotion or advancement are. They also want a leader who gives them a sense of importance—who makes them feel that they are needed members of the team. They like to work for leaders who are organized in their work—who plan their work, then work their plans—and who have well-defined jobs and keep everything in its place.

leaders who promote teamwork

Workers like leaders who promote teamwork in their department by emphasizing the positive rather than negative aspects of their performances, and who provide the opportunity to get their ideas heard and tried out.

Finally, employees like to work for leaders who are fair, impartial, and just in their dealings, thereby promoting a feeling of trust and security.

ARE LEADERS BORN OR MADE?

No one is a "born" leader. You may have certain capacities that enable you to develop into a leader, but you have to work at it. What are the capacities that you need if you want to lead others? No one can say for sure. However, if you look at good leaders, you will probably find that the common traits in the majority of them are as follows:

1. *Intelligence.* Leaders are usually a bit smarter or a bit more intelligent than their followers. This does not mean that a successful leader must have an excess of intelligence over his average follower. But it does mean that he is a bright and alert person with above average intelligence.

2. *Understanding.* Leaders need to have an understanding of and feeling for other people. Because leaders work with people and get things done through the efforts of others, they must be accurately attuned to the feelings of others, to their goals, and to their problems. A good coaching leader should be sensitive to the values of the entire group in addition to those of the individuals.

3. *Sociability.* Good leaders need to be active socially. They need to participate actively in group functions. They need to initiate actions for others and for the group as a whole.

4. *Communicability.* Good leaders need to be able to make themselves and their ideas understood by their employees. They need to be able to communicate messages accurately and clearly. If leaders can't communicate their "million-dollar" ideas, they are worthless.

5. *Ability to handle criticism.* If leaders are disturbed by criticism, they're headed for failure. A good leader can and does, however, take and welcome deserved criticism while shrugging off tactless, heavy-handed attacks from adversaries.

6. *Confidence.* Good leaders don't "run scared." They aren't afraid that they will be replaced if they teach someone else to do their job. Instead, they train their assistants thoroughly, teach them all the specifics of the job and help them to understand all its aspects, and finally, make the other employees aware of the assistants and their supervisory responsibilities. The confident leader will frequently let the assistant "try his wings" at supervising some job, then later let the assistant have a go at supervising the whole department. This training includes not only the productive aspects of the department, but also employee interviewing, employee training, and so on. And in all cases the confident supervisor coaches the assistant and explains how particular problems should be resolved.

   Having done all this, confident leaders can be absent from their jobs because of vacations or illness with no fear that work flow will slow down or that a mountain of problems will greet them when they return to work. Confident leaders are not trying to protect their jobs. They are not afraid of being replaced. They have confidence in themselves and thus are putting themselves in a position to be promoted when opportunities arise.

As you can see, you can work on, nurture, and develop most of these traits. You know that you probably have the native intelligence required to be a good leader. Therefore, using this native ability and intelligence, you can improve your capacity to understand others, increase your social activity, improve your communications skills, and develop your ability to accept criticism. Most people agree that with study and practice, a person can develop into a good leader.

You must remember, however, that a person's leadership capacity is relative to the intelligence, attitudes, and abilities of the workers in a particular work situation. This means that although you might be a good leader in one work group, you might not be able to be a leader in another work group. An individual who has the capacity to be the governor of a state and to lead legislators might be a miserable leader in a work group in a manufacturing plant. The capacity to lead is always relative to those being led. You can be a leader in *many* situations, but not in *all* situations.

HOW CAN YOU SPOT A POOR SUPERVISOR?

Obvious cases of poor supervision are easy to spot. But more often than not, it is difficult to detect a weak or poor supervisor. Marginal supervisors can and do use all sorts of techniques to hide or mask their lack of skill. Let's consider a few of them.[1]

This Is My Style.   When questioned or confronted, these supervisors cover up their inability by saying things like "My job is different," or "This is my style," or "This job takes a special approach." Then they'll say something like "What you think and say about my department may be true, but I stand by my results. They speak for themselves. We don't all use the same approach to supervision. This is the way I do it." The supervisor saying this relies on your agreement that what matters is results, not the way they are accomplished. Frequently the boss will "buy" this approach and leave the "muddlers" alone.

Doing Other Jobs.   Some supervisors compensate for a poor job by doing tasks that are highly visible and that can be done well. It may be organizing retirement dinners or Christmas parties, meeting guests and showing them around, or giving the VIPs from corporate headquarters the royal treatment. In all of these tasks, the boss gets lots of attention. Of course, while such supervisors are doing all these things, their jobs have to slide. But they have an excuse. And their boss accepts it because—well, who else could do these extra things so well? The fact remains that the marginal supervisory performance goes on, but is hidden by other self-assumed jobs.

[1] For a complete discussion see "Why Inept Bosses are So Hard to Spot," *Management Review*, August, 1980, pp. 23–6.

Two-Decade Dot.   This is the supervisor who has been on the job for years and years, but always out of sight, lost in the hierarchy of the organization. When such supervisors finally come to light for a promotion, their performance is poor, but "You can't fire someone who has been with the company for 20 years." So she's left alone because "Dot's been here a long time and has probably done a lot of good work." Poor supervision is thus overshadowed by longevity.

WHAT ARE SOME POINTS TO REMEMBER ABOUT BEING A LEADER?

Remember that leadership is the capacity to get others to follow you willingly and to do what you want them to do. As a leader, you will be called upon to make decisions that will be unpopular with some of your employees. You can't, therefore, be a "good Joe" to everyone. What you want to strive for is your employees' respect and their satisfaction with your leadership. Leading is, to a degree, a lonely job, but at the same time a rewarding one. You will have a sense of accomplishment for your company and for your workers. You will possess status and prestige among your friends in the community as well as among the employees at work. And, of course, you will have a higher income with the higher (and more difficult) job.

As a leader you will always depend on your employees for support. In fact, without their support and cooperation, you cannot lead. Thus, the authority or control you have over your employees is what they give you. Resist pulling your rank, therefore, except in cases of real demand. If you are just, fair, and impartial, you will earn the support and respect of your em-

leadership check points

ployees, and you won't have to pull your rank by telling them that you are the boss and they must do what you say.

Know where you are going and how you are going to get there. Then communicate this to your employees. Make the goal important and exciting, and show how it is possible to accomplish it. You'll get greater support if they perceive your decisiveness and sense of direction.

Handle different employees in different ways. Be firm and authoritative with the insecure and dependent type of employee as well as with the pushy and hostile employee. Be cooperative and willing to discuss problems with your cooperative, aggressive, and willing worker. Be democratic and give a free rein to employees who are self-starters, who know their jobs, and who work best with the least supervision. In any critical or emergency situation, however, always use the authoritarian approach. If the boat is sinking, you don't want to call a conference to discuss who should dip water!

Show courage and persistence. Don't back off from danger, resistance, or opposition.

Don't try to take credit for what the group has done. Most great leaders are modest and are quick to give credit to others for their accomplishments. Good leaders don't have to say how good they are—the loyalty of their followers and the group's work will speak it "loud and clear" for them.

Employees respond positively to leaders who don't try to give themselves
all the credit.

37

LEADING AND
SUPERVISING
OTHERS

Be genuine. Don't project a "know-it-all" air. If you don't know the
answer to a problem posed by an employee, say so. Then ask the employee
for his opinion. If he doesn't have an answer, tell him you will get an answer
to the problem and will let him know. Getting help and suggestions from
others makes for better human relations.

Be consistent. Your employees will want to be able to predict what
your answer will be today as well as tomorrow. Always show enthusiasm for
a job well done and disapproval for slovenly work. Don't sometimes avoid
the job of disapproving because it is unpleasant.

Try to understand your employees. Try to put yourself in their shoes;
if you do, you will be able to predict their needs and responses. You will
know your employees better and can give them more appropriate advice
and instructions.

Finally, always be fair and just. Treat all of your employees in the
same way. Don't show favoritism. Having a "teacher's pet" in your department will cause dissension among your employees and could destroy a good
team that you have worked hard to build.

QUESTIONS FOR DISCUSSION AND REVIEW

1. What qualities do you need to be a good leader? Explain each.
2. Which three qualities of leadership do you think are the most important? Why?
3. What traits indicate a poor leader?
4. What is a work group leader? Who appoints him? Is he important to a
   smoothly operating group? Why?
5. Explain the difference between job-centered and employee-centered
   leadership.
6. Describe the four types of leaders. Which type is best? Why?
7. How do leadership patterns affect the way people work together?
8. Do you think leaders are born or made? Explain your answer.
9. Explain some important points that you should remember if you want
   to be a good leader.
10. What sorts of actions indicate a poor leader/supervisor?

A Case Study
THE CASE OF THE OILY RAG

Ben Adams had worked eight years for a textile firm specializing in double knits when he was
promoted to supervisor of the packing and shipping department. Although he had been well

liked by the men prior to his promotion, an incident that occurred raised a question in his mind.

His story goes like this. The men in the packing and shipping department, according to him, had fallen down on their jobs, and were "goofing off" at least 30% of the time before he was made their supervisor. Aware of this, he instituted a strict work program, telling every employee work group exactly what to do, when he expected the job to be completed, and what their next job assignment would be. This information was communicated by a departmental "work order" that he designed. Men who were caught away from their assigned work areas without excuses were subject to layoff or dismissal. Reporting late to work from rest breaks or lunch periods also brought reprimands from him.

The men, sensing that he was trying to make a good showing, tried to cooperate with his "new broom" approach until the day he caught one group cleaning up in the washroom a good 10 or 15 minutes before lunch time. He immediately sent them back to their work stations with a promise of a penalty deduction from their pay. According to the men, this was the last straw; they knew that their old buddy had deserted them.

The next day, as Ben walked through his department checking up on his men, a dirty, oily rag sailed through the air in some mysterious way and hit him squarely in the face. In a fit of rage, he vowed to fire the individuals responsible for the act. Although the men declared their innocence and suggested that perhaps the rag had been thrown from one of the moving arms on a packing machine, it was obvious that they were amused by the incident.

1. What was wrong with Ben Adams's supervision?
2. How should he have behaved in his new assignment as supervisor of the packing and shipping department?
3. What action, if any, should he take about the incident of the oily rag?
4. If you were Ben's boss, what advice would you give him?

A Case Study
BUNNIES BURGERS

As president of Bunnies Burgers, Ken Johnson was always on the lookout for a potential manager for one of the chain's outlets.

Founded in 1972, the chain had grown from sales of $230,000 during its first year to current annual sales of $673,000,000. It was known as the leader in its field, and no small part of its success was due to the shrewd and capable management of Mr. Johnson. In his words, "Our most valuable asset is our employee. And our most valued employee is a qualified leader who can manage one of our food centers." He believed what he said and spent the greatest part of his time in looking for, interviewing, and recruiting potential managers.

His latest applicant was a young man named Robert Nicosea. Robert's experience was not too exciting: work in a supermarket as a checker, and summer work during school intersessions as a construction laborer and as a clerk in an accounting firm. Not too impressive a record, to be sure, but what struck Mr. Johnson was Robert's burning desire to get ahead—to succeed, to make something of himself.

Robert's job in the supermarket was head checker, and as such he was responsible for hiring, training, and manning the eleven registers. The job also entailed checking out each register daily to be sure that the tapes and the money checked. The store manager wrote a glowing account of Robert's job performance but did indicate that he was a little impatient to move ahead—to get promotions and salary increases.

When interviewed by Mr. Johnson, Robert exhibited an almost contagious enthusiasm for honest work, belief in his fellow man, and a desire to move ahead on the job. According to his personal data sheet, Robert Nicosea was the leader and informal spokesman for his local bass fishing club, and in addition was president of his town's Young Man's Fellowship Group. When asked about his prior work and his current involvement in other groups, Robert pushed them aside as only routine—nothing to brag about.

When Mr. Johnson asked Robert why he wanted to be the manager of one of their outlets—why he thought he would be a good leader—Mr. Nicosea thought for a moment and replied, "First of all, I know I can do the job. I've had experience in food handling in a supermarket, and I know figures and book work. Also, I think I know how to handle employees. I believe that people who work for you like to see their boss have a strong hand and exercise sound and strong control. They like a supervisor who is not afraid to make decisions and will make them quickly. They like a boss who runs a taut ship. And I think that all of these things apply to me.

"I don't mind sticking my neck out. I'm not afraid to make a decision. And I surely don't mind telling an employee to do something—to give instructions. Furthermore, if an employee doesn't follow through with what I give him to do, I don't mind reprimanding him, even firing him if he doesn't prove that he can do the job.

"I believe that I'm a born leader. I've always wanted to tell others what to do. Even when I was a little kid, I always wanted to lead the rest of the kids on my block—to tell them what we would do, to be the captain of the outfit.

"For these reasons, Mr. Johnson, I know that I could be one of your best managers within a year. I'm sure that I can run one of your outlets and increase business and profits. I'm a hard worker. I don't mind long hours, hard work, and tough goals. Give me the chance, and I will prove to you that I can get results."

Thanking Mr. Nicosea for coming to see him, Mr. Johnson indicated that he was interviewing several other candidates and would let him know his decision within a couple of days. The two shook hands and Nicosea departed.

Mr. Johnson was clearly impressed with Mr. Nicosea. But he wondered whether or not Robert Nicosea would fit in as the manager of a fast foods outlet. Did he have the leadership abilities he was looking for, or would he be too dictatorial in running an outlet catering to the eating public?

He was mulling over these ideas when his secretary announced the arrival of another appointment.

1. Would you hire Robert Nicosea? Why?
2. What leadership qualities do you see in Mr. Nicosea? Are they the type of qualities that would be effective in a fast food outlet?
3. Do you see any qualities that could be detrimental to Mr. Nicosea's success in Bunnies Burgers?

A Case Study
HELEN GOODMAN, FORELADY

Helen Goodman had been maintenance forelady at the local telephone office for six years when she was confronted by all of her employees at quitting time. After a few comments by their speaker, they presented a long list of complaints to Helen. She received the list, thanked them, and the employees left.

The group impressed her as not militant, but quite serious. She could not shrug off the incident as insignificant. Through the years, her theory had always been that the "complaining soldier was the happy soldier." Therefore, she had frequently passed off an employee complaint as a superficial gripe from a basically happy employee.

As she thought back on her work in the maintenance department, she recognized that from time to time she had gotten complaints from individual employees, perhaps more than the normal number. However, she had dismissed them casually because she did not believe they were serious. Now, confronted by a long list of complaints from all of her employees, she really "sat up and took notice," as one of the men said.

The complaints from the employees varied; the following are typical examples:

1. You don't understand us or maintenance work.
2. You are distant—we never really get to know you.
3. We are never sure you pass our suggestions up the line.
4. You show partiality to the female employees.
5. You are more concerned with the show that the maintenance department will make than you are with supervising the maintenance employees.
6. You follow the rules too strictly.

1. Judging from the list of complaints, what major problems exist for Helen Goodman?
2. What corrective action should she take? Why?
3. Do you think she has potential to continue as a successful leader/supervisor? Why?

A Personal Case Problem

You have been asked to speak before a local civic club on the topic of leadership. They specifically ask that you describe what a good leader is like.

1. What will you tell them?
2. How will you describe a top-ranked leader?
3. What negative aspects will you tell them to avoid in selecting a leader?

3

USING TIME WISELY

This chapter explains—

- How time is a resource
- How time is wasted
- How to use your time wisely
- How to save time
- How computers help to save time

Like everyone else, you've been allotted only sixty minutes for every hour. How well you use these sixty minutes determines your success. Any supervisor can do virtually anything if given enough time. But the supervisor who moves ahead is the one who does the most in the least time. He uses his time wisely.

How many times have you said, "There aren't enough hours in a day. I just don't have enough time"? Many supervisors feel this way, stating that they need 25 to 50 percent more time to do a really good job. Stop for a moment to consider that everyone has the same amount of time: 24 hours every day. Although you can't add any more hours to a day, what you can do is use these 24 hours in the wisest, most effective way possible as a supervisor. Knowing how to use time effectively is one of the greatest skills that any supervisor can have.

IS TIME A RESOURCE?

Is time a resource? You bet it is! All supervisors work with four vital resources. They work with their *employees*—directing their efforts. They work with all sorts of *materials* (buildings, machines, raw materials)—using them, changing them, fabricating them. They work with *financial resources*—wisely investing them. They work with *time*—trying to make every minute count to get maximum output in the least time. Think of these resources as the supervisor's big "M":

a supervisor's resources

M en and women
aterials
oney
inutes

You can't do your job without any one of them. How wisely you use each one determines your degree of success as a supervisor. Although your boss may determine to a large degree the amount of men and women, materials, and money you have at your disposal, your time is your own; how you use it is up to you.

Despite the importance of using time wisely, however, many supervisors give it the least consideration and, therefore, mismanage it the most. Their time is frequently unplanned, uncontrolled, and uninspired. They think they know how they use their time, but in reality they have no idea where their time goes.

CAN YOU SPOT SUPERVISORS WHO DON'T PLAN THEIR TIME?

It is easy to spot supervisors who don't plan the use of their time. They say they have to be in ten places at once, or they claim they need 36 hours a day to do their work. What they're really saying is that either they don't know how to plan and use time wisely, or they don't understand what their job as a supervisor is.

Supervisors who don't plan their work—who don't plan how they will use their time—often complain about not having enough time. They are the ones who kill their days doing wasteful and unnecessary things. Are you this type of supervisor? How do you spend your day? If you don't have a precise picture of what you are doing, you need to make an inventory of how you use your time. Such an inventory would show how many meetings you attend, how much time you spend in coffee breaks, how much routine clerical work you are doing (that someone else could do!), and so on. An inventory of what you do would show how you are spending your time and point out where you may be wasting it.

evidence of not
planning

HOW IS TIME WASTED?

Time not used productively is wasted. To see if you are wasting time, mentally review the things you do during the day that are nonproductive— things that are time wasters. You will probably recognize such time wasters as:

Socializing

Jumping from one task to another

Meeting visitors

Shooting the breeze

Attending unnecessary meetings

Coffee and cigarette breaks

Lengthy telephone calls

Reading junk mail

Completing needless forms

Doing personal work.

These, and similar things, cut supervisory efficiency. Why, you might ask, are supervisors involved in these time wasters? Why are they killing time? When you study their actions, you will probably find the following causes for their poor performance:

time wasters

- They have not clearly established work objectives in their own minds. Therefore, they flounder.
- They have not set work priorities. They jump from one task to another.
- They have too many interruptions and visitors.
- Their employees are "incompetent," so they have to do additional work.

"When it is not used productively, time is wasted."

- They lack the needed information to do the work properly.
- They are poorly organized.
- They have made improper task assignments to their employees.
- They procrastinate.

Although incomplete, the above list gives you some idea of how supervisors let a priceless resource—time—slip away. They fail to perform the single most important task that would enable them to make optimal use of time: they fail to adequately plan their work day.

HOW SHOULD YOU PLAN YOUR DAY?

First, make a list of your time wasters. Then, look carefully at each item and cross off those over which you have no control. For example, if your boss requires you to attend useless meetings, cross this off your list. You have no control over this loss of time. When you finish, you'll probably find that very few items are crossed off your list—that most of your time wasters are things you can control. This being true, it follows that you are in the driver's seat and can, therefore, do something about the wise use of your own time. In other words, *wise time management starts with you.* You've got to learn to manage yourself and your time wisely. Even if you are a highly skilled person, have a vast amount of experience, and have the innate ability to supervise, you can't supervise well unless you first manage yourself wisely. To do this, you need to start by taking stock of yourself and finding out what kind of supervisor you are.

WHAT SUPERVISORY STYLE DO YOU USE?

There are all kinds of supervisors, of course. Some have one set of characteristics, some another. To help you determine what kind you are, consider the following supervisory styles.

Are you the type who likes to *be in charge?* Do you like to be on top of everything? Are you the type who makes quick decisions and tells employees what to do? If you are, then you are the type of supervisor who doesn't like to let go of things. You either fear to or fail to delegate. You don't want to let someone else do the job. You believe no one can do the job as well as you can, so you try to do it all. As a consequence, you find there aren't enough hours in a day. Suddenly you find you aren't supervising—you're working. You aren't delegating. And you aren't using your time wisely.

Are you the *impulsive, highly energetic* type? Do you try to cover the waterfront? Are you everywhere? Always moving? Always making quick decisions? Always action oriented? If so, you may be so energetic, so physically active, that you don't take time to think about and plan your day and your work. You react rather than act. What you need to do is plan your work, then work your plan. Instead, what you are doing is managing yourself by impulse and energy.

supervisory styles

Or are you the *easy-going, socially warm* type of supervisor? If its excessively important to you to be liked by your employees, you may spend most of your time promoting interpersonal relations. In so doing, you neglect the overall job of supervising your department.

Finally, are you the *submissive type* who always defers to the boss? Do you spend most of your time trying to find out what the boss wants? In doing this, time slips away from you.

Perhaps no single supervisory style fits you, although you may see yourself possessing some combination of these traits. If so, flesh out the picture by jotting down on a piece of paper all of your attributes—good and bad. Analyze this list and keep adding other attributes as they occur to you. This may take several days, but once completed, you will be able to study your supervisory style and spot weaknesses that you weren't aware of. Once you are aware of these weaknesses, you will be in a position to eliminate them. If, for example, you find you are the impulsive type, you can make an effort to think things through more carefully. If you see that you want to be on top of everything, you can systematically start delegating—letting others do part of the work.

When you have discovered your supervisory style, your next move is to find out precisely how you spend your time. Do this by charting the way you spend your day. Make a supervisor's time-analysis chart for yourself.

A time-analysis chart (Figure 3–1) is a sheet of paper on which you list vertically the hours in your workday in 15-minute intervals, 8:00, 8:15, 8:30, 8:45, and so on. Make a separate chart for each day. Then, as you go through the day, keep an account of what you do, and record it next to the appropriate time intervals. Be conscientious and accurate. Don't estimate and try to make it look good. Remember, you are trying to find out how you *actually* spend your day—not how you *think* you spend your day.

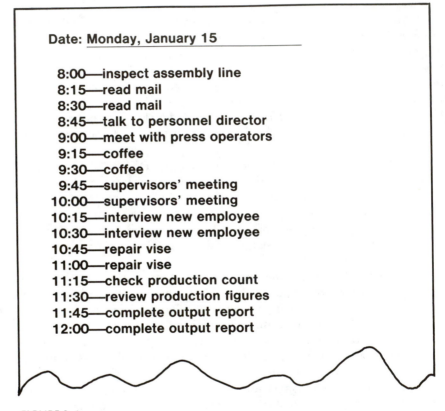

Date: Monday, January 15

8:00—inspect assembly line
8:15—read mail
8:30—read mail
8:45—talk to personnel director
9:00—meet with press operators
9:15—coffee
9:30—coffee
9:45—supervisors' meeting
10:00—supervisors' meeting
10:15—interview new employee
10:30—interview new employee
10:45—repair vise
11:00—repair vise
11:15—check production count
11:30—review production figures
11:45—complete output report
12:00—complete output report

FIGURE 3–1.
A supervisor's time-analysis chart.

At the end of a week, summarize the number of minutes you spent doing different things each day. You might find, for example, that you are spending eight hours each week reviewing and discussing your employees' work with them. This means you spent 20% of your week doing this. Maybe you'll find that you spent ½ hour each morning and ½ hour each afternoon at coffee breaks—12½% on this. And so on.

By analyzing your time-analysis chart, you will find out what you *are actually doing.* Now ask yourself what you *should be doing.* Are you doing everything you should? Can some of your work be discontinued for more important things? It's your job and you know it best, but remember that you should give at least 60% of your time to supervising the work of your department. Do you find that you are doing too many special jobs "that only you know how to do"? Special jobs that crop up can ruin your effectiveness as a supervisor. If you aren't careful, you may find that you are spending 50% of your time on them, when 10 to 15% is a better time allocation.

As you review the sheets, ask yourself whether or not you are spending an excessive amount of time on coffee breaks and other activities. Search for places where you should be spending more time. Search for activities where you could save time, thereby making it available for more critical activities. Ask yourself if what you do has to be done by you. Can your employees do some of it? How much of your routine work could you assign to one of your employees? Now look at the supervisory work that you alone need to do. Are you spending enough time on that? Are you using your time wisely?

Finally, ask yourself whether you have time to think, to be creative, to plan ahead. If your answer is no, then rework the way you spend your day. Eliminate what is unnecessary. Reassign other jobs. Make time for the important job of supervising!

*using a
time-analysis
chart*

HOW SHOULD YOU PLAN AND USE YOUR TIME?

After you've made and analyzed a time-analysis chart of your day, try *budgeting* your time. Use your desk calendar or a sheet of paper, and plan what you will do with your time for each day in the week. Divide the day into half-hour intervals. Your budget for Monday might read something like this:

- 8:00– 8:30 inspect presses, check oiler
- 8:30– 9:00 inspect copy machine
- 9:00– 9:30 interview new employee
- 9:30–10:00 attend monthly staff meeting
- 10:00–10:30 attend monthly staff meeting

*budgeting your
time*

and so on.

Making a general budget like this is planning for what you want to accomplish. What are you trying to do is allocate or budget your time by breaking it down into categories of how you will use it. Note that in the illustration you have allocated:

- One hour for inspection, 12½% of your day.
- One-half hour for interviewing, 6¼% of your day.
- One hour for meetings, 12½% of your day.

At the end of each day decide what budgeted things must be done tomorrow. List these "must-be-done" things in order of priority. Finally, put them on your general time budget for the next day.

If you wish, you can prepare a more precise budget by using actual starting and ending times instead of the half-hour intervals discussed above. To make this more precise budget, you first estimate the amount of time you will need to perform the various things you wish to accomplish. You might, for example, allocate 8 minutes to answer a letter, 4 minutes for a phone call, 25 minutes for a meeting, and so on. After making these time allocations, you set starting and ending times for each budgeted job. For example, you may have eight letters to answer, so you set the starting time at 8:55 A.M. and the ending time at 10:00 A.M. (eight letters @ 8 minutes each). Do the same thing for all your budgeted tasks, leaving some extra time as a cushion between jobs. By thus making a timetable with starting and stopping deadlines for all your regular tasks, you'll find that you will accomplish much more work during your normal work day. Without such a plan, however, you will find that unimportant tasks may drag on without a deadline, and at the end of the day you will have accomplished very little.

Prepare either a general or a precise budget like this every day for a week. At the end of the week compare your budgeted time with the actual time you used as shown on your time-analysis chart for the same time period. This comparison will show you how well you used your time— whether you accomplished everything you planned to in the time allocated. If you didn't, ask yourself what you could have done that you failed to do, or what you did that you shouldn't have done. Questions like the following will help you decide where you need to make changes:

1. What did I do that my employees could have done just as well or better?
2. What things did I do that were required by my job?
3. What things did I do that were not required by my job?
4. How much time did I spend on paper work? Could someone else have done it?
5. What things should I do to be a good supervisor? Did I allocate enough time to do these things?
6. What things did I put off until a later date? Why?
7. What things did I do that could have been left undone?
8. Do I do the same things over and over? Why?
9. What things do I do most efficiently? Why?
10. What things do I do most inefficiently? Can I improve here?

These, and similar questions about how you used your time, will help you formulate a plan for more effective use of your time. You will find that by searching for better ways to use your time, you will use it more wisely. You will get more done. And you will be a better supervisor.

Making a time budget like this is a plan for what you want to accomplish. It might not work out exactly as you hoped at first. If not, make the necessary adjustments until you have a plan that allows you flexibility, but still provides you with a way to spend your day effectively. *Plan your work—then work your plan.*

ARE THERE OTHER THINGS YOU CAN DO TO USE TIME WISELY?

To further use time wisely, try the following:

Get in the Time-saving Habit.   Make up your mind to use your time more wisely, then set up a routine to do it. Don't let any opportunity to make better use of your time slip by. It will take a great deal more time and effort to recover an opportunity than it will to act at the time it occurs. The more you seize opportunities to better use your time, the better you will become at it. Soon it will become second nature. Resolve, therefore, to make better use of your time, then start doing it!

Don't Get "Snowed" by the "Urgent."   Many supervisors find themselves almost snowed under by the "urgent," the must-be-done-now tasks. If you don't watch yourself, you'll spend all your time putting out these "urgent" brush fire emergencies and let the really important things go undone. Think back on some of your recent "emergencies." Viewed from a later perspective, do you find that most of them were actually minor projects given the status of major crises? One measure of good supervision is the ability to distinguish between the unimportant and the urgent. When something "urgent" comes up, don't automatically jump. Refuse to be snowed; refuse to be managed by crisis. Take time to see the "urgent" task in its overall perspective. Then give it the proportionate share of time it deserves. Remember that haste makes waste.

tips on using your time

Combine Similar Jobs.   For example, select a certain hour and write all your letters at that time. Don't spread them throughout the day. You'll waste time getting ready to start on each letter.

Learn to Say No.   Someone is always asking you for an hour of your time. Don't hesitate to say no. Tell them you'd like to help but that you are already overcommitted. Don't hesitate or hedge. If you do, you'll end up doing something you don't have time for.

Don't Procrastinate.   Make up your mind with due speed; then tell your employees what you want done. If you haven't made up your mind, if you are "still thinking about it," you obviously don't know what you want done, your employees don't know, and nothing gets done about it.

plan your work

Be Specific.   When the Personnel Department calls, for example, and wants to know when you can interview a prospective employee, don't say, "Any time this week." Look at your calendar and set a time that will provide you with ample time to devote to the interview; otherwise the prospect might show up in the middle of a grievance session. Ask your assistant to "get this done on Tuesday," not "when you get around to it." Make a note of it on your calendar for Tuesday to remind yourself to ask your assistant about it.

Watch the Open Door.   Too many supervisors waste their time shooting the breeze with first one person, then another. They have a policy that says "You can always see me. My door is always open." This sounds good but is a sure way to ruin your plan and waste your time. See people if necessary, and be polite; but when they just drop in to tell you about their latest vacation plans, ease them out with "I'm sure enjoying your visit, Gerry, but unfortunately I've got to get a report ready for the boss. Let's continue this later."

Don't Trust Your Memory—Make a List.   Jot down reminders of things you need to do. If necessary, make yourself some "things-to-do" folders—one for each day, one for each week, and one for each month. Then, as you think of something that needs to be done on Wednesday, scribble yourself a note and drop it in the appropriate folder. When that day arrives, pull out the folder to see what you need to do. When you're away from your desk, always carry a pocket pad and pencil to jot down reminders. Then put the reminders in the appropriate folder when you return to your desk.

Use the Exception Principle.   The *exception* principle will make your work easier by calling to your attention only those things that need your action. It works this way. Suppose you want to be sure that the #4 shear is working at a high rate of efficiency. Its normal output is about 1600 pounds a day. You tell the operator to let you know whenever a day's production falls below 1500 pounds. In this way your attention is needed only when production drops. And as long as you're not called, everything is OK. The exception (in this case, less than normal production) is called to your attention.

The exception principle is easy to use on many parts of your job. First pick out the job you are concerned about, such as the number of units shipped, the number of letters filed, the number of accounts posted, etc. Next, decide what is an acceptable level of daily performance for your department, such as shipping 112 units, filing 75 letters, or posting 250 accounts. Then set up a system so that you will be notified when the performance drops below the acceptable level. In this way, you won't waste your time on things that do not need your personal attention and action.

Delegate.   Examine everything you do, and ask yourself questions like: "Is it necessary for this to be done? Can it be eliminated? If not, can one of my employees do it, thereby freeing me for more important matters?" If you don't have an employee who can do it, can you train one to do it? By systematically going through your job in this way, you'll probably find that

always try to delegate

you're doing some things that can be eliminated and that you can assign much of what's left to your employees.

You may think this is passing the buck. But remember, you can't do it all. That's why you have people helping you. People won't think you are lazy; neither will you lose control of your job by delegating. As a supervisor, your job is to get things done through other people. So start getting things done by assigning other people the routine jobs that you have been doing yourself.

If you find yourself using the following excuses for not delegating, take another look. They're probably *excuses* only and not valid reasons:

1. My subordinates are too inexperienced to do this. I have to do it myself.
2. It takes more time to explain the job and farm it out than it does to do it myself, so why go through the routine?
3. I can't afford to have my subordinates make a mistake for which I will be responsible.
4. This job is different. It demands my personal attention.
5. My workers are all busy, too, and don't have time for additional load.
6. I don't have anyone who will take the responsibility for work like this.
7. I got where I am today doing this type of work, and I don't plan to stop now.
8. If I pass it on to a subordinate, I'll lose control of the job. I won't know what's going on.
9. People will think I'm lazy—that I'm just passing the buck.
10. No one knows exactly how I want this job done.
11. If you want a job well done, you've got to do it yourself.
12. This job is too important to trust to a subordinate.
13. Doing this sort of thing is my occupational hobby, and I don't plan to turn it over to someone else.
14. I've got to OK the final product anyway, so why not do it to begin with?

Use Three Baskets for Paperwork. When you use the three-basket system, label one basket "Do today." Label another "Do next week." And label the third "Do when there's time." Now when anything comes to you, the first thing to do is decide its urgency—"today," "next week," or "sometime later." Put it in the appropriate basket (or drawer). Don't leave work until you have done all "today's" things today. On Monday of each week, take the material from basket number two, and decide what part you will get done on each day of the week. Then stick to the plan. When you have free time, check basket number three.

Think Before You Act. I once knew a supervisor who always managed to jump into the middle of every problem and thrash about furiously, not really knowing what he was doing or what should be done. The moral here is don't rush into action without doing a little thinking and planning. Be willing to take time out to think and plan what needs to be done, rather than diving in headfirst in an attempt to be *doing something*. At times like this, doing nothing is better. If you'll only take time to reflect on your work, you'll probably see shortcuts and timesavers that you would not otherwise discover.

"Use the three-basket approach."

Even in emergencies when someone yells, "Fire!" don't rush head-on into the problem without thinking: "Where is the fire? Where are the closest extinguishers? How should the alarm be turned on?" Deciding the answers to these and similar questions would probably take no more than 45 seconds, and they would be 45 seconds well spent in thinking before you act.

rules to use

Stay Off the Phone. You'll be surprised how much of your time is spent on the phone, just talking and waiting for the other fellow. Spending as much as 25 or 30% of the day on the phone is not uncommon for many supervisors who have made no attempt to plan their work. Try to limit your calls to three minutes. Some conversations will take longer, but shoot for three minutes. You should use the phone to save your legs, but conduct your business first; then if the other fellow is a talking machine, ease your way out by having "someone waiting for instructions."

Tackle the Tough Jobs First. Most supervisors who tackle the tough jobs first get the most work done. Those who postpone the tough jobs soon find work piling up, and they really get behind. Studies have shown that many supervisors spend their time doing things they like to do or are good at, rather than working on the tough jobs first. Check your priority scale. Do you put off the tough or unpleasant jobs as long as possible? This type of job may be easy to do—like a monthly efficiency report—but it's a job you don't relish. Tackle the tough or unpleasant jobs first—when you are at your peak of energy, when you feel your best.

Start the Job. Even if you can't finish the job, start it today. An unfinished job is much more of a motivator than an unstarted job. When was the last time you were able to wash only half of your car?

Plan Tomorrow Today. Never leave your place of work until you have looked over what you will have to do tomorrow and have made plans about how it will be done, when it will be done, who will do it, and so on. You will find that when you come to work in the morning, nothing motivates you better than having a plan of action for the day. Lacking a plan, you'll waste time trying to get something going.

Analyze Your Work Every Month. Review every job that you do at least once a month to see if it is necessary, if it can now be eliminated, or if it can be combined with another job. See what you can do to rearrange or cut down on a job. Study after study has shown that supervisors who don't take time to analyze their work in order to eliminate some of their activities and improve the work sequence of others are the ones who virtually always are ineffective in utilizing their time.

Set Aside Some Time to Think Each Day. Allow some time to think each day. It may be only 15 minutes at the beginning of each day, but set this time aside *without* interruption. Use it to think through your job—to look ahead at what needs to be done. Try to think in broad terms of planning your work, improving your operations, and in general trying to work "smarter," not harder.

At the End of Each Day, Review What You Have Done. Review your activities at the end of each day. Ask yourself why *you* had to do the job. Could all or part of it have been done by someone else? If so, make plans as to how you will handle the job next time. Then stick to your plans.

CAN COMPUTERS HELP YOU SAVE TIME?

Computers can indeed help you save time—*if you let them*. Some supervisors, however, are afraid of computers. They don't understand them and don't know what they can do. They even fear that the computer will control or limit their actions, thus restricting their freedom to move about, make decisions, and supervise employees. And, of course, some supervisors don't trust computers at all. So they keep two sets of records, one by hand and one on the computer! This fear, however, is not justified. Lack of understanding of what a computer is, how it can be used, and what programs are available cause many technically excellent applications to be overlooked by supervisors. In order that this won't happen to you, let's take a brief look at what a computer is and what it can do for you.

WHAT IS A COMPUTER?

Essentially, a computer is a programmable electronic device that can store, retrieve, and process data. In other words, a computer takes information (data) such as a list of names and automatically works on it—i.e., processes it into various forms. It may, for example, give you an alphabetical list, or it may produce a list that organizes the names from the shortest to the longest. It does all this without your help—it's automatic.

parts of a computer

Computers are made of four devices. One is an *input* device such as a keyboard to "type" information into the processor. You would use the keyboard, for example, to get information (like your list of names) into the computer. A second component is a *processor.* This works on (processes) the information that you put in the computer. The third part is a *memory* device that stores or retains information (the list of names) that you type into the computer. The fourth is an *output* device that gets the processed data (an alphabetical list of names, for example) from the computer. Frequently seen output devices are video screens (a TV-like screen) and printers (like a typewriter), which print or type the information on a sheet of paper.

WHAT ARE HARDWARE AND SOFTWARE?

Hardware and software are parts of a computer. The *hardware* components are the parts you can see and touch—like the keyboard (the input device), the video screen (the output device), and accessories like printers used to print the alphabetical list. *Software,* by contrast, consists of electrical instructions, which you cannot see or touch. Software is vital to the computer's operation because it tells the computer what to do. For example, it can tell the computer to count the letters in each name in your list and print out a list of names arranged from shortest to longest. Software usually comes in the form of cassettes, floppy disks, or plug-in cartridges. We'll talk about them later.

IS SOFTWARE CRITICAL?

As mentioned, software is vital because it tells the computer what to do. Without software, the computer would do nothing with the list of names that you gave it. Software can tell your computer how to figure sales taxes, how to balance your bank account, how to list names, and so on. Where do you get the software instructions to give your computer? You buy them from stores as computer software packages. You can readily find specially developed software for lawyers, insurance agents, brokers, hospitals, banks, or for any other number of professions, agencies, and purposes. These instructions come on cassette tapes (magnetic tape) or *floppy disks.* Floppy disks are sometimes called *diskettes.* Floppy disks are about the size of a 45-rpm record and are floppy or flexible, hence their name. Like magnetic tape, these disks have a magnetic coating that stores information.

need for software

Some computer software also comes in the form of *plug-in cartridges* like the game cartridges you can buy to play games at home on your TV set. You can't, however, use cartridges on all computers.

HOW CAN SUPERVISORS USE COMPUTERS?

You as a supervisor can use a computer in lots of ways that will enable you to save time and make better decisions, and therefore be a better supervisor. A computer, for example, can serve as a filing system for important information about your employees, sales, safety practices, inventory, and so on. You can enter important dates, facts, or things to do in your computer, and then each morning when you come to work you punch a button and the computer tells you what needs to be done that day. The computer, for example, might tell you to start a certain employee training program on that day. It might also remind you to wish a certain employee a happy anniversary. It might tell you to review the safety practices of your employees or to check the accuracy of a special quality control practice. The list goes on.

Your computer can store and process all types of records. For example, it can store and prepare all sorts of accounting information and reports, thus informing you of inventory levels, profit levels, cash flow, and so on.

If your job as a supervisor deals with a lot of paper work like printing, sorting, matching, etc., then computers can save you a tremendous amount of time. They can be a real help when you have to make business decisions based on a lot of incoming information. In fact, the ways computers can help you are limited only by your imagination. You or your company's computer specialist can dream up all sorts of ways that computers can make

how computers help supervisors

your job easier, less time consuming, and more effective. Computers can free you from dozens of routine time-consuming tasks, thereby giving you time to supervise your employees. Computers can do all sorts of jobs relating to general ledger work, accounts payable, accounts receivable, payroll, and inventory management.

Virtually every organization uses some system of inventory management. Whether this pertains to office supplies, medicine, or products produced, a computer can help you by giving you daily inventory status reports and a report showing what is on order and when the items will be received. The computer also provides you with an analysis of various items in terms of usage, cost, turnover, etc. It can show usage by weeks, by months, compared to the same period last quarter, or compared to the same period last year. It can give you year-to-date information on items ordered, shipped, sold, used, etc.

The computer can also save you time in preparing a written report or speech. Using your computer, you can quickly compose and edit your material. You can put sections from old reports into the new one, delete sections of your new report, make last minute changes, get the spelling corrected, and then send the "final report" via the computer to several other supervisors (in the same building, across town, or even out of state) for their comments and suggestions. All this can be done within minutes—not days or weeks. Thus, computers can support supervisors faced with multiple projects, assignments, and decisions.

In the area of engineering, a computer can help you save time by giving you plant and production information that will allow you to keep on top of daily operations. It can also provide you with data such as routing information, specific parts information, bills of materials, production control information, capacity requirements, manufacturing scheduling, materials control, inventory management, purchasing control, and so on.

IN WHAT AREAS CAN COMPUTERS HELP YOU SAVE TIME?

Computer applications are endless, but the following list will give you some ideas of the possible ways computers can help you save time, thereby enabling you to do a better job of supervising. You can use a computer for:

> maintaining inventory control
> preparing employee payrolls
> developing accounts receivable
> developing accounts payable
> preparing cash flow reports
> maintaining company tax records
> controlling security systems
> generating production control data

monitoring patients and their vital signs

office word processing

generating quality control reports

maintaining and preparing employee tax records and W–2 forms

handling routine correspondence

generating information and reports about expenses, costs, etc.

editing written documents

maintaining and updating mailing lists

maintaining and updating lists of customers and their use of products or services

training and educating employees

simulating economic activity

computer applications

analyzing data such as portfolios of stocks and bonds by comparing today's prices, earnings, and dividends to those over the past six or eight years

training employees by simulating actual work conditions in organizations such as hospitals, nuclear plants, subways, airlines, etc., where on-the-job training is not practical because it would endanger other people

figuring loan interest rate comparisons

calculating taxes for small businesses

keeping patient histories

analyzing real estate investments

keeping case files for doctors, attorneys, etc.

computing departmental efficiencies in rank order

The above are merely suggestive of the thousands of things that computers can do for you to make you a better, more effective supervisor.

ARE YOU MAKING THE BEST USE OF YOUR TIME?

Perhaps you are thinking that you are already doing your job well, that there are no frivolous parts that could be eliminated, shortened, combined, or put on a computer. Maybe you've already analyzed your job and eliminated the soft spots. If this is where you think you are, then ask yourself the following questions:

1. *Am I a detail hugger?* Do I check up on small details that are important to some jobs but have little meaning for mine? Examples are things like: "How long does it take to change ribbons on your typewriter, Sally?" "How much string do we use per year in tying up packages?" "How many of our employees drive full-size cars?"

best use of time

2. *Am I constantly on the go?* Do I find that the only way to get things done is by doing the work myself? Am I spinning my wheels rather than getting help from others or from a computer?

3. *Am I a conference caller?* Do I have to get everyone's opinion before I can make a decision? Is every decision I make so important that I have to have a meeting of my key people to discuss it?

4. *Am I always thinking about what we could do, not what we are doing?* Using your imagination and some daydreaming are important ways to discover new approaches to your job; but when you spend all of your time thinking about what you are going to do tomorrow, and thus accomplish little today, you aren't making the best use of your time.

5. *Do I need more time?* If you reduce the time it takes to do the individual parts of your work, you can save time on the whole job.

6. *Do I avoid using my computer?* Using your computer will give you more time to handle other problems, as well as enable you to do your work in less time.

7. *Do I have a hang-up?* Do I love figures or statistics or solving personnel problems so much that I neglect all the other parts of my job?

8. *Is my desk always overflowing with work?* Do I spend my time routinely working through stacks of paper, reading, approving, disapproving, signing, and routing papers put in front of me? Couldn't someone else do this for me?

If you answered yes to many of the questions above, take another look at yourself. Chances are you are wasting the day by doing everything except supervising people. Make a conscious effort to correct these personal deficiencies by planning and using your own time more efficiently.

QUESTIONS FOR DISCUSSION AND REVIEW

1. Explain how time is a resource.
2. How do supervisors waste time? Explain.
3. What can supervisors do to help themselves use their time more wisely?
4. Explain what a time-analysis chart is and how it is used.
5. How should you plan and use your time?
6. Explain the things a supervisor can do to use time wisely.
7. How does *delegating* help you use your time best?
8. How can tackling the tough jobs first help use time wisely?
9. What is meant by getting "snowed" by the "urgent"?
10. How can you spot supervisors who don't use their time wisely?

A Case Study
MATT HINSHAW'S PROBLEM

Matt Hinshaw didn't like it when his boss told him he needed to pay more attention to the work in his department, that he needed to concentrate on the important things and leave the rest to other people. "I don't know what he expects," Matt thought. "I never loaf, and I always work overtime—have more to do than one man *can do*. He must want a superman to run this department. It's more than one man can do." With that, he turned his attention to the work of the day.

As the whistle blew, he checked his work stations and saw two empty spots. "Wonder what happened to Slim and Mavis," he mused. Then he noticed that four stations weren't operating. "Wonder why? Before I wade into this, I'd better take an ulcer pill." After a walk to the fountain for water, Matt remembered the weekly report that he always made out. Of course his secretary could do it, but he felt that these production figures should be kept from her, and besides, if everyone knew what was going on, he might lose control.

After the weekly report, Matt turned his attention to what he thought of as his "fun job," computing each employee's efficiency on the basis of the number of rejected products. He knew his secretary could do this as well as he could, but he enjoyed doing it, and it didn't take too much time. In the middle of his computations, he remembered about Slim and Mavis, and went to check on them. Mavis had come in late, but Slim wasn't at work. Matt decided he would have to double up on Slim's work by putting one of the stockmen there.

Forty-five minutes later, he was back at his desk waiting for his secretary to finish typing his weekly special report to top management. He always personally took this to the front office and delivered it to the "top boys." In this way he could have a cup of coffee and butter up the bosses some.

During his lunch break, he talked with other supervisors about their work, asking for tips on how to get things done. One suggested that he stop going to the routine supervisors' meeting each week. It just took time. Matt knew that Joe Dawson would like to have the assignment, and it would be good training for him since he had been picked to be acting supervisor during Matt's absences. But Matt had always kept this job for himself because he was afraid something would happen that he should know about.

When he got back to his desk, he reviewed the weekly stock report prepared by his storekeeper, which he telephoned into central records at the home office in Chicago. It usually took about 15 or 20 minutes. Joe Dawson could do it, but Matt always believed it should be an accurate report, and he didn't want the big boss to jump on him because of inaccuracies.

Later, his secretary put a stack of routine forms in front of him, and as he systematically signed them, he wondered what his boss would say if he saw all the things that he (Matt) had to do during the day. Maybe the boss would stop saying he needed to pay more attention to the work in his department.

1. What is Matt's major problem?
2. If you were Matt's boss, how would you handle him?
3. What do you think Matt should do?

A Case Study
THE JANIE HENNIS CASE

Janie Hennis was determined to be a good supervisor. When she was promoted to supervisor after working 6 years in the shipping department, she made up her mind to do everything possible to be liked by both her employees and her bosses.

She knew that she understood the technical aspects of her work—and was respected for it. But her concern was to be liked and, therefore, have her employees do a good job for her. Mulling over this, she decided on several things she could do to achieve this objective.

She always visited with each employee briefly each day in order to stay on good terms. Always generous with her time, she never turned away an employee or associate who wanted to talk. Other employees in the plant knew that they could count on Janie to give them a helping hand when they needed one. Her office door was always open and the welcome mat was always out. As a consequence, her office was a popular spot to congregate for a break or discussing a problem.

An avid talker, she frequently received telephone calls from other supervisors asking her opinion on how to handle some of their particular problems. In short, Janie achieved her objective. She was quite popular.

With her new position, however, she found new problems. Supervision was much more time consuming than she thought it would be. She had to stay after work virtually every day to catch up on the really important things. The less important ones she put off to work on later. A part of every weekend was consumed with company problems.

After eleven months as supervisor, she began to sense subtle pressure from her supervisor to be more on top of things, to get things done more promptly. As she watched the other supervisors leave at 5:00 P.M. each day, she wondered how they did it—and still managed to be on top of their jobs.

1. Was Janie a good supervisor? Why?
2. What major flaws do you see in Janie's concept of supervision?
3. As a consultant, what suggestions would you offer Janie Hennis to help her get on top of her work?

A Personal Case Problem
HOW DO YOU SPEND YOUR DAY?

Keep a log of how you spend ten consecutive hours of one of your days. Be honest with your report and record your major activity during each quarter hour. When you have finished the ten-hour log, go back over this diary of your day and classify each activity as productive or nonproductive. Eating lunch, for example, would be classified as productive, while taking an afternoon nap would probably be nonproductive. Compute the percent of your time that you were nonproductive. If you spent about 3 hours in nonproductive activity, for example, this would mean that you spent 30% of your time nonproductively. Next, check each nonproductive activity to see whether it was necessary, whether it could be eliminated, or whether someone else could do it just as well.

If you can eliminate the nonproductive activity or assign it to someone else, draw a line through it. Having completed this, count the number of hours you could have saved by eliminating the activity or assigning it to another person. Calculate this percentage. For example, if you could save 1½ hours out of three hours that were nonproductive, you would save 50% of your nonproductive time.

Bring this time-saving exercise to your next meeting and compare your day with those of other members of the group. Who made the most savings in time? Why? How did they do it?

4

THE BIG JOB: COMMUNICATIONS

This chapter explains—

- Why good communications are important to you
- How you can communicate more effectively
- Why communications break down
- Your role in good communications
- How to put it in writing

✳ The better you communicate, the better you supervise. In fact, the skill and expertise with which you communicate are in direct proportion to your skill and expertise as a supervisor.

✳ In managing your department, you will need to communicate with employees to explain the work that must be done, discuss who is to do it, show how it should be done, and so on. Supervisors must give orders or directions to employees, describing what they should do and what is expected of them.

Not only do good communications tie together a group of employees, thereby making them work as a team, good communications also tie together various component parts of an organization. They promote understanding, they increase efficiency, they promote harmony, and they improve control. For example, without communications, the sales organization would not know what to sell, production would not know what to produce, and finance would not know the amount of money needed. In all of our organizations, communications serve to transmit information from one person to another, so that we will know what to do. Communications also help us form opinions about the company as a good (or bad) employer. Through communications we are motivated to perform certain jobs with skill and vigor, and communications help to orient us in our social and economic environment. All of these types of communications are a part of and are important to the job of supervising others.

WHAT IS A COMMUNICATION?

importance and definition

A *communication* is simply the transfer of information and understanding from one person to another. It is successful only when a mutual understanding takes place—when both the sender and the receiver of the communication understand it. It is not necessary that the two parties *agree* with an idea in order for them to have a successful communication. It is, however, necessary that they *understand* an idea in order to have a successful communication.

When a communication involves you as a supervisor and your employees, it is often called an *employee communication*. This is a big part of a supervisor's job. In fact, it is so important that most first-line supervisors spend between 50 and 60% of their time communicating with their employees.

Communications, of course, can take place in many ways. You can communicate directly by talking or writing, or *indirectly* by gestures (thumbs down, meaning "no good"), by actions (a pat on the back, drumming your fingers, or tapping your foot), by facial expressions, by tone of voice, and so on. In fact, more than half of our communications are indirectly expressed through facial expressions and body movements.

We don't necessarily communicate when we talk. Although speech is the most frequent form of communication, we still make a lot of mistakes when we communicate by talking.

Words are symbols that we use to transmit ideas to another person. In oral communications, you have to *conceive* of an idea first. Then you have to *choose and say the words* that you think will communicate your idea to another person. And, finally, before a communication has taken place, the other person must *understand* your meaning of the words.

Suppose, for example, that your car breaks down and you want to get a ride to work with a fellow employee. You might say, "Joe, can you pick me up in the morning?" To which Joe might reply, "Sure," thinking that you are asking him if he is physically strong enough to lift you off the floor (pick you up) during the morning hours. In this instance, communication has not taken place because the other person did not understand the meaning of your words. Or suppose you say, "Joe, how about stopping by my house after work for a drink?" You might mean a cup of coffee or a soft drink, but Joe might say no because he thought you meant an alcoholic drink. Communications have to be *understood* before they are communications.

speaking vs. understanding

DO WORDS MEAN DIFFERENT THINGS TO DIFFERENT PEOPLE?

Most of us "hear" with our hearts as well as with our ears. This is because we may give words added meaning that is not intended. You usually don't say *mill* workers and *clerical* workers, for example, because these words might have a negative emotional connotation to some people. Rather, you might say *hourly* and *staff* employees. Or instead of saying that *union membership is compulsory* to work in a plant, you might say that you have a *union shop.*

Because we have this tendency to "hear" with our hearts, you have to be careful in communicating to others to be sure that they understand what you mean. To do this, you should try to learn ahead of time how others feel about certain situations and what their "hang-ups" and biases are so that you can express yourself with words and ideas that say to them the true meaning of what you have in mind.

word overtones

WHAT IS FEEDBACK?

When you communicate through writing, you can never be sure whether or not the persons receiving your letters or notes understand exactly what you are saying. You can't see their expression (a smile, a puzzled look) when they read it. In other words, you don't have any feedback. You can't check to see whether they understand the message. When you talk to people face to face, however, you can observe their expressions. You can ask whether

need for feedback

the message is understood. You can repeat yourself so that the person you are speaking to can grasp the true meaning of your words.

Because of feedback, two-way (face-to-face) communication is a better way to get ideas across to others than one-way communication, where the other person doesn't have the opportunity to ask questions. As a result, most communication by supervisors is oral, two-way communication.

Two-way communication is valuable because it gives the other person an opportunity to question and speak freely. In fact, you may find in two-way communication that the other person is critical of your ideas and says so quite frankly and openly. This would not be true in a one-way communication. To be a good supervisor, therefore, you should promote open, face-to-face communications between yourself and your employees, encouraging them to ask questions freely and to express their ideas openly.

WHY BOTHER TO LISTEN?

How many times has a parent or teacher said to you, "You're not listening to me!" How many times have you said that to others?

All of us need to become better listeners so that we can understand and communicate more effectively with our employees. Good listening changes the entire relationship that exists between the supervisor and employee. As a good supervisor, you not only need to listen to the *words* an employee is saying, you also need to work with an employee so that you can understand the *meaning* the employee is placing on his words. Listening is hard work. It is easy for us to "close our ears" or "listen with only one ear" when we have other things on our minds. Sometimes when others talk to us, we are not interested in what they are saying and don't pay close attention. When we listen in this frame of mind, we are not going to get the message regardless of its importance.

listening—a basic of communicating

Good listening, therefore, is basic to good communication. Inasmuch as you have to be mentally alert to the words being spoken, listening is a mental activity. As a consequence, you will find it easier to listen intelligently if you face your employees while they are speaking. Give them your full attention. Don't let your eyes wander about the room. Don't mentally complete sentences before your employee does. Don't try to frame a response to your employee's statement before you have heard it all. Such actions will hamper and even break the intended communication. People can sense when you are not giving them your full attention, which creates barriers to full and clear communications.

WHAT ARE THE RULES FOR LISTENING?

Recognizing that it is important to listen attentively and sympathetically, we should endeavor to go by the following rules for good listening.

1. *Be interested in the message.* Give the sender your full attention. When you are listening to others speaking to you—*listen.*
2. *Resist distractions.* Be completely attentive to what is being said.
3. *Look at the speaker.* Don't let your eyes wander about the room, look at the floor, or out the window. When your eyes wander, your mind will too.
4. *Don't let personal biases turn you off.* Sometimes you may not like the way a person approaches you, or you may not like the sound of a person's voice. These biases can cause you not to hear the correct message. As a supervisor, you will need to get the true and correct message about what is being communicated. You should not, therefore, let your biases and preferences cause you to fail to pay proper attention to what the other person is saying.
5. *Try to understand the words and the implied message.* Just getting the facts is not enough. Try to listen with your heart as well as with your ears and thereby get the real implications. For example, an employee might talk to you about wanting to quit or getting a transfer because of the type of work she is doing. Yet when you analyze the work in the department she wants to transfer to, you can see it is the same type she is now doing. The real message, therefore, might be that she can't get along with her work partners, or that she thinks you are unfair in assigning jobs. Try to understand the whole message—the implied meaning as well as the actual words.
6. *Work hard to understand difficult ideas or material.* Don't shut your mind to what is hard to grasp.
7. *Don't hesitate to ask questions.* Be sure you understand what the other person is saying. Don't let outside distractions (from a noisy machine, a ringing telephone, or another person waving to you) cause you to miss the meaning. When such distractions do interrupt, don't be afraid to ask questions. The person doing the talking felt it was important enough to talk to you and should, therefore, welcome this sign of interest and attention on your part.
8. *Be nonjudgmental.* Listen to and accept what the other person is saying. Let the other person's words and thoughts enter into your stream of conscious listening without judging them and preparing a rebuttal.

HOW CAN YOU TEST YOUR LISTENING SKILLS?

In a lecture at the University of Iowa, Professor Ralph Nichols of the University of Minnesota once suggested that you could measure your listening skills by answering the following questions with a yes or no. See how well you measure up.

1. Do you try to make others think you are listening to them whether you are or not?

2. Are you easily distracted from what a person is saying by outside sights or noises?

3. Do you take notes on what a person is saying?

4. Can you usually assess the quality of what a person will say by his appearance or how he says it?

5. We know that a person thinks four times as fast as another person talks. Do you use this excess time to think about other things (your reply?) while still maintaining the central idea about what is being said?

6. Are you receptive to facts and figures rather than concepts and ideas in a speech?

7. Do certain words or phrases "turn you off" so that you can't listen clearly to what is being said?

8. If you don't understand or are annoyed by what a speaker is saying, do you question the speaker or try to figure it out in your own mind?

9. Do you try to avoid hearing something that you figure would take too much time and trouble to figure out?

10. If you ever decide that a speaker is not going to say anything worthwhile, do you "tune him out" and think about other things?

For every no answer to the above questions, give yourself ten points. A score of about 80 is excellent.

WHAT ARE THE CHANNELS OF COMMUNICATION?

Virtually every organization has two ways in which information is transferred to employees. One is the *formal* channel set up by management, and the other is the *informal* channel often called the *scuttlebutt* or *grapevine*.

Formal Channels.   Formal channels usually follow the company's organizational lines of authority from the top person to the bottom of the totem pole. Communications and directives may go down this line of communication as well as up. In theory, there should be a two-way flow. In practice, however, this is often not true. Although orders and directions tend to flow from the top down without interruption or distraction, the flow of information from the bottom up is often sidetracked or stopped. A supervisor, for example, may feel that a certain piece of information should not be passed on up the line to his boss because (1) he doesn't want to bother him with trivia or (2) he may feel it would not reflect well on his ability as a supervisor. Upward communications are usually questions, complaints, or grievances, and many supervisors consciously or otherwise tend to stop the flow of such communications.

channels to use

In addition to communications up and down the line of authority, we also find formal communications that are horizontal; that is, they are be-tween employees or supervisors on the same level. These horizontal com-munications are necessary in order to coordinate the work of various individuals within a section or coordinate the work of various sections within a department.

Informal Channels.   Regardless of the formal channels established, an *in-formal* channel of communication variously known as the grapevine, rumor mill, or scuttlebutt always exists. It is born of both curiosity and insecurity. It grows out of people working and talking together about their jobs. It is natural for it to exist because all of us want to "be on the inside" or know what the latest information is. The grapevine thus provides a channel for employees to express their apprehensions or wishes in the form of rumors or speculations.

News that comes from the rumor mill, the grapevine, or the scuttle-butt is typically more gossip than truth, is unreliable, unconfirmed, and un-authenticated. Despite this lack of reliability, it draws people like a magnet, and rumors fly. We find it everywhere: in social circles, in small towns, in churches, in schools, and in businesses. The information generated by the rumor mill not only is unreliable, but also constantly changes in character in order to suit the purposes of the individual passing it on. For these and simi-lar reasons, the "gospel" passed along by the grapevine as the "unmitigated truth" is typically incorrect.

As a consequence of the above, the grapevine should never be used to give information to employees. Tell them yourself. Don't rely on others. In fact, the grapevine is found to be most active in companies where supervisors do not communicate openly and freely. If you don't tell your employees about job changes that will affect them, if you don't combat rumors, the grapevine will begin to manufacture speculations, and rumors will fly in all directions. Most employees would rather get the story straight from you. As a supervisor, therefore, you can do much to stem the flow of rumors by answering all questions as promptly and truthfully as you can. If employees know that they can get the right information from you, this will do much to scotch the rumors.

WHY DO COMMUNICATIONS BREAK DOWN?

Communications break down because barriers often exist that hamper or distort the flow of communications between people. These breakdowns in communications frequently can (1) cost time and money to the company, (2) cause employees to lose work, (3) create misunderstandings, (4) cause a breakdown in team effort, and (5) seriously damage morale. Because of these serious consequences of poor communications, you should attempt to recognize and overcome barriers that might cause you to be an ineffective communicator.

barriers to communications

Choice of words, which we have already mentioned, can cause a breakdown in communication. Status can also be a barrier to clear communication. Employees listening to their supervisor talk about sales quotas may evaluate what they hear in relation to their own positions and background—not their supervisor's. They may also assume that the supervisor doesn't understand them and their needs because the supervisor has never had to work, as they do, nor has he or she been in their financial position. As a consequence, they may not hear (or at least they may pay little attention to) what the supervisor is saying. Status also keeps us from speaking freely to those "up the ladder" from us. When we are in the presence of the big boss, for example, we may not express our thoughts, ideas, or complaints because he or she is so far removed from us on the company's status scale.

When communications take place over some distance, misunderstanding often occurs. Telephone conversations, for example, are not as effective as face-to-face communications because you cannot see expressions, gestures, and other body signals that help the speaker communicate the true meaning of a message to you. And since you cannot see these additional means of communicating, you are not in a position to ask questions and check on meanings that you might otherwise do if you were talking face to face.

Sometimes as a supervisor you may be prejudiced against a person. You may, for example, already have your mind made up about this employee's ability, and you might let this prejudgment show. You might, for example, say to the employee, "You probably won't understand this, but I'll try to explain it to you." The employee, knowing that you have no confidence in his capacity to understand, as shown by your statement, may make little effort to understand.

Or a supervisor may block communication by saying to an employee, "Where did you get such a wild idea?" Even a good idea—and communication—would probably die with such an introduction.

Another barrier to effective communication can be caused by either the "know-it-all" attitude on the one hand or the "I'm-so-inferior" attitude on the other hand. A person might consider himself such a know-it-all, so superior, that he feels that others don't know what they are talking about— and as a result, he doesn't bother to listen. At the other extreme, an employee who feels so inferior that he thinks he cannot understand what the boss is trying to tell him sets up a barrier to good communications and understanding by failing to listen.

Sometimes age indirectly acts as a barrier to communications. The older supervisor, for example, may have a different hairstyle from that of the young employee. They both understand the words that are being spoken, but because they are alienated by a generation gap as expressed in their choice of hairstyles, neither one accepts the other person for what he is, and good communications are hampered.

We all have known individuals who see themselves as being a certain type of person with a certain social status or position. Any communication that might tend to threaten this position of prestige would cause a breakdown in communications. Calling such a supervisor by first name, for example, might cause a breakdown in communications.

Physical disabilities and inadequacies should also be considered when we talk to others. Persons who are hard of hearing, for example, may have difficulty hearing what we are talking about. They may even feel we are talking in a low tone to frustrate them. Such feelings can obviously create resentment as well as erect barriers to good relations and communications.

HOW DO YOU OVERCOME COMMUNICATIONS BARRIERS?

Overcoming the barriers to communications mentioned in the previous section is more a matter of common sense than of any special skill. On occasion, we all use the techniques needed to overcome these barriers. The trouble is that we don't use them enough. What we need to do is become aware of the barrier problems, and then more frequently utilize the techniques that we already know.

Face-to-face talks are always better than other forms of communication. Talking directly to a person enables us to ask simple questions during our conversations in order to clear up any misconceptions. Watching facial expressions, such as a frown or a raised eyebrow, can also give a clue to lack of comprehension. Expressions of bewilderment or misunderstanding are good feedback clues. If a friend looks quizzical when you are explaining the floor plan of a house, this feedback is your clue to explain it again or perhaps make a drawing of it.

Simple, clear, clean-cut language does much to break down barriers to understanding. When we talk with others, we aren't out to win a speaking contest. Long, complicated sentences and words are sure to cause confusion. Avoid them at all costs. Use language that the other person can readily understand. For example, don't use "exactitude of verbiage" when what you mean is "precise words."

Repetition is another way to overcome communications barriers. For instance, repeat a message several times using different words. Try to say the same thing using simple expressions that the other person may readily understand. The frequency and degree of repetition will depend, of course, on the other person's experience, his background, and the nature of the message.

Try to place yourself in your employees' shoes. In other words, try to understand their feelings, their opinions, and their attitudes. We call this *empathizing.* If you understand how your employees feel, you can communicate to them in ways that they can understand.

Always be genuine and concerned about the welfare of your employees and about the possible effect that the communication will have on them. Whether you are "chewing out" employees for taking too many coffee breaks or simply reminding them that lunch is from noon to 1:00 P.M., the way you express yourself and your obvious concern for the total long-run welfare of your employees will have a positive effect on the way they receive and understand your conversation.

Remember to choose your words carefully. Different words mean different things to different people. Don't ignore the message your body communicates. Good body posture with your head held high communicates assurance and confidence. Poor posture with lowered head denotes shyness or a cowed approach. Crossed arms and legs and leaning back could convey dislike, whereas leaning forward with arms not crossed indicates interest and liking.

Be sure to make eye contact with your employee. Looking an employee straight in the eye communicates the message that you are honest and forthright. And don't forget to keep an appropriate distance between the two of you; being too close will place your employee on guard; being too far creates an air of distrust. Finally, in terms of your "body message," don't use annoying motions (fixing your hair, patting your foot). They always cloud the message that you are trying to get across.

When possible, choose a physical location that will help, not hinder, good communications. Talking over problems in a quiet office, free from noise and distraction, is quite different from trying to talk about problems on a print shop floor. There are, of course, emergencies, and we cannot always choose the best spot to talk. However, we should be aware of what makes a location a poor place to communicate with others.

Indeed, differences in culture make for differences in communication. Language is only one aspect of this communications problem. Customs, cultures, and mores also play an important role, as does body language. For example, if you wave goodbye to a Filipino he may interpret this as a call or summons, a common gesture in their land. Did you know that:[1]

- The typical thumbs-up American gesture is offensive to Arabs?
- It is not unusual for Arab men to walk hand in hand as well as kiss each other on meeting or leaving? Knowing no sexual connotation was intended, you would not give a disapproving glance at Arab men kissing.
- The left hand is thought to be unclean by some cultures? Knowing this, you would avoid eating with your left, or unclean, hand.
- In China it is not considered ill-mannered to stare?
- The American "OK" gesture has an obscene meaning to a Brazilian?
- Showing the soles of your shoes to an Arab would insult him?
- You should never give anything with a chrysanthemum symbol to an Argentenian? It suggests death.

Opportunities abound to make communications errors because of an individual's cultural background. As a supervisor, it is up to you to know your employees and their backgrounds, and to understand the cultural influences that make them react the way they do to your actions and communications. Seek help. Use your public library. And if you blunder, don't hesitate to apologize.

WHAT IS A SUPERVISOR'S ROLE IN GOOD COMMUNICATIONS?

The communications climate in your organization depends to a large extent on you. If you as a supervisor establish sound and clear communications with your associates and employees, an air of healthy open exchange will exist.

Although every person is involved in communications and has a responsibility to communicate effectively, as a supervisor you are the one on whose shoulders will rest much of the responsibility for the success or failure of a firm's communication program. The supervisor, like everyone else, communicates with others. In addition to this, however, you are charged with maintaining a good climate for communications among your employees. You are responsible for seeing that your employees understand each

[1] Dick Schaaf, "The Growing Need for Cross-Cultural and Bilingual Training," *Training/HRD*, January 1981, pp. 85–6.

other, their jobs, and their objectives. You are also the key person responsible for communicating between your department and other departments in the company. You are, in effect, the linking chain between departments, and as such you must realize that the total communications climate in a company is no stronger than the weakest supervisor.

"How well a supervisor communicates is in direct proportion to his skill as a manager."

In a large company, clear communications might well be stopped or hindered by a supervisor who is weak in communications skills, thereby preventing a clear concept of the boss's wishes from reaching the rest of the organization. In like fashion, a first-line supervisor is responsible for good communications and understanding within his unit. Despite the importance of communications, however, and despite the fact that supervisors recognize the problem of good communications, most supervisors would readily tell you that poor communications cause more problems and troubles than any other single item.

the supervisor's part

Communications that are effectively and properly made can have a healthy and positive effect on the climate and production of an organization. And the supervisor is the key person in this chain. An employee typically cannot understand a statement any better than the supervisor explained it. Poor communications make for poor understanding, and poor understanding makes for poor cooperation. An employee, for example, can't be expected to generate enthusiasm and support for a new wage payment plan if his supervisor didn't explain why the employee would be better off financially under the new plan.

As a supervisor you will need to be a better communicator than your average employee because your scope of influence is greater. You may well have fifteen or twenty employees depending on you for clear instructions, and your influence on the firm's success is, therefore, very great indeed. Through your communications, you can have a significant influence on production, morale, quality, and profit—because your communications affect a large number of employees.

Supervisors, therefore, should always be informed. If as a supervisor you do not know and understand, you cannot communicate effectively to others. And if you are asked a question that you cannot answer, you should not be afraid to say, "I don't know the answer to your question, but I will find out and let you know." In addition to being informed, supervisors should be genuinely concerned about how they communicate with others. To say they are concerned about good communications is one thing; to show that they are concerned by practicing good communications is another. An employee readily sees this difference; he should not be left wondering what the supervisor said.

As a supervisor you should gain your employees' confidence by being consistent in your communications—you should not say one thing today and another thing tomorrow. This confidence that your employee has in you will make for easier communications between the two of you. What employees hear depends to a large degree on their confidence in you as a supervisor. If they have confidence in you, they will accept the communication at face value. If they don't have confidence, they will begin to read and search between the lines for hidden meanings. Did the supervisor mean this or that? Why was it said the way it was? Was the supervisor trying to tell me something? These and similar questions are the type that arise to hinder and impair clear and easy communication when the supervisor does not have his employees' confidence.

Remember that the road to supervisory failure is paved with good ideas that were poorly communicated.

HOW CAN A SUPERVISOR AID UPWARD COMMUNICATIONS?

One area that the supervisor needs to be particularly concerned about is upward communications. As we have said, communications and orders come down the line easily, but information from the worker that needs to go up the line may be sidetracked unless helped.

Many supervisors don't seem to realize how difficult it is for their employees to talk to them. The supervisor, of course, feels free to walk over to the employee and talk to him. But the prestige and status of the two are different. The employee may be a blue-collar worker and because of his dress may hate to go to the boss's desk or to the front office in his work clothes.

Some supervisors, because of their years of experience, are frequently able to express themselves more easily than their employees, and as a result, the employees may hesitate to initiate a conversation. Then, too, the employees don't know their supervisor and the supervisor's job as well as the supervisor knows the employees and their jobs. Because of this, the employees cannot speak with the same understanding and assurance.

Another barrier to upward communications is the fact that the super-

*making
communications
easier*

visor controls the employees' jobs and pay. Employees, therefore, may be hesitant to say something that may in some way affect their jobs. In other words, employees are dependent to a large degree on their supervisor, and this may cause them to hesitate to "speak up" to the boss. For these and similar reasons, the upward flow of communications is hampered and in many cases is stopped altogether.

As a supervisor you should be aware of the existence of the above as well as other communications problems. Do all you can to make it easier for the worker to "speak his mind." Try to create a climate of mutual understanding and trust so that your employees will feel free to communicate more openly. Practice listening intently to what your employees are saying. Don't hesitate to ask questions so you will be sure of what your employee is really saying. If possible, avoid communications when you are angry, hot under the collar, or annoyed; or when your employees are emotional, near tears, or angry. You both will do a better job of communicating if the discussion can be delayed. You can also promote employee communications by making employees aware of company rules. Rules, for example, can be used to instruct employees on what should or must be called to your attention. For example, rules such as the following can be used to encourage employees to talk to their boss:

1. Employees should inform their superior of any change in their work that would require coordination or notification of other departments.
2. Employees should keep their supervisor informed of any controversies that might cause trouble between units in a plant.

You can readily think up other rules to aid upward communications.

In addition to these approaches, management should also establish alternative channels of upward communication—channels other than through the employee's immediate supervisor. Many companies, for example, have industrial chaplains, counselors, suggestion systems, opinion surveys, and open group meetings where employees may feel free to express themselves. These are excellent alternative channels of communication.

What we have discussed here are *techniques* that supervisors can use to enable employees to express themselves freely. But better than all these techniques is the strong desire on the part of supervisors to have their employees express themselves openly and freely. This genuine desire by supervisors to have free communications can be promoted only through the creation of a climate of free expression—a climate where the supervisor openly encourages all employees to communicate, and where the supervisor takes and shows a genuine interest in their ideas, suggestions, and complaints. As is true in so many other instances, the supervisor is also the key person here in the promotion and encouragement of the important and necessary upward flow of communications.

As a supervisor you can't know too much about employee communications. You supervise your employees by communicating to them, and the skill with which you communicate will be reflected in the skill with which you manage. To be a good supervisor, therefore, you need to muster all of the skill you can to influence your employees—your work team—to do what is needed to accomplish the goals you have communicated to them. There is no one *best* way to communicate to everyone. Depending on the person, the situation, and the information to be covered, you communicate in different ways to different people. Your communication may be a smile or a pat on the back to one employee; it may be a brief talk to tell others what a good job they are doing; or it may be a formal letter to another.

You can, however, *over*communicate. Like the man who wears suspenders, a belt, and a safety pin to hold his pants up, you can overdo it. Communicate enough to let your employees know everything necessary, but not so much that they will "tune out" old blabbermouth when you start talking. Talk to them about things they want to know about and are interested in—their jobs, their pay, the things that affect them at work. But avoid controversial nonwork subjects such as politics and religion.

communicate clearly

Be sure your employees understand what you are saying. Check on their comprehension by asking questions about what you have said. Choose exact words to say what you mean. Instead of asking your employees to "work harder," you might ask them if they can increase their production from 600 to 650 units per day.

Be a good listener. This is a big part of good communications. Don't interrupt employees when they are telling you something. Let them have their say—let them get it off their chests. Don't try to outguess them and help them along with their comments. Listen carefully to what is said. Try to understand their reason for talking to you. Give their comments thought; then give them your reply.

HOW DO I PUT MY WORDS IN WRITING?

There comes a time in every supervisor's job when spoken words and gestures aren't appropriate or aren't enough. You've got to get it in writing. It may be a report to the boss on why your department's overtime pay is above the average, it may be a letter to a customer explaining how your product is superior, or it may be a note to an employee expressing disapproval with her job performance and putting her on formal notice that unless improvements are made she will be fired. Whatever the reason for putting it on paper, you can do it if you will follow a few simple ideas about how to write effectively.

HOW LONG SHOULD A WRITTEN COMMUNICATION BE?

Good writing is concise. You shouldn't use unnecessary words in a sentence any more than you would use unnecessary parts in an automobile engine. Say what needs to be said in a few words. Then stop. This is not to say that you should write in short sentences and avoid details or explanations. It means you should use enough words to communicate your message—but don't use extra sentences and words that don't add to what you are saying. Make every word do its part—make every word add its meaning to what you want to say.

WHAT ABOUT GRAMMAR AND SPELLING?

Use a dictionary to check on the spelling of a word—or use another word that you know how to spell. Grammar presents more of a problem.

get it edited

There are many rules of grammar pertaining to the English language. You probably follow most of them through habit. However, if you have questions, get someone (your spouse, a friend, a secretary) to look over your writing for errors. Everyone needs this—even great authors have editors check their writing for grammar and spelling. Follow their example and don't hesitate to have your writing edited.

WHAT STYLE SHOULD I USE?

It is easier and more effective to write using your own speaking style. You wouldn't say, for example, "My first visit to see the Red Sox play will always be remembered by me." Instead, you would probably say, "I'll never forget the day I first saw the Red Sox play!" When you sit down to write, speak your thoughts mentally (or aloud), then put them on paper. This should enable you to write more easily as well as make your writing more alive—more interesting and easier to understand.

make it sound like you

Avoid negative statements when possible. For example, don't say, "John is not very often at his machine on time." Leave out the negative and say, "John is usually late getting to his machine." Most of us don't like being told what is *not*. Instead, we want to know what *is*. In like manner, you should avoid using negative words. Don't say that he is not honest. Say that he is dishonest. Instead of saying that Sally did not remember to come to the party, say that Sally forgot to come to the party. Your style will be improved if you avoid negative statements as well as negative words.

Write naturally. When you write, use the words you typically use in speaking—words that come to you easily. Don't try to sound highbrow by using fancy words that are not typically in your vocabulary.

Read what you have written and revise it or rewrite it if it doesn't sound correct to you. Be sure that your ideas build on or follow each other logically. Start from the beginning. If you are writing about a building, begin with your thoughts about the foundation first, and proceed to build on each thought until you get to your thoughts about the roof. Group your thoughts about the same subject (the foundation, for example) into a paragraph. Thus, one paragraph would contain your thoughts about the foundation, the next paragraph would contain your thoughts about the floors, the next the walls, and so on. This gives your writing a logical progression and makes it easier to read and understand.

ARE THERE IMPORTANT RULES FOR WRITING?

There are lots of rules for writing—so many, in fact, that you could get so involved with them that you'd never get anything written. Several common-sense rules, however, have been found to be helpful by many writers.

1. *Organize Your Thoughts.*   A simple plan for organizing your ideas is to answer the questions, who? what? when? where? and why? For example, suppose you want to write to your boss about the need for a departmental picnic. Your outline for writing might be:

> Who?—The employees in the furniture department and their families.
>
> What?—A family picnic and sports outing. Each family brings covered dishes. Participate in swimming and softball.
>
> When?—Any time in July, but near the 4th would be best.
>
> Where?—Anywhere sanitary facilities, picnic tables, swimming, and recreation areas are available. One good spot would be the Jones Mill Pond.
>
> Why?—Promote a team spirit and sense of belonging among the employees in the department.

Following this outline, you could easily write a well-organized communication.

2. *Be Specific.*   The best way to hold the attention of your reader is to be definite and specific. Most of us prefer the definite and specific to the vague. Consider, for example, the following:

- At his retirement dinner, Joe Black evidenced a pleased air of satisfaction when he received his well-deserved reward for his years of service.

Contrast this with:

- Joe Black broke into a wide smile when he put on his gold retirement watch.

3. *Make It Clear.* Remember that you are trying to communicate an idea to another person; therefore, make your writing easy to understand. This rule is more important than any other. Even though you may have misspelled words or used incorrect grammar in your communication, you have done what you set out to do if your meaning is clear. If you get confused in a sentence, rewrite it. Don't try to correct it or patch it up. Usually you've gotten too involved to see what needs to be altered.

4. *Don't Overdo It.* Don't "gild the lily." When you've said it simply and clearly, leave it alone. Ornate, elaborate, overblown words can be nauseating and frequently cloud your meaning. When you overstate your point, your reader is immediately put on guard with such thoughts as "Is this communication sincere?" or "Is the writer trying to fool me?" Even one or two overstated ideas in a report or letter can put the reader on guard about your other ideas or cause him to lose confidence in the rest of your report.

5. *Don't Be Breezy.* Flippant writing lacks sincerity and promotes mistrust. It conveys the impression to the reader that the writer was high or dreamy—not in full possession of his mental faculties. Imagine your reaction to "Well, old buddy, here I am again asking you to sweeten the pot in the annual pay review coming up for y'rs truly!" Contrast this to the following: "In view of my above average performance this year, Mr. Jones, I request that my pay scale be changed from Administrative Assistant to Director." Which one would you seriously consider?

6. *Be Concise.* This does not necessarily mean be brief. It means omitting the nonfunctional words. It means avoiding involved words and sentences. Conciseness adds punch and force to your writing. Contrary to what some people evidently believe, good writing is simple and direct. A well-written sentence contains no unnecessary words or phrases. For example, compare the following:

"Referring to your recent communication of April 23rd . . ." versus "Your letter of April 23 . . ."

or

"There is absolutely no doubt that you will find . . ." versus "Doubtless you will find . . ."

or

"May I call to your esteemed attention the fact that . . ." versus "Let me remind you that . . ."

7. *Write for your Reader.* Use words and terms your reader can readily understand, interpret, and visualize. Don't use technical terms when writing to the lay person.

8. *Tie in your Writing to your Reader's Experience.* If you are trying to sell fertilizer to a small farmer, tell him the amount he should apply to an acre of corn and how much it will increase his yield. Don't talk to him about marginal analysis, cash flow, and profit maximization. Although these concepts may be important to him, he doesn't think in these terms, and what you say, therefore, may not be relevant to him when you use them.

HOW DO YOU WRITE A BUSINESS LETTER?

If you are writing on a blank sheet of paper, use the form shown in Figure 4–1. If you use company stationery, you should omit your address (shown in the upper right-hand corner of Figure 4–1) but add the date. All other parts of the letter are the same. When composing the body of your letter, keep in mind what we have stated previously concerning good writing style, rules, and composition.

WHAT FORM SHOULD I USE IN MEMOS AND REPORTS?

The memo form your company uses should be followed. Many firms have memo pads or stationery for you to use with a printed heading showing:

Date: _____
To: _____
From: _____
Subject: _____

Forms for reports vary from company to company. A title page and a table of contents (such as that used in the front of this book) may be used for long formal reports. These may be omitted, however, in short informal reports. In both types, however, a letter of transmittal is used, with the report attached to the letter.

For a letter of transmittal, you should use the form shown in Figure 4–1 and indicate in the body of the letter what you are attaching (a copy of the report), why you made the report (who requested you to do it), when you did it, etc. Use the who, what, why, when, and how approach previously discussed.

The report itself should be typed, double-spaced, on 8½″ × 11″ paper, with normal margins. Break long reports into sections, similarly to the way this book is broken into chapters and sections. Be sure to follow the writing tips previously discussed.

Many managers like a brief summary of a report on the first page. With such a summary, your boss can quickly tell what your report is all about without wading through the details. The summary contains your main findings and what action you recommend.

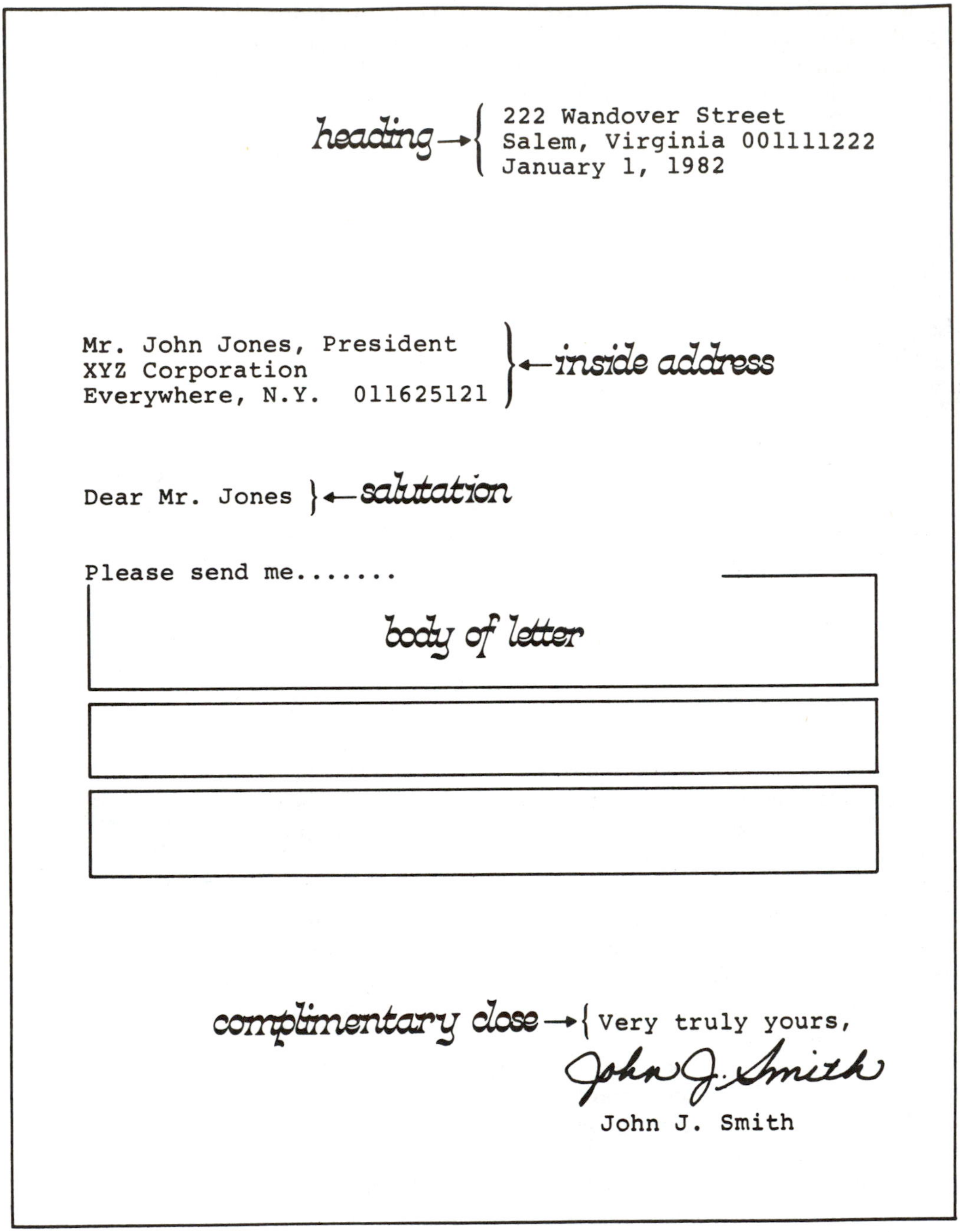

heading →{ 222 Wandover Street
Salem, Virginia 001111222
January 1, 1982

Mr. John Jones, President
XYZ Corporation   }← *inside address*
Everywhere, N.Y.   011625121

Dear Mr. Jones }← *salutation*

Please send me.......

body of letter

complimentary close →{ Very truly yours,

John J. Smith

John J. Smith

FIGURE 4–1.
Parts of a business letter.

In your report, you should put your conclusions and recommendations first, followed by the supporting details to back them up. When you do this, your boss can have in mind what you concluded and then read the facts on which you based your conclusions.

HOW CAN I EVALUATE MY WRITING?

After you've written a report, memo, or letter, read it over with the following questions in mind:

1. Did I need to write the communication? Is it necessary?
2. Is my communication timely?
3. Did I have all the facts in it?
4. Did I say it concisely and clearly?
5. Is my communication logically organized?
6. Did I use terms and language my reader will understand?
7. Did I use twenty-dollar words when five-cent ones would do the job better?
8. Did I put my statements in positive form?
9. Did I put related words and ideas together?
10. Is my writing natural? Does it reflect me?
11. Did I use ten words when four would do the job better?
12. Did I use spelling typically found in ordinary writing?
13. Did I explain when I didn't need to?
14. Did I avoid cute or pretentious words?
15. Did I avoid slang and dialect unless they were needed for clarity?
16. Can my communication be easily understood?

If you can answer yes to all of the above questions except 7, 11, and 13, then your written communication should be an excellent one.

WHAT ARE THE EFFECTS OF GOOD COMMUNICATIONS?

The effects of good written and oral communications within a department or a plant cannot be easily measured; however, they are reflected in several ways. For one thing, an employee's attitude toward the company and his job will be improved, as will be his morale, his cooperation, and his job satisfaction. With this healthier work climate, other more tangible effects may also result. For example, employee turnover, as well as absences and lateness, may be reduced. In retail establishments, a reduction in returned purchases and customer complaints may result. Well-written communications and reports can do much to enhance your chances for promotion, as well as call your qualifications to the attention of those reading your communication. None of this, however, is meant to imply that good communications is the answer to all problems. It is to say, however, that when a healthy attitude toward work and a free climate of communication exist in a company, it is natural that these other happy results should follow.

QUESTIONS FOR DISCUSSION AND REVIEW

1. Explain the importance of good communications to good supervision.
2. What is a "communication"?
3. Do your words always communicate? Give an example of words that might not communicate.
4. What is feedback in communications? Give an example.
5. Why bother to listen?
6. Why is two-way communication best?
7. List the seven rules for listening. Explain each.
8. What is a formal channel of communication? An informal channel? Give an example of each.
9. What causes communications to break down?
10. What is a supervisor's role in good communications?
11. What barriers to communications should you be aware of?
12. How do cultural backgrounds make a different in communications?
13. How long should a written communication be?
14. What style of writing is best?
15. Explain the eight rules for writing.
16. Explain the parts of a business letter.
17. What form should you use in preparing memos and reports?
18. How can you evaluate your writing?
19. What can a supervisor do to aid upward communications?
20. What effect can good communications have on a business?

A Case Study
GRACIE'S COMPLAINT

Jane Carlos was generally regarded by the girls in the typing pool as being a fair and just supervisor. She distributed the work equitably on the basis of quantity as well as difficulty. However, one recent employee, Gracie Haywood, seemed to have difficulty right from the beginning.

From time to time the other girls had seen Gracie Haywood crying at her work. When they offered to help, she replied, "Oh, it is nothing. I'll be all right."

Gracie was an excellent and careful typist, and Jane was pleased to have her as a member of the pool. She didn't, however, show Gracie any favoritism. After three months, Gracie applied to the personnel office for a transfer to another department—any department where typing needed to be done. In the transfer interview in the personnel office, Gracie told her story.

From the beginning she was tense, afraid she would not make a good employee and afraid she would lose her job. When Jane Carlos hired Gracie, her instructions were brief and to the point: "Do your job; don't talk; don't slip away to the restroom for an extra break; don't come in late; don't wear perfume; don't wear pants suits; and don't flirt with the men." After six weeks on the job, Ms. Carlos had sent Gracie a note to be in her office at 9:45 A.M. the next day to discuss her work.

Ms. Carlos handled the appointment in her usual, routine, businesslike way. She cautioned Gracie about several errors and carbon smudges, then told her she was being moved to the wide-carriage typewriter starting the next Monday. When asked if she had any questions or complaints, Gracie managed to say, "No, ma'am," and got back to her typewriter as quickly as she could.

Her work on the wide-carriage typewriter worried Gracie. It involved lots of tabulation and tables, and as a consequence her output dropped considerably. This worried her, and she was sure Miss Carlos was keeping a record of it and would soon descend on her with rebukes.

Because of bus problems, Gracie had been a few minutes late a couple of times. She had always gone straight to Ms. Carlos and explained the reason for being late, to which Ms. Carlos always replied, "Don't let it happen again." For these and other reasons, Gracie said she didn't feel that Miss Carlos liked her or approved of her as an employee, and, therefore, she wanted a transfer.

When the personnel interviewer called Jane Carlos to say that Gracie wanted a transfer, Jane couldn't understand why. She indicated that Gracie was one of the best, most promising typists she had hired in ten years.

1. What was the basic problem in the typing pool?
2. What mistakes did Jane Carlos make?
3. What should Jane Carlos do now?

A Case Study
THE CHRISTMAS PARTY

The annual Christmas party for the Baker Tire Company was being held this year on December 22. As was typical, it was an all-family affair, with spouses of all employees invited to attend and have fun. At the end of the party, Santa Claus always appeared with bags of goodies for the small children, presents for the spouses, and bonus checks for the employees. Mr. Goodman, the owner and manager, always said a few words on the occasion. After a polite round of applause, the wishing of Merry Christmas, and a handshake with Mr. Goodman, the individuals usually left for home.

This year was no exception. Everything went as usual. Then Mr. Goodman rose and made the following remarks.

"Fellow employees and friends. Tonight marks the 25th Anniversary of the founding of the Baker Tire Company. It has had twenty-five years of existence. Some years were good; some were trying. But in all, they have been good years for most of us. Some few of us, of course, haven't always worked with the Company. And some of you will not be here next year.

"This year has been a difficult one financially. Inflation has constantly eaten into profits, and expenses have pushed steadily upward. All this has had a dampening effect on profits, and as a consequence we are not in as strong a position as we have been in the past. The only hope I can see for a continued strong growth and a financially sound business is for us to cut expenses. This means we will have to reduce labor costs—along with any other expenses that we can control.

"I know that many of you are restless. Some of your children are hard to manage at this hour and you want to be on your way, but I did want this opportunity to say a few words to you. This business is our entire lives. We all have to nurture it as we do our children, if we want to see it develop and grow.

"I know that most of you have heard from the grapevine that business has been increasing at a decreasing rate and that profits and bonuses will suffer this year. Part of this rumor is true.

"I am very concerned over those who will remain with me through the future years. I want to see your children develop into strong and loyal young people. I want to see them married and establishing homes of their own.

"New ideas call for new wage plans, and I hope that in the coming months we can generate new ones.

"Finally, let me wish you all a Merry Christmas. In summary, this has been a memorable year, and I am happy to give each of your employees a bonus 'remembrance.' " With that, Mr. Goodman called out names, and the various employees came forward to get their checks.

When they later opened their gifts, every employee found that his bonus had been increased significantly over last year's bonus. When the party broke up, some families started drifting toward the door to shake hands. A good many of the employees, however, started gathering in small groups and talking. "What did the old man mean? Will some of us be fired?" were the types of questions they were asking.

1. What do you think Mr. Goodman had in mind for his message? Why do you think this?
2. What errors or mistakes do you see in his speech? Why do you think he said it in the way that he did?
3. If you had to correct or make suggestions about changing his remarks, what would you suggest? Why?

A Personal Assignment
WRITING A LETTER

Write a letter applying for a supervisory position that is open in one of your local companies.

Write a letter to your boss thanking him for the recent promotion and salary increase you received.

Bring these two letters to your next class meeting for discussion and criticism of your writing.

A Case Study
THE UNWRITTEN LETTER

Suppose that you have asked one of your supervisors to write an important letter by noon. At 2:30 P.M. you inadvertently find out that the letter hasn't been written. Your immediate reaction is to call the supervisor on the carpet. But on second thought you make yourself a list of ways to approach the problem. Your list includes:

1. Ask him if the letter has been written.
2. Ask him if the letter has been mailed.
3. Ask him why the letter has not been written.
4. Tell him to write the letter immediately.
5. Tell him to write the letter immediately and let you see it.
6. Explain the urgency and importance of the letter and suggest that he get it done right away.
7. Recognize that he has been busy with a machine breakdown, but tell him the letter needs to be written.

1. What would you be communicating to your supervisor when you used each of the above approaches?
2. Which approach would you use? Why?
3. Which approach is the best to communicate your feelings to your employee? Why?

A Personal Case Problem

Copy several paragraphs from a magazine or book. Rewrite the paragraphs to see how much you can simplify them and make the material easier to understand. In reworking the material, remember to strive for clarity, conciseness, and readability. Bring this material to your next meeting, and see whether other members of the group can improve on your writing.

PART TWO
PEOPLE PROBLEMS

5

GETTING YOUR EMPLOYEES MOTIVATED

This chapter explains—

- What employees look for and need in their work
- How you can recognize the important areas of motivation
- The characteristics of the supervisor who motivates best

Whamen your employees come to work for you, they bring with them certain needs or wants that affect how well they do their job. They want to be treated courteously and fairly, for example, and want to do interesting work. They also want good working conditions and fair pay. These wants are called *motives*. They are the things that make employees want to do what they do. In fact, virtually everything they do is to satisfy some need or motive. If your employees don't do something, it's because they see no personal advantage in doing it. It doesn't satisfy some want. It doesn't motivate them.

Your job as a supervisor is to get things done through others—to make them want to do their jobs. The main problem you face in this endeavor is actually discovering *what motivates your employees*. Let's look at this problem.

WHAT KINDS OF NEEDS DO PEOPLE HAVE?

All of us have different needs or wants. Jim, for example, might work hard because he gets a feeling of accomplishment from what he is doing. Tillie might work hard because doing her job well makes her feel important. And Dick might work hard because he enjoys being with a gang of people. Psychologists have classified these wants or needs into five groups.[1] If we look at these five classifications briefly, we will understand better why we want to do the things we do.

Basic Physical Needs. These are the basic necessities of life—food, shelter, clothing, rest, reproduction, and the other physical needs. They are instilled in us by nature in order for us to survive.

individual needs

Safety Needs. Once our basic physical needs are somewhat satisfied, our thoughts turn to the need to protect ourselves from danger, to be secure. We want freedom from worry about our future welfare, and normally this means job security to most of us. We want to feel that our jobs are secure and that we will have an income until we retire.

Social Needs. All of us want to feel that we are "in"—that we are a member of or belong to a certain group. This need is the social need. This need to belong, to be a part of the group, and to be accepted and respected by other members of the group is a strong urge in all of us.

Esteem Needs. Closely related to the social need is the need for self-respect. All of us feel this need when we want recognition, status, achieve-

[1] A. H. Maslow, *Motivation and Personality* (New York: Harper & Row, 1954), Chapter 5.

ment, or a sense of accomplishment. It is basically respect for yourself. You feel that you are doing what you were put here to do. Esteem needs are very powerful needs because they relate to our feelings of worth and importance.

"The main problem you face as a supervisor
is discovering how to motivate your employees."

Self-Realization Needs. Self-realization needs are what the psychologists call the highest order of needs. After the first four needs have been somewhat satisfied, then we experience the need for self-realization. We want to feel that we have accomplished things to the best of our abilities—our potentialities. When we have met this need, we say to ourselves that we have become all that we are capable of becoming. When we have met this need, we have been fully creative and are occupied in performing to the limits of our capacities. Not many of us turn to this need, because we are so busy trying to satisfy *social* and *esteem* needs.

All five of these different needs, however, are active to some degree at all times. We don't, for example, satisfy social needs and then move on to esteem. Frequently we are striving to satisfy both of these, along with satisfying our basic physical and safety needs.

WHY ARE WE AS WE ARE?

Every person is different. You are different from any other person anywhere in the world. As the saying goes, "They broke the mold when they made you." What causes us to be different? In fact, several things do.

A major influence is our *biological makeup.* Age, sex, weight, height, and physique are factors that have an important bearing on our personality and makeup. If a man is large and strong, he will probably be a mild mannered individual. He doesn't have to tell people he can lick them. It's obvious. If he is small in stature, he may need to compensate and may be "touchy." People can't run over him. He may be the cocky, belligerent, "bantam rooster" type, always ready to pick a fight. Most physical characteristics are hereditary in nature.

individual differences

Psychologists also tell us that our *childhood* plays a large part in determining our later adjustment and personality. Such factors as feeding patterns, environmental conditions, family units, and training patterns are things that affect our personality and adjustment.

Finally, the broad *culture* in which we grow up has a profound influence on making us the way we are. Our American culture, for example, stresses freedom of choice, competition, equal opportunity, and rewards for accomplishment. We are born and brought up to think and act in many ways different from people brought up in other cultures. In America, for example, we have a strong regard for a good day's work, whereas in some cultures work is looked upon as something to be avoided whenever possible.

We are a product, therefore, of our inherited physical makeup, our early childhood, and our culture. These factors make us what we are, and as a supervisor you should recognize that these are a part of your employees' personalities and should be utilized to the best advantage.

HOW DO YOU GET OTHERS TO WANT TO WORK FOR YOU?

Your job as a supervisor is to get others to do things *because they want to do them.* In other words, to be a successful supervisor, you must provide your employees with the opportunity to satisfy their own needs. They will work for you because by doing so they will satisfy certain needs.

When you think about it, you realize that most everything you do is directed toward satisfying some need. Getting a drink of water as you pass a fountain, for example, satisfies a physical need. You might not be very thirsty and, therefore, your need for water isn't strong—but you still have the need. If you go without water for twenty-four hours, then your need for water gets stronger, and it exerts a powerful influence on what you will do to get a drink of water. This illustrates a point about needs and supervision.

opportunity to satisfy needs

An employee's need that has been satisfied remains relatively quiet, but if the satisfaction of a need is withheld or denied, the need will eventually dominate your employee's behavior.

Although we can readily see and understand the need for water, which is a first-level or physical need, it is not so easy to see and understand social and esteem needs, which are third- and fourth-level needs. Like the need for water, however, if these social and esteem needs are completely unsatisfied, they may well dominate the behavior of an employee. As a supervisor, therefore, you need to provide your employees with the opportu-

nity to satisfy their needs. But before you can provide this opportunity to
your employees, you must first of all be aware of what motivates them.

95

GETTING YOUR
EMPLOYEES
MOTIVATED

WHAT HAPPENS WHEN NEEDS ARE NOT SATISFIED BY JOBS?

When employees' needs are not satisfied on the job, the employees may try
to overcome this lack by doing things that have a bad effect on their job performance. For example, frustrated employees who cannot satisfy some of
their needs on the job may say to themselves, "What the heck. Why beat
my brains out doing this job?" and then simply resign themselves to doing
just a passable job. They will only do enough to draw their pay and will seek
the opportunity to satisfy their needs off the job. Or the employees might
react in the opposite manner. Instead of resigning themselves to the situation, they might react in an aggressive manner with outbursts of temper,
negative attitudes, or even fighting. In either instance, poor job performance results and may mean that the employee will quit or be fired.

*poor job
performance*

DOES JOB PLACEMENT HELP SATISFY NEEDS?

To get others to want to work for you, you will have to place them in jobs
that will allow them to satisfy some of their strongest needs. This may mean
reworking jobs to make them more complex, more challenging, and perhaps
more satisfying to the employee. It may mean changing an employee from
an independent job where a need, such as the need to belong, cannot be satisfied, to a job working with a group of people where this need to belong
can be satisfied. Matching employee needs with jobs is a very difficult process. Once you've come to understand what employees' basic needs are,
however, you can teach yourself to be more sensitive to these needs and try
to match these employees with jobs that offer them the opportunity to help
satisfy their needs. If you do this, you will have made a giant step in the process of getting others to want to work for you.

*matching jobs
and needs*

HOW DO YOU HANDLE JOB BURNOUT?

Sometimes you may note that an employee who was formerly doing an excellent job no longer performs with the same enthusiasm and diligence.
There's a lack of motivation. This may be the signal that the employee is
suffering from job burnout. Watch for such symptoms as lack of enthusiasm,
a drop in job performance, a decrease in output, taking abnormally long to
do a routine job, lack of interest, and losing a temper easily and quickly. All
of these tell you that your employee needs a change—needs additional motivation. What should you do? If possible, make changes in the job—per-

*symptoms of
job burnout*

haps add new tasks. Adding new dimensions or duties to a job so that the work is more demanding will do much to eliminate job burnout.

use work circles

Another helpful approach is to try getting employee teams (or work circles) involved in solving their own work problems. Let them tackle the job of how to eliminate an annoying facet of their work. Getting them thus involved in group decisions will increase job interest as well as increase the probability that the decisions they make will be more firmly followed, will last longer, and will probably be excellent solutions to difficult situations.

WHAT DO EMPLOYEES WANT FROM WORK?

A lot of time and money have been spent trying to determine what employees want from their work. Some people say that money is the first need. Others say that working conditions come first. If you ask the employee what is most important, you get one answer. If you ask the supervisor what is most important to the employee, you will probably get another answer. To show you how different the answers are, look at the results of the following survey of thousands of employees in many different industries.[2] In this survey, the foremen were asked to rank ten job factors in the same way they thought their employees would. Then the employees were asked to rank

importance of job factor

these same ten factors in order of their importance to them. The results show that many foremen didn't understand what workers wanted out of their jobs.

Employee Ranking	Item Being Rated	Supervisor Ranking
1	Appreciation of work well done	8
2	Feeling of being "in on things"	10
3	Sympathetic help on personal problems	9
4	Job security	2
5	Good wages	1
6	Interesting work	5
7	Promotion and growth in company	3
8	Personal loyalty to employees	6
9	Good working conditions	4
10	Tactful disciplining	7

You shouldn't look at this report and say that money, good working conditions, and loyalty to employees are unimportant. These factors are extremely important, as you well know, and companies must continually strive to be competitive in these areas. In fact, all ten factors are important needs to every employee. Most of the time, however, employees *expect* a company to provide good working conditions, fair pay, opportunity for growth, and interesting work. Since most companies *do* attempt to provide

[2] W. C. Menninger and H. Levinson, *Human Understanding in Industry* (Chicago: Science Research Associates, 1956), p. 12.

these needs, and since the employees have been somewhat satisfied in these areas, they ranked them on the lower end of the scale. The low-ranking needs are very important, however, and if they aren't satisfied (like the need for a drink of water), they will surface and dominate the behavior of the employee. The interesting part of the survey—and what is important to you—is that inasmuch as employees expect and usually get their basic needs satisfied, their important wants are in the areas of social and esteem needs. This should tell you that these are the areas to which you as a supervisor should pay most attention.

WHAT ARE THE IMPORTANT MOTIVATION AREAS?

As a supervisor you should recognize that employees need and expect good working conditions and fair pay. Government regulations set minimum wage standards, and competition usually forces employers to establish acceptable working conditions and competitive wages. Therefore, since these lower-level needs are usually satisfied, you should turn your attention to satisfying your employees' other needs. These needs include the following:

Treat Your Employees as Individuals.   All of us like to be treated as individuals—not as numbers or cogs in a wheel. You like to have people show personal interest in you. As a supervisor, therefore, you should not get so wrapped up in your other duties that you neglect your employees, forgetting that they are individuals with feelings and opinions they might want to talk about. Most employees welcome the opportunity to talk over their ideas and opinions with their supervisor. The smart foreman, therefore, is the one who finds time to listen to his employees. It makes them feel good to tell someone, "I was talking to the boss the other day, and I told him exactly what I thought he should do about our office layout." The employee likes to be thus identified with the firm's leadership, thereby satisfying the need to feel important. During these talking sessions, you can also point out and emphasize the importance of the individual to the company, and what the employee is doing to help the company make progress. This makes employees feel that they are more than just cogs in a wheel. It helps raise their self-esteem.

higher-level needs

Be Sincere with Praise.   Some supervisors don't like to praise employees and don't want the employees dependent on praise for motivation. These supervisors state that their job is to run their departments and not to be one-man cheering squads for individual employees. Hollow praise, of course, can be quickly detected and is useless, but a genuine compliment can be a great motivator. All of us appreciate praise and recognition for a job well done. What we don't like is the routine remark, "Thank you for your effort," though this is better than no thanks at all. Consider, instead, what your reaction would be if your boss told you, "Hank, I really appreciate the outstanding job you did in pushing the Grayblock order through. You were great in the way you handled your gang, and I still don't see how you got those presses running so well. Keep up the good work."

You should be sure the praise is justified, however. Employees know when they've done a good job or a mediocre job. If you praise them for mediocre or poor work, your flattery will have a hollow ring, and they'll regard it as so much applesauce. The rule is *be genuine and sincere in your praise and recognition of individuals.* This will help satisfy their esteem needs.

Promote Participation. All of us want to be "in" on what is happening, and nothing helps boost our social and esteem needs like having a part in making a decision. Good supervision, therefore, calls for us to invite employees to help set goals and standards. Employees who have a part in setting up a goal or a program work harder to bring about its success because it is their own program. It is one that they helped develop. They helped set it up, and you don't have to "sell" them on it or push them to meet quotas.

Satisfying the need to be in on things is why this approach, called *management by objectives,* is so successful. This will be discussed in more detail in Chapter 14.

Make the Work Interesting. Many jobs in both government and industry are monotonous and boring. As a consequence, employees in these jobs lack interest in their work—though they like their surroundings, their fellow workers, and the company. Lack of interest coupled with boredom and monotony can lead to all sorts of problems. As a supervisor, therefore, you should identify these boring jobs and work to make them more acceptable. One approach is job enlargement, where interest is created by increasing the number of tasks performed by the employee on the job.

Job rotation is another possibility. Employees swap jobs with other employees for, say, a couple of hours and then go back to their old jobs for two hours, then swap again, and so on. Like job enlargement, job rotation helps relieve monotony and makes the work more interesting. These, and other ways you can think of, indicate the approach you can use to relieve job monotony and make the work more interesting.

Promote Cooperation and Teamwork. Promoting teamwork and cooperation helps your employees satisfy their social needs. The basic buddy system is an example of a system used extensively in youth organizations to encourage one person or buddy to help the other. The buddies are always together, willingly helping and making mutual sacrifices. This same sort of teamwork could well be promoted in your department if you have groups of employees dealing with each other in frequent face-to-face communication. If encouraged by you, these employee groups can form and promote social bonds of friendship and team spirit, thereby enabling them to get their jobs done in better ways. When this cooperation and teamwork develops, and your employees know that they belong to and are vital members of a team, it does much to help satisfy their social needs.

This type of cooperation and teamwork is best promoted by the supervisor who can be freely approached by his employees, who listens carefully to their problems and ideas, who remains calm and stable under trying conditions, who is always willing to help his employees, and who tries to build up his employees' egos and security needs. This is a good prescription that is hard to follow, but you will find it well worth your effort.

Provide Opportunities for Growth. The opportunity to grow promotes self-esteem, and the alert supervisor can usually find ways to provide this opportunity. It may mean letting employees learn more difficult jobs while doing their regular work. It could be encouraging employees to go to night school to enlarge their skills and thus qualify for better jobs. Or it could come about by delegating to an employee the authority to do some job. The delegation would give him a chance to "show his stuff." It should broaden his capacities and make him a more valuable employee, thereby strengthening the whole work team. When an employee is growing in a job, he is typically a motivated and happy employee.

IS THERE A FORMULA FOR MOTIVATING PEOPLE?

Despite all that we know about motivational areas and why we are what we are, we still don't have a magic formula that will motivate people to work. There are no shortcuts, no gimmicks, to securing employee cooperation. One of the best approaches to getting people to work with you, however, is to remember the following:

*motivational
needs*

1. Communicate with your employees and praise them.
2. Consult with your employees about their work.
3. Encourage your employees to participate in setting goals and jobs.
4. Counsel your employees about teamwork, opportunity, and so on.

Make these four concepts so much a part of you that they become second nature. Be sensitive to people and their needs. Use empathy to try to understand the other fellow's point of view before you act. Talk with and listen to the other fellow. Remember, *you only learn when you aren't talking.* Try to get others to participate in some of the decision-making processes. Try to know and understand people because only then will you be in a position to help them with their personal problems. Making some of these simple ideas a part of you will do much to help you get others to work for you.

HOW CAN YOU MOTIVATE YOUR EMPLOYEES?

The supervisor who motivates best is not the tough one or the superior one who uses fear. Both of these types tend to make employees resentful and may even make them unconsciously reduce their work pace. The best motivator is not the one who constantly harps on production and output. Instead, higher production usually results when less emphasis is placed on output and more emphasis is placed on the individual. Supervisors who motivate best are not the ones who play their cards close to their chests and make all the decisions. In fact, this type of supervisor usually gets the least cooperation from employees.

As a supervisor you will motivate your employees best if you follow these guidelines:

supervisory motivation

1. *Establish realistic goals* for yourself and others—goals that are worthwhile, challenging, and attainable.

2. *Make decisions only after relevant participation* by your subordinates. You should seek and be seriously interested in their thoughts and ideas. As a result, your employees will not hesitate to offer suggestions and work with you fully to get the best possible outcome.

3. *Seek and give feedback* to your employees about how they are doing, the progress they are making, and the problems that are coming up. Because of your open communication and feedback, your employees will be motivated to perform well. They will openly evaluate their progress and not hesitate to seek changes when they think they are needed.

4. *Resolve conflicts* with good judgment, understanding, and openness. Focus on solving the conflict rather than placing the blame. Attempt to understand the problem and determine the best solution. Approach your employees with the spirit of "Let's see what we can do to straighten out this problem." This approach and your fairness promote a more relaxed and trusting relationship between you and your employees.

5. *Always communicate* to your employees, explaining what is being done and why it is being done. Talk honestly and openly about how you feel about things. This process of open and continuous communication lets the employees know what's going on inside of you. They will feel they know and understand you better, thus promoting trust and confidence.

6. *Always listen* to what your employees tell you, try to understand what they are saying, and make good comments about their ideas. Don't hesitate to question them and ask them, "How about explaining that again to me?" Being listened to makes your employees feel important and also makes them more willing to listen to what you say.

7. *Be genuinely interested* in your employees as individuals and be interested in their growth and future progress. Talk this over with them and offer suggestions where appropriate.

8. *Be open and sincere in your praise*, reprimand in private, and praise in public.

9. *Control your temper.* When you are angry, don't brood but openly approach the person you are angry with and say, "Barbara, I didn't like the way you handled that problem. Tell me why you handled it as you did instead of following our regulations." This gets the two of you talking, and what could have been a major crisis can be disposed of as a minor problem.

10. *Be open-minded,* always willing to listen to new ideas—even those that are different from your own. You should not mind criticism and should readily admit your mistakes. In other words, you should try to be the type of person you'd like to have as a friend.

11. *Use reprimands only when necessary,* and even then deliver them in private. Use them to educate and correct—never to punish an employee.

12. *Make jobs as interesting and desirable as possible.*

13. *Don't be afraid to delegate,* and willingly give credit to your employees for a job.

14. *Don't try to get work out of your employees by threatening them.*

15. *Don't be afraid to admit that you are wrong* and your employee is right.

16. *Actively seek the opportunity to promote your employees*—even if it means losing them.

17. *Try to run an orderly department,* bringing system to an otherwise confused situation.

18. *Be big enough not to compete* with your employees for credit. Let your employees bask in the spotlight for a job well done.

19. *Don't be condescending.*

20. *Don't be a know-it-all.*

21. *Eliminate unnecessary threats and punishment.*

22. *Provide your employees with flexibility and personal choice.*

23. *Give your employees support when they need it.*

24. *Encourage and help your employees to set their own personal goals.*

25. *Make sure your employees see how doing their jobs will enable them to satisfy their own needs*—reach their own personal goals.

WHICH APPROACH TO SUPERVISION IS BEST?

From all that we have said, which approach to supervision is best?

1. To appeal to the lower-level needs (physical and safety needs).
2. To appeal to the higher-level needs (social and esteem needs).
3. Some combination of the two.

Probably, you shouldn't appeal to one level entirely and ignore the other. You could, of course, emphasize the lower-level needs. Or you could emphasize the higher-level needs. The question we need to answer is, "Which ones should you emphasize?"

A number of years ago Professor Douglas McGregor wrote *The Human Side of Enterprise*,[3] in which he stated that supervisors appealed to either their employees' lower-level or higher-level needs, depending on what the supervisors visualized their employees' needs to be. For example, if as a supervisor you thought that everyone was primarily concerned over pay, job security, etc., then you would supervise in a way that would appeal to their lower-level needs. But if you thought most employees were more concerned over the higher-level needs, then you would supervise in a way to appeal to their social and esteem needs.

lower- vs. higher-level needs

To illustrate his ideas, McGregor listed the two extreme ways supervisors could think about people. He called these Theory X and Theory Y. At one extreme is the Theory X supervisor, who appeals to employees through their lower-level needs. The Theory X supervisor believes the following about people:

Theory X

1. The average human being dislikes work and will avoid it if he or she can do so.
2. Because people dislike work, they have to be coerced, directed, or made to work by threat of punishment in order to get them to do what is needed for the organization.
3. The average person would rather be told what to do, wants to avoid responsibility, has relatively little ambition, and wants security above all.

At the other extreme is the supervisor who appeals to employees through their higher-level needs. In contrast to Theory X, above, this supervisor believes the following:

Theory Y

1. It is as natural for people to exert themselves physically and mentally at work as it is for them to play and rest.
2. The threat of punishment and external controls are not the only ways to get employees to do what is needed by the organization. Employees will exercise self-direction and self-control to achieve objectives they believe in and want to achieve.
3. The degree to which employees are committed to objectives depends on the rewards associated with achieving them.

[3] Douglas McGregor, *The Human Side of Enterprise* (New York: McGraw-Hill Book Company, 1960), pp. 33–43 and 45–57.

4. Under proper conditions, typical employees not only accept responsibility, but also seek it.

5. Using imagination and creativity to solve problems is not something that just a few bright people can do; instead, most of us have that ability.

6. Most employees' mental capacities are only partially used in business.

We recognize that Theory X and Theory Y are two extreme positions and that very few supervisors will exactly fit either one mold or the other. Therefore, instead of trying to motivate their employees by using only Theory X or only Theory Y, most supervisors will probably take a middle approach but will *lean* in the direction of either Theory X or Theory Y. In other words, they will use some of the ideas from both theories, but they will emphasize one approach to supervision (one theory) more than they will the other. The question is, What type of supervision motivates employees best? Do workers respond best to supervisors who lean in the direction of Theory X or to those who lean in the direction of Theory Y?

Supervisors who lean towards Theory X and try to motivate using the Theory X approach may be letting themselves in for trouble. They think they've got to strictly control and supervise their employees, and believe the best way to motivate them is through money, discipline, and the exercise of authority—appealing to lower-level needs. This may be the case in some situations, but it rarely holds true in our society today.

Supervisors who motivate using the Theory Y approach have a much higher regard for their employees. They trust them and believe that the employees will do what is necessary to get the job done with efficiency and dispatch. They don't think they have to stand over their employees to get them to work. They think that, given the proper conditions and understanding, employees will respond to the type of treatment that appeals to their higher-level needs.

Most modern managers agree that Theory Y has much to offer. In fact, most of the evidence indicates that if you use this approach, you will accomplish the greatest good. Thus, if you want to be a better supervisor, you should, in general, lean in the direction of Theory Y. It's not a magic answer, but if you lean toward the Theory Y approach, you will probably get the best in overall quality and performance that could reasonably be expected in the long run. Some individual employees, of course, may need to be supervised using the Theory X approach. They will only respond to discipline, authority, and money. But for employees as a whole, leaning in the direction of Theory Y should prove to be your best approach.

WHAT IS THE BEST APPROACH TO MOTIVATION?

From all we have said, you can see that there is no *one* how-to-do-it approach to motivation. People are much too complex to have some formula applied to them across the board. In fact, when you come right down to the basics of motivation, you'll discover that you really can't motivate your employees; instead, your employees must motivate themselves. After all, motivation is that certain something *within* an employee that incites him to act. All you can do, therefore, is study, talk to, and get to know your employees personally. By doing this, you will be able to find out what their needs are and then provide them with a work environment in which they can satisfy these needs. This is truly the essence of motivation, and all the suggestions made in this chapter are aimed at helping you develop a work environment where your employees can become motivated for the most positive long-run effects.

QUESTIONS FOR DISCUSSION AND REVIEW

1. List and explain the five types of needs that all of us have.
2. Explain why we are all different.
3. How do you get others to want to work for you?
4. What do employees want from work?
5. Discuss the most important motivation areas.
6. What is one of the best approaches to getting people to work with you?
7. What are the characteristics of the supervisor who best motivates his employees? Explain each.
8. Which approach to supervision is best? Why?
9. What is a Theory X supervisor? Explain.
10. What is a Theory Y supervisor? Explain.
11. What is the best approach to motivation? Explain.
12. What is job burnout? How can you handle it?

A Case Study
BEN BROWN AND HIS SUPERVISORY STYLE

Ben Brown was sure he was right. His approach to supervising his employees had always been a no-nonsense, tough-but-fair, close-to-the-chest approach to supervision. His output had been consistently good over the years, and he firmly believed that the best way to motivate a worker was through his pocketbook.

A recent company survey, however, showed that Ben's department was way below the company average on such things as appreciation for work performed, ease of communication with supervision, job status, loyalty, personal help and understanding by the supervisor, and feeling of belonging. Privately, Ben was somewhat concerned over his low ranking, but publicly he passed it off as just another "screwball personnel popularity contest."

He wanted to be liked and accepted by his employees, but he knew what he had to do to get the work out, and productivity came first. He set high output standards and closely supervised every one of his fourteen people, pushing the work through his department at top speed. Of course, training was a problem for him. As he explained it, "You can't get decent help these days. They're never satisfied—always leaving to look for greener fields." He often complained that if he didn't have to train so many new employees, he could increase production by 30%.

Last week, Ben's supervisor, Mr. Gilmore, talked with him about his low rating and gave him an article to read that explained the Theory Y approach to supervision. Today, Mr. Gilmore talked with Ben again about Theory Y management. But Ben expressed doubts that Theory Y supervision would work. It was overly permissive, too democratic, and gave the employees too much of a voice in their work. Ben strongly believed that his employees were supposed to do what he told them to without back talk. His attitude was that they were to work and try, but never question or reason why.

Mr. Gilmore didn't push Ben, who was too good and loyal an employee; during his 32 years with the company he had turned in a consistently good work record. Yet he wanted in some way to reach Ben and get him to approach Theory Y management with an open mind. After leaving Ben, Mr. Gilmore wondered if he should attempt to change him, and if so, how he should approach the job.

1. Do you think Ben was a good supervisor? Why?
2. Do you think Mr. Gilmore should try to motivate Ben to incorporate some of the Theory Y approach in his supervision? How?
3. Despite his good record of output, are there any signs other than those in the survey that indicate that Ben's employees are not too happy with his supervision?

A Case Study
ROUGEMONT COMPANY

The Rougemont Company owned and operated eighteen textile plants employing a total of 5400 employees. Many of these plants engaged in the same types of textile operations, such as spining, throwing, dyeing, weaving, etc.

The company was founded in 1938 and got its real start during World War II. During and immediately after the war, the management, in an effort to round out and complement their activities, acquired a series of small mills scattered over a radius of 300 miles from the home office. In acquiring these plants, the Rougemont Company maintained, insofar as possible, the same local administrative and operative officials, the same policies, the same labor, and in every way attempted to make the local unit autonomous. Each plant was considered as a profit center, and each plant manager operated his plant in the way that he thought best for sound business operation and maximum profits. This practice was apparently successful, and the company continued to grow.

Sixteen months ago, however, a textile union began a campaign to organize the company's eighteen plants. The union has not, to date, been successful in its mission. Many of the employees expressed the feeling that they would wait and see what the management of the Rougemont Company planned for them before they definitely decided on union representation. Even though the union has not succeeded in its drive, it has planted some seeds of doubt and distrust in the employees' minds. For example, it has demonstrated to the employees that no consistent wage scale has been adhered to by the company. The union showed that employees performing the same work in different plants received wage differentials as great as 26% in some situations. Even within some plants, it was pointed out that no systematic attempt had been made by the company to establish fair and just relative wages. In one plant, for example, the union representatives pointed out that the plant janitor was making 3 cents per hour more than employees who were doffing. (Doffing is a job requiring manual dexterity in removing and placing bobbins on textile machines.)

Many of these wage ills, of course, were acquired with the various plants. And some of them were brought about because several plants were brought together under one common owner. How the company acquired the troubles, however, was of no interest to the union. But what the company did about them was vital to organized labor.

1. What steps do you think the Rougemont Company should take to answer the union charges?
2. Would correcting the inequities motivate the employees in any way? How?

A Case Study
SUREFIT HOSIERY MILLS

As supervisor of the boarding[1] operation at Surefit Hosiery Mills, Louise Henderson had 21 employees reporting to her. Louise, known as the "top sergeant," was considered a "real square" by her employees. She seldom joined them for coffee, and never joined them to celebrate a birthday or anniversary with cake and punch. Generally, they thought of her as stern, distant, and bottom-line oriented. No matter what the request, Louise always considered it in light of its impact on the bottom line—profits.

To Louise's credit, she seldom had serious problems with her employees. The only negative feature of the boarding operation was its average output. No matter what Louise tried, the department's production rate remained about average. Sometimes with special contests, output would increase, but it soon resorted to its average position. Whenever Louise had to be away, she left Mabel Henry in charge. Mabel was mature, an excellent and loyal employee, and seemed to get along well with everyone.

Three weeks ago Louise had major surgery and left Mabel in charge. With the boss away, the employees immediately jumped on Mabel to get new chair cushions and some additional lights. Mabel checked with Mr. Rhodes, the plant manager, about the possibility and to her surprise he readily agreed to the request. Within a week, new lights were installed and new chair cushions were in place. With this accomplished, the employees asked Mabel for a radio so they could listen to news and weather reports, along with their favorite program: "John Henry Jones and His Country Five." Mr. Rhodes saw no harm in the request and immediately OK'd the purchase and installation of a radio.

When Louise returned to work and saw the changes, she told Mabel, "You certainly didn't

[1] Boarding is the term used when ladies' hose are slipped over a form for inspection.

lose any time in spending money while I was gone." Mabel merely smiled and pointed to the production charts. For three consecutive weeks they showed that output had reached a new high for the plant.

1. Why had output increased so drastically?
2. Will production probably remain at the new level? Why?
3. What would you do now if you were Louise Henderson?

A Personal Case Problem

Your community has just completed building a small civic center. It looks much like a home from the outside, but the inside has a lot of open space for meetings, displays, art shows, etc. The city has requested four local civic organizations and two garden clubs to undertake the job of landscaping the center. The town will seed the lawn, but wants the six organizations to purchase and plant shrubs to show off the center to its best advantage. You have been appointed to head up a committee of representatives from each organization to get the landscaping done.

1. Where will you turn for a landscaping plan? How will you get it?
2. How will you proceed to divide the work among the organizations?
3. How will you motivate the various organization members to contribute their dollars and their efforts to this undertaking?

6

PUTTING HUMAN RELATIONS TO WORK

This chapter explains—

- How human relations affect supervision
- How you should treat your employees
- How you can rate yourself on the human relations scale

Many managers seem to think that all they need to do to be good supervisors is to tell employees what to do and provide them with the tools and materials necessary to get the job done. Nothing could be farther from the truth. Employees are human beings like the rest of us. They have basic drives, needs, and wants that they seek to satisfy through their work in your department as well as through their outside contacts. As a supervisor, therefore, you will need to know how to handle people, how to influence them to do the things that you want done, and how to get along with them. One of your top-priority jobs, therefore, is to try to continually improve the relationships that exist between you and your employees. Remember that a firm is made up of *people*, that what you get accomplished is through *people*, and that your personal success as a supervisor will depend on how good a job your *people* do for you.

Thus, although you work with people, dollars, materials, and time, your employees are by far the most important. In fact, your success depends on them. Loyal employees who have the ability to feel, to think, to plan, and to make things happen are by far your most valuable asset. At the same time, however, people are difficult to motivate, control, and inspire.

WHAT DO WE MEAN BY HUMAN RELATIONS?

Some people say that practicing good human relations simply means applying the golden rule. Others say it is the application of psychology to people—sort of winning friends and influencing people. Some define human relations as an ethical approach to personnel problems. Others say it is what takes place (the relationship) between workers. All of these factors are a part of good human relations.

*motivating
employees*

To a supervisor, practicing good human relations means getting employees to work together harmoniously, productively, and cooperatively to achieve economic as well as social satisfaction. It means *motivating employees to want to do productive and personally satisfying jobs.* Note that we have said that the supervisor's job is to *motivate* his employees, not to *drive* or *push* them to do their jobs. This is a key part of human relations—to motivate people. You can see, therefore, that practicing good human relations is more than backslapping, more than "being a nice guy," and more than glad-handing.

WHAT MAKES EMPLOYEES DIFFERENT?

Employees who work for you are members of your organization only *part* of their time. They are also members of a family, members of a church, members of a club, and citizens of a community. Knowing this, you should recognize that you cannot change employees simply by bringing them into a plant, having them punch a clock, and assigning them a place to work. Employees still have their own physical and mental makeup. They still have their own feelings about things. Even though they work for you, they still have their own personal problems and attitudes. And you must remember that these feelings and attitudes come with them to the job, and that they will continue to be influenced by their associations in other organizations.

When you assign people to jobs in a retail store or a manufacturing plant, you should remember that you have limited the freedom of those individuals. Employees may, for example, be required to stay in one location. If they are the type of people who like freedom to move about, this may frustrate them. Or if their actions are paced by a machine, this may irritate them if they are by nature people who like to change their work pace. And, finally, if employees are forced to associate and work with certain individuals with whom they would not normally associate if left to their own choice, this, too, would limit their freedom. Such limitations as these may produce problems for some employees and, therefore, hamper their effectiveness in working with others.

Other employees, however, adapt themselves more readily to their work environment, and often these are the employees who are the easiest and most pleasant to work with. As a supervisor you should be aware of the individual differences that your employees bring to their jobs, recognizing that these differences might make the employee frustrated and discontented. By taking these diffferences into account when employees are initially placed on jobs or are later transferred to other work, the alert supervisor may well ward off trouble and create a healthier, happier work force.

*employee
differences*

In addition to these individual differences, some employees come to the job with a predetermined set of requirements that the job should fulfill. It might be that the job should appeal to their social status, or it might be that the job should satisfy their need to belong—to be part of a group. These and other expectations make for differences in the way that employees look at their jobs, how they react to them, and how effective they are. For example, some employees may look at jobs quite differently from others. Their job may be a temporary thing after school—perhaps a source of extra money and social contact. It may not be their chosen work, and they may not have other people dependent on them for support. On the other hand, some workers are the chief breadwinners in their families and are responsible for their welfare, thus affecting their job requirements.

Age likewise influences individuals. Older employees are often more security conscious than younger ones, and as a result they are more interested in maintaining their present positions than in transferring to other positions with unknown opportunities.

These are a few of the individual differences you will find among your employees, and they serve to point out to a degree why different employees have different needs, different attitudes, different personalities, and different demands from their jobs. As a supervisor, try to recognize these needs so that you will be in a position to effectively deal with them and thereby create a harmonious and well-directed work force.[1]

WHAT DO YOU NEED TO REMEMBER WHEN WORKING WITH OTHERS?

As a supervisor, you will be working with and leading people. Because you will be supervising and leading your employees, you should remember several basic facts about them as individuals.

1. Remember that all individuals are different. They are different in thousands of ways. Just as their fingerprints are all different, so are they different in other ways. From the day of their birth, they develop differently. They each have their own individual minds, their own individual thoughts, their own personal ideas about life, and their own wants and needs.

   Because they *are* individuals, therefore, the study of human relations starts with the individual. It starts with *you* as a person. You may be part of a work team, but remember that the team is made up of individuals like yourself, and the team exists and has power because of the individuals who make it up. The *team* cannot make decisions. The *individual members* of the team are the ones who make decisions.

the individual on your team

2. Remember that when you are working with a person, you are working with the *whole person*. You might wish you could employ him as a *hired hand*, but you can't. Even if you want only his hand to work for you, you also get his mind and his thoughts. You get his desires and motivations. You get the reflections of his home life, which affects his work even though it is separated from his work place. As a supervisor, you should remember that every employee is different and that you must work with each of them as a whole person.

3. Remember that all normal behavior by an individual is *caused* behavior. It is caused by what the individual needs or wants. Employees do things because they feel that by doing so they will achieve some goal that they feel is worth working for. Your employees are not motivated by what *you* think they ought to do and have, but by what *they* think they ought to do and have. To you, the things that your employees want and the reasons they want them may appear foolish. To them, however, the needs are important and are very real. Because they are important, these needs affect your employees' behavior and, therefore, the way they react to you and their job.

4. Remember that people are not machines to be knocked about and

[1] This section adapted with permission from Claude S. George, Jr., *Management for Business and Industry* (Englewood Cliffs, N.J.: Prentice-Hall, Inc., 1970), pp. 320–21.

thrown out when you are through with them. Every human being needs to be treated with dignity and respect. No matter what a person's job is, no matter how "low" you may think it is, an individual deserves to be and should be shown the proper respect for his choice of jobs and his own abilities.

If you will always keep these four aspects of people clearly in mind, you will find that your understanding of other people and your ability to work with them effectively will be significantly improved. For example, when you recognize that people differ from each other, you will not try to categorize them or put them in certain molds, such as he is a "good mixer," or she is a "cold fish." You won't try to handle every person in the same way because you will recognize that you are working with or supervising the whole person—an individual who is unique. You will more clearly recognize the dignity of work and better understand the respect another human being deserves.

HOW DO YOU AFFECT YOUR EMPLOYEES' ATTITUDES?

Your job as a supervisor is to get things done through people, and your effectiveness will be measured by how productive your employees are. You are dependent on them for your success. Inasmuch as this is true, your employees are your most valuable resource and should, therefore, be treated with respect and consideration.

Most employees want to please their boss, and your employees will probably strive to do what you want them to do. Remember that working for you is one of the most meaningful aspects of their lives and that they hope to find personal satisfactions and rewards from it. Whether or not they find these rewards depends on you as a supervisor and how well your style of management relates the job to them. Remember that your employees are the only ones who can decide how hard they will work. Remember also that this decision is closely tied to the way you understand them, the way you treat them, and the way you help them. The effective supervisor, therefore, is the one who can create a work climate in which employees willingly strive to do their best.

*your impact on
employees*

DO YOU UNDERSTAND YOURSELF?

It has been said that if you want to understand others, you should first understand yourself.

When you begin to know yourself, you have taken the first step toward understanding others. When you recognize, for example, that you have certain attitudes about how you should dress, how fast you should work, and how as a supervisor you should behave, you then realize that others, too, have ideas about dress, work pace, and supervision. You recog-

"The effective supervisor creates a work climate in which employees willingly strive to do their best."

GEE, THANKS BOSS!

nize that you are not the only one with goals and ambitions who works for them in an aggressive manner. Your employees, too, have ambitions and goals that they are working for with equal vigor. Understanding yourself will enable you to understand others, and when you come to understand other persons, you will be in a position to treat them fairly and justly.

know yourself

This is certainly true of the relationship that exists between supervisors and employees. Whenever you become critical of what others have done or said, first ask yourself what *you* have done to help create the situation that needs correcting. More than likely, you will find that some of the blame is yours. If not, shift your point of view and look at the situation from your employees' point of view; this will enable you to better understand them and their problem. As a result, you will treat your employees and the situation with understanding, compassion, and integrity because you know how you would like to be treated in similar circumstances.

Understanding yourself means looking at your strengths as well as your weaknesses. It is easy to see your strong points, but you have to work harder to see your bad points. You should recognize that you have limitations and hang-ups just like the next person—that you have such things as a short fuse or a quick temper, that you may be prejudiced against female employees, and so on. When you recognize these types of shortcomings, you will be in a position to try to control them and thereby be a better supervisor.

You will recall that we previously talked about understanding others by putting yourself in their shoes. When you do this, you are *empathizing;* that is, you are trying to see the problem from the other person's point of view. This does not mean, however, that once you see the problem from their point of view, you agree with them and decide in their favor. It means that once you understand and see the problem from their point of view, you are in a better position to deal with it effectively and fairly. You are in a position to appreciate their point of view and their feelings without getting yourself involved in their personal lives. When a problem arises between two employees, for example, you can empathize with both. You can truthfully say that you understand each person's point of view, that you understand the problem, and that you understand why each feels the way he or she does. Once you have achieved the ability to truly empathize, you will be in a sound position to make a clear and fair decision. And having made your decision, you will be in a position to state in clear terms why you made the decision and, if necessary, why the decision could not be made the way they wanted it.

the other point of view

We have said that all normal behavior is *caused*—that there is a reason for behavior. As a supervisor, you should try to recognize and understand the cause of your employees' behavior. The reasons why your employees do things may not be logical; they may not be reasonable; they may even be ridiculous in your mind. But they are important to the employees and are the cause of their actions. The challenge facing you as a supervisor, therefore, is to understand why particular employees behave the way they do, and not to turn off their actions as absurd or ridiculous. In fact, when you state that actions by others are absurd, you may well be admitting your own inability to see their points of view—to see the reasons for their action. If you are unable to see the reasons for their action, then perhaps you are at fault as a supervisor.

A good supervisor must work at empathizing with his employees. You should make it so much a part of yourself that it comes as easily as shaking hands. It should be so much a part of you that you will be able to quickly settle a dispute, prevent a grievance from arising, or shed new light on a tough problem.

HOW WELL SHOULD YOU KNOW YOUR EMPLOYEES?

The better you know your employees, the better you will be able to understand them, their points of view, and their problems. As a supervisor, therefore, you should make every effort to see and understand the whole person. You should know about your employees' families because they are parts of them and influence your employees' work and behavior patterns. If you know the sizes of your employees' families, the ages of their children, what

115

*the whole
person*

their names are, where they go to school, what their accomplishments are, and so on, you will know and better understand your employees.

In like manner, you should know something about the employees themselves. Where are they from? What work experience have they had? Do they have special skills or hobbies? What are their educational backgrounds? What are their goals and ambitions? Knowing these types of things about employees enables you to talk with them about the possibility of better placement within the company, about their opportunities for advancement, or, if they aspire to be supervisors, whether or not they have the educational and personal makeup that the company requires.

To be a good supervisor, it is almost impossible to know too much about an employee. Knowing the types of things mentioned above, you will be in a better position to understand your employee, to understand his problems, to see his point of view, and to empathize.

SHOULD YOU TRY TO CHANGE YOUR EMPLOYEES?

The fact that employees differ widely in their abilities and capacities is a fact of life that you must face. Some of your employees will have real mechanical ability, whereas others are almost lacking in mechanical aptitude. Some may be bright, others dumb. Some may be quick to catch on to a new job, whereas others are slow learners. People are different, and as a supervisor, you must learn to accept people as they are.

Your employees, of course, bring their differences to the job, differences they have developed over their years of living and countless experiences. It would be unrealistic, therefore, for you to try to remold or change them. You must accept people as they are and work with what they have. If

*accept people
for what they
are*

you try to do otherwise, if you try to change them, you will face a life of needless frustration.

This is not to say that you should ignore your employees—that you should not attempt to help your employees help themselves. With your friendly help and suggestions, some of their mannerisms or poor work habits, for example, might well be improved in time. Accepting people as they are does not rule out trying to help them. You accept an employee as a person and as a sensitive human being—not as a commodity that you can remold. The supervisor who sees this difference, who accepts employees for what they are but is willing to try to understand and help them, will succeed because of his handling of the human problems of supervision.

WHAT IS DIFFERENT ABOUT WORKING WITH GROUPS?

Good human relations results from knowing how to work with groups of employees as well as with individuals. As a supervisor, of course, you will find that much of your time is spent working with groups of employees. These may be *formal* groups, such as assembly teams, or they may be *informal* groups, such as blackjack clubs that play cards during breaks and lunch periods. Formal groups are set up by management to enable employees to work together on a job. Informal groups are formed by employees who have some common interest. Inasmuch as you will be supervising people who work and play in groups and who achieve their personal needs through groups, you should have some knowledge of what groups are and how they work.

Groups differ greatly in the attraction they hold for members. Some groups are loosely formed and members drift in and out, such as the blackjack group. Other groups are highly cohesive; they are strong, enduring, and highly effective. They command and get active support from their members. In highly cohesive groups, pressure will be put on extremists to conform to what the *group* thinks should be done. A group, for example, may have its own output standard which differs from that set by management, and pressure is exerted on the members to meet the group's standard. In highly cohesive groups, some of the members will try hard to get the nonconformist to change. However, if the members fail and the nonconformist refuses to change, then the members will give up trying to influence him. Instead, they will "cut off" the dissenter and will no longer accept him as belonging to the group. These things do not hold true, however, in less cohesive groups.

One peculiarity of groups that you should recognize is that the people who are most vocal and try the hardest to influence the other members of the group are usually the ones who are most willing to accept the opinions of others. This may seem contradictory to you at first, but it is a characteristic of the behavior of employees in groups. If one employee wants desperately to influence the others, if he wants to be the leader and spokesman, then he will be most willing to accept the views and suggestions of the other employees so that he can "lead" them. The stronger the ties of the group and the more cohesive it is, the more this rule holds true. If it didn't work this way, then the employee who was vocal and said things the group did not agree with would soon be cut off from the group if he did not accept their views.

These are characteristics of all groups, whether they are formal or informal. Recognizing and understanding these group characteristics are important from a performance point of view. A highly cohesive, closeknit group that agrees with and supports your ideas and production standards can influence its members to do better work than they might otherwise do. And likewise, if there is disagreement, the members can be influenced to do poor work. As a supervisor many of your goals will be achieved through your employee groups; you should, therefore, carefully study and analyze your employees' actions in groups in order to make your work groups operate as harmoniously as possible.

*group
attractions*

Make sure that the size of the group is appropriate to the task to be performed. In general, the smaller the group, the more effective it can be. Large groups make for less individual employee participation in group activities. Large groups open the way for increased employee disagreement and provide a basis for a growth in antagonism among employees. As a consequence, employee satisfaction typically drops as the group gets larger. Therefore, if your group can be kept small (no larger than, say, 8 or 10), then your chances for good group-centered leadership will be enhanced.

group size, leadership, and behavior

Group-centered leadership is supervision in which you treat all of your employees in a group as important individuals, building and maintaining their sense of importance. In addition, you recognize that any group-oriented problems should be discussed and dealt with by the group in a participative way. In other words, you should not solve group problems in a unilateral fashion. Involve the group.

Finally, always analyze your group's behavior patterns when the members are not performing up to your expectations—for example, when output is too low. When this occurs, first of all be sure that the group understands what needs to be done—what they are expected to do. Then ask yourself whether there are any physical problems interfering with their output. Are machines running properly? Is raw material up to standard? If nothing emerges here, then ask yourself why the group is not performing the way you want it to. At this point, make sure the group understands why achieving the expected goal will be beneficial rather than detrimental to them. Explain to all the employees why achieving the output goal will be in their best interests, how it will help them realize their personal goals, and how it will enable the company, and therefore the employee, to be successful and prosperous.

IS A QUALITY CIRCLE A GROUP?

Quality circles, a Japanese innovation, are relatively small groups of employees who work together under the same supervisor. The basic idea is that the employees and the supervisor get together to study, analyze, and solve quality problems. The key to success is voluntarism. A quality circle might, for example, voluntarily tackle the job of finding out why four percent of their output is rejected. Or it might analyze why they have problems making a certain part to specifications. The circle (or group) of employees meets at lunch time or after hours to discuss their problem and find a solution for it.

Obviously, most employees aren't qualified to jump right in and tackle a quality problem. Usually, therefore, a quality circle begins by receiving specialized training about product quality. Later they decide on a quality problem to work on. Meeting once or twice a month for a few hours, the group can get staff help on specific questions if they wish. The primary emphasis in quality circles is to get employees involved in their work and in solving quality as well as other problems that they experience. In short, a quality circle is a system of group awareness, group-reached decisions, and group rewards in the form of personal enhancement and peer acceptance. For quality circles to be effective, their supervisors should be knowledgeable in the group leadership skills discussed above.[2]

employees solve problems

WHAT DO EMPLOYEES WANT FROM THEIR JOBS?

All of us have certain basic needs that we want fulfilled. We all need food, clothing, and shelter, and we all have the same desire for self-respect, recognition, and self-esteem. Individual employees, however, place different weights or values on different needs. A starving man, for example, places a high value on food, whereas a man with plenty of food but little clothing places a high value on clothing. If you know the different needs or wants that individual employees have, you will be in a better position to do an effective job of motivating and supervising them. You can, perhaps, help each employee to satisfy his or her needs, thus becoming a better employee.

Although different employees have different wants and place different values on these wants, studies have shown that the basic wants or desires of the average employee will include the following:

1. *Fair pay.* Most employees want fair pay for their work and comparable pay for comparable work. Employees resent others getting more money for the same or comparable work. They also want their pay to be in line with that in the community. A deviation from the norm is a sore spot and may well be a source of employee discontent and dissatisfaction.

2. *Recognition as an individual.* Employees want to feel important in the eyes of their fellow workers. They want to be recognized for doing a good job. Words of encouragement, a pat on the back, or a pay increase could help supply this need.

3. *Opportunity for advancement.* Most employees want the opportunity to move ahead on the job. New employees frequently look for this in seeking a job. Moving ahead is vital, and blind-alley jobs may explain why an employee is dissatisfied and may eventually quit. In addition to the opportunity to advance, most employees want *job security* to go with it—they want to feel secure enough in their jobs that they can

job needs

[2] For an interesting article see William J. Storck, "Participative Management Brings Employees into Problem Solving," *Chemical and Engineering News,* March 26, 1984, pp. 10 ff.

plan ahead, buy a home, and settle in a community. This is particularly true of the employee who is the head of a household and is supporting several other people.

4. *Interesting work in a good place to work.* This factor will be high on many workers' lists. Safe, clean, pleasant working conditions are desired along with employee facilities such as parking lots, cafeterias, lockers, and shower rooms. A good place to work, however, is to little avail if employees are not interested in their work. Various jobs, of course, hold different attractions for individual employees. What is one person's pie is another one's poison. You should exercise real care, therefore, in choosing and placing employees in jobs.

5. *Acceptance by the group.* The desire to belong is strong in most workers. As was stated before, employees seek social acceptance and approval by their fellow workers. If they do not get this, their morale may be low, their efficiency lacking, and their productivity suffering. Not only do employees need to belong to employee groups, they also need to feel that they belong to and are a *part of the company group*—that they are "in." All workers want to feel appreciated and needed by the company to the extent that they participate in discussions about possible shift changes or a new method of work. Getting this information directly from supervisors rather than through the grapevine will do much to make employees feel a part of the company group.

6. *Good and just leadership.* All employees need to have confidence in their superiors. They want to work for people who know their jobs, who are sure of their decisions, and whose actions are impartial and fair.

The weights placed on these needs and desires by various workers will differ. As a supervisor, you will need to recognize these and other individual needs and the different weights that each employee places on them. Opportunity for advancement might be of first importance to one employee, whereas job security might be most important to another. It won't be easy for you to identify individual wants, so be on guard. What employees say they want and what they actually want may be two different things. They might, for example, express dissatisfaction with their pay, but their real need is to be accepted by the other employees. Recognizing these and other wants can help you understand why employees behave as they do, as individuals or as members of a group. To practice good human relations, you should be aware of these desires and insofar as possible create conditions favorable to satisfying most of the major desires of the individuals. Supervisors who strive to do this contribute considerably to making a group of employees get along well together and work in an efficient and harmonious manner.

Years ago supervisors never even heard of human relations. Employees were paid to do a job—to do what they were told to do without back talk.

Today the picture is different. Every successful supervisor is typically expected to possess and practice basic human relations skills. As a supervisor, you should:

1. Keep your employees informed about everything that will affect them. Use bulletin boards, news letters, departmental meetings—anything you can think of to get the information across to them. Keep them so well informed that they can never say "I never know what's going on around here."

2. Make your employees want to do things. Supervisors should be leaders, not drivers. Employees who work for drivers do things reluctantly because they are pushed into it, whereas employees who work for leaders are cooperative and enthusiastic because their supervisor makes them want to do things.

3. Give credit where credit is due. This is nothing more than letting each employee know how he or she is doing. It means giving an employee a pat on the back when deserved.

4. Praise in public, damn in private.

5. Don't be afraid to speak, to socialize. We are all in the same boat: no one employee is "better" than the next. Remember that there are no castes in America.

human relations skills

6. Don't play favorites.

7. When you're wrong, admit it. No supervisor loses face by admitting an error—if errors don't pop up too often.

8. Listen courteously to an employee's ideas. They may be wild ideas, but don't let the employee know it. If not thwarted by you, the employee's next idea may be a winner.

9. Let employees take part in decisions. This is particularly true for decisions affecting the employee. When employees feel that they had a part in making a decision, they will be much more likely to go along with it with enthusiasm.

10. Never hesitate to build up the importance of an employee's job. All of us like to feel that our jobs are important—even critical to the success of the department.

11. Express confidence in your employees. Most of your employees will live up to what is expected of them. If you show confidence in them, if you let them know you expect them to do their best, then that is what they usually will do. We tend to perform in accordance with what is expected of us.

WHAT CAN YOU EXPECT FROM GOOD HUMAN RELATIONS?

Human relations takes place between one person and another—between employees and supervisors, or between fellow workers. By practicing good human relations, supervisors will be able to help their workers satisfy some of their needs. A supervisor might, for example, introduce a new employee to the blackjack club members, saying, "Fellows, this is Joe Brown, a new employee on the punch press. He is a great worker and a humdinger at blackjack. How about showing him the ropes and dealing him in?" This might make Joe a member of the group and thus satisfy his need to belong.

human relations
impact

Practicing good human relations, of course, doesn't mean that everybody will be all smiles and happiness. We all have our problems, but practicing good human relations enables us to work around the difficulties that problems present. What you should aim for in your work is to have:

1. Peace among your employees.
2. Openness and understanding.
3. A friendly air between workers.
4. Employees expecting and receiving a fair, just hearing and decision.

Achieving these human relations objectives will pay off. The rewards may be difficult to measure, but rest assured that they are there. Practicing good human relations may mean that a difficult problem of employee coordination or a problem of poor work performance can be avoided—can be stopped *before* it starts—rather than be patched up at a later date. Practicing good human relations may mean uninterrupted work rather than a slowdown or stoppage. Thus, practicing good human relations will manifest its value in numerous ways that will provide you with the personal satisfaction of a job well done, as well as provide your employees with the opportunity to develop and practice their talents to the fullest.

HOW HIGH DO YOU RATE ON THE HUMAN RELATIONS SCALE?

Your job is to supervise the employees working for you in your department. In doing this, you will have an opportunity to test all of your human relations skills. Answer the following questions honestly to see how high you are on the human relations scale. Give yourself 4 points for each yes answer. A score of 80 or better places you high on the scale of practicing good human relations with your employees.

1. Do you know each employee well?
2. Do you talk to your employees about their homes, their hobbies, and their families?
3. Do you tell your employees how they are getting along?

4. Do you give them credit when credit is due?
5. Do you tell them in advance about changes that will affect them?
6. Are you open-minded? Do you ask for suggestions?
7. Do you respect all jobs and make them seem important?
8. Are you courteous in your treatment of your employees?
9. Are you honest, impartial, and fair in your dealings and judgment?
10. Do you treat your employees with dignity and make them feel that they are a part of the company group—that they belong?
11. Are you generally cheerful?
12. Do you try to be a good listener?
13. Do you always consider every complaint?
14. Are you equally strict (or lenient) with all employees?
15. Do you praise good work and criticize poor work?
16. Can you say no to employees without making them feel antagonistic toward you?
17. Can you empathize—see the other person's point of view?
18. Can you give clear and easily understood orders?
19. Do you explain why changes have to be made?
20. Do you do everything you honestly can to get your workers promoted or transferred to better jobs?
21. Do your employees come to you freely with job or personal problems?
22. Do you try to explain your employees' jobs and their relation to the whole company in order to show the employees that their jobs are important?
23. Can you freely accept personal criticism from your employees about how you operate as a supervisor without getting upset?
24. Do your employees respond positively when you talk to them about doing a better job?
25. Do you know yourself as well as you know your employees?

QUESTIONS FOR DISCUSSION AND REVIEW

1. Define human relations.
2. Explain how employees are different. Give examples.
3. What is meant by "working with the whole person, not the hired hand"?
4. Explain what is meant when we say "Normal behavior is caused behavior."
5. How do you affect your employees' attitudes?
6. How does knowing yourself help you to understand others?

7. What do we mean by empathy? How does empathy help a supervisor?

8. How well should a supervisor know his workers? Why?

9. Should you try to change people who work for you? Should you try to help people who work for you? What is the difference?

10. Generally, what things do most employees seek from their jobs? Explain why each of these is important.

11. Comment on: "Practicing good human relations means that everyone is always smiling and happy."

12. What should you expect to come from practicing good human relations?

A Case Study
THE CASE OF THE PERFECTIONIST SUPERVISOR

Bart Richmond is supervisor of the Plating Department for the Southern Liberty Company. In his mind, his department is the best-operating and best-disciplined department in the whole company. And he views himself as being a tough but fair supervisor, with his only real problem being that he can't get reliable help. "They always come in like a new broom," he states, "but within a couple of months their work begins to slip, and within six months they move on to other jobs."

Bart is a perfectionist who expects everyone to work the same way. He is a stickler for following rules to the letter, never making exceptions regardless of the reason. For example, one company rule states that an employee will not be paid for a holiday if he is absent on the day prior to or following the holiday. Henry Sizemore, who will retire next year, failed to show up for work on the day following July 4. He had stayed with his wife who had an emergency appendectomy on that day, July 5. Despite his age, his years with the company, and his superior attendance record, Bart treated him exactly as he did the new motorcycle rider who was also absent at a race on July 5. "You've got to be firm and fair—treat them all alike," was the way he put it.

Likewise, he views everyone as an individual who is entitled to his privacy. He never talks to his employees about their outside work or hobbies unless he feels these activities are interfering with their work in the Plating Department. "What the employee does outside of work is his own business," Bart says. His only concern is what the employee does on his job in the Plating Department. However, when an employee's output drops, Bart is quick to talk with the employee and "jack him up." He feels an employee is paid to perform at a satisfactory level, and if he doesn't, Bart is the first to point this out. As long as the employee's work is OK, he never bothers him.

Bart doesn't believe in coddling people. In his view, his employees are paid to do their work, and he expects them to do it. When he got a new man from the personnel department, Bart put him to work where he was needed without discussing the position with him, assuming that the employee wanted to work or he wouldn't have applied for the job.

Despite the fact that he is just, never stands in an employee's way in promotions, and treats all of his employees with the same degree of firmness and fairness, Bart's production record has gradually slipped during the past eight months. In his mind, the reduction in output is directly related to the "poor help" that the personnel people send him. "The guys I get are picky and choosy about what they want to do and will leave at the drop of a hat," Bart explained. Other departments, however, haven't experienced these same problems.

1. What do you think is the problem in Bart Richmond's department?
2. What human relations mistakes do you think Bart is making?
3. If you were called in to give Bart help, what would you tell him?

A Case Study
LAZERBEAN'S

As supervisor of inventories for Lazerbean's, a large chain operation, John Rogers had six separate storerooms under his control. Two of the six storerooms were located in the Auto-Servi-Center where automotive products were sold and repairs were made, with the remaining four storerooms located in the main building, which housed various departments in a six-story building.

The storerooms were specialized in their inventories and were located near the particular areas using their supplies. As a consequence, the six storerooms were fairly widely scattered throughout the Lazerbean complex of buildings and floors.

In organizing these storerooms, Rogers had appointed one employee to be head storekeeper in charge of the operation of the particular storeroom as well as of the other employees working in it. Although those in charge were not called supervisors, they were recognized as having potential for promotion to supervisory positions and were paid wages higher than the other employees.

One Saturday during the noon lunch hour, Lazerbean's District Manager, Mr. J. J. Swamore, came by Rogers's office and asked to be shown through the various storerooms. Rogers had developed a reputation in the Lazerbean chain as one of their outstanding supervisors and organizers. Because of this, Mr. Swamore was interested in seeing how Rogers organized and controlled his operations. It was obvious from Mr. Swamore's comments that he was much impressed with the operations of the storerooms, the layout of the rooms, the personnel assignments, and the manner in which material was controlled.

Everything went well until they entered the upstairs storeroom in the Auto-Servi-Center building. Here they found the room open with no one apparently in attendance. As they walked through the back of the room, they found the head storekeeper sound asleep on a pile of cleaning rags. Rogers was embarrassed for himself, ashamed of his storekeeper asleep on the job, and indignant that the District Manager had come upon the scene. As Rogers started for the storekeeper, Mr. Swamore suggested that they continue with the inspection, indicating that he (Rogers) could deal with the sleeping employee later.

As soon as the inspection was completed, Rogers returned to the storeroom and found the employee still asleep on the rag pile. He awakened him, and without waiting for any explanation, fired him on the spot.

In his exit interview in the personnel office, the employee indicated that he liked his job, was sorry he had fallen asleep, and would like another chance. He stated he had been up the previous night with virtually no sleep because of a sick wife and baby.

1. Should Rogers have fired the storekeeper under the conditions? Why?
2. If you were Rogers, what action would you have taken? Why?
3. What effect would your actions have on other employees? What effect would Rogers's actions have on other employees?

A Case Study
TODD RICHARDSON'S GROUP PROBLEM

Todd Richardson was still angry when he related the following story to his wife on Friday night. She listened attentively as he recounted the details. According to Todd:

The fourteen employees making up the bearing assembly group had worked together for 26 months without any problems. Their work was of good quality and productivity had been high. Jim Johnson, one of the older members of the group, was an especially good employee. Always on time, always there, he had a way with both men and women in the group that made everyone like him.

Because of his seniority with the company, Jim was promoted last week from the assembly job to one with more responsibility and higher pay—one which could possibly lead to an administrative or supervisory job. The group employees were sorry to see Jim leave, but were happy for his promotion. On his last day the group had a small "farewell" party for him during the afternoon break.

Most group members considered Jim's job the best and most desirable one in the bearing assembly process. When he left, therefore, several changes were made within the bearing assembly group, moving some of the senior employees to better and higher paying jobs in the group. A new employee, Elizabeth Jennings, was routinely added to the group to do a routine job.

Things appeared to be settling down to normal by Thursday. But on Friday "all hell broke loose." Of the group's output, 23% was rejected because of poor quality, and accusations started flying about. Several employees blamed the poor quality on Elizabeth Jennings's work. Three of the women in the group came to Elizabeth's defense. Some of the men accused the women of sticking together and not putting the blame where it was deserved.

At this point Todd stepped in and told the group in no uncertain terms to shape up or ship out. He said that if both quality and quantity of output were not improved, he would replace the poor employees with some who would and could produce. Todd's actions smothered the flame of anger, but in no way was it extinguished.

On Friday afternoon something happened within the group that really caused tempers to flare. The resulting heated arguments led to a work stoppage and even caused employees on other teams to stop work and watch the fight in the bearing assembly group. When this occurred, Todd moved in, ordered them back to work, and stood by to make sure his orders were followed. The group reluctantly resumed working for the last 45 minutes of the day. After work some of the old hands told Todd that they couldn't work under such tension and bickering, and were going to apply for a transfer if something wasn't done.

As Todd explained to his wife, "It all happened because I worked to get a promotion for one of my best employees." In Todd's mind, he was damned if he did and damned if he didn't. If he had refused to promote Jim Johnson he would have had problems, and when he did promote Jim he had problems. Todd was troubled and wondered what his best course of action would be.

1. What really caused the problem in the bearing assembly group? Why?
2. Could the problems in the group have been foreseen and thus prevented? How?
3. What do you think Todd Richardson should do now? Why?

A Personal Case Problem

One of your friends, Melba Little, comes up to you and says that studying human relations is a lot of bunk—that human relations is nothing but a high-sounding word for "how to skin friends and influence people." Melba further states that you are really not being ethical or honest when you practice human relations—that you say things you really don't mean just to get people to do things for you.

1. How would you reply to Melba?
2. Would you try to explain human relations to her? Why?
3. What points about human relations do you consider the most important to stress to Melba?

7

THE SUPERVISOR AND MORALE

This chapter explains—

- How your supervision affects morale
- How to measure morale
- How you can help build morale

Napoleon knew the importance of morale. He recognized that an army's effectiveness depended on its training, its size, its experience, and its morale. But to him, morale was more important than all the others combined. The same thing holds true in other organizations.

WHAT IS MORALE?

Morale is your state of mind—how you feel about things. If your morale is "good" or "high," you feel good about things. You are optimistic. You work with enthusiasm and energy. And you feel that you are making progress. Low morale is just the opposite. You feel "down" or "low." You have a negative attitude toward your work.

Many things can affect your morale: your health, your work environment, your family experiences, your supervisor, the company you work for, and so on. Your reaction to these and many other factors causes you to feel a certain way about things. Morale, therefore, is the result not of a single attitude or feeling, but of a combination of several or many factors.

WHY IS MORALE IMPORTANT?

How you feel about your job—your attitude—plays a large part in determining your success on the job. In fact, most supervisors will tell you that an employee's poor attitude or low state of morale accounts for more job losses than does inefficiency on the job. The same thing, of course, applies to supervisors as well. Many of the supervisors who fail are those whose state of mind or morale is low. They don't understand that their state of morale is contagious—that what they say and how they say it affects the morale of their employees. And, of course, all of this affects the productivity of the firm, the quality of the product, and the ultimate success of the organization as well as its employees.

WHY DOES MORALE VARY?

Some of us are very intense in everything we do. We don't do anything halfway. If we decide to do something, we enter into it with 100% enthusiasm. If we aren't given this opportunity, we don't like it, and our morale suffers. Other people, however, may have a sort of take-it-or-leave-it attitude. They are indifferent as to whether or not they do something. They are seldom highly excited or very low. Theirs is a steady monotonous existence. There are also people who are moody—bright and happy one day, down and depressed the next. Their morale varies with their moods.

We all have different ideas about things. We have developed attitudes from our experiences at home, at school, and with friends. Some people, for example, may have been taught that "idle hands are the devil's workshop" and that they should always approach work with vigor and a positive frame of mind. Employees with this background are not happy and do not have good morale unless they are working at a meaningful job. Other people, as a result of their home environment, may find work distasteful and put a high premium on leisure time. Their morale is highest when their jobs provide leisure time for other activities.

approach to work

"The way you manage employees has a direct bearing on their morale."

As you can see, these and other similar factors are the reasons you feel the way you do about things. These are the types of things that affect your attitude about your job and your morale.

DOES SUPERVISION AFFECT MORALE?

The way you manage and supervise employees has a direct bearing on their morale. As you know from experience, morale is always present in some degree. Sometimes it is high, at other times low. But it is never absent. It always exists at some point between extremely good and very poor. What you do as a supervisor affects the point where your employees' morale will be on this scale.

As a supervisor, you can't use your authority to make your employees have high morale. You can't buy it. The only thing you can do is help create a climate in which high morale can develop. Good morale grows out of good human relations, good employee motivation, respect for the individual, recognition of individual differences, good supervision, good communications, understanding, counseling, and other good supervisory practices.

Because of the importance of good morale, you should be concerned with the level of morale among your subordinates. You, more than any other person, affect the morale of your employees through your day-to-day contacts. It is a long-run proposition—not something that can be cultivated by a brief pep talk. Good morale comes about as a result of long-run actions taken by you to create a work environment in which your employees will willingly participate.

authority and morale

Morale may vary from day to day. It may spread in a contagious manner, but it can erode quickly if something is wrong. As a supervisor, therefore, you will need to exert your energies to maintain a satisfactory level of morale among your employees. Good morale among your workers will mean a happier, healthier work force, one that tackles jobs with a better work attitude. With good morale, better production and better product quality typically result.

Your employees are all individually affected by the morale you help to develop. Good morale for your employees makes their work a pleasure, not a chore. Good morale makes working with others a source of satisfaction rather than a source of ill feelings. Employees with good morale are usually pleased with their jobs, have confidence in their abilities to get their work done, and participate willingly in getting the work out. These factors are all important to employees because they make their day of work a pleasure rather than a miserable experience. They are likewise important to the supervisor because quality products and good productivity can be expected from employees who have a healthy attitude toward their jobs. One of the major tasks of a supervisor, therefore, is to build or create a departmental climate where high morale can develop and grow.

DOES WORK CLIMATE AFFECT MORALE?

Look around at your employees and their work areas. What "feel" do you get? Is it organized, structured, systematic? Are your employees at their respective positions performing their jobs with little talk and show of emotion? Or is the "feel" one of lightness, informality, and openness? Are your employees working, but still smiling and talking with other employees? Do they look like they are enjoying their jobs?

environment and morale

The climate in your department has a lot to do with your employees' morale and how well they do their jobs. People are naturally gregarious— they want to be with others. And the hum and clutter of a busy and friendly work place can create a climate of vitality, of progress, of being alive. All of these things affect your employees' morale. They feel more satisfied about their jobs. The more that social scientists discover about human beings, the more they realize the importance of the work environment and its effect on people's morale and productivity. As a supervisor, therefore, your job is to build an environment in which friendly employees can work together effectively. While there is no 1–2–3 list to tell you what to do, your common sense will lead you in the right direction. In this chapter we'll discuss many of the things you can do to enhance morale in your department.

WHAT INFLUENCES MORALE?

Almost anything you can think of can have some bearing on morale. Some things are under the control of management; others are not. As a supervisor, for example, you can do little to change the family relationships that your employees experience at home, their associations with friends, their hobbies, their ability to repair a faulty water heater. Yet these things affect an employee's attitude. An argument with a spouse can easily cause an employee to face the day in a negative mood. The lack of success and frustration in repairing a water heater may likewise cause an employee to approach work with less than a positive attitude.

WHAT CAN A SUPERVISOR DO TO IMPROVE MORALE?

Although you cannot do anything as a supervisor to control the above factors, you should be alert to their existence and do whatever you can to reduce their impact on your employees. One of the best things you can do to help ease the impact of outside events on your employees' morale is to help them "get it off their chests." Encourage your employees to talk to you about what is bothering them. Just telling their problems to others seems to help, and in the process you may be able to help your employees put their problems in proper perspective, or even point out an alternative solution. You might, for example, give your employee a good tip on how to repair the water heater. With a possible solution in mind, the employee will probably stop worrying and concentrate on work with renewed vigor and a more positive frame of mind.

Employee morale is also influenced by factors that are within management's control. These include such things as job security, adequate compensation, good working conditions, interesting work, and recognition for a job well done. All of these factors affect morale, and neglecting any one of them may cause the extra effort you put in on the others to go for naught. For example, if you neglect to give recognition to your secretary for his good work, for his help and loyalty, and for a job well done, his morale may suffer even though he is well paid and works under good working conditions. So take time out and say to him, "Jim, you are really a great secretary. Don't know how I could manage all of these things without your help. Even

*things that
affect morale*

though I don't always tell you, I want you to know that I do appreciate all your efforts and everything you do to make things run smoothly here."

Employee morale is particularly affected by what you as a supervisor do and the way you act. Your general approach to supervision, your direction, and your leadership all have a direct effect on your employees' morale. For example, expressing appreciation to your employees for their good work will exert a positive effect on their morale. If you talk with them and show them how important their work is to achieving the overall company objective, they will have a healthier mental attitude toward their jobs. The *way* in which you do these things—the way you act—likewise affects their morale. If you compliment an employee's work with a lighthearted, off-the-cuff remark, it will not have the impact that a serious compliment would. Consider, for example, how you would feel if your supervisor said to you, "Oh, by the way, that repair job you did the other day was O.K." Contrast your reaction if instead he had said, "Joe, I want you to know that management appreciates the skill and speed you used in repairing the press. Because you did such a good job, we'll be able to ship the government order on time. All of us are grateful to you."

If you as a supervisor lose your temper, show that you are worried, or indicate that you are unsure of yourself, these factors, too, will affect your employees' morale. If employees see that their supervisor is angry and worried, the employees, feeling that things are not going well in the department, will be depressed and their morale will suffer. As a supervisor, therefore, you should remember at all times to lead in a positive way. You should acknowledge your difficulties and should seek your employees' help to correct an error that has been made, rather than try to hide your problems and show that you are worried. Remember that "worry begets worry" and that confident leadership creates a work climate where morale can be high.

WHAT OTHER FACTORS AFFECT MORALE?

In addition to the above, there are eight aspects of an employee's job that have a direct bearing on the employee's morale. In supervising your employees, try to keep these in mind:

1. Be certain your employee understands what you expect, the goals you have in mind, the policies you expect the employee to follow, and the consequences of deviations.
2. Show your employees why it is important for them to understand and be committed to achieving the goals.
3. Give recognition so that your employees will know they are not cogs, but are needed individuals who will be rewarded for good work. Give your employees credit that is rightfully theirs.
4. Be truthful. Never rationalize or tamper with the facts.

5. Make employee assignments to an appropriate work team. Employees who are put in a warm, cooperative, cohesive work team will have higher morale.

6. Make your employees responsible for their work. The more they feel responsible for their jobs and for their productivity, the greater their pride in their workmanship and the higher their morale.

7. Be people-centered in your supervision rather than production-centered. Employees who see that you have them at the center of your supervisory practices will be more cooperative, will have higher morale, and will be better members of your work team. There is no surer way to cripple morale than to constantly center your focus on output.

8. Be courteous to your employees. Show a genuine consideration for their wishes and feelings.

HOW DOES MORALE AFFECT PRODUCTIVITY?

Some people think that high morale and high productivity go hand in hand. This is not always true. Generally, however, there is some positive correlation between the two; that is, if morale goes up, productivity usually goes up. If morale goes down, productivity usually goes down too.

*morale and
work*

Your morale reflects your attitudes about many things, some of which do not influence productivity. For this reason, we can't say that an increase in morale will always increase productivity. It is fair to say, however, that high morale puts employees in a frame of mind to be productive, and if good supervision and good working conditions are also present, then productivity will usually go up.

Employees' have high morale only when their happiness, their satisfaction, and their personal adjustments make them want to contribute their efforts to reaching the company's goal. Reaching the company's goal, of course, enables them to reach their own goals of food, clothing, a home, and so on. A good supervisor, therefore, should always try to show employees that they will personally benefit, that they will reach their own goals, if they will help the company to reach its goals of producing goods. It is possible, of course, to have good productivity and low morale, but it is highly questionable whether this condition would last for any length of time. Low morale, reflecting negative attitudes, would sooner or later affect output.

CAN YOU MEASURE MORALE?

It's difficult to measure morale because morale is an attitude or frame of mind. It is how you feel about something. However, as we have said, maintaining high morale is important to supervisors because high morale results in a better, happier, more satisfied work force, one that produces better products at a higher output. Managers do, therefore, try to measure morale through morale surveys, opinion surveys, or attitude surveys. All of these terms mean the same thing. In a morale survey, questions like the following are asked.

opinion surveys

1. Do you like to work for this company?
   ☐ Dislike.
   ☐ It is O.K.
   ☐ Like the company.
   ☐ Very happy working here.
2. Does your supervisor keep you informed about what's going on?
   ☐ Never.
   ☐ Rarely.
   ☐ About half the time.
   ☐ Yes, always.
3. Does your supervisor listen to your complaints or gripes and handle them quickly and fairly?
   ☐ No. Very unsatisfactory.
   ☐ He tries but doesn't do enough.
   ☐ He handles them well.
   ☐ I never have any complaints.

By analyzing the answers to these and similar questions, management can tell how its employees feel about their jobs, what parts of the jobs they feel strongly about, how they feel about their supervisors, their attitude toward the company, which departments are weak, where training needs are apparent, where poor communications exist, and so on. It is important for management to take immediate action to correct tlese problems once they find out what they are and where they exist. By correcting them, supervisors can help create a better work climate where employee morale can be shifted to a more positive position.

WHAT ARE THE ADVANTAGES OF A MORALE SURVEY?

In addition to showing management how employees feel, morale surveys also give employees the opportunity to say what is on their minds. They enable them to communicate freely up the line. This can be important because it tells management what the employees are thinking, and it makes the employees feel better because they are provided the opportunity to get some things off their chests. Morale surveys are also important because they indicate to employees that the company is interested in them and their opinions—that the company cares.

Morale surveys have another advantage: they focus management's attention on morale and its importance to the company, making supervisors "morale-conscious."

As a morale-conscious supervisor, you will be in an excellent position in your company to sense and control the attitude among your rank-and-file employees. You can talk with your employees and learn why they feel the way they do. You can help your employees see another point of view. You can teach your employees new ways of looking at things, both by example and by talking with them. For example, Sam, a newcomer, might think the company is unfair to him because he has been assigned to the oldest press on the floor. It is an old and slow machine, and as a result, his output is low. He gripes about this and thinks it is unfair. A good supervisor recognizes Sam's gripes and helps him see the situation from the company's point of view. Sam is the youngest man in the department, still a "learner." His supervisor explains that all new employees are put on the slower press until they get the hang of the job, usually about three months. After this they are transferred to newer and faster equipment where they can meet their production quota. With this explanation, Sam's attitude changes. He can see that the company is giving him an opportunity to learn and to make his mistakes on a slower machine, and he knows that as soon as he develops skill on the job, he will be assigned a newer machine.

ARE THERE SIGNS OF LOW MORALE?

You don't always need a morale survey to tell you how well things are going in a company. You can also tell that morale is low by signs such as the following:

1. High labor turnover.
2. No respect for supervisors.
3. Low productivity.
4. Excessive waste.
5. Large number of grievances.
6. Large number of accidents.
7. General lack of cooperation.
8. Poor quality of production.
9. Low regard for the company.
10. Excessive lateness.
11. Excessive sick leaves.
12. Leaving work early.
13. Long lunch periods.
14. Excessive one-day absences.
15. Loss of interest and enthusiasm.

Of all the workers in a company, assembly line workers, by and large, are apt to have the lowest morale. Because of the monotony of their jobs, they generally find little satisfaction in their work. Frequently they feel they are overworked, not appreciated, and have little or no opportunity for advancement. These same things can be said about other workers; however, assembly line employees seem to be most subject to low morale. Since the supervisor is in most frequent contact with these employees, he or she is in the best position to help improve their attitudes. The supervisor should, therefore, keep these signs of low morale in mind and should take immediate steps to change the conditions and help change the attitude causing the low state of morale.

WHAT CAN A SUPERVISOR DO TO HELP BUILD MORALE?

As you can see, it is of utmost importance to you as a supervisor that your employees have high morale and positive attitudes about their jobs. You might wonder what you can do to help satisfy a worker's needs. For one thing, you can develop an understanding and appreciation of your employees as persons, seeing their individual qualities and capacities. You should treat them courteously at all times and let them know that they are needed and valuable members of the work team. Give them credit where credit is due. Criticize employees when it is justified, but do so in private, not in front of their fellow workers.

building morale

Talk over your employees' jobs with them, getting their ideas and suggestions for changing and improving those jobs. Be sure that their pay is just, fair, and in line with pay for comparable jobs in the community. Look after general working conditions, making sure of comfort, safety, and cleanliness. Periodically talk with individual employees about their job performance, their progress, and the opportunities that might lie ahead for them. Point out their need (if any) for additional skills, training, or education in order for them to take advantage of future opportunities.

You can make your employees' jobs more interesting. Short-cycle jobs are monotonous. See what you can do to add variety to a job. Most employees like this. If possible, let the worker decide the pace to be maintained. Change the job so that the employee completes a whole unit, rather than simply adding a cotter pin to the assembly. If none of these changes are possible, see what you can do to rotate employees on a scheduled basis among several jobs. For example, let the typist run the duplicating machine for an hour, while the duplicating machine employee operates the postal room, and the postal clerk does the typing job.

By doing these and similar things, you will have the opportunity to raise the level of morale among your employees, and at the same time you will be able to observe and study them for indications of dissatisfaction. As a supervisor, you are in a position to constantly study and observe the attitudes and behavior of your employees. You can listen to what they are saying as well as to what they are implying. You can sense changes in their attitudes toward the company and their willingness or unwillingness to cooperate.

Because of your close day-to-day contact with your employees, you should know them well and should be able to sense and observe minor changes in their morale. The closer you are to your employees, the easier it will be for you to recognize changes in morale before they grow to the point of disrupting the work of your department. It is in this area of day-to-day supervision that you can do the most to raise and maintain the level of morale in your department.

QUESTIONS FOR DISCUSSION AND REVIEW

1. What is morale? How does it affect you?
2. Explain how morale varies among different people.
3. Can a supervisor affect the morale of his employees? How?
4. How does a supervisor's morale affect his employees' morale?
5. Does morale affect productivity? How?
6. How do you measure morale?
7. What good does it do to measure morale?
8. Are there signs when morale is low? Name some of them.
9. How can a supervisor help build morale?
10. Of what value is high morale to a company?
11. How does work climate affect morale? Explain.

A Case Study
ALLISON AUTO PARTS

In 1927, Henry Allison opened his first auto parts store in connection with his garage and service station. He sold high-quality products at fair prices and in the years that followed developed a reputation as a reliable source for replacement parts.

With continued growth in the auto parts business, he sold his garage and service station and in 1934 opened a mail-order auto parts store. By 1954, his staff had grown to 60 salesmen, 15 warehousemen, and 5 office employees.

Mr. Allison was an iron-fisted man who ran a "tight" shop. His word was law, and everyone knew it. His hiring practices were simple. If an applicant for a job wore a hat, he concluded that the man would make a good salesman. If he did not wear a hat, Mr. Allison, depending on his mood, might consider him as a possible warehouseman. He always asked a prospective employee, "Do you repair your own car?" If the prospect answered "no," he was turned down for the job. When an applicant was hired, Mr. Allison personally took him into the store or warehouse, depending on his assignment, and told him precisely what he wanted him to do. Then he turned the employee over to the supervisor. Any worker who contradicted or strongly disagreed with Mr. Allison was fired without question.

Allison Auto Parts had no formal system of pay or merit increases. Instead, every employee was paid what Mr. Allison thought he was worth, and his pay was increased whenever Mr. Allison thought it should be increased. Mr. Allison was a firm believer in hard work and didn't "baby" his employees with fringe benefits, paid vacations, or sick leave.

In 1967, Mr. Allison's son Dick came to work in the business as vice-president and general manager. In school, Dick had taken some courses in personnel and human behavior and felt that the company's personnel practices were not ideal. His first act was to devise an application blank for all employees. One was filled out for each new applicant, and to complete the files, he also had one made out for each old employee. In addition, he made arrangements with a local physician to give every new employee a physical examination to determine his physical fitness for the work. Dick also wanted to install an employee as well as a supervisory training program, but he was not able to convince his father of such a need.

Labor turnover during the past ten years had increased from 6 to 26%, and absences had increased in proportion. Although most employees who left the company said they did so because the work was too hard, they also stated dissatisfaction with their jobs, and some complained about pay. When Dick checked the average wage, however, he found that it was above the community average for similar work.

In trying to figure out the cause of the trouble, Dick decided that what was needed was a system of job specifications. He also indicated that he thought morale could be improved by an employee suggestions system. Mr. Allison vetoed the idea of job specifications but agreed tentatively to an employee suggestions system. Accordingly, Mr. Allison placed on the company bulletin board an announcement indicating that a suggestions system was in effect and that employees should make their suggestions to their supervisors. If an employee's suggestion was adopted, he would be awarded a cash bonus to be determined by the value of the suggestion to the company.

After a month and a half had passed with no suggestions, Dick found that several had been made, but the supervisor in question had decided they were of no value and, therefore, had not passed them on to Mr. Allison. Dick then got his father's permission to install a new suggestions system, and during the next month over 41 suggestions were received covering such topics as changes in manufacturing methods, changes in plant layout, job classifications, employee leaves, vacations with pay, a system of promotions and transfers, and materials handling. Mr. Allison patiently read each suggestion aloud to his son and explained why it could not be adopted. When employees heard nothing from their suggestions, they stopped submitting them. Labor turnover continued to increase, up to 32%.

Dick Allison knew that employee relations and morale were getting out of hand, but he could not decide what steps he should take next.

1. What do you think the trouble is with Allison Auto Parts?
2. What would you do to correct the situation?

A Case Study
GENE HUBBARD

Gene Hubbard had been in business for four and a half years. Opening up his office supply store with virtually no capital, he had worked night and day to make it a success. It had grown, was well accepted in the community, and Gene felt that with his nine employees he could now afford to work less and enjoy life more.

But things didn't seem to work out for him that way. There always appeared to be problems that he personally had to solve—a customer who didn't get what he ordered, an employee with a personal complaint or grievance, employees not showing up for work at the designated hour, and thus the list went on.

Gene was a self-made man and really didn't know what to do. He wanted to give his employees authority to make decisions, to run his store, but he didn't trust them. He felt that they couldn't be relied upon to do what they were hired to do. In fact, in his mind they weren't worth the pay that they received each week. It seems that every one of them had complained about his or her job, indicating they were all overworked and not appreciated. He always laughed at the employees when they started talking along this line, telling them that what they needed to do was to roll up their sleeves and get to work. This usually shut them up and they returned to their jobs.

In fact, this was one of the things that always annoyed Gene—that his employees were always complaining, telling him that they needed a better washroom, or that they wanted an area where they could sit down for a coffee break or eat their lunch. He laughed at such ideas, telling them that this was a place to work, not a home where you could lounge around. In Gene's mind, his employees just didn't seem to appreciate all that he was doing for them. They always wanted more.

It seemed to him that they had forgotten what their status was before he gave them a job. Most of them had been unemployed, looking for work, and with families to support. They had forgotten that he had found them at the unemployment bureau and had offered to give them the opportunity to make something of themselves.

Gene wanted to have a prosperous business. He wanted his employees to like him. And he wanted to be known as a successful businessman. But he didn't know how to go about telling his workers what he wanted from them. He had never been "good with words," and he figured his actions would tell them a whole lot more than any fancy words. He always stayed an hour or so after the store closed, for example, and he hoped some of them would too. But he found that, instead of staying late, two of them had slipped out ten minutes early last Tuesday. However, he figured he had stopped that type of action by docking their pay and letting everyone else know about what they had been trying to get away with. He had said on many occasions that he didn't plan to treat any of his employees with kid gloves.

1. Do you think that morale was high or low in Gene's store? Why?
2. What would you say were the main qualities that Gene Hubbard possessed as a supervisor?
3. If you were hired as a consultant to help Gene Hubbard, what advice would you give him?

A Case Study
A STATE OF MORALE

When Dorothy Fagge was first hired in the shipping department to box and ship hose at the Apex Hosiery Mill, she was quite happy with her work. Most of the employees were about her age, and they talked and had a lot in common. Within a couple of weeks, however, Mr. R. J. Pennington was transferred to the shipping department as the new supervisor, and the "new broom started sweeping clean."

His first change was to stop coffee breaks. The women missed their coffee chats, so they started bringing coffee to work in thermal containers. With their own coffee, three or four would get together at odd times and have their private coffee chat. When the new supervisor saw this, he mumbled something to the employees about how what they needed was fewer coffee breaks and more work breaks.

Next he jumped on the employees for putting pictures on the walls—pinups, movie stars, grandchildren, scenes from foreign countries, you name it and it was there. Claiming they were a fire hazard and unattractive, he ordered the pictures removed. One by one they came down.

The straw that broke the camel's back was his order to stop wearing perfume and tight-fitting jeans to work. The younger women thought he had really gone too far this time, but complied with his order.

Within three weeks, however, two of the better employees had quit and three others had asked for transfers to the stockroom. With only a skeleton crew, shipping lagged and customers began to complain about incorrect and missed shipments. Mr. Pennington was on the spot.

1. Do you think Mr. Pennington could have accomplished his objectives without upsetting his employees? How?
2. Is this a morale problem or a supervisory problem? Why?
3. What would you do now if you were Mr. R. J. Pennington? Why?

A Personal Case Problem

Decide for yourself whether you think the following statement is true or false: "Motivation is more important for a smoothly running department than morale is." Discuss (or debate) this with a member of your group who feels the opposite of the way you do. Let the entire group (or class) listen to the comments you and your opponent set forth to defend your positions. Have the class then choose the individual who made the most convincing presentation.

Repeat the above for several class members. Do you detect any shift in class opinion as to which is more important? If so, why do you think this shift has occurred?

8

YOU, UNIONS, AND PUBLIC POLICY

This chapter explains—

- Why unions are attractive to some people
- How unions operate in collective bargaining
- A supervisor's relationship with unions
- What you should know about public policy regarding labor

Today labor unions are just as much a part of our society as the family and the morning paper. Unions have both legal status and social approval. As a supervisor, therefore, you will probably have to deal with unions. It may be that your employees are union members, or you may deal with other firms whose employees are unionized. In either event, unions are an integral part of the management scheme, and you should recognize, understand, and work with them effectively.

WHAT IS A UNION?

A union is an organization of employees that seeks to improve its members' social, economic, and political interests through the process of collective bargaining. Most unions emphasize improving wages and conditions of work. They seek through collective bargaining to get better pay, better fringe benefits, and better working conditions for their members. In addition, some unions seek to improve the workers' status by influencing political action in the local, state, and federal governments.

types of unions

Some unions are craft unions and only accept members from a single occupation or trade, such as carpenters. On the other hand, industrial unions represent all workers in a particular company or industry regardless of what jobs they perform. The United Automobile Workers is an example of an industrial union, where one union represents all workers in the automobile industry.

WHY DO WORKERS JOIN UNIONS?

One reason that workers join unions is that one employee alone doesn't have much of a chance trying to bargain over wages with a giant company. The firm can get along without the worker and can tell him to take the wages offered or leave. The worker's only bargaining strength is that he can quit. This obviously is not much strength for an individual, but when all workers join together and say they'll quit, they have some power over the company. Employees join unions, therefore, for *greater bargaining power.*

bargaining power

Another reason is the *need to make themselves heard.* Most employees want to be more than a cog in the wheel. They want the supervisor to listen to them and their ideas. They want a voice in the operations and procedures of the enterprise. The union gives them this voice.

Some workers are coerced to join unions as *a condition of employment* in businesses where unions have contracts specifying that employees must join the union within a certain period of time or be fired.

People are social, friendly creatures whose actions are influenced by what others do. If all the other employees are joining a union, a given person will, too. Therefore, being "in," *being a member of the group,* or being identified with the organization that the employee feels is to his benefit is another reason employees join unions. This satisfies the social need discussed in Chapter 5.

need to belong

Employees also join unions because they want to eliminate or at least *minimize favoritism and discrimination.* In some companies, a few employees may be given the soft jobs, given the new machines, or shown favoritism in other ways. Most workers resent this, and through unions they can press for equal treatment, equal opportunity, and equal pay for equal work.

WHY DO SOME EMPLOYEES REJECT UNIONS?

Inasmuch as 75% of the labor force does not belong to any union, not everyone is in favor of unions. Why not? A lot of employees feel that *unions are socialistic or collectivistic in nature.* They distrust them and somehow feel they are "un-American" and contrary to the American concept of individual initiative, individual freedom, and free enterprise. They feel that employees ought to stand on their own feet, get ahead by their own abilities, and fight their own battles.

*collectivistic
nature*

Other employees reject union membership because they can see *no good reason to join.* They are happy with their jobs and their pay, and they see no reason why they should have to join a union and pay dues every month to fatten the union treasury.

Professional people typically reject unions because they feel that union affiliation would be *beneath their dignity.* Instead, they seek out and join their own organizations such as the American Medical Association, American Association of University Professors, and the American Bar Association, whose objectives are much the same as the unions'—to represent their members and better the members' positions.

Unions are typically composed of blue-collar workers because many white-collar employees feel that it is *below their social status to belong.*

Finally, some employees reject unions because they *prefer to be associated with the managerial side.* This is particularly true of white-collar employees who work closely with the supervisors and managers and who tend to accept the management point of view. They feel their future lies in advancing upward in managerial circles and think that union membership might hamper this possibility.

HOW DOES THE UNION AFFECT THE SUPERVISOR?

The way you as a supervisor deal with your employees is considerably changed after the union comes in; you can no longer deal directly with an employee over such things as hours of work, adjustment in pay, and working conditions. The shop steward is the one who speaks for the employees and is the person you must deal with.

The supervisor is no longer the "cock of the walk" after the union

restriction of freedom

comes in. Instead, you must now make sure you do nothing to violate the union contract. You are bound, so to speak, by the written word. For example, you may not be able to shift a worker from one job to another with the freedom you did before. If you ask an employee to perform a task that requires better skills in some respects than the job the employee has been used to, both the union steward and the employee will demand a higher job classification. If you wish to let two or three employees go because business is slack, you can't lay off the worst workers. Instead, you may have to let those with the least seniority go. In other words, the freedom of action of supervisors is considerably restricted.

Another effect on the supervisor is that you now *must* treat every employee alike. If one punch-press operator gets safety shoes at company expense, every employee operating similar machines must also be furnished safety shoes at company expense. All employees assigned the same jobs get the same pay, except for seniority increases. Supervisors can make no differentiation.

"With a union present, a supervisor can no longer deal directly with his employees about hours of work, adjustments in pay, and working conditions."

SIR, THE SHOP STEWARD SAYS WE CAN'T PAINT THIS ROOM UNTIL MONDAY MORNING

Instead of dealing with dozens of employees, you now deal mainly with the shop steward. If you want to know your employees' preferences for vacation, you ask the steward. If you want to know their reaction to job rotation or job enlargement, you ask the steward. In one sense, this simplifies your job because the shop steward usually knows the employees and has a "feel" for their true opinions, and thus gives a fair picture to you. Because of this, you can easily check with the steward about questions regarding such things as working conditions, safety equipment, how to operate an employee suggestion system, and so on.

Decisions that supervisors used to make have a tendency to be centralized when the company has a union. For example, a small change in work methods or the way a complaint is handled is no longer controlled by the supervisor because such things might be in violation of the union contract or cause a grievance. Because of this, management tends to take the authority for these and similar decisions away from supervisors and centralize them in the industrial relations department. This is particularly true in the handling of grievances. In many companies, the union contract specifies that the first point of contact over grievances will be between the steward and the supervisor. In practice, your authority as a supervisor to handle the grievance frequently resides in the industrial relations department, and before you can give a definite answer to a question, you have to check with industrial relations. In multiplant companies, this centralization of power is even more noticeable because management wants to make decisions with all plants in mind, not with just one department in mind. Afraid that the supervisor will do something to cause a work stoppage, top management in many instances has virtually taken away the power to discipline from the supervisor.

Thus, as a supervisor you really lack authority and status in many instances. Although technically you are a member of the management team, you may feel forgotten because you are frequently left out of contract negotiations. In addition, you are often made to look ridiculous to your employees because your superiors' concessions to union demands may contradict what you tell your employees.

Finally, given the many ways in which unions affect supervisors, you sometimes find your salary lower than those of some of your employees. This condition usually results from pay concessions made in union agreements pertaining to hours worked, overtime, and the like.

The above examples are illustrative of a few of the ways that unions can affect you and your supervisory job.

WHAT ARE A SUPERVISOR'S RIGHTS WHEN THE UNION TRIES TO ORGANIZE?

When unions move in and try to organize the workers in a company, what can you as the supervisor do? What rights do you have? There are a lot of things you can do and a lot you can't do. We'll discuss a few of them.[1]

When union organizers appear on the scene, you can correct any un-

[1] Adapted from Claude S. George, Jr., *Management for Business and Industry* (Englewood Cliffs, N.J.: Prentice-Hall, Inc., 1970), pp. 362–64. Reprinted by permission of Prentice-Hall, Inc.

true or misleading union propaganda but cannot ask an employee to talk in private about the union. You can, however, talk to employees openly, on company time, and in groups, just as long as the talk is not held during the twenty-four-hour silence period held before each election. During this period, however, you can mail material to employees' homes.

In talking with your employees, you can point out the disadvantages of a union, such as monthly dues, fines, wages lost from strikes, and so on. You cannot, however, threaten the loss of a job, reduction in pay, or discontinuance of any past benefit if an employee joins or favors a union. Neither can you use language that could be construed to be intimidating or language that would keep a worker from joining a union. You can, however, talk with your employees, telling them about any of your personal union experiences and can even show how the employees' present wages and fringe benefits compare with those in unionized shops, emphasizing that unions cannot do anything for workers that they cannot do for themselves. But in this talk, you as their supervisor must not do or say anything that might be interpreted as restraining or interfering with an employee's right to participate in union activities. In fact, you cannot do anything that would imply to employees that you are keeping an eye on them to see whether they are participating in the organizing activities, nor can you ask them to tell you what they think about unions.

supervisory rights

You can, of course, insist that unions carry on their unionizing activities outside the plant work areas and during nonworking hours. Unions, however, do have the right to distribute pamphlets dealing with items of union interest, including political matters, provided it is done in nonworking areas and at reasonable times. You may ask your employees to notify you if the employees are in any way threatened or coerced by a union member or organizer. You can also point out to your employees that a worker does not have to sign a union-authorization card or even talk to the union organizers unless it is his or her voluntary desire, and if a union-authorization card is signed, the employee is under no obligation to vote for the union.

When you see any of your workers taking part in unionizing activities, you cannot in any way discriminate against them or deny them their right to solicit other workers except during working hours and in work areas. In other words, if the solicitation is in outside areas and during nonworking hours, you cannot interfere. You cannot stop a worker from soliciting other workers, even on company property and during working hours, unless management can clearly show that it is interfering with their jobs. In addition, you cannot threaten in any way to discipline or fire a worker for favoring or joining a union, nor can you threaten to close, move, or in any way reduce operations in a plant if the employees join a union.

As a supervisor you can, of course, talk to your employees, but you must be careful about what you say. You can, for example, discuss the usual seniority provisions present in most union contracts, pointing out how they would serve to stifle the progress of ambitious and skilled employees, but you must not imply that if the worker does not join the union, he will be promoted, given a raise, or rewarded in some manner. You cannot imply or state that you will not deal with a union in order to discourage your employees from joining, nor can you ask your workers to report to you the names of other workers, including themselves, who are either union members, favor unions, or are participating in union activities. As a manager, you can legally *listen* to this type of information if it is told to you voluntarily, but you cannot ask any questions about it.

A supervisor has the right to point out in conversations with employees that the union will probably try for a union shop, which will force all employees to join the union whether or not they so desire. As a supervisor you can suggest that if employees join a union, they will be paying for benefits they are already getting. You cannot, however, discriminate between union employees (and those thought to be union employees) and nonunion employees by giving the soft jobs to those who object to unions, saving the harder and more unpleasant tasks for the union members or those suspected of favoring the union.

Finally, as a supervisor you may advise your employees that they need not attend an organization meeting announced by a union organizer. In fact, under these conditions, you may call a meeting of your employees and advise them that the company has complied with all requests from the Labor Board and that the employees are not obligated to attend the announced union meeting. You should also point out that each worker must individually decide whether or not he or she will attend the meeting and that, whether in attendance or not, it will not affect the employee's employment status.

WHAT IS COLLECTIVE BARGAINING?

When authorized representatives of management and the union get together to bargain over and agree upon wages, hours of work, and working conditions, the process is called *collective bargaining.* By law, the process involves four steps:

1. Recognition of the appropriate bargaining unit.
2. Bargaining in good faith.   *legal aspects*
3. Meeting proposals with counterproposals.
4. Incorporation of the findings in a written contract.

The company must recognize the union chosen by a majority of its workers who voted in a government-certified election. The company must also bargain in good faith. It is not bargaining in good faith if it does any one or a combination of the following: meets with the union with no intention of reaching an agreement, refuses to bargain because its competitors haven't bargained, or claims the union is irresponsible and sets up unreasonable conditions before it will bargain. If the company fails to offer constructive counterproposals to the demands made by the union, it is not bargaining in good faith. Finally, it is unfair under the law if the company refuses to sign a written contract after reaching an agreement.

The actual bargaining is probably the least understood part of the process because it goes on in some hotel room or lawyer's office behind closed doors. The bargaining is given little publicity and is fraught with tension and emotions. Some people say it is like a high-powered poker game where the stakes are high. Actually, it is a bargaining process where the proposals and counterproposals are traded and bartered until the two sides finally reach an agreement. What the union usually strives for is to maximize the members' incomes, provide for job security, improve and maintain good working conditions, and make provisions for the continuance of the union.

HOW IMPORTANT IS THE SUPERVISOR TO COLLECTIVE BARGAINING?

As a supervisor you are very important to collective bargaining. In fact, you are usually the first contact between employees and management and between the union steward and management. What you do and say and the way you act concerning labor matters are of vital interest to the company. Your actions are not for your department alone, but have company-wide implications. If you neglect or ignore an employee's grievance, assign jobs in a thoughtless or unfair way, or encourage an employee to ignore safety practices, reports of your actions will probably find their way to the bargaining table as issues in future contract negotiations. You may, in fact, take actions that could precipitate a strike or get the company charged with breaking the union contract. Because of this, you are the key person in determining how testy the collective bargaining process will be.

a key person

Called upon to make decisions about and interpret the labor agreement, you are in a pivotal position. You aren't expected to be a "labor contract lawyer," yet you've got to know the proper responses to employee requests and union charges. If you don't, you may cost the company millions of dollars. Therefore, whenever you are in doubt about what attitude you should take, what the company's position is on a matter, the interpretation of a union contract clause, or how you should handle a request, you should get the answer from your boss or from the industrial relations department. You shouldn't guess. You should be sure of your ground first and then move.

HOW CAN A SUPERVISOR HELP WITH COLLECTIVE BARGAINING?

A supervisor can help with collective bargaining by making suggestions about union relationships. These suggestions should be specific and given well in advance of the start of the bargaining process. Many companies encourage their supervisors to give the management team suggestions throughout the year—any time the situation comes up and the supervisor has it clearly in mind. In this way, every suggestion can be evaluated with respect to how it would affect all other departments. Supervisors are especially encouraged to make suggestions about the three areas they are most heavily involved in: wages, seniority, and discipline.

WHAT RELATIONSHIP SHOULD EXIST BETWEEN A SUPERVISOR AND THE UNION STEWARD?

As a supervisor, you should by all means be friendly and cordial. Don't be anti-union. But don't forget that as the supervisor, you are in control of your department. The union steward's job is to protect his members' rights, and your job is to protect management's rights.

The steward has no authority to tell you what to do or boss any employees in your department. He may give you strong advice that you may later wish you had followed. But all he can do is advise. If possible, however, gain the steward's confidence and cooperation. This could be a mutually satisfactory agreement where each could help the other. You could keep him posted about what your plans are so that he can tell his members. And he can give you help by getting the workers to cooperate with, for example, a new work plan that you want to try out.

Try to work with the steward. Remember that the company has a contract with the union and that unions are a permanent part of our society. Don't waste time trying to annoy the steward or buck the union. Spend that same energy trying to find ways that the two of you can live in harmony.

WHAT IS PUBLIC POLICY?

So far, we've been talking about your relationship with unions. But don't get the idea that dealing with unions will be your toughest job. It won't be. During the last decade or two a great many public laws have been passed on both federal and state levels which erode your administrative freedoms and demand special attention and action on your part. Most companies are aware of, and typically abide by, the National Labor Relations Act, the Labor–Management Relations Act of 1947 (Taft–Hartley), the Fair Labor Standards Act of 1938, and the Labor–Management Reporting and Disclosure Act of 1959. These acts, therefore, will not be discussed. What we will be most concerned with are the more recent acts dealing with minorities, equal opportunity, discrimination, and the like.

Every manager today needs to be especially aware of this country's laws—its public policy. They are technical and difficult to implement at times. Yet, the supervisor who glosses over or ignores them leaves his company and himself open to a host of legal complications and suits. You should, therefore, be aware of these laws and make sure that you are not unnecessarily jeopardizing your company and your employees by not abiding by them.

WHAT LEGISLATION DEALS WITH DISCRIMINATION IN EMPLOYMENT?

Title VII

Title VII of the 1964 Civil Rights Act, as amended by the 1972 Equal Employment Opportunity Act (EEO), is critical for a supervisor to be familiar with. This legislation prohibits discrimination in pay, terms, conditions, or privileges of employment on the basis of race, color, religion, national origin, and sex. Furthermore, it is unlawful for you to limit, segregate, or classify employees or applicants in *any way* that would deprive or even tend to deprive them of employment or status because of race, color, sex, religion, or national origin. This applies to all individuals, private as well as public companies, state and local governments, employment agencies, and labor unions.

WHAT IS EEOC AND WHERE DOES IT FIT IN?

EEOC's job

The Equal Employment Opportunity Commission (EEOC) consists of five members appointed by the President of the United States. It was set up by Title VII. Its purpose is to investigate complaints and enforce the laws pertaining to discrimination. It does this by attempting to get the two sides in the complaint to agree. If this fails, the EEOC takes the case to court for enforcement. Thus, if one of your employees or applicants brings a complaint against you, the EEOC will investigate the complaint and, if necessary, file charges against you (or your company) on behalf of the employee or applicant. With this power, violations can be brought into court quickly. To help you work within the framework of the law, the EEOC has developed special guidelines regarding selection procedures, records, inquiries, and affirmative action. You, or your industrial relations department, should be familiar with these guides.

If state or local laws also prohibit discrimination, the EEOC lets the local body have jurisdiction. However, if these local agencies do not satisfy the two parties expeditiously, the charges are referred to the EEOC for resolution.

HOW DOES AFFIRMATIVE ACTION APPLY TO YOU?

As we have seen, EEOC attempts to assure that no one is discriminated against because of race, color, religion, sex, or national origin. In other words, people should be hired on the basis of their qualifications, with everyone having an equal chance for the job.

Affirmative action (required by Executive Orders 11246 and 11375) goes another step in the process and requires you to attempt to recruit, hire, upgrade, and promote those in minority groups. Its purpose is to eliminate the present effects of discrimination practiced in the past. In brief, the steps typically recommended for complying with an affirmative action program include:

1. Put in writing an equal employment policy and affirmative action commitment statement that the company plans to follow.
2. Appoint a top company official to serve as the company's affirmative action officer, charged with the responsibility and given the authority to direct and implement your affirmative action program.
3. State publicly, both inside and outside the company, that you are an affirmative action employer. Provide all concerned parties with copies of your affirmative action statements. Publicity can include meetings, manuals, training sessions, posters, newsletters, pay envelopes, employee handbooks, advertisements, letters to recruiters and recruiting sources, and so on.
4. Survey your company and analyze female and minority group employment by department and job type. Once you know the current status of minority group employment in your company, you will be in a position to recognize areas in the company where minority groups or women are either under- or overemployed in relation to the relevant job market. This job market could easily be defined as national in scope.
5. Set goals and schedules for hiring minority group members and women. Identify the discrimination barriers presently existing in your company and set goals for eliminating them.
6. Develop and implement an affirmative action program to achieve the goals set forth in item 5.
7. Organize an internal auditing system that will monitor the progress being made to achieve your affirmative action goals.
8. Develop and provide support programs and services inside and outside the company that will help achieve the overall objectives of affirmative action.

steps to comply with affirmative action

IS IT EVER LEGAL TO DISCRIMINATE?

It is legal to discriminate under two circumstances: first, if you can show that discrimination is necessary for the safe and efficient operation of the business, and second, if you can show that discrimination is a bona fide occupational qualification. If you were hiring a preacher, for example, you would require a specific religious background. Sex would not be an issue when hiring models of women's fashions. You can readily think of others.

Even if you can prove ignorance of the law in discrimination suits, you

legal discrimination

are still liable for discriminatory practices. Even if you prove you made every attempt to abide by the law, you are still liable. If you can prove you made every effort to design a test that does not discriminate and it was found to be discriminatory, you are liable.

ARE THERE OTHER EMPLOYMENT LAWS YOU SHOULD BE AWARE OF?

There are several other employment laws which, although not as difficult to comprehend, are nevertheless important. For example, the Equal Pay Act of 1963 specifies that all employers who are subject to the Fair Labor Standards Act must give equal pay to men and women who perform similar work.

The 1967 Age Discrimination Act makes it an offense to discriminate against people between the ages of 40 and 65. The law was amended in 1978 to raise the voluntary retirement age from 65 to 70 years.

OSHA

The Occupational Safety and Health Act of 1970 (OSHA) places broad responsibilities on you for providing your employees with a safe and healthy work environment. As a result of this act, companies involved in interstate commerce are required to:

1. Provide a work place free of recognized hazards.
2. Comply with health standards set forth by the Secretary of Labor.
3. Keep records of all employee injuries and deaths.
4. Provide physical examinations and check-ups for employees exposed to certain harmful substances.
5. Open their plants for inspections.
6. Post in a prominent place copies of any violations of the Occupational Safety and Health Act of 1970.

Employees who report complaints to the Secretary of Labor are specifically protected by the Act from discharge or any other punitive action by an employer.

The safety standards that companies are required to abide by are those created and administered by the Secretary of Labor. When the Secretary receives a complaint from an employee or his union, the Secretary investigates the situation. If he finds the company guilty of safety and health violations, the Secretary may issue a citation specifying the violations and what the remedies should be. The company can disagree with the citation and appeal to the Occupational Safety and Health Review Commission for relief. If the Commission finds the company guilty, it has the power to assess penalties up to $10,000 for violation of a standard, administer penalties of $1,000 per day for continued violations, and assess a company $20,000 for willful violations resulting in the death of an employee. The Commission can also levy a fine of $1,000 to persons giving advance notice of inspections, as well as fine individuals up to $10,000 for providing false information.

If you have a government contract or subcontract in excess of $2,500, you will be subject to the Rehabilitation Act of 1973. In essence, this act requires you to take affirmative action to hire the handicapped. It also expects employers to make reasonable accommodations for applicants' and employees' handicaps. For example, ramps and wide doors should be provided for wheelchairs. Likewise, toilet facilities, fixtures, etc., should be suitable for use by the handicapped.

HOW DOES EEO AFFECT YOU?

For you, as a supervisor, EEO means:

- Meeting EEO goals and timetables will probably be one of the main items that will make you successful in the eyes of your superiors.
- Replacing thoughts like "It won't work here," "It's nothing more than unnecessary government interference," or "Why bother if it doesn't make work easier or employees more productive?" with "It *will* work, and it will not impede production."
- Focusing on behavior and skills consistent with the objectives of EEO; don't feel confused by legal jargon.

EEO parts

- Focusing on your actions rather than your thoughts. You may not believe a woman can be a good auto mechanic, but she certainly can be, if trained and given a chance!
- Applying every rule, law, or guideline to the operation of your department. Make them relevant. Make them meaningful. Make them work.
- Replacing overt (open) and covert (not disclosed) discrimination with a healthy attitude for equal opportunity.
- Reading everything you can pertaining to EEO, and attending meetings or seminars concerning it, so that you will be in a better position to understand the laws and do a better job of supervising.

QUESTIONS FOR DISCUSSION AND REVIEW

1. Explain what a labor union is. Why is it important for a supervisor to understand unionism?
2. What are the major reasons employees join unions?
3. Why do some employees reject unions?
4. What impact does unionization have on a supervisor?
5. Explain collective bargaining.

6. Explain a supervisor's rights when a union tries to organize the workers in a company.
7. What role does the supervisor play in collective bargaining?
8. How can a supervisor help with collective bargaining?
9. What kind of relationship should exist between the supervisor and the union steward?
10. Explain the legislation that forbids discrimination.
11. Explain the part played by the EEOC.
12. Explain affirmative action.
13. Discuss some other employment laws a supervisor should know.

A Case Study
JOE MANN VERSUS THE UNION

Joe Mann, supervisor of the testing department for Ace Electric Company, was upset because John Gordon, one of the lead testers, was absent again, the third time this year. And this time Gordon hadn't even bothered to call in sick, as he had on the other two occasions. This meant a disruption in the testing program for the government job that had to be shipped tomorrow. He'd have to make some emergency changes to get the work done, which would mean a decrease in his department's efficiency record and a loss in pay for him.

In fact, as Joe Mann thought over the events, he got even angrier. The Fourth of July had been on Monday of this week, which had made a long weekend for his crew, and a short work week. So Mann had explained the need for an all-out effort on the testing of the government job, and Gordon, knowing all this, had taken an extra day—not even bothering to call in. Mann made up his mind that he'd "fix" Gordon when he did return to work.

At 10:30 A.M. on Wednesday, John Gordon finally punched in. Joe spotted him and immediately walked over to his position. "Joe, you've pulled this 'sickness' stunt once too often," he told Gordon. "You'll get no pay for Monday July 4th, for Tuesday July 5th, which you missed, and I'm suspending you without pay for today and tomorrow. I don't want to hear any of your excuses. Just punch out and report back for work on Friday."

John Gordon made no reply, but his look of disgust and contempt was evident. On his way out, he stopped by to see Ollie Jefferson, his union steward, to give him the story and ask him to see what he could do to help him.

When Ollie approached Joe Mann about the case, Joe lit into him with both barrels. "John Gordon was deliberately fouling up the testing procedure," he shouted. "He's been absent twice before this year, supposedly for sickness, and now he stretches a long weekend by taking an extra day and a half, not even bothering to call in. He's always one of the last to return from a rest break, he 'jaws' with the others too much, and in general he's an agitator. The union contract allows suspension for poor attendance, and that's exactly what I'm doing. Maybe it will teach him a lesson."

Ollie opened his mouth to protest, but decided to hold his tongue. Instead, he simply replied, "Mr. Mann, you are dead wrong about John. This suspension is illegal. John Gordon is right and you are wrong."

The union filed a written grievance, and when it came to the hearing, Ollie Jefferson stated that Joe Mann had blown his stack without the facts, that Mann had just *assumed* that John Gordon had stretched his long weekend arbitrarily. Actually, what had happened, he explained, was that John took his wife to the hospital at 6:00 A.M. on July 5th, stayed by her side during an emergency operation, and remained at the hospital until she came back from the recovery room at 9:30 A.M. on July 6th. Knowing that she was all right, he immediately reported back to work. Although it was true that the union contract called for forfeiting the holiday pay if an employee was absent on the day prior to or following the holiday, Ollie stated that the facts in this case called for an exception to the rule. Furthermore, the other absences, he stated, were because of actual sickness as shown by a doctor's written statement. Finally, Ollie indicated that Joe Mann apparently "had it in" for John Gordon, by accusing him of being the last to return (but not late) from rest break, of talking with other employees "too much," and of being an agitator.

"I submit, therefore," Ollie stated, "that John Gordon was misjudged, that his supervisor was more interested in getting even with him for petty things, and that this absence was used as an excuse to suspend him without pay."

1. How well do you think Joe Mann handled his problem? What do you think he should have done?
2. How should "returning last from rest breaks, excessive talking, and agitating" be handled by Joe Mann?
3. How would you decide this case? Why?

A Case Study
ABE SALEM AND THE UNION

Abe Salem walked into his office to find the union steward and two of his employees waiting for him. "What's the problem?" he asked.

John Hickory, the union steward, started the discussion with a blast at management. "Damn it all, Abe, what are you trying to do to us?" John demanded. "Just when we thought we understood each other, you tell Ed Johnson, here, that he'll be fired if he joins the union. You know this isn't so. You know it's illegal to do this, and I'm going to have your hide for this. I've overlooked too many slips on your part already, and I'm waking up to the fact that they were all planned.

"Take the time last week," he continued, "when you made my men leave the loading platform during their lunch hour, telling them to talk about unions and to carry on unionizing activities elsewhere. You know this isn't right as well as I do. Then on Monday you tried to get Sadie Jones to stop talking about unions on the sewing line while working. You know that they carry on a constant stream of conversation all day long. You name it and they talk about it. If Sadie wants to talk about unions and try to get others interested in it, I say more power to her.

"But the straw that broke the camel's back was when you indicated to Ed here that if he was in favor of unions, he could look for a job elsewhere. Oh, you didn't come right out and say it in so many words, but Ed said that you really gave him a hard look when you overheard him say that the union would see to it that all of its members got their just deserts in pay from you, and that union membership would assure equality of opportunity and equal pay for equal work."

"Now wait a minute, John," Abe countered. "You've got it all wrong. I don't know who has been feeding you this pack of lies, but let me set the record straight. Yeah, I did talk to Ed and Jim here about what your union was and what changes it would make. I told them in no uncertain terms that your union was for seniority and that in most of your contracts, seniority means that ambitious employees like Jim and Ed here might well be stifled in their progress in the company. You know as well as I do that seniority provisions give opportunity for promotion and pay increases to the senior man—not to the junior man in the group. So, if your men want to get ahead based on ability, and not seniority and pull, then joining the union isn't the way. And I'll also say to you and any other employees that joining the union is a waste of money—you'll be doing nothing but paying for a benefit you are already getting.

"And one more thing I want you to get straight," Abe stated, "is that I can say what I damn well please to my employees. And for your information, I am going to have a meeting on Friday with all my employees in the cafeteria and give them the straight dope on you and your union. I'm not going to pull any punches. If the truth hurts, then you'd better prepare to get hurt." With that, Abe turned and left the three men sitting in his office.

1. Comment on Abe Salem's actions. What did he do wrong? What did he do right?
2. How do you think Abe Salem should have handled the meeting?
3. Do you think that John Hickory had any grounds for complaints? On what basis?
4. What advice would you give John Hickory as to how he should conduct himself at future meetings like this?

A Case Study
JEFF BARNES'S PROBLEMS

Jeff Barnes kept his appointment with Ross Craven, the personnel manager, promptly at 9:00 A.M. He opened the meeting with "Ross, I need your help and guidance. I'm completely confused about government requirements and regulations, and I'll be darned if I know which way to turn." Thirty minutes later, Ross recognized that the problems facing Jeff Barnes could not be easily solved.

Jeff had just installed a new machine in his department. The employees he could choose as operators included Darlene Thomas, a black woman with three years of service; Herbert Rascoe, a white man, who had been working for Jeff for eleven years; Takuo Setsuzi, a Japanese-American with seven years of experience; and "Pete" Decosta, a Hispanic with two and one-half years of experience with the company. Jeff had heard there were certain government regulations to be aware of in making this choice. He wanted an explanation.

His second problem concerned a complaint he had recently received from Ruth Gordon about pay and position. Ruth contended that, in her job as the only black Secretary/Associate, she performed the same work as whites with the same title, but received a lower rate of pay. Furthermore, she contended that the company would not promote her—that she was simply a token black who made the company look good. When Jeff checked her pay, he found other Secretary/Associates with equal service receiving 5 to 8% more. He felt, however, that stronger qualifications and additional skills qualified them for higher pay.

His third problem concerned the possible rehiring of a minority employee who had been crippled in an auto accident and confined to a wheelchair. "Should I take her back, Ross? She can still type, but what about steps, rails, door widths, toilet facilities, desk height, etc.? Do we have to rebuild the office so she can come back to work?"

His final problem concerned Louise Jordan, one of his hard-working and loyal employees. Jeff explained to Ross that, during meetings, he typically asked employees to volunteer or stake out claims for special work assignments of interest to them. When no employee expressed an interest in a particular assignment, Jeff did the best job he could of putting the right employee on the right job. Louise was a quiet individual who kept to herself. As a consequence, few, if any, of the other employees were aware of what Louise did. Recently, Jeff overheard gossip that Louise looked busy but did very little—that she wasn't pulling her fair share of the department's work load and that she was being shown partiality by Jeff.

1. If you were Ross Craven, what words of advice would you give Jeff Barnes?
2. What would be a legal basis for your replies to Jeff Barnes?

A Personal Case Problem

Assume that a group of your employees met you after work one day and said, "We don't agree with the way things are being done around here. We see prejudice and inequity playing a large part in the way decisions are made. We are, therefore, going to get a union to represent us, and we wanted you to be aware of what we are doing."

1. What would be your immediate reply? Why?
2. What would you do within the next few days?

9

HOW TO HANDLE DISCIPLINE AND SETTLE GRIEVANCES

This chapter explains—

- The steps you should take to promote self-discipline
- The different types of disciplinary action
- How to handle complaints and grievances

If any one factor can make or break supervisors, their actions in meting out discipline will be close to or at the top of the list. Thousands of workers go through life and are never a party to a grievance, but virtually everyone is subject to some form of discipline when they spoil some piece of work, break some rule, or have a run-in with another employee.

WHAT IS DISCIPLINE?

Most of us think of discipline as the use of authority to reprimand, to punish. This is one type of discipline. But discipline is far more than this. When we say that the Jones Company has good discipline, we mean that the workers understand and abide by the company's rules. In its broadest sense, discipline involves any action that attempts to generate compliance with rules and regulations. Thus, a training program to get employees to obey reasonable rules is one aspect of discipline. In this sense, then, discipline is the state of affairs that exists in a company. It is a condition that exists in a company where workers act according to recognized codes of behavior set forth by the organization. Discipline is good when employees willingly follow the company's rules and regulations. This is what the Navy calls a "taut ship."

"If any one factor can make or break a supervisor, the way he metes out discipline will be close to the top."

OH NO, MR. SILVERS, I LIKE WORKING FOR YOU FINE, BUT MY NEW JOB HAS A WINDOW WITH A VIEW.

Although closely related, discipline is not morale. As we learned in Chapter 7, morale is a state of *mind*, an employee's attitude. Discipline, on the other hand, is a state of *affairs*, an employee's conduct. The two are closely linked, however, because the level of morale (the state of mind) affects the employee's conduct. When morale is high, you generally have fewer disciplinary problems than when morale is low. Of course, it is possible to have absolute compliance with rules and regulations—hence, good discipline— but at the same time to have poor morale. When this condition exists, however, it is usually under strict conditions of fear and force, such as could be found in a military unit or under dictatorial authority. So although morale and discipline are related, they are not the same thing.

state of affairs vs. state of mind

HOW DO YOU BUILD A CLIMATE FOR GOOD DISCIPLINE?

Good discipline grows out of a good work environment, a good state of morale, and a mutual feeling of respect, cooperation and consideration. Virtually all the things we know about human relations, communication, motivation, leadership, and supervision have an impact on the overall climate or work environment that influences employee behavior. If all these things have led to a positive work environment, then morale will be high, and self-discipline will be good. If you as a supervisor have generated a negative work environment, both morale and discipline will suffer.

need for disciplinary climate

It would be unrealistic, however, to say that just because you do everything right, all employees will be good and no one will ever break a rule. There is always something or someone that will require your attention. Some rule will be bent or broken, and how you handle these infractions will determine how other employees will handle themselves.

MUST SUPERVISORS DISCIPLINE EMPLOYEES?

Discipline is necessary, but it's tough for most supervisors to apply the principle of sound discipline. In fact, most supervisors don't even think about discipline until they are faced by an infraction of a company rule. They know that discipline is one of their responsibilities, but they seem to ignore it until something happens that calls for corrective action. And then, in too many cases they tend to jump in, show the employee who is boss, and clobber the guy.

Like it or not, supervisors must maintain control in their departments. What every supervisor would like, of course, is for each employee to voluntarily follow company rules and regulations whether the supervisor is there or not. This can happen when the supervisor, through sound leadership and expert teaching, has developed a state of affairs where discipline is good.

WHY DO YOU HAVE TO DISCIPLINE?

Although most employees generally comply with the organization's rules, it seems that there are always one or two who try to get away with breaking them. Those employees who refuse to be mature enough for self-discipline have to be handled by you as their supervisor.

Taking disciplinary action is an unpleasant task, but one that is inherent in your supervisory job. To avoid further infractions of company rules, you have to use your authority and take positive action to correct the rule breaker. If you don't, other employees who have a tendency to break rules may also move in that direction when they see that one person can "get away" with it.

the rule breaker

Your problem is what disciplinary action to take and how to take it. The objective of discipline is not to punish an employee or get even. Instead, the purpose of disciplinary action is to improve the behavior of the offender so that the work environment in your department will be improved for all employees. As a supervisor, therefore, you should look upon a rule violation as an opportunity to help teach an employee to conduct him- or herself in the proper way. Your problem, of course, is deciding which course of action to choose that will teach the employee as well as provide immediate corrective action.

HOW SHOULD YOU CHOOSE APPROPRIATE CORRECTIVE ACTION?

judge overall impact

In deciding what disciplinary action to take, remember that your objective is not to change your employee's morals or character, but to correct the situation and prevent it from recurring. With these ideas in mind, try not to judge whether your employee's actions were morally right or wrong. Instead, try to judge the overall effect that your employee's actions had, and decide on the penalty in this light. In judging the overall effects, consider such things as the impact your employee's actions had on other employees, on morale, on the company's reputation, on employee safety, and so on. Then, having considered these things, choose an appropriate action—one whose severity is in line with both the "crime" and company policy, and one that, hopefully, will correct the situation and prevent it from occurring again. In disciplinary action cases, remember that you should never adjudicate an employee's offense before you have all the facts in hand. Once you have the facts, however, move swiftly. Prompt corrective action will have a greater impact on your employee, as well as show that you are not delaying because of weakness or favoritism.

As a supervisor you would like to have your department run so that you will never have to reprimand anyone. You would like your employees to always do the right thing, to always do what needs to be done. In fact, you would like everything to run so smoothly that you would never have to use any discipline.

Almost everyone agrees that following instructions and generally accepted rules of conduct is a part of every employee's job as well as responsibility. Most employees, therefore, can be counted on to do their part, to get to work on time, to follow instructions, and to abide by company rules. This is self-discipline. When employees understand the rules and regulations and believe that they are not unreasonable, they will usually abide by them with little or no prompting from you. Rules are thus "self-enforced."

employee cooperation

As a supervisor, however, you are the one who will have to generate the environment in which this state of self-discipline can exist. Your employees must know from what you say and do that they will have your help and support as long as they abide by company rules and regulations. In addition to this, however, you must set an example of self-discipline for your employees to follow. Obviously, you cannot expect your employees to impose self-discipline on themselves when you do not set the proper example. You can readily see that the supervisor who comes to work with alcohol on his breath will have a hard time explaining to his employees why they shouldn't do likewise.

WHAT STEPS SHOULD YOU TAKE TO PROMOTE A CLIMATE OF SELF-DISCIPLINE?

To promote a healthy climate of self-discipline, you should follow several well-defined steps.

1. *Make sure that all of your employees are aware of and understand the rules.* This is such an obvious first step, that many supervisors take for granted that "everyone knows this." But new employees, and sometimes even the older ones, have never heard of a particular rule until they break it. Some supervisors make it a practice to give all employees a copy of company rules and have them sign a statement that they have received, read, and understood the rules.

2. *Remain calm. Never lose your temper.* No matter how severe the violation, you should remain calm and in control. If you feel you are losing your "cool," then you should postpone action until you have regained your composure. How do you regain your composure? Hold your tongue and talk later. Do anything to stall for time. Tell the employee to meet you in your office in half an hour, or ask the worker to take a walk with you to your office or a rest area. Finally, remember

that never, never in a fit of rage touch an employee. It may be misinterpreted as a punitive move.

3. *Investigate, get all the facts, before making any decision and taking any action.* You should not ignore a breach of company rules. If you do, you are signaling to the other employees that you don't intend to enforce company rules and regulations. Neither should you go to the other extreme of moving in haste to take punitive or corrective action against a worker, as indicated above. Before you move, before you do anything, you must get a clear picture of what happened and why the employee did it.

4. *Explain your actions.* Tell your employees why you decided to take the actions you did.

5. *Take disciplinary action in private.* When corrective action is taken in public, the employee being censured will build up resentment over being chastised in public, and the situation may be blown all out of proportion to the infraction. The supervisor who reprimands in public is also asking the other employees to serve as a "jury" to approve of his action. If they feel that the punishment doesn't fit the crime, that the supervisor was too severe, they will side with the employee. This may lead to arguments with other employees and more disciplinary problems. Privacy, therefore, should be the rule for taking disciplinary action.

rules for taking disciplinary action

About the only exception to the privacy rule would be when an employee openly confronts you before the other employees. In this case, you would have to take quick and decisive action in front of the others or risk losing control of your department. If you fail to act decisively, you will lose your employees' respect, lose control, and do injury to the department's morale.

6. *Be consistent in enforcing the rules.* Rules were made for everyone to follow. Imagine the problem you would face if an employee approached you with the statement, "You didn't do anything to June when she was late last week. Why pick on me?" Of course, not every violation calls for the same punishment. Being consistent doesn't mean treating everyone in exactly the same way. It means that when an exception is made, it must be regarded as a valid exception by the employees. For example, the circumstances and conditions under which the incident took place, and the employee's intent, would influence and perhaps alter the type of reprimand. When June was late, it was because she had a flat tire. When Mildred was late, it was because she stayed in the ladies' lounge to grab another cigarette. Different reprimands would be called for here. One incident was an unintentional violation, the other willful. The consistency rule, therefore, means that under similar conditions and circumstances, the same type of reprimand should be used.

7. *Be firm but fair.* Being firm doesn't mean getting tough or throwing your weight around. It means not being pushed around, holding your position. Fairness applies to both the employee and the company. Being fair to an employee means being just. It includes explaining why the company has the rule, why the disciplinary action is being taken, and what you hope the action will accomplish.

8. *Always express your confidence that the employee will not be involved again.* Remember that the objective of a reprimand is to teach, not to punish. You should, therefore, always show your employee that you are confident that he or she will correct the problem. Ending a disciplinary session on this positive note can help remove any bitterness or resentment that the employee feels.

9. *Tell your employee how to appeal your decision.* Don't hide company rules about appeal. Be sure to tell your employees that you won't hold it against them if they do appeal your decision—*and mean it!*

ARE THERE DIFFERENT STEPS IN DISCIPLINARY ACTION?

Many companies today are fostering the idea that discipline should be progressive in nature, moving in steps from a minor reprimand for the first offense to discharge as the final action. Step one in disciplinary action usually starts with an *informal talk* for the first offense or a relatively minor infraction of rules. It gives you, the supervisor, the opportunity to discuss the employee's behavior in an informal, friendly way, emphasizing how well the employee has performed in the past and how pleased you have been with the employee's cooperation, but at the same time pointing out the employee's obligation to abide by the rules. If this friendly talk doesn't work, the next step is to recognize the violation and give the employee an oral reprimand.

The *oral reprimand*, step two, is firmer than the friendly informal talk. Here you are all business, pointing out that the employee's behavior could lead to ultimate dismissal unless corrective action is taken. During the oral reprimand, you should place the employee on notice that you will not tolerate continued violations, and that if they continue, the employee will be subject to more stringent disciplinary action.

A *written notice* is step three. This is a formal written warning that becomes a part of the employee's permanent record. It is a forthright statement of what the employee did and the consequences that can be expected from such an incident in the future. In unionized firms, this is an important step because it can serve as evidence in a grievance case.

If none of these steps have worked, your next move is to try step four, a *disciplinary suspension.* In a disciplinary suspension, the employee is laid off for several days or weeks, depending on the severity of the offense. Some employees don't respond to oral and written reprimands, but facing a Fri-

*progressive
steps in
discipline*

day without a paycheck gives them a shock. They begin to recognize the seriousness of the situation and the need to comply with rules and regulations, and will thus return to work with a better understanding of them. Suspension, however, doesn't always work like this. The employee may build up resentment while away from work and return in a more recalcitrant mood than when he left. For this reason, some companies refuse to use disciplinary suspension.

Finally, *discharge* is the last step in progressive disciplinary action. When an employee is discharged, the company loses a large investment in a skilled employee who knows the company. In addition to the loss of investment and of the employee, the company will have to replace the old employee with a new employee, which means an additional training expense as well as the expenses incurred in the disruption of production. You should take every reasonable step, therefore, to modify and correct an employee's infractions before resorting to discharge.

Be sure, also, that you are on firm ground when you do fire an employee. In unionized companies, discipline and discharge are two of the most touchy actions you can take. Many times a "fired" employee has been returned to the job because the supervisor couldn't prove beyond a reasonable doubt that the employee had broken a rule. Sometimes arbitrators will rule in favor of the employee because the supervisor did not give fair warning that the employee would be fired if he or she continued the actions in question. When you are having trouble with an employee, therefore, send the employee a memo or letter setting forth your concerns about his or her performance on the job, and suggest ways that the employee could improve. Also, invite the employee to discuss the situation with you to be sure that what you are communicating is understood. Be sure, of course, to keep copies of everything you write, and make notes about any interviews you have with your employee. These memos and letters, along with your written notice, will be of real value in such situations. Finally, be sure that the crime warrants firing an employee. For example, would firing an employee be a just penalty for being one or two minutes late to work on several occasions? Firing could conceivably be justified in this case, but in all probability some other type of punishment would be more appropriate.

HOW DO YOU TELL YOUR EMPLOYEES ABOUT COMPANY DISCIPLINARY POLICY?

Employees like to know in advance what the rules are and how they will be applied. The more they know, therefore, the better position they will be in to conduct themselves in accordance with the accepted rules of behavior in your company. This means that you should let the employees know the rules by doing such things as (1) posting them on bulletin boards, (2) distributing them in printed form, and (3) discussing them with your employees on any appropriate occasion. Discussing rules face to face with your employees makes for much better understanding than simply having employees read them on bulletin boards or in an employee handbook. When rules are discussed, questions can be asked and employees can understand *why* the rules are needed. Knowing the rules in advance, the reason behind them, and the consequences of breaking them, makes employees more receptive to abiding by them through self-discipline. You should, therefore, fully discuss all rules with your employees as a part of their orientation.

talk about disciplinary policy

In addition, you should not hesitate to discuss a reprimand that you have given an employee. This is not to say that you should tell the whole department every time you reprimand an employee, but you should freely discuss the circumstances behind a severe reprimand such as laying off an employee for several weeks or actually firing the employee. Telling employees the facts will prevent erroneous speculation and grapevine talk about why the employee was fired and, at the same time, show the employees that you were impartial and fair in the way you handled an infraction of the company's rules.

WHAT DO YOU DO WHEN AN EMPLOYEE DISAGREES WITH YOUR REPRIMAND?

Employees who disagree with your reprimand should have the right of recourse through a formal grievance procedure. In unionized companies, the steps in a grievance procedure are precise and well defined. These steps should also exist with the same degree of clarity in nonunionized organizations. The right of appeal is a real right and not just a formality, and supervisors should be mature and secure enough in their positions not to regard appeals as threats to their jobs. In like manner, supervisors should not tell employees that they have the right to appeal to higher management and then hold it against the employees if they do. Employees are human and need the right to appeal what they consider to be an injustice. Supervisors who discipline their employees properly will usually find that their actions are upheld by their own superiors.

WHAT IS A GRIEVANCE?

Handling grievances is just as much a part of your job as a supervisor as is hiring employees. Sometimes grievances can be so technical that you may feel more like a labor lawyer than a supervisor. Yet the skill with which you handle grievances is a direct measure of your ability to supervise.

At one time or another, each of us has complained or expressed dissatisfaction with some turn of events. These are not grievances; they are merely expressions of dissatisfaction. Grievances are complaints that have been *formally registered* with the employee's supervisor or some other management official in accordance with the recognized grievance procedures.

Grievances usually arise when employees think that they have been done an injustice. Maybe nothing wrong has been done, but if employees *think* that they have been treated wrongly, they can file a grievance.

dissatisfaction vs. grievance

The beginning of a grievance is an employee's expression of some complaint or dissatisfaction. The complaint may be either real or imagined, but from the employee's point of view it is real. Supervisors who brush aside such complaints as "routine gripes" are asking for them to be blown up eventually into full-size grievances. The sensitivity by supervisors to this possibility means that they recognize the key role that they play at this point in preventing grievances. Frustration, anger, and hard feelings are at a minimum at this point, and now is the best time to reach a mutually satisfactory solution.

If, however, the parties are unable to reach a satisfactory understanding at this beginning point, then the employee typically puts a grievance in writing to the supervisor. At this stage, the supervisor has to formally recognize and answer the grievance. The problem is still one between employee and supervisor; however, if the supervisor's answer is not satisfactory to the employee, the employee may then start formal grievance machinery, which takes the problem out of the hands of the employee and his or her supervisor. How the grievance is then handled depends on whether or not the company is unionized, and this will be discussed in the next two sections.

WHAT ARE THE GRIEVANCE PROCEDURES IN NONUNIONIZED COMPANIES?

steps in filing a grievance

Many companies have a published grievance procedure that guarantees an employee the right to file a grievance and to have it follow well-defined steps up to the chief executive. Company policy may further stipulate that employees who file grievances can do so without any fear of reprisal. Few if any employees, however, avail themselves of this procedure because they are keenly aware of the indirect means available to their supervisors to "get even" with employees who cross them—especially those employees who formally complain and thus question the wisdom and capacity of a supervisor.

Retaliation of this sort by supervisors may take the form of withholding a deserved merit increase, bypassing the employee for a promotion, consistently assigning the employee to undesirable jobs, or ultimately firing the employee on some other trumped-up charge. What can top management do to avoid this and make sure that an employee does get a fair shake?

First, be sure to have a written grievance procedure. Employees may not use it, but at least they know that management wants to be fair.

Second, set up some anonymous means for employees to air their grievances. This may take such forms as a committee that airs grievances given to it anonymously, open meetings where "problems" can be discussed in a nonpersonal way, or a community board or committee made up of disinterested third parties with the authority to resolve grievances. In each instance, what management is trying to do is enable employees to get their grievances aired without prejudice and possible retaliation. Unions have been able to secure this guarantee for their members by getting precise steps written into their labor contracts.

HOW ARE GRIEVANCES HANDLED IN UNIONIZED COMPANIES?

In unionized companies, one of the first people to be contacted by an employee in the matter of grievances is the shop steward. His or her function is to represent the employee in any complaints or grievances that the employee might have against the company. The shop steward is a specialist, well trained to prepare and present a grievance. In dealing with these union stewards, supervisors would do well to remember not to lose their tempers with them, not to ridicule, bluff, or make threats to them, not to stall or try to slow down the process, and not to make statements they aren't prepared to back up with facts.

If the employee and his supervisor are unable to reach a satisfactory agreement, the next step is usually for the employee and his union representative to present the grievance in writing to the next higher authority. At this level, usually a superintendent or division manager reviews the case and either supports or reverses the decision of the supervisor. If the boss supports the supervisor's decision, the grievance may be carried to top management.

*from supervisor
to arbitrator*

When grievances get this far, usually the best of the union's grievance handlers represents the employee. This might be the chief steward, the president of the union, the business agent, or a designated grievance committee. The case is typically heard by the plant manager, general manager, or president of the company. The case proceeds with the company's labor relations staff and the union's grievance specialists hearing evidence, presenting arguments, and conducting discussions. The top manager who must make a decision at this point must weigh the effects on the entire organization of supporting or reversing the decision. It is now a total company problem and not just a departmental or divisional one. As was indicated previously, this level is the last "court of appeal" in a nonunionized company. However, in a unionized company, if the case is not resolved in favor of the union, then the union may take any grievance to arbitration if it wishes to.

Arbitration consists of referring the case to a disinterested third party for a hearing and a decision. Most union contracts specify arbitration as the final step in the settlement of a dispute. An arbitrator, approved by both union and management, is chosen, and both sides agree in advance to abide by his decision.

The arbitrator conducts a hearing, similar in many respects to that in a court of law. It is not unusual for both sides to be represented by legal counsel at the hearing. Charges are made, witnesses are called, statements are heard, and the arbitrator weighs the evidence and renders a decision. At this point, supervisors have no control over the process other than to watch it and hope that their initial decision will be affirmed.

Sometimes union agreements stipulate that conciliation may be used. A conciliator makes no judgments and renders no decisions. His only role is to help both parties find a common ground on which an agreement can be reached. If the conciliator fails, then the only recourse is through the courts or the National Labor Relations Board.

HOW SHOULD YOU HANDLE COMPLAINTS?

Every supervisor will get some gripes and complaints, no matter how well the job is done. In fact, many management experts agree with the Army, saying that "a happy soldier is a complaining soldier." When employees don't express complaints, many take this to be a sign of suppression, indicating that the employees are afraid to speak out. In the best-managed companies, therefore, you can expect a number of employee complaints. Try as hard as you like, you can't satisfy everybody. You'll have some complaints no matter what you do.

When you get a complaint, however, the way you handle it may prevent it from becoming a grievance, moving through the steps we have just covered. If you want to do a good job in handling the complaint, be sure to remember the following:

1. *Never ignore a gripe or complaint.* Don't think that if you ignore a trouble spot, it will go away. Don't think that if you soft-soap an employee, he will forget his complaint and live happily ever after. It doesn't work that way. An unsettled complaint continues to simmer in an employee until it reaches the boiling point. He'll gripe to his friends and fellow workers, and they'll probably agree with him. This is when you'll have trouble—when you ignore a small complaint and thus allow it to fester into a major problem.

2. *Know your grievance procedures and follow them impartially.*

3. *Be tactful.* Don't dismiss the employee with the suggestion, friendly though it may be, that he or she has no basis for complaining.

4. *If you are in error, admit it.* Correct the circumstances surrounding the complaint, admit your error, and offer an apology.

5. *Don't try to laugh off a complaint.* This could change a complaint into a grievance, and a mad employee into a furious one.

6. *Treat the employee and his complaint as being serious and important.* Never brush a complaint aside with a "so what" attitude. Even if you know that there is no basis for the complaint, the employee thinks there is. Therefore, if it is important enough for the employee to bring

it to your attention, it should be treated as an important complaint by you.

7. *Don't withhold any concessions.* Concede any point that you can.

8. *Listen carefully.* Listening carefully to an employee's complaint not only shows respect for the employee, it may also enable you to find out what is really bugging him or her. For example, a typist may be complaining about his typewriter when his real complaint is that the file clerk upsets him and causes him to make typing errors. Listen carefully, therefore, to what is being said, and listen for hidden meanings.

9. *If an apology is called for, do so immediately.* Better to apologize for a complaint now than have it grow into a grievance later.

10. *Don't lose your temper.* When you're upset, you lose control. You don't think clearly. You may react hastily. Stay calm, therefore. If you feel yourself getting angry, delay the discussion until later in the day. But set a time to resume it.

11. *Don't decide until you have all the facts.* Although you may feel under pressure to render a quick decision, don't answer the complaint until you have investigated both sides. Get the facts—all the facts. And get them straight before you make a decision. Only then will you be in a position to make a sound decision. "Decide in haste, repent in leisure" holds true here. Remember that a small complaint and your hasty decision may become a major grievance.

12. *Speak to the problem.* When you answer a complaint, get to the heart of the matter. Answer the complaint head on. Don't try to avoid unpleasantness by talking all around the problem but never speaking to it. Be specific and definite in your answer. Make your statement so that there can be no mistake in what you mean.

13. *Explain why.* Always tell an employee why you made the decision you did. Whether you agree or disagree with the employee, explain why you took the stand you did. If you can't explain the logic in your decision, you had better think it through again before you give it.

14. *Express confidence.* Not every complaint is going to be settled in favor of the employee. Yes answers give you no trouble, but when you say no, you'll need all of your administrative skills to make employees understand and accept your decision in good spirit. After you've explained your decision to them, you should express confidence that they will accept the decision in the spirit it was made. Appeal to their reasoning, their sense of fair play, and their belief in equal treatment. Try to make them see the reason for your decision and agree to give it a try.

15. *Be fair, just, and honest.* Be sure that your decision takes into account both sides of the issue. Above all, don't play favorites. Get the facts, weigh them, and then render an equitable decision that is fair and just

to both parties. This can't be emphasized too much. Don't take sides. Get the employee's point of view clearly in mind before you make a decision. If you really understand the complaint, maybe you will make the decision in the employee's favor. Don't hesitate to change your mind when the facts support it, but don't horse-trade. Be fair.

16. *Always be available to your employees.* Don't be afraid to listen to complaints. "A stitch in time saves nine" was never truer than when it applies to nipping grievances in the bud. Keep an open door.

17. *Explain to your employees how they can appeal your decision.* Don't make it difficult for them to find out how to appeal a ruling they disagree with.

HOW CAN YOU AVOID COMPLAINTS AND GRIEVANCES?

Most complaints and grievances center around three areas:

1. Discipline.
2. Problems of promotion, seniority, layoff, etc.
3. Problems dealing with work assignments and job evaluation.

These are the areas you'll need to be extra careful with. Remember, too, that complaints and grievances are frequently symptoms of some other problem. The symptom may be a backache, but the problem may be a slipped disc. The symptom in a company may be that employee turnover is high. The problem may be that the employees don't think they are getting a fair shake in promotions and transfers.

keep employees informed

Handle all matters pertaining to these three areas with particular care, with extra caution, and with the utmost fairness. On all matters pertaining to these areas of sensitivity, be sure to keep your employees informed. Let them know in advance what changes are coming up and *why* the changes are being made. If you are going to have changes in raw materials, methods, working conditions, incentive pay, hours of work, and so on, tell the employees about these changes far in advance and tell them why. A thumping noise in the middle of the night may be frightening. But when you know the facts—that a limb is being blown against the window—the noise is of no concern. A shift in hours of work may be frightening (Are we going on short time? Will I be fired?), but when you know the facts (the company is starting a new project on a second shift), the shift in hours is of little concern.

Finally, be alert and sensitive to any situation that might cause a grievance. Recognize the breeding ground, and then correct the situation. Perhaps the best way to recognize these trouble spots is by looking at what has happened in your department in the past. Where have most complaints come from? What have most of the complaints been about? When you get a complaint that is out of the ordinary, poke around to see if a similar situation might exist elsewhere in your department. In other words, be on the lookout for trouble and trouble spots. The driver who watches out for trouble is less likely to have an accident than the driver who goes down the road looking to neither the left nor the right.

QUESTIONS FOR DISCUSSION AND REVIEW

1. Explain what is meant by discipline.
2. How does discipline differ from morale?
3. What is a "climate for discipline"? How does it affect discipline?
4. What do we mean by self-discipline? How do you develop it?
5. What steps should you take to promote self-discipline?
6. What are the recognized steps a supervisor should take in disciplining an employee?
7. Explain the different steps in progressive disciplinary actions.
8. What facts should you tell an employee about the company's disciplinary policy?
9. What is a grievance? What are the usual grievance procedures in a nonunionized company?
10. How are grievances handled in unionized companies? Explain each step.
11. How should complaints be handled? Explain each step carefully.
12. How can you avoid or minimize complaints and grievances?

A Case Study
HAZEL FRANCISCO'S PUNISHMENT

Hazel Francisco had worked for six weeks as a punch-press operator in a medium-size manufacturing firm. She liked her job, but felt that the safety trip on the press slowed down her work so much that she couldn't earn more than 5 or 6% incentive pay. One of her fellow employees said that if she tied down the safety trip, the press would work faster and she could earn more pay. Hazel tried it and it worked.

A couple of days later, her supervisor happened to pass by when she had the safety trip tied down, and he really "let her have it" for tinkering with the machine. She was so overcome by his language and his ranting and raving, that she didn't say anything.

When he left, she stopped her press and went to the rest room for a few minutes to recover from her bawling out. When she got back, her supervisor was standing by her press and "let her have it" again for being away from her job during work hours. This was too much for Hazel, who was conscientious and tried to do a good job. She started to cry, and at that, the supervisor told her that if she couldn't stay at her work place and work, he would find another person who could. With tears running down her face, Hazel started the press and began work. She ruined eight out of the next ten pieces she tried, at which her supervisor sent her home without pay for the remainder of the day.

When Hazel returned to work the following morning, she reported all this to her union steward who said that she had grounds for complaint and that she should immediately file a grievance. Hazel didn't want to make trouble. She liked her job and had about decided to drop the whole matter when her supervisor came by and said he hoped she had "learned her lesson" yesterday. That did it for Hazel. She decided right then to file a formal grievance with the company over the way she had been treated.

1. Do you think Hazel was justified in filing a grievance?
2. Do you think the supervisor was justified in taking the actions he did?
3. How should the supervisor have handled the situation? What did he do wrong?

A Case Study
DELWAY VACUUM CLEANER COMPANY

The Delway Vacuum Cleaner Company manufactured and distributed vacuum cleaners on a nationwide basis. Sales were made directly to consumers through field representatives. These representatives were not sales people on a commission, but were employees of the company who received a straight salary plus an annual bonus based on company profits and individual sales. The Delway Company was an old and reliable firm of 31 years, and its product was well established in the market. Because of its standing in the field and the fact that its representatives were not sales people in the strictest sense, the company had a strict rule against an employee's selling any other product, even noncompetitive ones.

Norman Ellerbe came to work for the company in 1975 and was given the Dallas–Fort Worth territory. In 1980, the district manager, Mr. Purvis, called on Mr. Ellerbe and indicated that his sales volume had not been keeping up with the increases in the comparable territories of Houston and San Antonio. Mr. Ellerbe was somewhat surprised to hear this, but indicated that he would attempt to do better.

In March 1981, Mr. Purvis wrote Mr. Ellerbe, indicating once again his dissatisfaction with Mr. Ellerbe's sales volume. He indicated that the dollar value in comparable districts had increased an average of 97% since 1980 and that Mr. Ellerbe's volume had increased only 72%. His letter was rather strongly worded, and he implied that if improvements were not forthcoming, the company would have to take "appropriate action." Mr. Ellerbe replied that he did not understand why his sales were apparently lagging behind other districts because he was calling on housewives and demonstrating the cleaners in the manner prescribed by the company. In fact, he indicated that he was making 18% more calls per day than the company recommended.

In January 1982, Mr. Hoffman, the division superintendent for the Delway Company, wrote Mr. Ellerbe, with a copy to Mr. Purvis, indicating that his sales were unsatisfactory and that unless he increased his sales by 20% within the next six months, the company would be forced to take "appropriate steps" to rectify the situation.

At this point Mr. Ellerbe called on his union representative, told him the facts, and asked if the company could arbitrarily fire an employee (as they had implied) because his average was 25% below other supposedly comparable territories. The union representative was incensed over the threats made to Ellerbe and stated he would immediately contact Mr. Hoffman.

When the union representative called on Mr. Hoffman, he was shown that quarterly sales of employees in comparable areas had now increased by over 123% since 1980, whereas Mr. Ellerbe's still lagged with only a 90% increase. Furthermore, Mr. Hoffman had just discovered that Mr. Ellerbe had been working at night selling aluminum cooking utensils and electric food mixers. When asked about these facts, Ellerbe indicated that he had worked eight to ten hours per day selling vacuum cleaners, that he was unable to meet his family expenses from his income, and that out of necessity he had started selling the other items on his free time in the evenings as a "second job." The union representative then pointed out that Mr. Ellerbe had been with the company since 1975, that he had performed long and faithful service, and that the company's rules had not been infringed upon inasmuch as Mr. Ellerbe had sold the other items on his own time. The meeting adjourned at this point, and this is where the matter now rests.

1. What actions should have been taken by Mr. Purvis? Why?
2. Should Hoffman have been called into the act? Why?
3. What decision would you recommend to Hoffman? Why?

A Case Study
THE RETIRED WATCHMAN

John Carter retired as night watchman at the local mill after working there 40 years. On his last day at work his supervisor came by, shook his hand, and wished him well in his retirement. At the end of his shift, John left work and went home.

At the end of a month he had heard nothing from the company and decided he would talk to his union steward. According to John:

1. Most employees were given some recognition by the company when they retired.
2. Usually, the employee's friends chipped in and bought him a present.
3. The company gave all retiring supervisors a gold quartz watch and a month's pay.
4. The local newspaper usually carried a story about people who retired.

John's complaint was that no one of these things had happened to him and he felt that he had been discriminated against by the company.

1. Do you think John Carter had a legitimate complaint? Why?
2. Do you think the company had a legal obligation to do more than it did? Why?
3. Do you think the company had a moral obligation to do more than it did? Why?
4. If you were the steward, what would you tell John?

As supervisor in a local firm, you have been asked to speak to a group of new employees about your company's grievance policy. You are not asked to go into detail on the technical aspects of grievance procedures, but instead to explain the company's position in handling grievances.

1. What would you tell these new employees?
2. What aspects of the grievance procedure would you emphasize? Why?
3. What aspects of the grievance procedure would you leave out? Why?

PART THREE
SUPERVISORY SKILLS

10

HOW TO SOLVE PROBLEMS AND MAKE DECISIONS

This chapter explains—

- How to identify and solve problems
- What errors you should watch for in making decisions
- A practical approach to making decisions

The job of supervising and managing employees is the job of making decisions—decisions about hiring new employees, about promotions, about training, about equipment, about productivity, about communications, about morale, and so on. In fact, when all is said and done, supervisors are paid for doing primarily one thing—making sound decisions. As a supervisor, this is your job. To do a good job, therefore, you must make good decisions because making good decisions is the essence of good supervision and the key to success as a supervisor.

WHAT TYPES OF DECISION MAKERS DO YOU FIND?

People make decisions in different ways. Some supervisors pride themselves on making quick decisions. You know this type. These supervisors give little thought and consideration to people's feelings, to analyzing the facts, or to the impact the decision will have on others. Their main concern is to do it fast and move on to the next problem, which frequently is caused by some other quick decision they have made.

At the other extreme are the supervisors who take weeks to decide on an answer that should have taken a few hours at most. They never get excited, always put off taking action, and tell you that things will work out O.K. in a few days.

Between these two extremes there are the middle-of-the-road supervisors who hesitate to make decisions that will upset anyone. They want to be everyone's friend and can't bring themselves to make decisions that would be against someone's wishes. They are the pussyfooting type who never make solid decisions. Instead, their answers are all watered-down compromises that seldom upset others and seldom really solve the problem.

making decisions

Sometimes we find research-type supervisors who refuse to make decisions until they have looked into every facet of the problem. They want all the facts before they move. Frequently, "all the facts" aren't available, so decisions aren't made—or it takes so long to get "all the facts" that the opportunity to take action has passed.

Of course, you will recognize other types of decision makers. There are the worriers who agonize over every decision, no matter how small (should we buy *one* or *two* boxes of paper clips?), and worry everyone else by asking their opinion when it really doesn't matter. Or the shy and timid types who never have the guts to face a problem head on. They sort of give it passing glances and try to fool themselves and others that they are "working on it."

What we are interested in here is not these types of poor decision makers, but supervisors who have an open and willing-to-learn approach to making sound managerial decisions. Some problems, of course, can be decided on by past experience. For example, past experience will tell you how much paint to order for stock and what colors consumers want most. Other problems that have to be solved are not so easy. They are the one-of-a-kind type that cause most of the difficulties that supervisors experience. Let's take a look and see how you should tackle this type of problem.

HOW DO YOU MAKE A DECISION?

If you were to ask various supervisors how they make decisions, they would probably say, "I don't know. I just do what has to be done," or "I have a gut reaction. There are no rules. I just do it," or "It is something that I do naturally. I don't know what steps I take." Despite what they say, however, they all agree that making good decisions means they are good supervisors. And even though they are not aware of it, virtually all good supervisors follow a fairly well-developed series of steps in their decision-making process. These steps to making a decision are:

1. Be alert to possible problems.
2. Clearly define the problems.
3. Systematically analyze the problem.
4. Solve the problem.

Let's examine each of these steps in detail.

Be Alert for Problems.   To be a good supervisor, you need to be sensitive to the possibility of problems developing. You should be aware that trouble is brewing long before it bursts into the open and becomes critical. You need to be alert to areas that will cause potential problems and to keep a sharp lookout. A good supervisor always tries to nip a problem in the bud and solve it in its early and easy stages rather than wait for a crisis to develop. For example, a disagreement between two employees should be settled to their satisfaction before the whole department takes sides and work is stopped.

sensitivity to developing problems

You might be wondering how you develop this skill. It's not hard to do. If you'll review most problems, you will find that some evidence or symptom that something was wrong appeared long before the problem itself surfaced. What you need to do, therefore, is systematically observe these small symptoms and see if they could possibly lead to larger problems. Once you get yourself used to thinking along these lines, you will become alert to any small symptoms that occur and can then do something about them. For example, if Kay's machine is producing a little more scrap than normal, what does this mean? That the machine is wearing out? If this is the trouble and the machine breaks down, it will cause a week's delay in production. Or does the excess scrap signal that you have a batch of poor-quality raw material that will run up costs and make poor-quality products? Or rather, does it tell you that Kay is having some sort of personal or morale problems that have affected the quality of her work? Whatever it is, this small signal should alert you to look into the matter and to make some corrective decisions before the problem gets out of hand.

"A good supervisor needs to be alert
to the possibility of problems developing."

In the same way, other symptoms of problems should not go unnoticed. For example, if you have a slight increase in labor turnover, look into it. Likewise, you should check such things as an increase in absenteeism, lateness, accidents, down time of machines, sickness, uneven performance, and employee restlessness.

Communications between you and your employees can also provide clues to future problems. If there are no communications where there used to be a free exchange, what is wrong? If an employee starts giving a brief "Good morning" instead of the old warm "Good morning, Harry! How are things going with you today?" this may signal some problems in the making. None of these incidents may be anything unusual, but each could be a signal that something is brewing. Check them out! Look into them. Train yourself to be alert to these and other signs that may point to larger problems.

Define the Problem.   Believe it or not, clearly defining the problem is frequently the biggest part of solving the problem. Once we know what the problem is, we can usually find an answer for it. If an automobile engine sputters and stops, for example, we might guess that the problem is no gas. So we put gas in the tank, but the engine still won't run. We next say our problem is that it needs new points. So we put in a set of points. The car still doesn't run. Finally, we put in a new gas filter, and the engine starts! We "solved" two problems that didn't exist, but we did not initially define and solve the real problem that was causing the trouble! Instead, we stumbled on it by trial and error. If we had checked the gas tank for gas, the spark plugs for spark, and the carburetor to see if we had gas going through it, we would have found the real problem: no gas was going into the carburetor.

problems vs. symptoms

And we would have found it *before* we had wasted a great deal of time solving nonexisting problems.

As a supervisor, you may be faced with all sorts of symptoms. You may recognize from reports dealing with waste, employee absences, machine breakdowns, and goods returned by customers, that something is wrong. You may feel frustrated, disturbed, and even dismayed at all the things you see that could be the root of the problem. But remember, you are like a doctor carefully analyzing all these symptoms before making a diagnosis: your job is to diagnose and state specifically what the problem is. Once you are sure of the problem, you can look for a solution. But before you start taking action, you need to know what the problem is.

You must be careful, however, not to treat symptoms instead of causes. For example, if your head hurts, you may treat the symptom (a headache) with an aspirin, but as soon as the effect of the aspirin wears off, you may find that your head still hurts. Later you find out that the real problem is eyestrain. You need glasses, therefore, to solve the problem and eliminate the headache symptom.

Another aid in defining a problem is to *listen closely* when an employee tells you about a troublesome situation. When this occurs, stop whatever you are doing and listen closely to what is being said. Ask questions and restate the employee's comments. Not only will this communicate that you are interested in what has been said, it will also enable you to be sure that you understand what you have heard. Finally, be careful not to put the employee down with a flip remark like "No problem; my eight-year-old could solve that." Remember that what you want to do is find out what the problem is, not show how smart you are.

Practice in sifting through facts, listening carefully, and defining the real problem will improve your problem-solving ability. The more you practice, the better you will be. And the better you are at determining the real problem, the more confidence you will have in yourself as a decision maker.

Analyze the Problem—Get All the Facts. After you have defined the problem, your next job is to systematically analyze it. To do this, you will need to get all the facts that are available to you. Until you define the problem, however, you will not know what information you will need. This is why it is so important for you to define the problem *before* you start collecting the facts. Once you have a clear definition of the problem, you can then decide what is important and what additional information you will need.

Some supervisors are always complaining that they can't make a decision because they don't have enough facts. This is frequently just an excuse for putting off a decision. You will never have *all* the facts. What you must do, therefore, is make decisions with the facts you have, plus those you can get without too much delay and expense. Without the facts, you are "shooting from the hip." You are making snap decisions, and the consequences may be disastrous.

understand the problem

Getting the facts that bear on a problem is so basic to good decision making that it is almost impossible to overemphasize the importance of this step. Even when it means delaying the decision somewhat, it is frequently worth it to get the facts.

To reach a sound decision, supervisors frequently need information or facts pertaining to a host of things in their company. For example, they may need to know what company policy is, what rules and regulations exist, and how similar cases have been handled in the past. They may have to seek the answers to questions like, Have any precedents been set? Do union contracts have any bearing on the problem? Are any excessive costs involved? What effect will a possible decision have on work procedures and on employee morale? And so on. These are the types of things that as a supervisor you will need to investigate. You will need to have a searching and questioning frame of mind so that important data that could have a significant bearing on the problem will not be overlooked.

Having identified the problem and gathered the facts, you then need to make sure that the problem was correctly identified. You need to review the situation to see whether the real problem has changed from what you originally thought it was.

At this point, with the problem defined, the facts gathered, and the causes of the problem understood, you are ready to try to solve the problem.

Solve the Problem. As the old saying goes, "There is more than one way to skin a cat." Likewise, there is more than one solution to most problems. For you to find the best answer to a problem, therefore, you will need to develop several possible solutions so that you can select the best one. This is a difficult step in decision making because you need to keep an open mind to all logical solutions to the problem. Most of us have certain tendencies, preferences, or preconceived ideas about how something should be done. As a supervisor, if you aren't careful, you may well solve a problem using your personal preferences or preconceived ideas without ever looking at other possibilities.

To solve a problem, most supervisors find it helps to take two steps:

solving the problem

1. Look at all logical solutions. Consider all the ways in which the problem can be solved.

2. Select the best solution from all the possible solutions that you recognize.

Let's look at these two steps in a little more detail.

Look at All Logical Solutions. At this point in making decisions, you need to make a firm rule that no decision will be made until all possible logical solutions have been considered. Remember that *the decision you make will be no better than the solutions you consider.* To do your best job, therefore, you should have as many solutions as possible to choose from, so that you will be sure to select the best. If, for example, you have to choose the color to paint a house and you only consider red, blue, and purple, you will probably not make a wise decision. If, on the other hand, you considered all shades of yellow, green, blue, red, purple, black, and white, then you would probably make a wise decision because these alternative colors (solutions) from which you can select one color (the decision) give you a greater selection to choose from. You have looked at all logical choices of color. You have considered all logical solutions to the problem of what color to paint your house.

Don't fall into the trap of seeing only one or two solutions to a problem. True, it is easier to choose when you have only two alternatives, just as it is easier to make a choice of ice cream if you only consider cherry and vanilla. If you consider 37 varieties, however, your decision will be more difficult to make. But the outcome will probably be better. The same is true of more complex decisions. Remember, the rule here is to always consider all possible solutions before you make a decision.

Select the Best Solution. Once you have looked at all possible solutions, your next job is to choose the best one. To do this, you will need to sit down and carefully consider each solution. Every alternative solution has some good points and some bad points. What you need to do, therefore, is size up each solution: recognize the good features that would help solve your problem as well as the negative aspects that the solution offers. To do this, try to visualize how using each solution would affect your department, your employees, and so on. Try to foresee the desirable as well as the undesirable consequences of putting each solution into effect. For example, try to foresee what effect the solution would have on production. Would it help production or slow it down? What effect would the solution have on your employees? Would it help morale or hurt it? What effect would the solution have on product quality? What expenses would be involved? Do you have the necessary tools? Would the solution be in line with stated company policy? These are the types of things you should consider for each proposed solution.

After having thought through each of your solutions in this manner, you will be in a position to see which one would work best for you and would cause the least amount of friction. The one that appears to have the most good points and the smallest number of bad points would be the one you would choose. This would be your best solution.

You must remember, however, that every decision involves some risk. There is no such thing as a "sure-fire" decision—one without any risk. No matter how carefully you have thought through the decision, things that you didn't foresee can come up and go wrong. So be prepared to work with the solution to make it work.

In choosing a solution, some supervisors rely on previous experience. This is not a bad idea, but you should remember that history does not always repeat itself. What worked before may not work this time. Although past experience is helpful to supervisors, it would be dangerous for them to follow it blindly without considering every possible solution. Conditions, people's feelings, and economic situations vary, and what worked last time may be a poor solution now.

HOW DO YOU MAKE ROUTINE DECISIONS?

common problems

Some problems occur frequently enough so that you can set up a routine way to solve them. For example, if an employee, Tom, were absent on the day prior to or following a paid holiday, should he be paid for the holiday? You might decide that if he were absent on both the workday prior to and the workday following the paid holiday, he should not be paid for the holiday. Or you might decide that if he were absent only on the day prior to the holiday, he should be paid for the holiday. Having set up this procedure, you would follow the same routine in deciding similar cases in the future.

Before you decide on a particular routine decision, however, you should go through the same procedures we discussed previously in order to determine which solution would be the best one. In other words, you should consider all possible routine solutions before selecting the best. In the holiday pay case above, for example, you should consider these possibilities:

1. No pay for any time not worked.
2. Pay for the holiday under any conditions.
3. Pay for the holiday only if the employee worked the day prior to and the day following the holiday.
4. Pay for the holiday if the employee worked either the day prior to or the day following the holiday.

Each of these four possible solutions should be evaluated, recognizing the impact it would have on employee morale, expenses, output, union negotiations, and so on. The choice would be the solution that had the largest number of good points and the smallest number of bad points.

HOW DO YOU MAKE QUICK DECISIONS?

Making decisions where you have time to think is not too difficult. In situations requiring quick decisions, however, you don't have time for the formal routines we've discussed. What do you do then? While there is no set way to handle these semiemergencies, the following approach has been found quite helpful by a great many supervisors.

- First, don't delay. Attack the problem right away. The longer you wait, the worse the situation may get.
- Second, don't spend time gathering excess data. Instead, think about why the decision needs to be made and what you want to accomplish—your ultimate goal.

- Third, if company policy or a routine you've previously used can help you get the answer, use it. Likewise, call on your prior experiences for help. Don't abandon what you learned from other problems. Using those experiences as precedents, recall what you did and what the results were. Select those aspects of the problem that are similar to the one you currently face, and see whether you can use the same procedure.

- Fourth, don't fail to use your employees. Tell those familiar with your departmental operation what the problem is, and ask for their ideas and suggestions. You're not asking them to make the decision for you—just to give you their advice and ideas. Weigh their ideas and opinions, select those that might help, and apply them to the situation.

- Finally, evaluate your best alternatives and their probable outcomes. Select the best one and make the decision.

CAN BRAINSTORMING HELP MAKE DECISIONS?

Brainstorming is the "ten-heads-are-better-than-one" approach to solving a difficult problem. It's a simple idea, but frequently turns up some pretty good answers to perplexing problems.

The first thing to do is get your group (any manageable number) together in a quiet place. Tell the group what the problem is that needs solving. Then ask them to throw reason to the wind in coming up with answers. Ask them to think wildly—without reserve—not considering such things as lack of funds, lack of space, etc. As suggestions and answers come forth, don't stop to examine them as to their feasibility. Instead, let every proposed solution, no matter how wild it may sound, serve to trigger another person's thinking. Keep this type of activity going for a set length of time, and then go back and examine every individual suggestion. Perhaps one or more suggestions can be combined and modified to come up with a pretty good solution to a perplexing problem.

think broadly

Just for a start, try brainstorming with a problem like "What use can we make of 100,000 empty coffee cans?"

ARE THERE BARRIERS TO MAKING DECISIONS?

You should be aware of several situations that can dampen or even stop you from making the right decision.

Watch for your inhibitions. Make sure that they don't blind your ability to perceive an innovative approach to solving problems. Your inhibitions can prevent you from getting practical, needed facts. Your inhibitions can even change the way you perceive the problem, the way you evaluate the facts, and the way you weigh their importance.

You should try to become aware of any cultural or socioeconomic biases that you might have. Make certain that your background doesn't make the decision for you. A cultural bias might lead you to consider only employees of a given sex or race for a job, when in actuality an employee of a different sex or race would be the better choice.

As a supervisor, you should make decisions based on sound reason—not emotion. Don't let fear block your making a decision. Fear of failure, fear of not being accepted, fear of making a fool of yourself, fear of not being liked, and similar emotional states might build a wall between you and a sound decision. We can't drain ourselves of all emotion, but we can become aware of it and thereby minimize its impact on our decision-making process.

Finally, strive for objectivity. Insofar as possible, make certain that you are being objective in making decisions. After you've made a decision, ask yourself questions such as the following to test your objectivity.

1. Did I make the decision while I was angry?
2. Did I brush aside facts or considerations that did not support the outcome I wanted?
3. Have I considered *all* the facts? Did I ignore some relevant ones because they were "unimportant"?
4. Does my decision fly in the face of good common sense? Would the village idiot have known better?
5. Did I make the decision and then try to gather the facts to support it?
6. Did I challenge and question all of my assumptions? Did I play the devil's advocate and make every assumption stand the test of objectivity?

WHY DO WE PUT OFF MAKING DECISIONS?

In many cases we put off making a decision for good reasons. Often, however, we put off making a decision because down deep inside we want to avoid making it. We don't want to face the consequences of the decision. You might, for example, be faced with making a personal decision about spending a large sum of money that will put you deeply in debt. You don't relish the thought of this and are, therefore, subconsciously looking for ways to put off making the decision. You look for all sorts of "legitimate" excuses. You may not be aware of what you are doing, but you are trying to avoid making the decision. Whenever you find yourself in this position of having to make a decision that you want to postpone, you should stop and ask *reasons to* yourself if you are trying to duck making the decision. To help you answer *postpone* this question, see if you are postponing the decision for any of the following *decisions* reasons:

1. You decide that there aren't enough facts to make the decision. Therefore, you decide to postpone making it until you can get *all* the information.

2. You decide that the decision is not important enough to bother with—then you assign it to a subordinate to make.

3. You assign the problem to a committee to decide. This will probably delay the decision indefinitely.

4. You undertake research on the topic to find out how such a problem was previously decided. This could cause the decision to be put off for months.

5. You postpone making the decision because of "illness" or a "more pressing problem."

6. You decide that you don't have the authority to make the decision— that it should be made by someone else.

7. You decide to wait until next week when you will have more time to devote to giving the matter your undivided attention. Next week, of course, seldom comes.

If you find yourself not making decisions for these and similar reasons, *be sure you understand yourself* and know what you are doing. Recognize that in all probability you are ducking the decision-making responsibility. Of course, if you actually want to delay making a decision, then any one of the above excuses could serve you well.

The rule, however, is to understand yourself and postpone making decisions only for good, sound reasons.

CAN COMPUTERS HELP YOU MAKE A DECISION?

A good computer can be a lifesaver to supervisors swamped by a number of complex decisions. Having a computer terminal on each supervisor's desk enables you to get data instantly from other supervisors or their computers, thereby speeding up or aiding the decision-making process. You might, for example, need pertinent information concerning the supply of special reports, parts, or forms in your company's main office in order for you to accurately project a budgetary figure for next year's requirements. The computer would enable you to get these data immediately.

If you have a large volume of information about such things as employees, sales, new services or products, medication, etc., you can use a computer to organize the information in several different ways so that you can use it to make better decisions pertaining to these subjects. In fact, the more complicated and voluminous these data are, the more help the computer will be to you in organizing, reorganizing, sorting, projecting, and scheduling the information so that you can use it in your decision-making process.

We don't make decisions just for the fun of it. A decision is made to solve a problem, and one of the most satisfying experiences that you can have as a supervisor is to see your carefully thought-out solution to a problem put smoothly into effect. This doesn't happen by itself, however. Instead, it involves a well-thought-out plan of putting the solution into operation. A *wise* decision that is *poorly* implemented is worse than a *mediocre* decision that is *well* implemented. As a supervisor, therefore, you need to carefully plan *how* your decision can best be implemented.

implementing your plan

Most of the time a decision will result in some type of change that will affect one or more employees. It is human nature to resist changes. A change moves us from a routine we know to one we don't know. Therefore we resent the change. A supervisor who recognizes this human resistance and carefully plans the implementation of his plan will be a successful supervisor.

Putting any decision into effect involves several steps:

1. *Plan* how you will put the decision into operation. You need to consider such questions as What needs to be done? Who will do it? How will it be done? *and* When will it be done? Many a good decision has failed simply because it was introduced at the wrong time. Decisions sometimes fail because the work is introduced out of sequence. By planning ahead, a supervisor can foresee possible trouble spots and can take action to avoid them.

2. *Communicate* the decision. Most decisions involve people, and the wise supervisor is the one who gets the employees who will be affected by the decision into the act. This may mean consultation during the decision-making process if the decision is one where an employee can help. It also means prompt communications to all affected employees. Any supervisor who has learned from one of his employees about a management decision to add a second shift will readily understand the need for prompt communications through the proper channels. This same sort of logic applies to the implementation of your decisions. Communicate them promptly to your employees, and try to get their support. Answer their questions carefully and truthfully. You will depend on them to get the decision carried out, and if your employees do not support your idea, they can make you as well as your ideas look pretty silly.

3. *Follow up* the process. No matter how well you have thought out a plan and how carefully you have discussed it with the employees involved, it is always possible for it to go wrong. Things may come up that you don't anticipate. Perhaps not everyone is doing his or her part to get the decision implemented. Maybe some group of employees has developed resistance to the change. Maybe raw materials are not coming in on time. These are the types of things that could make

the decision not go into effect smoothly. You will need, therefore, to follow closely every step in the implementation of your decision. Following up is your insurance that things are going according to plan, that your decision will be implemented. This is not to say that you have to be involved in every detailed step, but you should not give your employees a plan or decision and then forget it. Instead, you will need to make routine checks just to be sure that everything is going according to your plan. This is the point where small deviations can be caught that could save time and money later.

4. *Evaluate* your results. Did your decision achieve the desired results? If not, why did it fail? Where did it fail? All of us can learn by our mistakes, but we cannot learn unless we study our mistakes and see where we went wrong. Examining your failures, therefore, can point out errors to avoid so as to achieve future success. If you plan was successfully introduced, you should look at what you did that made it succeed—and then use these ideas again. By evaluating successful plans, you may also see some weak spots that you could improve upon next time, thus making your plan even more successful.

As was said at the beginning of this chapter, supervisors are paid to make good decisions. The only way to consistently improve your decision-making ability is to follow the procedures outlined above.

WHAT ARE SOME PRACTICAL TIPS ON MAKING DECISIONS?

Now that we have discussed the process involved in making and implementing decisions, let's look at some day-to-day practices that you might well remember.

1. *Decide whether the decision is a big decision or a small one.* If it is a big problem, give it the full treatment that we have discussed. Weigh all aspects carefully. Big problems deserve all the time, attention, and skill that you can give them. Little problems, on the other hand, don't deserve the trappings of a summit conference. If it is a small problem, don't spend hours agonizing over what to do. For example, don't spend hours trying to decide whether to give a coffee break at 10:15 or 10:30, or whether you should paint the employee lounge a beige or eggshell color. Major concern over little problems isn't worth your time, and if you are not careful, the small problems may take your attention away from more important matters.

aids to making decisions

2. *Don't make a snap decision.* Take time to get the facts, and then analyze them carefully.
3. *Rely on established company policy and practices where possible.* If company policy is to suspend an employee found drinking on the job, this is the answer if you face such a problem.

4. *Seek the help of others when you are in doubt.* Ask other people what they think, especially people who are well informed and whose judgment you trust. Seek the help of experts if the decision involves technicalities you are not familiar with. For example, don't try to solve a safety problem involving electricity. Instead, call the plant electrician or an electrical engineer to give you help.

5. *Avoid crisis decisions.* Most of the time, decisions don't have to be made under crisis conditions—even though you might think they do. Stop and consider the situation. Ask yourself when the decision has to be made. Then utilize the time available to make the best decision. If you do have a crisis, however, remember that you are the boss and your employees are looking to you for a decision. Don't panic. Instead, take a moment to go through the major decision-making steps we have previously discussed. Then give your answer to your employees.

6. *If a decision has to be made, make it.* Don't put off making a needed decision. This will only cause your work to pile up all the higher.

7. *Don't brood over a decision once action has been taken.* Evaluation, yes! Brooding, no! The thing is done. You can't be 100% right every time. Poor decisions are made every day, from the President of the United States on down. We are all human. This is not to excuse a poor decision. This is not to say we should not analyze a decision once we have put it into effect. What we are saying is, Don't worry yourself into ulcers trying to decide whether or not you made the right decision. As a note of consolation, we seldom make any really wrong decisions. Instead, most of the time it is a matter of how good (or how poor) the decision was. That is, it is a question of the degree of correctness of our decision. So once you've made a decision, put it into effect and don't worry over it.

WHAT DO YOU DO WHEN YOU'VE MADE A POOR DECISION?

When you've made a poor decision, don't ignore it or cover it up. It won't go away. And it is probably not the first or last poor decision you'll make. The main thing is for the large percentage of your decisions to be good ones. If so, then your overall average will be acceptable. Learn from your mistake. Ask yourself where you went wrong. Get advice from those around you concerning what you should have considered that you didn't, what you should have done that you didn't, what errors of judgment you made, and so on.

learn from poor decisions

After this analysis, decide what you should do now—the action you should take. Then tell your boss about your new plan of action. Explain to him why you have moved from the old decision and why it is important for you to make the change. In talking with your boss, don't try to shift the blame. You are responsible for the decision and for the error. Take the consequences.

Finally, get your employees involved in phasing out the old decision and implementing the new one. What you want to do is go from plan A to plan B with a minimum of confusion and loss, and your employees can make valuable suggestions and contributions.

QUESTIONS FOR DISCUSSION AND REVIEW

1. What types of decision makers can you recognize?
2. How does being alert for problems help you in your decision-making process?
3. Explain how defining the problem can help you solve it.
4. What part does analyzing the problem—getting the facts—play in making sound decisions?
5. What good does it do to look at all possible solutions to help you solve a problem?
6. How should you go about selecting the best solution to a problem?
7. What is the best approach to making routine decisions?
8. How can brainstorming help make decisions?
9. What subconscious reasons do we use for putting off making a decision?
10. Explain the steps you should take to put a decision into effect.
11. How do planning, communication, follow-up, and evaluation affect decision making?
12. What tips would you offer a supervisor about making decisions?
13. What barriers to decision making should you be aware of?
14. What should you do when you make a poor decision?
15. How can computers help you make a decision?
16. How do you make quick decisions?

A Case Study
DECISIONS! DECISIONS!

Gene Hamlin, the supervisor of the small-parts assembly line, had just returned to his desk from his weekly production conference to find himself faced with the following:

1. Mattie Smith, one of the best assemblers he had ever known, had been offered a job by a competitor at an increase in pay. She wanted to talk with Mr. Hamlin about opportunities in the company.
2. A note indicated that Mr. Ashmore, the plant manager, wanted to talk to him about a new departmental layout.
3. The digital tester on the subassembly line was giving "funny" readings. The employee wanted to know what she should do.

4. The welding group of four men said they were quitting work at 4:00 P.M. unless the company took some action to make the welding equipment faster and safer. They had already had two lost-time accidents this week.

5. A note from his wife requested that he call her immediately.

6. His secretary, according to her note, was sick in the women's lounge. She didn't know whether to go home or try to stick it out and wanted his advice.

7. The personnel director had three candidates for a job opening in the department waiting to talk to Gene.

When he reviewed all the things facing him, Mr. Hamlin heaved a sigh and put his head in his hands.

1. What priority should Mr. Hamlin give each decision?
2. Which problem should he tackle first, second, and so on? Why?

A Case Study
NEW LONDON FURNITURE COMPANY

The New London Furniture Company was a medium-size manufacturer of bedroom and dining-room suites, and in addition fabricated a small line of occasional living-room pieces such as coffee tables, end tables, and odd chairs.

In the fall of 1978 the purchasing agent, Mr. Henry Parden, resigned his job to accept the position of purchasing agent and vice-president with a similar company specializing in the manufacture of upholstered furniture. Because of the nature of the offer, Mr. Parden had to leave the employ of the New London Furniture Company with only a week's notice.

To fill his position, the company hired Mr. Burch Kelford, a long-time buyer for a chain of furniture stores. The officials of the New London Company felt that because of Mr. Kelford's familiarity with furniture in general, and their lines in particular, he would be able to assume Mr. Parden's duties without too much difficulty. On Mr. Parden's last day, Mr. Kelford reported for work, was shown around the plant, and was introduced to Ms. Virginia Bellamy, who served as the secretary for the purchasing agent, the designer, and the accountant. Insofar as possible, Mr. Parden gave Mr. Kelford an outline of his duties and indicated his plans for reorganizing the purchasing department. Because of the situation, however, his instructions to Mr. Kelford were necessarily brief.

During the following week, Mr. Kelford began analyzing the work of the purchasing section and found several disturbing facts. For example, a supply of core stock (lumber used as a base for veneers) sufficient to last for sixteen months was on hand. In addition, two boxcar loads had been received and waybills showed that six more were on the way. All available space at that time was being used to store this material, and he had real doubts as to where the additional material could be stored. Although he and Ms. Bellamy searched the files, they were unable to find a purchasing contract authorizing the shipments. On Wednesday, five rush calls from the assembly plant informed Mr. Kelford that the plant was out of drawer pulls, hinges, and braces for a particular dining-room suite and that unless a new supply could be obtained immediately, production of this item would necessarily stop. Later in the day, the accountant requested him to

OK a bill from a paint and varnish supplier. Upon checking, Mr. Kelford found that although the material had been received, no purchase order had been issued for it. Instead, he found that Mr. Parden's practice had been to allow the paint salesman to inspect the company's stock and ship whatever supplies he (the salesman) thought appropriate. As a result, Mr. Kelford estimated that the New London Company had an eighteen to twenty months' supply of various types of fillers, paints, and varnishes.

At various times during the week, several plant foremen brought Mr. Kelford bills for brushes, sandpaper, etc., indicating that they had practically exhausted their supplies and so had replenished them locally.

1. If you were Mr. Kelford, what immediate action would you take? Why?
2. What would be your long-range plans?

A Case Study
THE TYPING POOL

Several employees have complained to you that they are having trouble getting typing and other stenographic work through the typing pool on time. They also indicated that when they did get the work, it frequently contained errors and was generally poor in quality. They complained to Ruth David, the pool supervisor, but indicated that they have seen no improvement. They are now appealing to you, as Ruth's supervisor, for help. The complaint surprises you because you've never had any problems with the typing pool's work quality or speed.

1. What do you think is the nature of the problem in the typing pool? Why do you believe this?
2. Does your position have anything to do with the problem? Explain why.
3. What action should you take to solve this problem?

A Personal Case Problem

For more than a year you have suspected your employees of petty theft—nothing large, just small items. With 37 employees, however, this theft can amount to quite a sum of money in a year. You are not sure whether all of your employees are involved, or just a few. However, regardless of the number, you want to stop the illegal exit of tools and materials from your department.

1. Would you make a survey and get your employees' comments? Why?
2. Outline the steps you would take to make a decision on this problem.
3. Would you solicit your employees' help in solving this problem? Why?
4. How would you implement your decision?

11

HOW TO PLAN AND LEAD A MEETING

This chapter explains—

- A supervisor's role in meetings
- Why you need to hold meetings
- The fine points of speaking at meetings

Many supervisors readily admit that they attend too many meetings. They complain that most meetings achieve very little, take up too much time, and frequently run on and on without a purpose. In fact, some meetings, they complain, are a flagrant waste of time. Yet it seems that they have more and more meetings every day, and sometimes it appears that the only reason for calling them is that they haven't met in a month. However, despite all the noise made against meetings, there's no readily available substitute for them. Without meetings, it would be very difficult for an organization of any size to operate efficiently.

WHY DO WE HOLD MEETINGS?

We hold meetings because we haven't found a better way to get information across to employees and to get problems solved. There are, of course, many ways other than meetings to get information to employees, and there are ways to get employees' ideas about how to solve problems. We could, for instance, use bulletin boards, letters, and surveys instead of meetings. But employees like meetings best. They like to hear the story straight from the boss. And they like a chance to ask questions and express their own ideas.

need for meetings

In addition, an informal meeting is a great way to get employees to participate in departmental matters. They are more enthusiastic about carrying out directives and plans that they have helped develop than plans handed down from above. When you get a group of people together to talk about a problem that is of interest to all of them, there seldom is a dull moment.

Under a friendly atmosphere of exchange of experiences and opinions, better solutions to departmental problems will develop than could have been made by one person alone. A group of people bring a wide background of experiences and education to bear on a topic, and it is only logical, therefore, that a better decision can be reached. This is the brainstorming effect we discussed in Chapter 10.

Motivation and morale are typically improved when employees discuss problems and arrive at conclusions using face-to-face communications. Meetings can also bring about coordination among employees as well as departments. When members discuss and understand the other person's point of view, they usually are more tolerant of the problems that other employees present.

In addition to the above, meetings are also held for the following reasons:

1. To give subordinates the opportunity to express themselves and be in on making decisions.

2. To enable you to communicate your departmental "party line" to your employees and to explain why.

3. To provide a forum where friendly debate can take place to explain key problems or selected topics.

4. To teach others, by example, how meetings should be conducted.

5. To allow employees to indicate their emotional reactions to proposals or suggestions, allowing them the opportunity to hear all sides and arrive at compromises.

6. To promote teamwork by making all participants equal in the development of a final decision.

WHAT TYPES OF MEETINGS ARE THERE?

Four types of meetings are typically held in business situations:

1. *The Informational Meeting.*   This type of meeting is held to get information across to the participants. It may take the form of an address or lecture, or it may be visual, using motion pictures, filmstrips, slides, and so on. Although there is some discussion and questions may be asked, the major emphasis is on imparting information to the participants.

2. *Opinion-Seeking Meetings.*   These meetings are used when the supervisor wants the ideas and opinions of others to help make a decision. Typically, the supervisor asks questions, solicits employees' opinions, and wants to know how an employee would handle the situation.

varieties of objectives

3. *The Problem-Solving Meeting.*   A problem-solving meeting is called to get the facts before the group so that they can be considered and discussed, and a solution to a problem can be agreed upon. This type of meeting typically produces free and lively discussions. In problem-solving meetings, the group has been given the authority to make a decision, and even if their solution is not the best one, it is one they have agreed upon and one that will be implemented by them.

4. *The New-Ideas Meeting.*   The purpose of a new-ideas meeting is to *generate* new ideas, to *elicit* full participation in the development of new concepts. The purpose is not to take action, but to develop new concepts and ideas that may later prove useful.

WHERE SHOULD MEETINGS BE HELD?

Of all the factors that can make or break a meeting, nothing is more important than where you hold it. In fact, where you hold it is so important that *location*

the location can positively or negatively affect the participants and can make the meeting a success or a flop. Therefore, choose the meeting place carefully. Be sure it is comfortable and relatively quiet. Some companies provide conference rooms. A brief, informal meeting might even be held right in your own department. However, where difficult problems have to be tackled, meetings are most effective when they are held in a quiet, well-lighted, temperature-controlled room, arranged so that all the members can see and talk with each other. Chairs set in rows like theater seats are poor because people cannot speak to or face each other. A blackboard or other writing surface is frequently needed to list group ideas and to summarize what has been said. Finally, the area should be isolated so that the meeting will be free of phone and personal interruptions.

WHAT IS A LEADER'S ROLE IN THE VARIOUS TYPES OF MEETINGS?

importance of leader

Depending on the type of meeting, the leader's role will vary. An informational meeting needs a leader who is a good speaker, who can explain ideas, and who can get the group to agree to go along with what the leader is telling or "selling."

The opinion-seeking meeting requires a leader who can get people to express their ideas. As the leader of a meeting, you should have the ability to suggest questions that will stimulate the group and convince them of your sincerity in wanting their ideas. You need the ability to make every member feel that he or she has made a significant contribution to the discussion at hand.

The problem-solving meeting is the most complex of all and requires a leader with the greatest abilities. Your job here is to get ideas accepted, elicit discussion, get all the members to express their ideas, and keep the meeting moving on the target. You have to have the ability to tactfully shut up those who want to hog the show and to get the quiet ones into the act. When discussion goes astray, you have to move it back on target without offending the speakers. Your job is *not* to tell people what *you* think, but to get them to say what *they* think. The purpose of the meeting, after all, is not to learn what the leader thinks, but to get the group to express its ideas and solve the problem—to make a decision. As a good leader, therefore, you should deemphasize your own ego and, instead, constantly strive to secure maximum group participation. You have to artfully curb the talkative and stimulate the timid to speak. To keep the meeting in focus, you should write what people say on the blackboard so they can see the point. You should talk only enough to equalize participation and reflect the sentiments of the group.

Most of the time, the problem-solving meeting is at its best when discussion is high and members are participating back and forth with each other rather than with the leader. The leader's role here is to listen, make notes on the board, and occasionally summarize what has been said.

The leader of a problem-solving group needs to get the members to agree on a solution. If at all possible, the leader should try for a unanimous agreement. Otherwise, some of the members will be forced to carry out some action that they did not support or even openly opposed. Unanimous agreement, however, should not be sought when it would destroy the group or excessively prolong a meeting. It is frustrating for members who have already made up their minds to listen to extra hours of discussion trying to convince one or two members to go along with the decision of the group. In such cases, a minority report could be made to go along with the findings of the majority.

As you might well imagine, the leader of a new-ideas meeting should attempt to promote an atmosphere that encourages a free and easy discussion of the topic at hand. Such a leader should never criticize or evaluate an idea. Instead, the leader's role is to elicit ideas, encourage participation, and promote a full discussion of any concepts that the group may evolve.

WHAT ARE THE MAJOR STRENGTHS OF MEETINGS?

Probably the biggest byproduct of a meeting is that the participants feel more strongly motivated to carry out the decisions of the group. In fact, in a lot of companies, this is one of the reasons, if not the main reason, for holding meetings—that is, to get the participants to agree to carry out the decisions of the group. A person who participates in making a decision is much more interested in seeing it work and will work harder to see that it does succeed.

A second bonus from meetings is that nonparticipants are also more apt to go along with decisions made by the group than by an individual. Even superiors are more likely to abide by group decisions because they feel that controversies have been ironed out in the meeting and that the group should stand behind its recommendations.

motivation through participation

Meetings are also important to industry because employees are working together instead of simply talking together. Members begin to know each other by individual capacities and by jobs or positions. When this occurs, members begin consciously to want to work together as a team. Thus, the desire to cooperate is stronger, and the individual's team efforts are considerably increased. The group is more cohesive.

Meetings bring the talents of many different individuals to bear upon a problem. From their diverse backgrounds and experiences, these individuals should be in a position to bring out all pertinent facts and arrive at a sound decision.

Because of the thorough discussion that most problems get at a meeting, participants tend to have a better understanding of what everyone thinks, and they recognize all aspects of a problem. Understanding the complexity of the problem, they may see that there is no simple solution.

Finally, meetings are especially good at getting employees to innovate, think up new ideas, or brainstorm. As you know, brainstorming gets the members to express new ideas about a problem or product in a meeting. Their ideas in turn start other members thinking and communicating their ideas. Out of all the ideas discussed may emerge an innovation in the form of a new product or new concept that no one individual can claim as his own. It is a product of the entire group, each person contributing his idea to make up the whole.

WHAT ARE THE WEAKNESSES OF MEETINGS?

Meetings take up a lot of time, and many of them are unproductive. Meetings are complicated, and although the supervisor may wish for the simplicity of individual decision making, meetings are here to stay, and we may as well learn to live with them. It's no longer a matter of whether to have meetings, it's a matter of how best to use them.

Meetings take money as well as time. It's not uncommon for a meeting of fifteen people to last three hours. This means that 45 man-hours of effort at a large cost in dollars went into the making of an agreement or decision. When we see the outcome, we sometimes wonder if the money was well spent.

costs, time, and compromise

Meetings tend to make people seek the lowest common denominator of agreement, to compromise rather than take a stand that they would have taken individually. When we meet, we have a strong feeling or urge to reach an agreement. As a result, people compromise their feelings to reach this end. Of course, this leveling effect is not altogether bad. It serves to curb radical ideas and keeps the group from going off half-cocked.

Individual responsibility is not felt in meetings. Participants feel that the responsibility is shared among all the members present, and, as is frequently the case, "everybody's business is nobody's business." No one feels responsible as a result, and this somewhat limits the usefulness of meetings.

Even with these weaknesses, meetings are still an important part of our business and social lives. They serve an important and unique function that cannot be served by any other device.

HOW SHOULD YOU HOLD A MEETING?

The key to a good meeting is to plan in advance what you will do. First, *be sure you know why you are holding a meeting*. What is your objective? That is, what do you want to accomplish? After satisfactorily answering this question, ask yourself if some other technique could be used that would be less expensive.

If a meeting is still your answer, then you should *prepare a list of participants*. Be sure to include specialists from different areas in order to get proper representation as well as a balanced group for proper deliberation, but don't waste the time of people not concerned with the subject. Keep attendance to a minimum. Invite only those necessary for the composition or *mix of the group.* If possible, select participants who are about equal in rank and who have a stake in the outcome of the meeting. This will ensure that the participants will contribute to and benefit from the meeting. Avoid an imbalanced mix. A group that includes the plant manager, the controller, the division manager, and supervisors, as well as workers, would inhibit the participation of most of the workers as well as of the lower-level supervisors. Finally, the mix should include a stenographer to record minutes for later distribution.

Next, *prepare a discussion outline* listing the objective of the meeting, probable topics to be discussed, questions that you should ask, and materials and handouts that you will need. Doing this will force you to think the whole thing through in advance and will allow you to anticipate the participants' reactions to points of discussion. It also provides you with an agenda for the meeting, thus making it more likely that no important point is omitted.

*have objective
and plan*

List the materials you will need—materials like slides, demonstration models, or printed handouts. Be sure you have a blackboard or a chart pad handy. When you write things on the board for the group to see, you focus their attention on the topic. You can also use the board to list key points that are brought out in a discussion, as well as to summarize what the group has covered.

Choose a time and place. Select a time during working hours that is most convenient for everyone. Meetings held outside working hours are seldom effective because employees reason that if the meeting isn't important enough to hold on company time, the subject matter must not be too important.

Find a meeting place that is comfortable, quiet, and well lighted and that provides ample work space. Arrange the seating to form a "U" so that each participant will have maximum visibility, and to give the discussion leader better control. Be sure to *notify all participants* well in advance of the meeting.

When the day of the meeting arrives, *open the meeting on time by clearly stating the objectives* of the meeting. Indicate precisely what the group is expected to accomplish. If specificl items need to be considered, list these on the blackboard for general guidance.

Start the discussion by introducing noncontroversial material that the group can tackle without fear of ignorance. Then move toward the objective by helping members express themselves and by calling for illustrations to clarify points. Get the group to suggest different ways that the objective can be met. Then discuss each way suggested, looking at its strong and weak points.

Up to this point, you've gotten the meeting going, and a lot of discussion has taken place about different ways the problem could be solved. For the informational, problem-solving, and opinion-seeking meetings, the stage is now set to *get the group to compromise and agree.* This will test your leadership ability because you must get those who disagreed to reconcile their views and to agree to a position that is a compromise. You can tactfully point out faulty thinking, biased judgments, and narrow points of view. You can summarize positions, pointing out the advantages and disadvantages of each recommendation. With all this, you will need to keep up group interest and not let a good meeting become chaotic because of poor control.

"Before you call a meeting, be sure you know why you are holding it— what the objective of the meeting is."

OK IF WE PLAY CARDS UNTIL YOU COME UP WITH A SUBJECT?

Don't drag out a meeting. When you sense that the group has reached an agreement, ask them, "Are we in agreement, then, that this is what we should do?" If you get agreement, restate the proposal, summarize the conclusions, and ask if you have made any errors or omitted anything.

Then *close the meeting on time.* If some members want to continue the discussion, tell them that they are welcome to do so after the meeting adjourns.

DO YOU NEED AN AGENDA?

A well-prepared agenda distributed to members before the meeting will do more than anything else to keep your meeting from wandering off the track. In fact, more meetings fail because they lack an agenda than for any other reason. An agenda, therefore, should be distributed in advance telling the members why the meeting is called and what will be discussed.

The agenda, which is a list of topics to be discussed, should be carefully planned. Topics necessary to the purpose of the meeting should be listed in their proper sequence. In order to keep your meeting moving, set a time limit for the discussion of each topic.

Although the agenda establishes an outline and a time schedule, it should not be so rigid that it cannot be adjusted. Certain topics may take longer to discuss than anticipated, and some topics may arise that you had not foreseen. The agenda, therefore, should be planned with a degree of flexibility. You should use it to guide the discussion, as well as to point out to the group what remains to be covered. With practice, you will learn when the group has discussed a point sufficiently to move on to the next topic.

WHAT KINDS OF QUESTIONS SHOULD A LEADER ASK?

Depending on the response you want, you can ask various types of questions. To start off, you might direct a question to an individual who doesn't mind opening a meeting. However, be careful how you use directed questions because you might embarrass a timid member. Instead, you can use questions directed to the group in general, such as "What do you think we can do to correct this problem?"

If you want one of two answers, use a question like "John, would you give this person a merit raise or reprimand him?" This gives the respondent only two choices. If you want to stimulate his thinking and get his ideas, then say, "John, what would you do in this case?" If you want to provoke discussion and controversy, you could say, "To be successful, does a businessman have to be religious?" Then listen to the controversy that follows! Avoid catch questions such as "Have you stopped drinking on the job?" If the person answers with either yes or no, he is caught.

Don't let the group put you on the spot. When they ask you questions like "Boss, what is meant by a ratio-delay study?" throw the question back to the group by saying, "That's a good question, Sam. Henry, can you explain a ratio-delay study to Sam?"

*types of
questions*

Finally, use a yes-or-no-type question to get a commitment and then follow it with a "why, when, or where" question. For example, you might say, "Joe, do you think attending meetings like this is worthwhile?" He'll say either yes or no. Then ask, "Why do you feel it is (or is not) worthwhile?" You've caused him to tell you what he thinks; now you can get him to express his reasons for his belief.

WHAT DO YOU DO ABOUT MEMBERS WHOSE ACTIONS DISRUPT MEETINGS?

As a leader, what do you do about members who are compulsive talkers, or members who won't say anything, or participants who tend to argue over every point, or digress, or carry on private conversations? All of these individuals present problems for the leader. Perhaps a discussion of each would be of help.

The Compulsive Talker.   Some people just talk too much. They like to hear themselves talk, and it seems they use every meeting to monopolize the discussion. If you know this type in advance, seat him to your extreme right or left; then you can "avoid" seeing his attempt to get the floor. If he gets the floor, let him have a reasonable amount of time; then interrupt by saying, "You've got some good points there. Now let's hear what some other members think." If this doesn't work, set a time limit of, say, two minutes for any one person to hold the floor.

The Member Who Won't Say Anything.   Some people are timid and get all tongue-tied when they try to speak before a group. Don't embarrass this kind of person by asking a difficult direct question. Instead, ask questions you know they can answer, for example, a question about their work, their family, or how they handled a particular situation. Give them praise and a pat on the back whenever possible to help them get over their hesitation to speak out.

Private Discussions.   When one member starts a conversation with his neighbor that is disturbing to the group, what should you do? The best thing is to ignore it if possible. There are always people who are inconsiderate about other people's feelings, and you'll just have to tolerate them. If the conversation reaches a point where something has to be done, try interrupting the talkers by asking a direct question. Or you might stop speaking and wait for them to be quiet. If this doesn't work, you could say to the talkers, "If you have anything to say, please speak up so that everyone can have the benefit of your comments." And, finally, if you want to put them on the spot, ask them to summarize the last few proposals and evaluate their feasibility. They probably haven't gotten them clearly in mind and will have trouble. They'll get the point.

The One Who Argues over Every Point.   Participants who argue over every point can cause an otherwise good meeting to fall apart. You'll need a lot of skill to handle them. If you can, try to find out why they are against everything. Once you detect this, maybe you can handle them. Don't get upset by their criticism. Treat their caustic comments and questions as though they were normal and routine. If possible, rephrase and restate them so that they appear to be conforming with the group. If you cannot tactfully control them, then refer their questions to the group. They'll probably be disgusted with them by this point and will not pull any punches in letting them know how obnoxious they are. This should quiet them. If not, see if you can avoid having the person who argues over every point at your next meeting!

Digressions.   Irrelevancies tend to crop up in meetings that try the skill and tact of even the best leaders. When this happens too often, the meeting is sidetracked and progress is retarded. Your job as leader is to get the group tactfully back on the track. Several techniques can be used.

handling disruptions

You can say, "This is an interesting observation. How does this fit into our problem?" This may cause the group to see their digression and get them back on the topic of the discussion. Or, if possible, gradually tie in the remote discussion to the problem at hand, and thus lead the group back on the track. If this doesn't work, try summarizing what has been said up to this point. This should serve to orient them and focus their attention on the main discussion. You might have to point out, "This discussion is interesting, but may I suggest that we postpone it until next month's meeting when that topic will be discussed." If none of this works, you might have to simply rule the discussion out of order.

HOW DO YOU ACHIEVE GROUP PARTICIPATION?

As the chairman, your general attitude toward the group can do more to elicit group participation than any other single factor. After stating the purpose of the meeting and providing the group with the necessary background information, you should then invite discussion from the floor. This is a critical point in a meeting. You should create the impression that what everyone says is important and that you want everyone to participate. To get things going, you may have to pose one or two controversial questions, followed by some of the "what, when, and where" questions. Or you may invite individuals to express themselves about one of the problems under consideration.

If the group is rather large and you want everyone to participate, it is advisable to break it up into smaller groups. These small groups would then go off and meet separately to discuss and decide on an assigned topic. After a designated time, usually 20 minutes, the small groups report back to the entire meeting, stating their positions and why they hold them. This gives everyone a chance to speak and be heard. It also encourages those people who would hesitate to speak out in a large group to have their say in the smaller units.

SHOULD YOU TAKE A VOTE?

A lot of leaders think that you should vote if a solution has been agreed upon, and a lot of participants think that a vote is the democratic way to do things. Taking a vote, however, has drawbacks. For one thing, it accentuates the differences between people. This makes some of the employees uncomfortable—especially the minority. Also, if a person has committed himself publicly to a position, it is difficult for him to change his mind later without looking as if he is weak or vacillating. Finally, those in the minority who "lost" the vote cannot be expected to carry out the group decision with great enthusiasm. For all these reasons, it is better not to take a formal vote, but to work toward a consensus instead. Try to get the sense of the group, and state to them, "If I understand what you've been saying, it is that we should not proceed with the incorporation of the new product at this time. Is this correct?" Hearing no objections, you should further indicate, "Hearing no objections, then, I'll inform top management of your decision." This technique gets agreement and puts no one on the spot.

WHEN DO YOU CALL A MEETING?

You don't need to call a meeting every time you have a decision to make. Supervisors are paid to make decisions and take action. Meetings and conferences are time consuming. You should therefore solve run-of-the-mill problems by yourself. Only in situations where you need to involve other people to help solve or carry out solutions should you call a meeting. The rule to follow is, Unless you really need it, don't call a meeting.

WHAT ARE THE FINE POINTS OF SPEAKING AT MEETINGS?

The old saying, "Stand up so they can see you. Speak up so they can hear you. And shut up so they will like you," is pretty good advice. There are, however, some other points that you should consider.

If, for example, you are asked to brief your department on the advantages and disadvantages involved in the new retirement program, how will you go about it? Although there are no magic rules, several common-sense considerations, listed below, will make your job easier and better received.

1. Ask yourself what the objective of your speech is. Is your purpose to entertain, inform, persuade, get a decision, or get your audience to take some action? If you know what you will be trying to do, then you can "build" your meeting in a way that will achieve your objective.
2. Who will your audience be? Who are the key persons attending? Do they have any special quirks that you should be aware of? Do they have any major preferences or biases that you would be wise to avoid? If the big boss has a "thing" about slides and a darkened room, don't use slides.
3. Outline what you will need to tell the group in line with the objective of the meeting. Keep in mind what idea or central theme you will want the group to leave the meeting with. If you want them to remember that "the new retirement program is essential for high employee morale," then build your speech around that idea.
4. Remember that a read speech is a disaster. Don't read. Outline what you need to say, then *rehearse* your talk. Use your family, a friend, anyone as an audience for practice. Or practice your presentation by using a recorder and play it back to see what you said and how it

sounded. Keep rehearsing until you feel at ease with the material you have outlined. Don't try to memorize your speech. You might be like the high school debater who memorized his speech and had to start all over every time he forgot a line.

5. If you think that there will be audience participation or questions, try to predict what questions will be asked. Then prepare your answers in advance so that you can make a smooth presentation. When you get an audience question, repeat it for the rest of the group.

6. If you don't know the answer to a question, admit it. Then promise to get the answer and let the person know.

know our objective, your subject, and your audience

7. Tell your audience why the meeting was called. Then tell them what your part is—what you are going to talk about. Next, give your speech. Then summarize your remarks.

8. Avoid the hard sell. You can't ram new ideas through your audience with push and force.

9. In your speech itself, use humor if it applies, but don't drag in an old joke that will break the trend of thought. Use everyday words in your speech. Don't try to impress your audience with long words. Speak clearly and enunciate each word clearly. A lot of words sound alike but can have very different meanings.

10. We think and comprehend at the rate of 500 to 600 words a minute, but to be understood you should speak no faster than about 100 or 125 words per minute. Anything faster causes your audience to lose the sense of what you are saying, and they may have difficulty following you. The rule, therefore, is to speak clearly, distinctly, and not too fast. Slow down.

11. Look at your audience—not at the floor, the ceiling, or out the window. Move your eyes slowly from one person to another, letting them rest momentarily on each individual as you talk. If you feel uncomfortable doing this, then pick out a spot in the back of the room and talk to that spot. This is better than looking up or down. When you look at your audience instead of away from them, you maintain contact with them. You can see whether they are "with you" or whether they themselves are gazing at the ceiling or looking out the window.

12. In closing your speech, don't forget to summarize what you have told them. But be concise, not long-winded. Remember: if you want to give a good speech, use the "stand-up, speak-up, shut-up" rule!

IS BODY LANGUAGE IMPORTANT?

Body language is so important, that it can aid or impede your chances for success as a supervisor. Your body movements can tell another person how you feel about a topic or a question. At times, your body language may be in

*body language
signals*

direct conflict with your verbal expression, but more often than not, it expresses how you feel more honestly than your words do. It can thus lend credibility to what you are saying. Most people are quite good at interpreting body language, whether they are talking to you directly or listening to you speak at a meeting.

Employees can usually tell when the boss is "out of sorts" by the boss's body language. It may be a distracted look, a tense tone of voice, or the lack of eye contact. Whatever the clue, the boss's body language will tell the employee that today is not a good time to ask questions about buying a new typewriter. Your body language also tells your employees how you feel about life. If your shoulders are stooped, if you walk with a slow, hesitating pace, if you usually look down, your employees will glean that you are down and that life seems to be overwhelming you.

Most nonverbal messages, however, are sent by our facial expressions. We get a great many communications, for example, through a person's eyes—a form of body language. That's why people can "hide behind" dark glasses: what their eyes unwittingly express can't be read.

A more direct and obvious type of body language that can be used in face-to-face situations, both before and after meetings, is the act of touching another person. All of us live in little "space bubbles," and when another person gets too close to us or touches us, that person is penetrating our space. Who they are and how they do it sends messages. A pat on the back, for example, may be acceptable from a male supervisor to a male employee as a message of approval. To a female employee, however, it could have other connotations.

When people touch each other, their space bubbles are broken and they are more vulnerable to being influenced by the other person. If, for example, you are touched on your arm by another person, you are almost instantly more alert, more attentive, and more open to being persuaded by the other person's comments.

What you wear also sends messages. For example, would you trust a doctor wearing dirty blue jeans and a sweaty T-shirt? Or a nurse in a bathrobe? Or a banker wearing overalls? Not usually, though there could be extenuating circumstances. Typically, inappropriate clothes send negative messages and destroy a person's credibility.

There are, of course, many more subtle aspects to body language, but the above will give you an idea of what body language is and its importance in communicating your ideas to another person or to an audience.

HOW CAN YOU EVALUATE YOUR MEETING?

Ask yourself the following questions:

1. Was the meeting necessary? Was it the best way to solve the problem?

2. Did I prepare and send out a notice in advance giving time, place, and agenda?

3. Did I select an appropriate meeting room with the necessary props?

4. Did the discussion stick to the topic?

5. Was the meeting short enough to keep the group's attention?

6. Did the group make its own decision versus agreeing to the boss's wishes?

7. Were individual members limited in the amount of time they could speak?

8. Did most members participate in the discussion?

9. Did all aspects of a problem get covered?

10. Did I limit discussion by those trying to monopolize the meeting?

11. Did we discuss the problem thoroughly before suggesting solutions?

12. Were several solutions discussed before agreeing on one?

13. Were members encouraged to express their real feelings?

14. Was I able to minimize serious disagreements?

15. Did I keep the meeting on the track of discussing the problem and not personalities?

16. Was a consensus reached?

17. Was the outcome of the meeting and the action taken recorded and distributed to the participants?

18. Was the meeting worth the cost?

If you can answer yes to most of the above, you've run a good meeting.

QUESTIONS FOR DISCUSSION AND REVIEW

1. What are some of the reasons that we hold meetings?

2. Explain the nature and use of the four types of meetings.

3. Where should you hold meetings?

4. What role should the leader play in a meeting?

5. What are the major advantages of meetings?

6. Discuss the weaknesses that meetings have.

7. Explain what you should do in order to hold a good meeting.

8. What kind of questions should a leader ask a group? Why?

9. What should you do about a compulsive talker?

10. How do you break up private discussions?

11. How do you handle the person who argues every point?

12. How do you handle digressions?

13. What is an agenda? Why is it needed?

14. How can you get everyone to participate in a meeting?
15. Is a vote needed? Why?
16. What points should you keep in mind when speaking at meetings?
17. Explain the importance of body language.

A Case Study
PLANNING A MEETING

Assume that you are the manager of a large department in a retail store. You have just been informed of a major change in company policy that will affect your employees. You are faced with the problem of communicating and explaining this new change to your employees. You could write a letter or memo to them, but on second thought you decide to hold a meeting of your employees to tell them of the change and to get their suggestions about how the change can best be introduced.

1. What type of meeting would you hold for this purpose?
2. When would you hold your meeting?
3. Would you ask all employees to one big meeting, or would you hold two or three small meetings?
4. What kind of questions would you ask?
5. How would you conduct your meeting?
6. Are there any special things that you should be prepared for in your meeting?

A Case Study
HOLDING A MEETING

One of the best ways to learn is by doing; one of the best ways to learn how to conduct a meeting is to hold one. For this case, therefore, select a person from your class to hold a "meeting" to explain to his "employees" how to perform a job. Have six or eight members of the class act as the "employees." You can choose any job or task you want to, but select one that the "supervisor" should know. For example, have the supervisor explain to the group how to drive with a standard transmission or how to conserve electricity on the job.

When this "meeting" is completed, choose one or two more "supervisors" and some other "employees" to hold other meetings to learn about other jobs.

When these "meetings" are over, choose a class member to lead the class in a discussion of how well the leaders did.

Rate the leaders on how well they conducted their meetings.

A Case Study
ELECTRIC COMPONENTS CORPORATION

As his first assignment with the Electric Components Corporation, Dick Parker was placed in charge of the company's storeroom. The company, a large nationally known manufacturer, engaged in the design, fabrication, and sale of many types of electronic products. Amplifiers, recorders, speakers, and transmitters were just a few of its products. Commonly used parts in these products were stocked and issued from one centralized storeroom. Over 10,000 different parts were stocked, including screws, nuts, bolts, resistors, condensers, grommets, and so on.

As a recent graduate, Dick was anxious to "make good," and he incorporated several improvements. One of his problem areas was maintaining a sufficient stock of 72 different sizes and lengths of screws and nuts. He wondered as to the necessity for the various sizes and decided to see what could be done to reduce the number.

Upon checking the product specifications, he found that the design engineers had specified for each product that a screw must extend beyond the nut exactly two threads. This, he discovered, accounted in part for the large variety of screw lengths he was required to stock. Furthermore, he found that each design engineer chose whatever diameter screw he felt appropriate for the product, thus accounting in part for the variety in the diameters of the screws. In general, the number of threads per inch was fairly well standardized.

After talking with a large number of design and product engineers, Dick believed that the variety of screws stocked could be considerably reduced. He reasoned that the length a screw extended beyond a nut, if it were a reasonable amount, was immaterial in the functioning of a product and, except for items where appearance was a factor, made no difference to the customer.

Accordingly, he prepared a report for top management showing the excess dollars tied up in "needless" varieties of screws. The plant manager was impressed with the report and decided that a meeting should be called to discuss its possibilities.

1. Around what theme should the meeting be organized?
2. Who should call the meeting?
3. Where should it be held?
4. Who should attend the meeting?

A Case Study
COMMUNICATION IN THE BANK

As supervisor of the small-loans department in a large bank, you have a feeling that proper and needed information is not being disseminated among your employees as promptly or as effectively as it should be. You have discussed the problem with several of your employees, but no concrete suggestions have been forthcoming. You decide, therefore, to hold a meeting to try to get to the root of the problem, as well as to set up some routine or pattern to establish how the information flow should be handled.

1. Would a meeting be the best way to handle your problem? What other ways could you suggest?
2. Assuming that you want to hold a meeting, how would you go about making plans for the meeting?
3. Would you solicit help from your employees? Why?
4. Would a follow-up meeting be necessary? Why?

A Personal Case Problem

Assume that you are the supervisor and that the other members of your class are your employees. During the past several years your department has accumulated $406 that can be used in any way the employees see fit. You favor giving the money to the Salvation Army. You have heard, however, that some employees want to have a party while others favor purchasing play equipment for the town's municipal park. You have called a meeting of your employees to discuss what to do with the money.

Plan how you will hold the meeting, what you will say, and how you plan to try to get your employees to give the money to the Salvation Army or at least to a comparable charity.

Hold the meeting when your class meets next. After you have had your try at running the meeting, let several other class members try their hands in order to decide what to do with the money.

1. Which one ran the best meeting? Why?
2. Did the last meeting run smoother than the first? Why?

12

HOW TO SUPERVISE
SPECIAL EMPLOYEES

This chapter explains—

- How to give orders
- Signals that indicate that you are not doing a good job
- How age, sex, and professional status affect supervision

Your job as a supervisor is to get things done through others. How you supervise determines the results you get. If you want to get your employees involved in their work, if you want to get them going on their jobs, you've got to give them directions. Telling other people what you want them to do is the way you get your decisions and ideas implemented. It enables you to put your ideas into action. *How* you tell them what you want them to do— *how* you give directions—will determine how well the job will be done and whether or not you will succeed or fail as a supervisor.

HOW SHOULD YOU GIVE ORDERS?

Giving orders is so much a part of supervision that we sometimes take it for granted. Yet the act of giving any employee an order is a complicated and difficult task. It is more than simply saying, "Paint this red," because as a supervisor your skill in understanding and motivating your employee is reflected in how you give your orders. The words you choose, how you say them, your tone of voice—all of these factors help promote a climate in which work will be done. Because directing others is so important to you as a supervisor, let's look at six simple rules you should follow.

1. *Create the Right Climate.* Orders should be given in a climate and spirit of help and cooperation. Commands and brusque orders are the mark of an immature supervisor and seldom achieve more than a grudging compliance. As every supervisor knows, you will need all the cooperation and help your employees can give you, not just a reluctant compliance. You should, therefore, strive to create a climate of voluntary cooperation, respect, and understanding between you and your employees. This type of climate does not happen overnight, but grows out of fair treatment, a just handling of differences, and firm supervision. Where employees willingly and enthusiastically accept a directive, you can be sure that a climate of helpful cooperation exists.

*correct
environment*

Where employees do only what they are told, only what is expected of them, you will have a second-best climate of compliance, where work is completed without enthusiasm. Initiative, creativity, and suggestions from your employees will be lacking. Your employees will do only what you tell them—no more and no less.

The worst climate, of course, is one of open hostility. Orders are received with defiance, and employees do only what they have to because of the authority you have over them. They constantly look for opportunities to foul up the process and to embarrass you.

The first rule for giving good orders, therefore, is to create a climate of mutual understanding, trust, and cooperation between you and your employees.

2. *Make the Order Reasonable.* A good order is a reasonable one. It is one that your employees can physically accomplish without danger to their life or limb. Remember, however, that an order that would be reasonable for one person might be unreasonable for another. It would be unreasonable, for example, to order an employee to drive a tractor–trailer to deliver a product if his only experience was driving pickups. The same order, however, would be reasonable to an experienced and licensed truck driver.

Sometimes orders are given that stretch employees' capacities and make them learn something new. Reasonableness here is matter of degree. Generally speaking, however, you should remember that any directive given to an employee should take into account whether or not that employee is capable of accomplishing the task.

appropriateness

3. *Make the Order Understandable.* Any order that cannot be understood cannot be executed. Be sure, therefore, that your order is understood by your employees. What we are talking about here is the process of communication that we discussed in Chapter 4. As we saw there, the importance of good communications can't be overemphasized.

clarity

"Any order that cannot be understood cannot be executed."

How you communicate varies with the employee and the situation. For some employees you will need to "dot every i and cross every t" before they will understand what you want done. Other employees merely need a few key words to understand what you want them to do. Whatever the situation, be sure that the employees to whom you are talking understand your point of view and know exactly what you want done. To be sure that they do, don't hesitate to repeat what you have said. Not everyone gets the same meaning from words—so give your employees an opportunity to ask questions if their understanding appears to be hazy. In fact, to make sure your employees understand you, it is a good idea to ask them to explain to you what you want done.

4. *Choose the Right Words.*   When you give an order, choose the right words and say them in such a way that your employees enthusiastically accept your directions. Don't be like an army sergeant and issue commands. Instead, use suggestions or requests or instructions. Just because you say something like "Joe, how about giving me a hand with this new order?" in no way lessens the force of your directive. But it does make it more palatable to your employee.

word choice

At times, of course, a direct command or order is needed. In case of danger, for example, you might shout to Joe, "Run for your life!" Or if the employee is one who only understands and responds to direct orders, you might say, "You're behind in your production, Ted, and I want you to complete twenty good units by five o'clock." Most employees, however, regard themselves as adults and want to be treated with consideration. As a result, direct commands are seldom needed. Instead you might say, "Ted, you're a little behind the rest of the gang. How about seeing if you can catch up by closing time today?" Or if Ted is a perceptive employee who only needs a suggestion to understand what you want, you might only need to say, "I see you're a little behind, Ted."

Remember that on most occasions you will fare better if you *request* your employees to do something. Commands and orders are words that kill willing cooperation. In fact, some employees, backed by their unions, will refuse to cooperate under such conditions. The thing to remember, therefore, is to choose words that will give your orders a pleasant ring. Your employees will cooperate more willingly, and you will get a higher rating as a supervisor.

5. *Explain the "Why" of the Order.*   Always explain *why*. If there is the slightest chance that your employees will not understand why something needs to be done, be sure to tell them why. If you think about this for a moment, you will see why this is true. Employees who don't see why something should be done, who don't think it will help meet the goals of your department, will probably be reluctant to carry out your suggestion. And when they do what you want, they may do it half-heartedly, without enthusiasm, and slowly. On the other hand, if they understand why you gave them the order, they are more likely to pitch in and get the work accomplished with dispatch.

tell why

6. *Be Prepared for Problems.*   No matter how carefully you have gone through the previous steps in giving directions, you are bound to have some

problems. For example, some employees may not be listening and may miss the message. You will, therefore, need to talk it over with them to "catch them up" on what you have said and what needs to be done. Another employee may not have understood your choice of words, even though you tried to use easy-to-understand language. In order to minimize your problems, therefore, don't give a directive and forget it. Follow it up with questions. Talk it over with employees who don't appear to understand. And be alert for actions that could signal a lack of understanding. Remember, your job is to get things done through the efforts of others, and they can't take the proper action unless they clearly understand your orders.

follow up

WHAT SHOULD YOU DO WITH THE EMPLOYEE WHO REFUSES TO DO WHAT YOU SAY?

Suppose you have done everything that we have suggested so far, and one of your employees still refuses to do what you requested. What should you do? First of all, don't blow your stack. Don't lose your temper. Take a walk and cool off if necessary, but don't blast your employee. Stay cool and calm and try to review in your mind what has happened.

Ask yourself questions like, Am I sure the employee can do what I want done? Am I sure he understands what I said? Is he willfully refusing to do the job for some reason that I am not aware of? If you cannot understand or see why he won't do what you say, the best thing for you to do is to approach him directly: "Well, John, what's your complaint? Why don't you want to go along with my suggestions?" Maybe he has a good reason for not doing what you requested. Maybe he didn't understand. Whatever his reason, your questioning approach will give him an opportunity to talk it out. Maybe something you said or the way he interpreted it "teed him off." Your questioning approach, therefore, might give him an opportunity to let off steam—to get it off his chest—and he will then go back to work in a better frame of mind.

However, if an employee absolutely refuses to follow your request, if he is stubborn and won't cooperate, if he won't calm down, what should you do? You can, of course, penalize him or suspend him on the spot if the union contract permits. This is punitive action, however, and is bound to cause ill will that might affect the other employees, as well as be difficult for the penalized employee to overcome. If he is a good worker, your wiser course of action may be to modify your request to one that he will comply with. In this way, you will get him back to work, and later when he has calmed down, you can talk to him privately in a constructive manner. Remember that your job is to get work accomplished through the help of other people. You won't get your work done by firing or punishing your employees or by creating ill will between yourself and your employees. Be firm in your talk, but be big enough to work *with* him, not *against* him. If, despite all this, he still shows evidence of resistance, you will need to let him know that appropriate disciplinary action or dismissal will result if he can't work with you.

steps to follow

This is a last resort, however, and should be used only when everything else has failed.

WHAT DO YOU DO WHEN AN EMPLOYEE ASKS FOR THE ANSWER TO A PROBLEM?

Do you give employees the answer when they have a problem? Do you solve the problem for them? Most supervisors feel that this would be a poor supervisory approach to take. Solving a problem for employees is not constructive because it doesn't place the employees in a position to make a sound decision the next time they face a similar problem.

What you should do instead of giving them the answer is to lend the employees all the support and understanding you can. Do this by talking with them and getting them to see all the issues involved in the problem. Help them to come up with several alternative solutions to the problem. Then ask them to decide which alternative is best. In other words, don't *give* them the answer—help them *discover* the answer for *themselves*. If you do this, they will be in a better position to make a decision for themselves next time, and you will have more freedom to do your own thing.

help employee discover answer

However, this is not to say that you should never help your employees—that you should never solve their problems for them. What is being said is, "Don't volunteer your total help until your employees specifically ask you for it." Then at that point help them solve the problem by asking questions that will encourage them to explore alternative solutions.

All this may seem like the long way around the barn. You could solve the problem yourself and give your employees the answer much more quickly than you could get the employees to reason it through and come up with their own answer. This may be true in the one instance. But remember that you are training them to be better employees—employees who can make decisions on their own in the future. Of course, it may take more of your time in the short run to help them make a decision, but in the long run it will save you time because they will learn to decide for themselves.

This process is like the answer the little boy gave to the teacher when she asked him if he bought a cart for $6.92 and sold it for $8.24, whether he would win or lose on the deal. He thought for a moment and then said he would win on the dollars but lose on the cents. In helping an employee solve his own problem, you may lose on the cents (the short run), but you will win on the dollars (the long run).

DO EMPLOYEES' AGES MAKE A DIFFERENCE IN SUPERVISING THEM?

Up to the time employees are about 50 or 55 years old, age has little bearing on how you supervise them. From about 50 on, however, age does enter into the picture. Older employees form a separate social group because their interests change and their physical capacities change. They should not, however, be made to feel socially isolated, but should be accepted and respected for what they can do and for what they have to offer.

Older workers are important to industry. Not only do they provide about half of the needed labor force, they also bring skill, maturity, good judgment, and patience to many jobs. Older employees are much more stable than younger workers. They have gone through the period of changing jobs, usually have settled down, and are now prepared to stick to their jobs more than are younger employees. Older persons are usually work-oriented, have better attendance records, and are more loyal. For these reasons, they are valuable members of your work force.

Older employees do, however, have some drawbacks that you should recognize in supervising them. For one thing, their eyesight may be failing, which means that they may react more slowly or may require better light. Age also typically brings on some physical infirmities, which often slow down the older employees, reduce their strength, or cause them not to bounce back so quickly. You'll need to remember, however, that while the older employees may be slower, they typically make fewer mistakes. Although their vision is weakening, it can be corrected by glasses and good light. And although their strength is fading, they typically work with greater skill and consistency to compensate.

CAN OLDER EMPLOYEES LEARN NEW JOBS?

Some older employees may not be as highly motivated to learn new jobs as are younger ones. As a consequence, new jobs requiring the employee to learn new skills should be assigned only to those employees, young or old, who have demonstrated that they want to learn. There are times, however, when an older employee who wants to learn a new job may still have trouble doing it. Suppose, for example, that you have two typists working for you, one 55 years old and the other 22, with the older a more consistent typist who makes fewer errors. Now suppose you purchase a new machine with mathematical symbols—one that requires that the operator relearn some of the major keys on the keyboard. In this instance, the older employee would probably have difficulty learning the new keyboard because of thirty years of experience and skill on the old keyboard. This placement of the keys on the new machine would be in conflict with the strong skill that he already has. He could learn the new machine and job, but it would probably be more difficult for him than for the younger employee, whose skills are not set by years of experience. The wiser course of action would be not to change the older employee to the newer machine unless he expresses a desire to make the change. If you do make the change, you will need to be patient with the older employee, pointing out the similarities between the old and new machine, and giving encouragement and praise for progress.

*age and
supervision*

Otherwise, leave the older employee where he is. If not all your typewriters are being changed, why disrupt a senior employee's work? Leave his job alone. Put the younger person on the new machine. The older employee will be happier, and you will be smarter to keep him on a job where his thirty years of experience would not be wasted. Remember, however, that older employees should receive the same fair and equitable treatment that you give everyone else.

ARE OLDER EMPLOYEES HARD TO MOTIVATE?

As employees grow older, they may tend to become complacent—satisfied with the way things are. They may not be motivated to venture to new jobs or to try to master new skills. They may be satisfied with their way of doing things, with their skills, and with their job assignments. Because they are thus satisfied, they are good workers—loyal, consistent, always there. And it is difficult under these conditions to suggest to them that they should change their ways or improve the way a job is done. However, your job as a supervisor calls for you to try to motivate these older employees. Getting them to want to learn a new way to do a job better will depend on your skill in human relations and your salesmanship. It will require all the tact, skill, and persuasion that you can muster. You'll need to encourage them, praise them, overlook mistakes, and point out how others their age are using the new method. You'll need to show them that in time they can equal or exceed the production of younger employees.

To get older employees to try a new way of performing their jobs, you should first talk with them in private about the change, rather than in front of the other employees. If they agree to change, you should, if possible, place them in an inconspicuous location—one that doesn't call attention to their mistakes. Work with them when you can. It will make them feel better to see that you aren't too skilled and that you too make mistakes. Once they have gotten the hang of things and have gained some skill in the new job, you should begin to call their progress to the attention of other employees. By working with older employees in this manner, you will be able to "rehabilitate" them, so to speak, and make them more effective and up-to-date workers.

WHAT ABOUT WOMEN?

Women are excellent workers. They are loyal, diligent, and cooperative. They are good at doing intricate, fine work that is physically confining. They cannot, however, do all kinds of physical work that men can. For one thing, they are usually not as strong as men are. Also, every state has laws limiting the day as well as night hours they can work. Work before and after childbirth is regulated in some states, and other states have laws pertaining to rest rooms, laws requiring chairs for alternate standing and sitting, or laws stipulating the amount of weight a woman can be expected to lift. Despite these legal limitations, however, women can and do hold down virtually every job that men do. They are doctors, painters, lawyers, plumbers, judges, astronauts, masons, supreme court justices, welders, construction helpers, and so on. In fact, recent trends show that more than 6% of construction workers are women, more than 6% of the welders and flame cutters are women, and over 2% of the locomotive engineers are female.[1] Women are also making gains in the professions, according to a U.S. Department of Commerce report. In fact, women are particularly strong in the professions dealing with editing, reporting, accounting, college teaching, life and physical sciences, social sciences, medicine, and law. In the managerial area, women now hold nearly one-third of the nation's management jobs. They comprise over 17% of the nation's judges, over 50% of the managers in medical and health related operations, and over 47% of personnel and labor relations specialists.[2] In the past ten years the number of female managers has doubled, and during 1983 women filled over 70% of all new managerial jobs.[3]

equal treatment

Recognizing this movement of women into all corners of the work force, you should supervise women in the same way that you do men. All employees, both men and women, should be treated with tact and courtesy. You should likewise supervise both male and female employees impartially, treating everyone the same. This applies to the amount of personal attention you give each one, where you physically locate them, the equipment you assign to them, the types of jobs you give them, and so on. In other words, good supervision demands that *all employees* be treated impartially, equally, tactfully, and courteously. These then are the four watchwords that supervisors should keep in mind in supervising all employees: impartiality, equality, tact, and courtesy.

WHAT SHOULD YOU DO ABOUT SEXUAL HARASSMENT?[4]

Sexual harassment applies to both sexes and you should curb it immediately.

Whether you know it or not, it is illegal to make repeated and unwanted sexual overtures to an employee or a peer. Likewise, it is illegal to demand sexual favors from a subordinate. To curb sexual harassment, your first course of action is to post well-written and widely publicized policy statements and guidelines pertaining to it. In addition, you should have

[1] "The Condescending Male," *Durham Herald*, Sept. 19, 1980, p. 2.

[2] Census Bureau report quoted in *Durham Herald*, April 11, 1984, p. 9A.

[3] President Ronald Reagan in his State of the Union Address, January 25, 1984.

[4] For a complete discussion see Ron Zemke, "Sexual Harassment: Is Training the Key?" *Training/HRD*, February 1981, pp. 22ff. See also "Sex and Romance in the Office and Plant," *Wall Street Journal*, Nov. 29, 1982, p. 1.

stop it quickly

well-founded training programs for your employees, including strawbosses, line workers, and supervisors.

If an employee complains to you that he or she is being harassed, move quickly and positively to get it stopped. Don't ignore it as being only human. Either you or your company may be culpable if it is ignored. And don't think it couldn't happen in your department. According to a 1979 survey by a federal agency,[5] 25% of all federal workers—42% of the females and 15% of the males—reported that they had experienced some form of sexual harassment during the two years prior to the survey. And cases on sexual harassment are now flooding the courts, with awards running as high as the $140,000 which Ford Motor Company was ordered to pay in compensation for a supervisor's amorous verbal pursuit of an employee.

What constitutes sexual harassment? This is an unclear area. Some courts have ruled that physical contact must occur. Other courts hold that ear pollution (telling lewd stories and jokes) is sexual harassment. Still other courts indicate that nude pin-ups could be considered sexual harassment.

What should you do as a supervisor? At present there are no clearly defined legal steps that you must take. However, a good defense would surely include the following:

1. Be sure that a company statement has been given to each of your employees indicating explicitly that company policy does not condone sexual harassment of any type.
2. Be sure that detailed reviews are made of all your decisions to hire, fire, and promote so that your superiors can be certain that you have not been guilty of any supervisory misconduct or negligence along these lines.

steps to take

3. Make certain that channels of communication have been established and widely publicized whereby an employee could safely make a complaint of sexual harassment to management.
4. Once a complaint is made, you should make a prompt and thorough effort to discern the facts and resolve the issue.
5. Consult a lawyer to make certain that you have complied with all federal and state regulations.

Sexual harassment problems are serious and should not be taken lightly. Whether you recognize it or not, there is a strong similarity between sexual harassment and assault and battery, and personal liability is involved. Fraternization isn't the essence here, but offensive conduct is. You shouldn't attempt to establish a code of morality in your department. What happens between consenting adults is not your business. But what you should be concerned with is keeping your department free from offensive conduct on the job.

[5] Zemke, *op. cit.*, p. 27.

Professional employees such as doctors, engineers, scientists, nurses, and research workers are those with particular educational skills and training. They are different from other employees and can cause you a ton of headaches if you don't understand the differences.

First of all, they feel that they are different from other employees and that they should, therefore, be treated differently. They typically know the technical aspects of their jobs much better than anyone else and resent being told how to do things. They are proud of their chosen field and are usually self-starters; that is, they are typically more highly motivated than the average employee. As a result, they don't need anyone to "crack the whip" over them. In fact, they resent it. As a general rule, the more professional employees are and the higher their level of education, the more difficult they will be to supervise. Their loyalty is not to you but to their profession. The company comes second. As a result, professional employees don't feel tied to the company and are usually more susceptible to offers from other companies. In fact, it is not at all unusual for a professional employee to change jobs more frequently than other employees. You can see, therefore, that they are more likely to be touchy employees, and supervising them will be more difficult.

Professional workers expect to be treated differently from the average employee. They want personal recognition for what they do, they want greater freedom and more liberties than the average employee, and they want better working conditions than those furnished the other employees. They want to be respected as a member of their chosen profession and be recognized as a doctor, research scientist, or registered nurse—not as a company employee.

Inasmuch as they are self-starters, they are usually not clock watchers. They may get involved in problems and work long hours with no thought of extra compensation. They do, however, expect greater flexibility in rules regarding when they start to work and time off for personal reasons. Generally, a work situation that calls for clock punching is rejected by them.

degrees of supervision

Inasmuch as professional workers regard themselves as different from the average employee, they resent doing any "average" work. They feel that anything routine that a clerk or technician can do should be done by a clerk and that their talents should be used in a more productive way. They typically place emphasis on the chance for professional development above job security and money, so you can see why they are more independent and difficult to handle than the rank-and-file employee.

Professional workers are difficult to regiment, and almost all of them refuse to work by any time schedule. You can't tell a research scientist, for example, "I want you to invent a new method for making paper within the next two months." In like manner, you wouldn't tell a surgeon, "I'll give you fifteen minutes to take out my appendix." In both instances, you'd probably be told in no uncertain terms where to go.

HOW DO YOU SUPERVISE PROFESSIONAL WORKERS?

Recognizing all the above peculiarities, you may be wondering how you should supervise professional persons. There is no one right answer. In general, however, you should not supervise them too closely. Fortunately, since most of them are self-starters and are self-regulating, you won't have too many problems about professional persons "goofing off." You won't need to bear down on them; instead, you should try to act as an advisor, be a good listener, and serve as their link to higher management. Try to understand your professional employees, and provide them with reasonable services and liberties. Insofar as you can, give your professional employees challenging assignments and the opportunity to perform. When you have to say *the link to* no to them, be sure to explain why. They will then gain a better under-
higher standing of you and your managerial problems and not view you as a person
management who thinks exclusively in terms of profits.

If you could use only two ideas to determine how best to supervise professional employees, these two ideas would probably be:

1. Give the professional employees as much freedom as you can.
2. Give them worthwhile and challenging assignments.

Remember, however, that both of these ideas should be used with moderation, should be modified according to the individual you are supervising, and should be in line with company policies.

WHAT IS A TECHNICAL PROFESSIONAL?

Some individuals may think of themselves as professionals when in the strictest sense they actually are not. People in technical occupations such as draftsmen, surveyors, laboratory technicians, traffic managers, and purchasing agents, for example, frequently think of themselves as professionals. A better name for this group would be *technical professionals*.

These employees are your important, highly skilled, technical individuals who seek challenging jobs with the opportunity for professional growth. If you can provide this environment, they will overlook any shortcomings in the work situation. But if the work isn't challenging, they are apt to become critical of you, the way you supervise, company policies, and so on. While the amount of pay is important to the technical professional, even more important is that their pay be competitive and equal to others in the community performing the same work. Recognizing the importance of these employees, you might consider making it possible for them to participate in your profit-sharing plan, stock bonus plans, and other motivating options that you make available for management and professionals. In other words, technical professionals should be treated, insofar as possible, as professionals. You, however, will have to judge the degree of freedom they should be given and the difference with which they should be treated.

HOW DO YOU SUPERVISE WHITE-COLLAR EMPLOYEES?

Office workers have many of the same needs and desires that shop workers have, and supervising them is much the same. There are, however, some differences that you should be aware of. For one thing, office employees are frequently more status conscious than shop employees. Titles, locations, job assignments, and even their boss's status are more important to office workers than to shop employees. Office decor, color schemes, and decorating harmony are also more important to office workers. The degree of importance of each of these factors varies with each employee. Your job, therefore, is to study your employees, try to understand their needs, and then deal with each of these needs according to what you know about the employees as individuals.

This is not to say that pay is unimportant to clerical workers. It is as important to them as it is to shop employees. You should, therefore, be sure that your clerical workers receive equal pay for equal work and that your salary scale is comparable to the wage level in the community for similar work.

Many of your office employees will be women, and what was said before applies here: supervise all employees impartially, equally, tactfully, and courteously. Likewise, you will probably have both men and women who are career oriented working for you. Each will need stimulating jobs and good assignments wherein they have a chance to learn new skills and broaden their capacities. You should therefore try to broaden the job scope of career-oriented individuals. Give them additional duties. Let them try their hand at a more difficult or skilled job. And move them ahead when their skills fit new job opportunities. Be careful, however, not to shower this type of worker with too much attention. If you do, your other employees will become jealous of "teacher's pet," and office morale could suffer.

SHOULD YOU COUNSEL EMPLOYEES WITH SPECIAL PROBLEMS?

From time to time, all employees have problems that affect their work. In such instances, an understanding and cooperative supervisor who recognizes these problems can do much to help the employees get over this difficult time.

As a supervisor, what you should be concerned with in such cases is helping worried and unhappy employees get over their problems and thus be better workers. There are lots of things that worried employees do that may signal their state of unhappiness. A sudden change in behavior is a prime indication. For example, Tom used to smile and say, "Howdy" to everyone. Now he seldom speaks or smiles; something is wrong. Increases in an employee's absences and accidents may point to a state of worry. When these and other signals tell you that an employee is worried, you should try to help him get himself straightened out by listening to him talk in some counseling sessions.

listen carefully

WHAT IS A COUNSELING SESSION?

A counseling session is nothing more than a talk in private wherein you listen to everything your employee has to say before you make a comment. In these sessions, always listen carefully. Don't argue with what is said, and don't criticize your employee. Instead, try to understand what the employee is trying to tell you. Like an iceberg, only 10% of an employee's feelings show. The other 90% are below the surface. As a conscientious supervisor you should try to discover these hidden feelings through a detailed talk with your employee.

"Like an iceberg, only 10% of an employee's feelings show. The other 90% is below the surface."

By listening to what employees have to say, you may discover, for example, that although they are complaining about their pay (the 10% that shows), their real concern is about the sales territory you have assigned them (the hidden 90%). In counseling sessions, you discuss items that may be bothering employees, with the objective being to understand and decrease the resulting emotional problems. A good counseling session may provide employees with sound advice or with hope and reassurance. Or it may enable them to clarify their own thinking and thus become better employees. Such sessions can provide employees with a means to release their emotional tensions, supply a communications bridge between them and management, or simply serve to help them regain and clarify their perspective about their work, the other employees, and so on.

In beginning a counseling session with an employee, it is a good idea to try to put him at ease. Don't jump in and start asking questions. This will confuse the employee, put him on the defensive, and perhaps cause him to shut up. Instead, try to say something that will open up the conversation and allow him to talk freely. Ask questions you know he can answer. Ask about problems you know he will feel comfortable talking about. Get him to open up by asking a question like "What kind of dog is best for hunting quail—a pointer or a setter?" If he knows hunting, this type of question will open the way for him to talk freely about it, and he may relax and tell you some of his other problems, too. The session won't be brief. In fact, you should be prepared to spend 30 or 40 minutes. Anything less than that won't give you time to accomplish very much.

SHOULD YOU EVER USE PROFESSIONAL COUNSELORS?

In counseling sessions your job is to serve as a fact finder and listening post. Let your employees talk out their own problems and find some answers they can live with. Be careful, however, not to get in over your head. After you have had two or three sessions with a troubled employee and do not seem to be making any progress, don't hesitate to get the employee to go to a competent professional counselor. Sometimes, of course, it is difficult to know when you should try to help an employee and when you should suggest that he or she see a psychiatrist or professional counselor. If you have any question about how to handle the situation, it is better to err on the side of caution. The rule, therefore, is, if there is any reasonable doubt in your mind, *send your employee to a professional counselor.* The employee may be emotionally disturbed or psychotic and beyond your friendly help. In most communities of any size, you will usually find a fair number of psychiatrists, social workers, or clinical psychologists who can give your employee help. If you don't know of any, start by asking the company physician, the employee's physician, or your own personal physician whom he or she would recommend.

WHAT TYPES OF PROBLEMS DO YOU WATCH FOR?

Generally, the most difficult problems to identify and correct are personal problems. These range from money and family problems to problems with law-enforcement officials. Whatever these problems are, they bother the employees. For example, if Janie's mother has to go to the hospital for a serious operation, it may cause her to be absent or late, or it may result in an increase in posting and typing errors. Or if Joe is worried that his creditors are going to repossess his motorcycle, the quality of his work may suffer. This affects the work of your department as well as the work of other employees.

Personal problems may be interrelated with all sorts of other problems—all of which may have some negative effect on an employee's work pattern. Even though you may dislike it, it is a supervisor's job to try to help employees with such problems. It may be unpleasant, but remember that problem employees can do more harm than good if they are not helped. They are expensive to keep on the payroll. They are difficult to motivate. They may be demoralizing to other workers. And they are the most difficult to supervise. When you help such people solve their problems through counseling, you will be doing them a favor as well as making your own work easier and more rewarding.

Sometimes an employee's problems are so severe that the employee is a disruptive influence at work and is difficult to supervise. Morale for the whole department then suffers. If you know a person is that type before you hire him, you should avoid putting him on the payroll. If such a person already works for you, however, your job is to help him or see that he gets professional attention.

ARE THERE SIGNALS THAT YOU AREN'T DOING A GOOD SUPERVISING JOB?

No one signal will clearly indicate that you are doing a poor job of supervising. However, several factors combined might be telling you that something is wrong. Look at the following checklist. If two or more of these items apply to you, then it may be a signal that you are not doing your best.

1. Do you get complaints from your customers or other departments about the quality and delivery of your work?
2. Are costs increasing in your department that you can't justify?
3. Is the production output per employee decreasing?
4. Have you suffered any increase in the number of complaints or any unusual number of grievances within the past year?
5. Have you had to reprimand several of your employees during the past year for conflicts, hostility, and unjustified actions?
6. Do you find that you have to watch your employees more closely than you used to? That they are no longer self-starters?
7. Is there a general indication of apathy and disinterest among your employees about their jobs and the company?
8. When you hold employee meetings, do you find that attendance is

perfunctory with little real interest shown in the topic being discussed?

9. Do your employees misunderstand your instructions and not follow through on what you tell them to do?

10. Do you have any noticeable increase in absences, lateness, requests for transfers, or turnover?

QUESTIONS FOR DISCUSSION AND REVIEW

1. Why is giving orders important to a supervisor?
2. How should a supervisor issue orders? Explain each step.
3. What do you tell an employee who asks you to solve a problem for him?
4. What do you do with the employee who refuses to do what you tell him to do?
5. How does age make a difference in the way you supervise an employee? How does age affect learning a new job? How does it affect motivating an employee?
6. Is supervising women different from supervising men? Why?
7. Explain how supervising professional workers is different from supervising other workers.
8. Does a white-collar employee require different supervision? Explain.
9. What are the signs that you are not doing a good supervisory job?
10. How should you deal with an employee with special problems?
11. What is a technical professional employee?
12. How should sexual harassment be handled? Explain.

A Case Study
THE CASE OF MARGE BURNS

Marge Burns supervised 37 women employees who were assigned to typing pools in five different locations throughout the central agency's five-story home-office building. Inasmuch as she couldn't closely supervise the employees in every location, Marge had appointed a "lead worker" for each of the five locations to give out the work and answer questions.

Anita, the lead worker in the premium accounts pool, was one of the company's senior employees with over twenty-six years of experience. A career employee, Anita had always spoken up for the company. Her girls had always taken their coffee breaks and lunch periods promptly, were virtually never late, and had always worked overtime when required.

Six months ago, the company hired six new women—two commercial artists, one layout expert, one skilled copy editor, and two communications specialists—to do publicity and publication work. Their job was to prepare and supervise publication of all company reports and to give publicity to company news through the newspapers, TV, and other media. The work required a great deal of outside contact and work, with the women visiting outside suppliers, editors, and so on. Marge appointed the copy editor, Elizabeth Ware, to be the lead worker for the group.

From the very beginning, Elizabeth Ware's group seemed to feel that they were different from the other women employees. Although work hours were from 8:00 A.M. to 5:00 P.M., it was not unusual for individuals in the publicity group to start work anywhere between 8:00 and 8:45 A.M. They were equally lax about lunch periods. Their work, however, was excellent and had received good reviews by local publicity experts. As a result, the group was a highly cohesive one and worked well as a unit. It was not at all unusual to see their lights burning long after everyone had left the building.

The work of the publicity group, however, had not gone unnoticed by the other women employees. In fact, several of the lead workers reported to Marge Burns that their subordinates wanted to know how that "special group got by, coming in at all hours and taking any amount of time they wanted to for lunch." To cite another problem, just this week one of Anita's staff had refused to work past 5:00 P.M. to get a report out, stating that her workday was from 8:00 A.M. to 5:00 P.M. and she didn't see why she should break her back working past 5:00 P.M. when others in the company came in 30 or 45 minutes late with no punishment. As time passed, more and more women came in late in various groups, and the lead workers always gave Marge the same answer: the girls felt that if the publicity group could come in late, they could, too. Marge recognized that things were getting out of hand.

1. What caused the trouble for Marge Burns?
2. What do you think she should do? What steps should she take? Why?

A Case Study
WHITSET HOSIERY MILLS

Whitset Hosiery Mills manufactures one of the nationally known brands of high-quality ladies' hosiery. It is an aggressive and progressive company that is proud of its good employee relationships. In fact, it is not unusual to find two or three generations of a family working for Whitset Mills.

Inspecting women's nylon hosiery for flaws has traditionally been performed by women. The process consists of visually inspecting the hose for snags, runs, poor-quality seams, picked threads, and the like by "boarding," or placing the hose on a leg-shaped form and revolving it so that all sides of the hose can be seen. This is basically the inspection process employed by Whitset Hosiery Mills, and it is the one that has given them some recent trouble.

Actually, the women in Whitset Mills inspection room #4 have a thorough knowledge of hosiery inspection procedures. Most of them are between 50 and 60 years old and have been with the company for twenty or more years. Because of their long experience, they know what to look for and where flaws will probably occur. Output for the department formerly averaged about 200–250 pairs of hose per hour, with the better operators averaging 300–325 pairs per hour. During the past eight years, however, their inspection output has gradually decreased to a point where the inspectors are now producing an average of 150–200 pairs per hour. During this eight-year period, the company has tried a series of installations and adjustments to get the output back up to the old level: they changed the layout of the room; they designed and installed new "boards" on which the hose were examined; they installed a loud-speaking system and played any music the women wanted; and they changed the color scheme of the room. In each of these instances, output was increased slightly but quickly fell back to the old level in several days.

A member of the plant's engineering team suggested the installation of a new-type fluorescent light. This was done and proved to be no more effective than the other changes. A check of the intensity of light at the time of the installation showed that the level of intensity was equal to the minimum recommendations for this type of work.

After doing everything of this nature that they could think of, the plant officials were becoming discouraged. They talked to the employees, who indicated that they were going as fast as they could while still doing a thorough inspection job. The employees were aware that management wanted to raise output to the old level, but they claimed that with the new shades and deniers of nylon, seeing was more difficult, and it took longer to inspect. Management, however, discounted the idea because the same basic shades were being used and the denier had not decreased an appreciable amount. Nevertheless the employees stated that the stockings were more difficult to see and took longer, therefore, to inspect.

1. If you were on the staff of Whitset Mills, what supervisory action would you take? Why?
2. Are there any signs that supervision has not been as good as it might be?

A Case Study
GERALDINE'S PROMOTION

Geraldine MacIver was one of your best and most talented employees, so when an administrative position developed in your department, you put Geraldine in the job. This meant that employees who were formerly Geraldine's associates were now her subordinates.

From her actions, you have sensed that Geraldine is uncomfortable with her new supervisory job. You have noted, for example, that she is spending much more time socializing with her employees, especially during work breaks and lunch periods. You have also noted that she frequently has one of her employees at her desk deeply involved in a discussion. From casual remarks, you have learned that Geraldine is socializing with some of her employees after hours. Your concern is that Geraldine will not be able to develop and maintain a true supervisory relationship with her employees, nor will she be able to generate helpful relationships with other supervisors in the organization with whom she comes in contact. Geraldine is your first black female supervisor and you are anxious to see her succeed.

1. Do you think there is a problem here? Why?
2. Would the sex of Geraldine's employees make any difference? Why?
3. What, if anything, should you do to help Geraldine succeed? Why?

As the supervisor of the nursing unit of a small local hospital, you are experiencing problems with one or two of your registered nurses (RNs). Your licensed practical nurses (LPNs) are complaining that the RNs are not doing their fair share of "undesirable" work like bathing patients, emptying bed pans, etc. The RNs, on the other hand, complain that the LPNs sass the RNs, talk back, and never willingly do the work assigned to them by the RNs. One of the LPNs has accused a male RN of making "inappropriate remarks" to her—remarks that could be interpreted as sexual harassment.

1. What steps should you take to get to the bottom of the problem—to find out what the truth is and what is causing the discontent?
2. Which problem should you tackle first, the one dealing with "undesirable work" or the one dealing with "inappropriate remarks"? Why?

13

HOW TO USE PLANNING TOOLS FOR BETTER MANAGEMENT

This chapter explains—

- What planning is
- Why you need to plan
- How to use planning tools

Like it or not, as a supervisor you will have to plan, and if you fail to plan—you plan to fail. It may be a plan for tomorrow's work, or next month's vacation, or next year's sales. It may involve one department, or it may involve the entire business. Whatever its scope, planning is a function performed by every manager.

When supervisors make plans for the future of their departments, they project a course of action for some future period of time. It may be a complex plan for the efficient utilization of equipment next month or a simple plan for staggering work hours. Whatever it is, the aim is to achieve coordinated action so that a desired goal can be reached with minimum disruption.

Just because you plan, of course, doesn't mean that something will come true. However, without planning, the probability is remote that you will achieve a goal other than by accident. Plans are rudders that guide us toward given objectives. For example, if we want each employee to sell $500 worth of merchandise each day, some plan has to be developed to help make this come true. Just wishing for it doesn't make it happen. And although planning won't make it happen either, it will increase your probability of success by as much as 80%.

WHAT IS PLANNING?

Planning is a managerial function that every supervisor uses every day. It's not something you put aside for a rainy day and pull out when you have nothing else to do. When you plan as a supervisor, you typically:

planning actions

1. Take a realistic look at the future.
2. Try to accurately anticipate problems that will occur.
3. Determine alternative ways to handle and solve these problems.
4. Weigh the advantages and disadvantages of each alternative to see which one is best.
5. Decide on which course of action you will follow.

Planning, then, consists of looking ahead, thinking about the future, anticipating what will probably happen, and determining what should be done in order to be ready for it.

IS PLANNING EASY?

planning and the supervisor's job

For a lot of supervisors, planning is difficult to get around to but not hard to do once they get started. Whereas a lot of supervisor's work is physical in nature, planning is mental work. Physical work is easier for most of us than mental work. Planning, therefore, falls in the category of being harder than most managerial tasks.

DO YOU NEED A PLAN FOR SIMPLE JOBS?

When you really think about it, you'll see that you have to plan for everything you do. When you get ready to do something—say, wash your car—you have to plan for it and act on the basis of *facts*, not on guesses. For example, you may not be able to wash the car whenever you choose because others may need to use the car. You will, therefore, have to find out when the car will not be needed for an hour. You also have to plan how you will wash it—whether you will use a hose or a bucket of water. By getting the facts, you find that your family will not need the car between 2:00 and 4:00 P.M., so you plan to hose it down then. Before you act, however, you have to get the facts about the availability of the hose, bucket, and water. The water is OK, you find, and you have a bucket; the hose, however, has a split in it. This means that you will have to change your plan about hosing the car down, and instead you will have to wash it with a sponge and a bucket of water.

For the complex job of running an entire department, you would need to have your goals clearly established and have plans made whereby you can achieve your goals. If you don't have plans, the probability of your reaching your goals is remote.

WHO IS RESPONSIBLE FOR PLANNING?

Every manager is responsible for planning: the chairman of the board, the president, the division manager, and the first-line supervisor. Not everyone is involved in the same sort of planning, however. The president and other top-level managers are involved in planning about where the company will be next year or five years hence. They plan long-range company strategy, whereas first-line supervisors plan about the daily, weekly, or monthly operations of their departments, about how they can supervise their employees best, and about what will have to be done to ship the special orders next week.

HOW FAR INTO THE FUTURE SHOULD YOU PLAN?

How far into the future you should plan will depend on your level in the organization. If you are a member of top management, your planning will be for at least five years into the future. This type of planning will be broader in scope and have a far greater impact on the total firm than short-range planning. Middle management will probably be involved in planning that is more operational in nature than that by top management. Also, it will not look as far into the future—maybe eighteen to twenty-six months.

First-line supervisors make plans for work to be done by their own departments. Most of these plans are on a weekly or monthly basis and seldom project further than six months into the future. What this means is that as a supervisor you must find some free time, usually early in the morning or late in the day, when you can look over what your department is responsible for in the future so that you can plan or size up what has to be done in order to reach these objectives. Occasionally, you will be asked to project or plan your activities for a year or so in advance so that overall plans can be made to assure an adequate supply of, say, labor or materials.

WHAT, IN A NUTSHELL, ARE THE ESSENTIALS OF GOOD PLANNING FOR A SUPERVISOR?

We all know that the future is uncertain, and as a consequence, we have to make plans. Before you plan, however, you have to predict or project what the future will be like. Most of us are fairly good at predicting what will happen in the near future—like this afternoon, tomorrow, or next week. But the further we try to predict in the future—like next year or three years from now—the poorer our predictions become. For this reason, the further we plan in the future, the less precise our plans can be. Two essentials for a supervisor's plans, therefore, are (1) you should not project your plans too far into the future, and (2) you should make them clear, easily understood, and concise.

Another essential for supervisory planning is that you should include allowances in your plans for any changes that might come up. You might, for example, plan to have a picnic in the park this afternoon and then have to change your plans because of rain. In other words, you need to make contingency plans in case something changes. A contingency plan for the picnic, for example, might be to hold the picnic in your recreation room in case of rain.

essentials of planning

Finally, supervisory planning calls for you to be precise about *what* is to be done, *when* it is to be done (today, tomorrow, next week), *where* it will be done (at the work place, in the stockroom), *how* it will be done (steps, processes involved, tools to use, etc.), and *who* will do it (list the employee by name).

As the supervisor, of course, you have to remain flexible because these plans may have to be changed as conditions change. An employee may be absent, a machine may break down, or raw material may not be available—all of which would mean a change in plans. But the important thing for you as the supervisor is that you have a plan—that you know what needs to be done and how you will do it. You have thought through the problems and have decided on how to handle them. A supervisor who plans his job carefully is seldom caught by surprise. And the supervisor who plans his job is the successful supervisor.

WHAT ADVANTAGES CAN A SUPERVISOR REASONABLY EXPECT FROM GOOD PLANNING?

When you as a supervisor give some thought to the future and make specific and concise plans about it, you will find that your employees' jobs are coordinated so that disruptions are minimized and schedules are more easily met. When plans are set forth on paper, you can spot areas where no one is responsible for the work or where two or more people are supposed to be doing the same thing. Thus, duplication or omission is avoided by having a plan. Inasmuch as the employees know what to do, they have a better mental outlook and feel that things are "under control," and consequently morale is better. By planning ahead, the best employee can be placed on the most difficult job—that is, the 16-cylinder man can be assigned to the 16-cylinder job and not to the 2-cylinder job.

rewards

Planning the work and then following the plan gives you better control over employees and costs. You know what your employees are or should be doing, and by utilizing their efforts most effectively, your operating costs will be kept at a minimum. Since you know what will be done in the future, you can take adequate steps to ensure that needed tools and materials are available to meet your requirements. And, finally, good planning should enable you to operate your department at a high level of quality and efficiency and at minimum cost.

MUST YOU PLAN?

Some supervisors say they don't plan when they actually do. They may not recognize it as planning, but they are always staying "one jump ahead." They are good enough to do this mentally; therefore they say they are not planning when they actually are.

Most of us aren't smart enough to keep it all in our heads. We have to put our plans down on paper so that we can study the plan, spot flaws, and make changes. If you want to be a good supervisor, therefore, you will need to plan.

CAN YOU SPOT SUPERVISORS WHO DON'T PLAN?

There are lots of "signals" that tell you supervisors are not planning their work. When delivery dates and schedules are missed, for example, or when some work gets overlooked, poor planning is usually the case. When you look around and find some employees not working and their equipment idle, poor planning is probably the cause. When employees are working at a slow pace, it is probably because they don't have anything else to do, and they are stretching out their work—again, the result of poor planning. Any time you see a supervisor in a "crash program" going around like the proverbial chicken with its head cut off, it's probably because little or no planning has been done.

"There are lots of signals that tell you supervisors are not planning their work."

DO PLANS EVER FAIL?

Plans often fail. Just because you plan doesn't mean that you will meet your goal. Lots of things can make plans go astray. Strikes at a supplier's plant might mean a delay in the receipt of materials. "Acts of God," such as floods, fire, and lightning, may cause delays. Having employees out sick or having key employees quit could throw a monkey wrench into your plans.

Or maybe the plan itself is poor and wouldn't work under any conditions. Some supervisors don't understand the fundamentals of planning, and although they've tried, their plans are inadequate.

Just because plans can fail, however, is no reason not to plan. Even with major catastrophes, the probability of reaching your goal is better under planned conditions because you know what has to be done and you know what should be done, who should do it, how it should be done, etc.

And you know all this because you had a plan that you were following. Now all you have to do is modify the plan in light of the inflicted change; you don't have to start from the beginning with no plan at all.

WHAT HAPPENS IF YOU DON'T PLAN?

If the situation is bad enough, you may lose your job. Certainly you will lessen your chances for promotion. If you can't plan and operate your own department, the chances that you could do well with a larger job are pretty poor. This is how your boss will see it, and promotions will probably not come your way.

poor operations

If you don't plan, your department will probably be one of the poor departments in the company, and consequently your employees will not take pride in their work. No one wants to be on a losing team, and good employees, therefore, might transfer. This means your department's record gets poorer, its costs go up, and you get pressured by top management to "get on the ball"—to increase production and lower costs. Harried and pressured, you start on the "fire-fighting" routine. The confusion that results, along with employee dissatisfaction, might cause an increase in accidents. And thus the snowball grows larger and larger—all because, as the supervisor, you would not or did not take a little time to think through your work and make some plans.

WHAT KINDS OF PLANS SHOULD A SUPERVISOR BE INVOLVED WITH?

As a supervisor you should be involved with every kind of plan that affects your department. Top management should ask you to participate in setting goals for your department, and you should make certain that they are realistic since you are in the best position to know the department's capabilities and potential.

plans that affect the department

You should also have a part in developing goals and plans affecting various operations in your department, such as a plan to reduce scrap by 3%, a plan to reduce employee absences by 10%, a plan to reduce employee turnover by 2%, a plan to reduce expenses by 15%, and so on. For each of these, you will need to determine how the goal will be reached and what your overall plan of attack will be.

In like manner, you should be involved with plans concerning the scheduling of work, the development and maintenance of a trained work force, the organization or reorganization of the people and work in your department, the systematic replacement of old equipment with new machines, and so on. In other words, as supervisor you should be a part of any plans that have anything to do with the work of your department. This is true whether the responsibility is yours or that of a specialized staff. In either case, you should be a party to the development of the plan and should have the opportunity to review, change, and finalize a plan involving the work and processes in your department.

WHAT PLANNING TOOLS CAN YOU USE?

Perhaps one of the simplest and easiest-to-use tools is the Gantt chart. First developed by Henry L. Gantt in the early 1900s, it was first widely used by supervisors during World War I to aid in planning and controlling operations in war materials plants.

On a piece of paper, you can easily construct a Gantt chart like that in Figure 13–1. List each activity you want to consider at the left side of the chart on one of the horizontal lines. Let the vertical columns represent any time interval (hours, days, etc.) you wish. Figure 13–1 shows a plan for painting a house. Note that the *plan* calls for the scraping and sanding to be completed by Tuesday noon. The *actual* time required to scrape and sand was all day Monday and Tuesday. As work starts and progresses, you fill in the *actual line* opposite the appropriate activity.

Gantt charts

You can use Gantt charts in a variety of ways. You could, for example, use one to plan and schedule a project through a plant, with departments or machines listed on the left. The scheduled (planned) time is shown opposite the appropriate department or machine. As work progresses, you draw a line representing the actual time taken opposite the appropriate activity to show the status of the job. As you can see, when you make a Gantt chart,

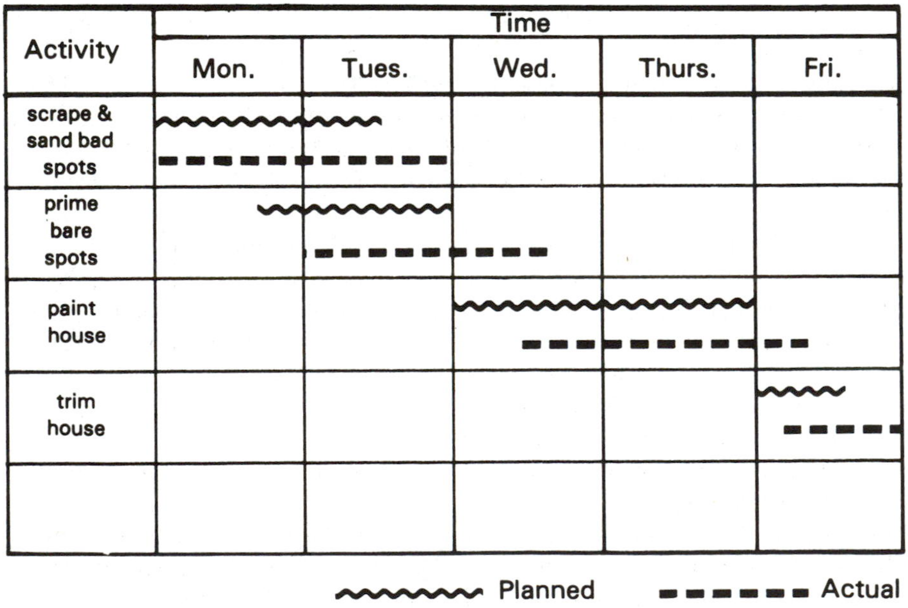

Activity	Time				
	Mon.	Tues.	Wed.	Thurs.	Fri.
scrape & sand bad spots					
prime bare spots					
paint house					
trim house					

〜〜〜〜〜 Planned   ▬ ▬ ▬ ▬ ▬ Actual

FIGURE 13–1
Gantt chart for painting a house.

you (1) plan what needs to be done (the activities), (2) show when each segment of the job should start, and (3) determine when the overall project should be completed. Then, as time passes, you add your "actual" lines to show how your plan is progressing, how actual operations compare with what you planned, and whether you are ahead or behind schedule. In this way, your chart serves as both a planning tool and a control tool.

HOW CAN BREAKEVEN CHARTS BE USED?

The breakeven chart is another tool that will help you plan. It can show you the probable outcome of a course of action and thus allow you to proceed with your original plan or change it to meet new eventualities.

Suppose you plan to produce a new type of loaf bread in your bakery. Your best cost estimates show the following:

Estimated sales of new loaf		$9,000.00
Cost of producing 10,000 new loaves	$5,000	
Cost of selling new product	900	
Overhead expenses	1,600	
Total expenses		7,500.00
Estimated net profit		$1,500.00

From these figures, you can easily construct the breakeven chart shown in Figure 13–2.

First, you draw your sales revenue line starting at zero (no sales, no revenue) and run the line through the point above 10,000 loaves on the horizontal scale and opposite $9000 on the vertical (dollar) scale.

Next, draw your fixed-cost line. As your cost estimates show, your fixed costs are $1600. Regardless of how many of these new loaves you bake, your fixed costs remain constant. Therefore, you draw this line parallel to the bottom of the chart starting at the $1600 point on the vertical scale.

Finally, you draw your total cost line. If you don't produce any of this new bread, you still have an overhead expense or fixed cost of $1600; therefore, you start your total-cost line at $1600 on the vertical scale. Your total expenses for baking 10,000 loaves of new bread are estimated to be $7500; therefore, you draw the total-cost line from the starting point ($1600) through a point above 10,000 loaves and opposite $7500.

breakeven analysis

You are now ready to "read" your breakeven chart. It shows you that you will break even (no profit, no loss) if you can sell approximately 5150 loaves of the new bread. If you sell over 5150 loaves, you will make money. For example, sales of 12,000 loaves would give you $2000 in profits. You can make other assumptions about costs and chart them. Suppose, for example, that the price of flour goes up 25%. You could increase your manufacturing cost appropriately, draw a new total-cost line, and then read the effect this price increase would have on your breakeven point and what the profit would be at various levels of output.

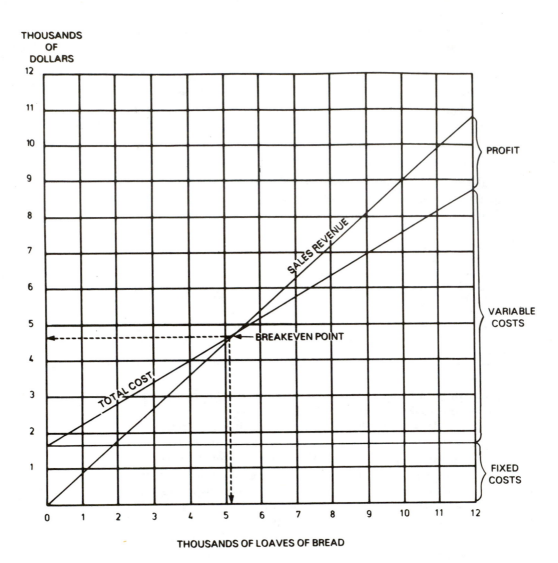

FIGURE 13-2
Breakeven chart for producing a new type of loaf bread.

You can also figure your breakeven point mathematically. Using the above figures for bread, you can figure the breakeven point as follows:

$$\text{BE Point} = \frac{\text{FC}}{1 - \dfrac{\text{VC}}{\text{Revenue}}}$$

$$\text{BE Point} = \frac{\$1600}{1 - \dfrac{\$5900}{\$9000}}$$

$$\text{BE Point} = \frac{\$1600}{1 - .65555}$$

$$\text{BE Point} = \frac{\$1600}{.3444}$$

$$\text{BE Point} = \$4645$$

Or in terms of loaves of bread, the breakeven point would be $4645 ÷ $.90 = 5161 loaves of bread. The 90¢, of course, is the selling price for a loaf of bread—$9000 divided by 10,000 loaves.

HOW CAN PERT BE USED?

You can also use the Program Evaluation and Review Technique, commonly known as *PERT*, to help you plan. PERT is basically an adaptation of network theory. A network is a detailed "picture" of what should happen in order to complete a project or job. A network of a young man getting a date, for example, might look like:

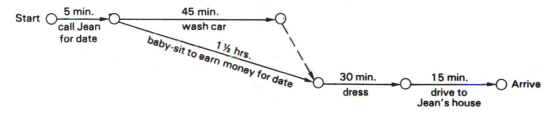

The overall time from start to finish is two hours and twenty minutes, and two acts were performed simultaneously: washing the car and babysitting. As you can see, this network for a date is a schematic model giving a picture of what must be achieved, the interrelationship of the various parts, a mathematical aspect (time), and an idea of some of the problems involved. As a supervisor, you can likewise construct a network showing an overall plan for a particular project, clearly indicating the events that must take place before the end objective is reached. In this way you get a clear, easily understood description of the total operation. It shows you why some events must follow others, why a particular event cannot be done now, why the total operation takes so long, and so on.

network theory

WHERE CAN YOU USE PERT?[1]

PERT is not the type of planning used in highly repetitive manufacturing. It is, instead, of major value in one-of-a-kind projects. In many departments today, special projects developed through research need overall planning

[1] The following sections on PERT were adapted from Claude S. George, *Management for Business and Industry* (Englewood Cliffs, N.J.: Prentice-Hall, Inc., 1970), pp. 603–8.

and control. PERT is of real value in those cases for planning the initial set-up for manufacturing a product.

When using PERT, you first identify all tasks that make up a project. This means that *every* job must be visualized in a manner clear enough to be incorporated in a network similar to the one shown above. Obviously, this forces clear thinking, a penetrating analysis, and a detailed breakdown of each job involved in a project. This "in-advance" analysis and thinking is in itself of major value to good planning. It forces you to consider all facets of a project or product and make plans to integrate the various parts into a meaningful whole.

*steps in using
PERT*

Second, construct a network with each job logically related to all other jobs. Be sure that jobs that can be performed concurrently are so indicated and that you do not consider a job completed until all jobs preceding it in the network are completed.

Third, make time estimates for each job in the network, showing (1) the most optimistic time that would be required if everything worked perfectly; (2) the most likely time that will be required to perform the job; and (3) the most pessimistic time that would be required if everything that might logically go wrong does.

Fourth, calculate a critical path through the network. This critical path is the overall time it will take to complete the project. It is the longest path in time through the network.

Fifth, as the project progresses, compare the actual performance on the project to the estimates of times shown on the network. This constant review provides you with control.

Made up of the above five steps, PERT is simple in theory. In application, however, it is fairly complex but can effectively be applied with a little effort. In developing a network for a project, an *event* is represented by a circle. An event takes no time and represents no work; however, it does signify that something has occurred. The completion of the typing of a letter would be classified as an event. The actual typing of the letter would be an activity. An *activity* like typing a letter involves time and labor. An activity is represented in a PERT network by an arrow and connects two events. Figure 13–3 shows a schematic of a network incorporating these concepts.

In this PERT diagram, no work can be started on any other event until event B has occurred. After completion of event B, work can be started on the activities following event B leading to events S, R, C, and D. Note that event C cannot occur until events A, B, S, and R have occurred, and so on.

*constructing a
PERT diagram*

After a network of the project has been established, your next step is to assign time values to each of the activities linking the events. You need to know, for example, how long it will take to perform the activity leading from event A to event B, the time from B to C, and so on. These time values for projects can be estimated by those individuals most familiar with them. If the activity between events A and B, for example, were concerned with the development of blueprints for a building, then the architect would be the one to estimate the time that would be required for this activity. If the

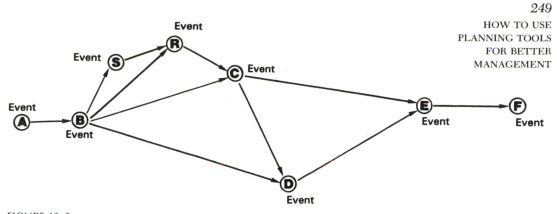

FIGURE 13–3
Schematic of a PERT network.

activity between events B and C were concerned with purchasing materials for the building, then you would turn to the purchasing agent as the person best qualified to give you the time that would be required to perform the activity. And so on it would go throughout the network.

Three time values are estimated by these people for each of their particular activities:

1. The shortest time it could possibly take to perform the activity—the most optimistic time estimate.
2. The time it will probably take to perform the activity—the most likely time.
3. The longest probable time that it will take—the most pessimistic time.

These three time estimates for each activity are usually given in weeks, but any appropriate unit of time can be used. Once determined, these time values for each activity can be added to your chart in Figure 13–3 above the line for the activity involved. It is much simpler, however, to work with only one time value on the chart rather than three. In PERT, therefore, a time value is chosen that appears to be representative of these three times. The most likely time could, of course, be chosen. However, rather than use the most likely time, it has been found that an *expected time* can be calculated using the three time estimates previously discussed. This PERT *expected time* is the time that divides the range of probable times in half. Thus, there is a 50–50 chance that the actual time will equal or exceed the expected time. The formula for calculating the expected time is

$$T_e = \frac{B + 4M + P}{6}$$

where

$$T_e = \text{expected time}$$
$$B = \text{best or most optimistic time}$$
$$M = \text{most likely time}$$
$$P = \text{most pessimistic time}$$

Thus, if $B = 4$ weeks, $M = 6$ weeks, and $P = 10$ weeks, then the expected time for the activity in question would be

$$T_e = \frac{4 + 4(6) + 10}{6}$$
$$T_e = 6\frac{1}{3} \text{ weeks}$$

By using this formula and calculating expected times for each event, the network is considerably simplified inasmuch as one time rather than three is used.

When you have calculated expected time values for each activity and recorded them above the activity line, your chart will appear as in Figure 13–4.

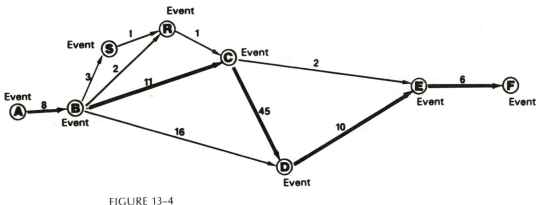

FIGURE 13–4
Completed PERT diagram.

WHAT IS A CRITICAL PATH?

You are now in a position to determine the critical path. The critical path in a network is that sequence of interconnected events and activities which will require the greatest amount of time between the start and completion of the network. In other words, the critical path is the longest "time path" through the network, using the expected time values for each activity as a guide. In the above chart, the longest time path and therefore the critical path is indicated by heavy lines, and requires 80 weeks to complete (8 + 11

determining critical path

+ 45 + 10 + 6 = 80). This is called the critical path because any delay in completing the activities along this path will delay the completion of the project. Some of the other activities not on the critical path, however, often can be delayed a week or so without affecting the overall time of the project. In other words, these activities have excess or slack time in their schedule.

WHAT DOES SLACK TIME TELL YOU?

After the critical path, probably the second most valuable computation to you in the PERT technique is the determination of slack times for activities. Slack time is the maximum delay that you can tolerate in performing an activity and still not delay the completion of the overall project. It is the difference between the expected time value for an activity and its latest allowable time. Inasmuch as the overall completion date is determined by adding the expected time values along the critical path, it follows that only activities off the critical path can have slack time.

Slack time for an event can be calculated by adding the total expected time from the beginning of the network to the event under consideration, and subtracting this from the latest allowable time that will not affect the critical path event times.

Using the above network as an example, you can determine the latest allowable time for event R as follows. You see that event R must be completed one week before event C because the activity leading from R to C requires one week to perform. You also know that event C must be completed 19 weeks (8 + 11 along the critical path) after the beginning of the project. This tells you that the latest allowable time for the completion of event R is 18 weeks, or one week before the necessary completion of event C. Eighteen weeks, therefore, is the latest allowable time for event R. However, by totaling the expected time values from the beginning of the project to event R, we see that it will be complete in 12 weeks (8 + 3 + 1 = 12). This means that if everything goes according to schedule, event R will be ready or will have happened at the end of the 12th week after the beginning of the project, or 6 weeks ahead of time. This excess time is called slack time. When excessive amounts of slack time are found in a network, this tells you that you have assigned too many resources (men and women, materials, and machines) to perform these jobs—that these jobs or activities will be completed too far in advance of their required date. In the illustration, for example, excessive amounts of men and women and materials have been assigned to achieving event R, so much so, in fact, that it will be completed 6 weeks ahead of time. Under such conditions, you should look at the possibility of transferring some of these resources to perform more critical activities, perhaps those along the critical path, thereby decreasing the overall time required for the project. Not only would such shifts serve to reduce the overall project time, they would also result in a better balance and use of resources among several alternatives. Good planning!

IF PLANNING IS SO IMPORTANT, WHY DON'T MORE SUPERVISORS PLAN THEIR WORK?

Most supervisors are in a tough spot, serving as a buffer between top management and the employees. They are constantly called on to justify the actions of employees to management and top management's actions to their employees. Many supervisors, therefore, simply state that they don't plan because they don't have time to do it. And the supervisor who "doesn't have time to plan" is usually the one who needs it the most.

lack of understanding

When supervisors cite time as the reason they are not involved in planning, they're usually too busy putting out "brush fires" to develop an overall plan of "fire prevention." Or they may say that there are so many physical demands on their time that they don't have time for the mental work involved in planning. Both of these excuses point to the need for planning. Time spent in planning pays off in preventing the "brush fire" emergencies, thus cutting down on physical work and leaving time for the equally important but less pressing mental work.

Some supervisors don't plan because they have never had any instruction in planning, have never thought about it, and don't have the foggiest notion about how they should go about it. This may be an excuse for today, but not for tomorrow. Every supervisor can avail himself of help, either from experts in the company, from evening courses, from individual study, or from talking and working with supervisors in other companies who are involved in planning.

Remember: if you fail to plan—you plan to fail.

QUESTIONS FOR DISCUSSION AND REVIEW

1. Why do we need to plan?
2. What is planning? Is it hard to do?
3. What type of jobs do you need to plan for? Why?
4. Who is responsible for planning?
5. How far into the future should you plan?
6. What are the essentials of supervisory planning?
7. What are the advantages of supervisory planning?
8. How can you spot a supervisor who doesn't plan?
9. What kinds of planning should a supervisor do?
10. Explain how a Gantt chart is a planning tool.
11. How do you use breakeven charts?
12. What is PERT? Explain how it is used.

A Case Study
ALLEN MANUFACTURING COMPANY

The Allen Manufacturing Company, located in South Plains, manufactures and distributes small electric tools such as hand-held electric drills, light drill presses, hedge clippers, sanding machines, buffers, etc.

The company is well established and has operated at 80% of its capacity since 1974. Sales last year amounted to $1,000,000, but gross profits were only $100,000. When Mr. Allen, the president and owner, began checking into the cause of this rather low gross profit, he found that the manufacturing and distributing costs had increased. He found, for example, that labor costs last year had risen to $500,000 and that the costs of raw materials had increased to $300,000.

At the next staff meeting, Mr. Allen presented this problem of dwindling profits to his staff and asked for their recommendations. The Chief of Manufacturing suggested that the trouble was that the products were priced too low, and suggested, therefore, that an across-the-board price increase of 25% would place the company back in a sounder profit position. The Sales Manager, however, objected to the rosy picture painted by the Chief of Manufacturing, and indicated that a 25% price increase would surely reduce sales. The Chief of Manufacturing regretfully agreed with the Sales Manager, and the two of them estimated that the proposed price increase would reduce the utilization of plant capacity by 10%.

The Chief Engineer, on the other hand, indicated that he did not think it would be wise to attempt any price increase at this time. Instead, he proposed to make some improvements in the old operating equipment, purchase some new labor-saving machinery, and incorporate processing changes. In fact, he estimated that with an increase in fixed costs of $100,000, he could reduce labor and material costs by 25%.

Mr. Allen pondered the two proposals: one to increase prices and suffer a reduction in volume; the other to purchase new equipment, thereby increasing fixed costs but reducing out-of-pocket expenses.

1. How would you go about making a decision in this case?
2. What action would you suggest that Mr. Allen take? Why?

A Case Study
BEAMON PLATING COMPANY

The Beamon Plating Company specialized in cleaning and plating all types of small metal objects. Its service was good, its prices were reasonable, and its work was guaranteed. As a result, it enjoyed a healthy business—mostly from industrial concerns located within a 500-mile radius. Some of its work, however, consisted of silver-plating and gold-plating objects of art as well as silver services and the like.

Several hazards exist in any plating shop, and due precautions must be taken. Fumes from the plating tanks, for example, are very dangerous and can cause sickness, and even death, from prolonged exposure. To preclude such a mishap, the management of Beamon Plating installed one of the most efficient air exhaust systems obtainable. In fact, air purity tests showed that the air in the plating room contained less toxic gases than air elsewhere in the plant. In addition, three emergency showerheads were installed beside the plating tanks. In case an employee spilled acid on himself, he quickly stepped under the closest shower and pulled a chain. This automatically opened a valve sending a full-force shower over him, thus dissipating the effects of the acid. The company also furnished all its plating room employees with special uniforms, rubber boots, rubber aprons, and rubber gloves. These protected the employees from the plating fluids and acids.

Chemicals used in the plating tanks were purchased in 50-gallon drums, and acids came in large glass containers called *carboys*. Both the acids and the chemicals in drums were stored under a shed which was 150 feet from the main building. Other less bulky items such as cadmium balls, soda ash, etc., were stored in a small storeroom in the plant. When material from either of these storerooms was needed, any one of the employees who wasn't busy at the time was sent to get the material. If it was not too heavy, the employee usually carried it by hand. If it was heavy or bulky, the employee could choose one of the several handtrucks that were always available. Occasionally, the material fell off and spilled on the floor. In several instances, an employee dropped material on his feet, causing a lost-time accident. Some of the workers complained of straining their backs from lifting, but this could not be positively linked to lifting the material for the plating shop.

Despite all the precautions and the provision of protective equipment, the company had some trouble in the plating room. Several of the employees almost refused to wear the rubber boots and aprons provided by the company. In fact, they removed them quite frequently, claiming they were bulky, hot, and uncomfortable. Management realized that this was a dangerous practice, but if the employees would not wear the safety equipment, management admitted it did not know what to do about the situation.

Several accidents of a minor nature occurred recently. For example, one of the women who wired parts to racks so that they could be individually plated, stuck one of the sharp parts into her finger. This would not have happened if she had been wearing the gloves furnished by the company.

Although this may be looked upon as a minor item, the Beamon Plating Company does not want its employees to forget that serious injuries can occur. It also wants them to realize that the company is trying to provide maximum protection for its workers during their workday.

1. What do you think of the safety program of the Beamon Plating Company?
2. What changes, if any, would you recommend? Explain why.

A Case Study
DEPARTMENTAL UPDATE

Walking back to his automobile, Bill Thomas was elated over how the annual company meeting had turned out. He had asked for funds to update his department, but no specific amount was mentioned in his request, nor were specific changes recommended. As he explained to the Board, his divison had consistently been one of the most profitable in the company year after

254

year, but it was now at the point where it needed to be refurbished and reworked if they expected these same results in the future. Based on his past success, and having confidence in his ability, the Board, after much discussion, voted to allocate $16 million to his division for a new addition to the building and for updating his equipment and layout.

There was, however, one hitch. Before the Board would release any of the money, they wanted to see a detailed plan on what Bill planned to do.

1. How would you advise Bill Thomas to proceed?
2. What planning tools do you think he should employ? Why?

A Personal Case Study

In a bull session with other supervisors yesterday, the topic of planning was discussed. One supervisor said he never planned and that in his opinion it was a waste of time for first-line supervisors to go through the motions of planning so that their department would look good on paper. The supervisor then turned to you and said, "Don't you agree with me?"

1. How would you reply? Would you agree that planning is to some degree a waste of time?
2. What advantages to planning would you point out?
3. Would you try to convince the supervisor that he was wrong? How?

14

HOW TO USE MANAGEMENT BY OBJECTIVES

This chapter explains—

- How MBO works
- How you can use it
- What benefits you can expect from it

If you've ever tried to push a piece of string, you know it is almost impossible. But moving a piece of string by pulling it is easy.

Your employees are like this, too. You can get only so far by pushing them. But you can make great progress if you lead them to a way to reach a goal or objective. A technique for doing this is called *Management By Objectives*—MBO for short. It works well and has found ready acceptance in many business organizations.

WHAT IS MBO?

MBO is the process through which supervisors and employees jointly establish work goals to be accomplished within a given time period. It has two aspects. MBO is (1) an attitude or belief about how to set objectives or goals, and (2) a tool of supervision.

MBO is an attitude inasmuch as the supervisor and the employee believe that *together they should determine goals* to be achieved by the employee. This is in contrast to the usual work situation, where the employee has no part in setting a work goal. Instead, the supervisor typically tells the employee what objective has been set for the employee to reach.

MBO is also a tool of supervision inasmuch as *specific objectives* are set which are to be accomplished within a *certain time* with the *employees being held directly responsible* for accomplishing the objectives. When using MBO, for example, a supervisor might explain to a typist that the supervisor's departmental goal is to reduce departmental expenses by 3% during the next quarter, and then ask the typist if she would help him meet that goal. The two of them then discuss ways in which the typist could help meet the departmental goal of a 3% reduction in expenses. The typist *setting* might, for example, suggest that she could set as her personal goal the typ*employee* ing of 76 letters per day. If the two of them agree that this would be a good *objectives* objective, then it is set up as the typist's goal. In similar fashion, objectives would be set for other employees in the department, with all of them contributing to reducing the department's expenses by 3%.

As you can see, the supervisor and the employee *together* have agreed upon:

1. A specific, measurable goal.
2. A time period within which the goal is to be accomplished.

WHY DOES MBO WORK?

MBO has several features that almost all employees like. Most employees, for example, like to have a part in determining what they will do. They like to voice their opinions and be a part of the process. They like to suggest changes they think are appropriate. MBO allows them to do these things. And when an agreement is finally reached, they feel good about it because they had a part in it. As a consequence, they agree to do it. They commit themselves, and having done this, they strive to keep their word. This is what appeals to the employees—what makes MBO work. Instead of being told what to do, *the employees participate in establishing personal work objectives.*

*employee
participation
and
responsibility*

Another appealing feature of MBO is that the employee, such as the typist, can reach the objective by her own initiative and work. She alone is responsible for accomplishing the agreed-upon goal. If she consistently reaches her daily goal of 76 letters, then she will be rewarded for her success by a promotion or a pay increase. If she fails, she would not be surprised by demotion. Thus, the employee's progress and success is in her own hands. She isn't dependent upon someone else.

Finally, MBO works because employees are brought into the decision-making picture. By participating, they belong—and morale is improved. They are made a part of the team that determines what needs to be done, how it will be done, when it will be done, and who will do it.

ARE OBJECTIVES EVER CHANGED?

Objectives are quite often changed. In fact, for new projects it is not unusual for employees and supervisors to be so enthusiastic about possibilities, that overly ambitious goals and procedures are agreed upon. Later, when they attempt to put them into practice, they might find that resources and specifications were not as generous as they thought they would be. When this happens, the supervisor and the employee get together to take another, more realistic look at the job and the goals. *Together,* they decide upon a new specific objective with perhaps a new time frame within which the objective is supposed to be met.

Objectives that have been in effect a long time are also changed when work conditions, processes, materials, etc., make changes necessary.

IS MBO FOR EVERYBODY?

MBO can be used virtually everywhere that objectives can be measured. The president of an organization can use it to set objectives for the supervisors who report to him. They, in turn, can use it for their subordinates. And virtually every supervisor can use it with his employees where measurable objectives can be agreed upon. It can be applied in almost any type of organization—business, religious, social, etc. It can be used in virtually every work situation where specific, measurable goals can be established.

Although MBO can be applied in most organizations, there are times when it won't work well and you'd be wise to postpone its use. For example, if your company is about to make some major organizational change such as a change in products manufactured, a merger with another firm, or a move to a different location, don't try to apply MBO. Under these conditions your employees will be more concerned with what their new jobs will be, or perhaps with keeping their jobs, than they will be about generating enthusiasm for some new program that you want to introduce. Likewise, if your organization is heavily involved in, say, a unionization move, or if there is unrest caused by political infighting, then the introduction of MBO should be put off until the organizational climate is calm and clear. And, of course, MBO should not be attempted if the firm's managers do not fully support the MBO concept of employee participation in the establishment of work goals.

CAN MBO BE EASILY APPLIED?

MBO can be as structured or as informal as you wish. The more structured it is, the more involved is its conception and installation. In some organizations, MBO is a highly structured approach with precise formats for establishing goals, precise review schedules, and precise review techniques.

At the other extreme, MBO can be as informal as "we just get together and decide what needs to be done and who will do it." Some supervisors think this approach may be a little too relaxed. Most companies have found that MBO applications work best when goals and review sessions are held on a regular and somewhat formal basis.

IS MBO WORTH A SUPERVISOR'S TIME?

Without question, MBO is worth the time spent on it. In fact, the more time you spend on MBO, the better it usually works. If you devote time to it and work hard at it, you'll find your employees will be more satisfied with it. Along with this you'll also note an improved relationship developing between you and your employees, with greater success in reaching specified goals. In addition, the more your employee works with you, and the more improved your relationship becomes, the greater will be the employee's satisfaction with you and your supervisory style. And the more satisfied an employee is with you as a supervisor, the more satisfied the employee is apt to be with the MBO process. This all adds up to improved employee satisfaction, improved morale, and a well-run department for you—*if you make it work*. For it to be successful, however, you as the supervisor must feel that MBO is important to you and your employees. And you must give it adequate (but not excessive) time and energy to keep it going.

Some supervisors simply don't want to change their way of doing things. They have always done something in a certain way, and they resist the work and trouble involved in writing down goals, keeping records, etc. They feel that MBO is just a new idea to take up an unreasonable amount of their time without proportionate results.

Some supervisors resist MBO because they feel they are losing some of their managerial authority. What these supervisors don't seem to understand is that their goal should be to have a smooth-running department and produce a good or service at minimum costs. Instead, they seem to see their personal goal as that of playing the big shot in the department—of being the one who tells everyone what to do. This same supervisor typically sees his employees as being incapable of making decisions about their jobs and objectives.

Of course, some employees and supervisors don't like the thought of their work being measured and reviewed. As a consequence, they resist MBO. Some supervisors, too, dislike facing employees periodically to discuss with them how their work is progressing—pointing out failures or shortcomings. Inasmuch as this review is unpleasant to many supervisors, they resist MBO, knowing that the employee review is an integral part of it.

WHAT KIND OF EMPLOYEE OBJECTIVES DO YOU SET?

Every objective should be so clearly and simply stated that the employee easily understands it. It should be concise, clear, and specific. In addition, the objective should be capable of being measured. A poor objective, for example, would be to "reduce defects in your work to a minimum." This objective is poor because the goal is not clear or specific, and you would never know whether or not your employee had reached the goal. For example, if an employee had ten parts rejected because of defects, is this bad? Did the employee reach the goal? Or suppose ten parts were rejected because they would not function properly. Is this worse? Did the employee reach the goal? If the number of rejects were reduced to five, did the employee reach the goal? There is no way to know the answer to these questions because the goal is not specific. It doesn't tell you what a "minimum number of defects" is.

If, instead, the goal stated for your employee is to "reduce the number of parts rejected because of flaws in the finish to 1% and the number of functional rejects to 3% of daily output," then you could answer the questions. You have an objective that is clear, concise, and capable of being measured.

In addition to the above, you should also remember the following when you are formulating an objective:

1. Make the objective reasonable—one that can be met.
2. Make the objective stretch the employee's ability.
3. Be sure the objective incorporates the employee's ideas and suggestions.
4. Be sure that the objective is one that the employee regards as fair.
5. Make the objective mesh with the resources you have available.

HOW IS AN EMPLOYEE'S PERFORMANCE REVIEWED?

The employee and the supervisor *together* review the employee's progress at specified intervals. Every month, for example, the supervisor might review the typist's performance in relation to the agreed upon goal. If performance is below the specified objective, the *two of them* would discuss it and explore any problems that may have arisen and determine what can be done to help her meet the goal. Or the employee might see ways to improve the process, and thereby change the objective of 76 letters per day. These improvements, like any problems discovered, would be considered by both the employee and the supervisor; and changes, if needed, would be agreed upon.

Review sessions are good in that they make both the employee and the supervisor aware of progress that could be made, of changes that should be made, or of adjustments that need to be made. And, of course, if the system is working fine, then this is pointed out in the review session.

HOW DO YOU CONDUCT A PERFORMANCE REVIEW?

Set a specific time and place to meet with your employee. Be sure the location will provide privacy and no interruptions. Prepare yourself by reviewing the employee's performance and the agreed-upon objectives.

When the employee arrives, put her at ease. The atmosphere of this session should be the same as that in talking with the employee to establish her objective. In each instance you are trying to help your employee understand the problem and reach agreed-upon goals. You should, therefore, indicate that you want to support and help your employee—not serve as her judge and jury. *Both of you have a mutual interest in the goals and how well they have been achieved.* Be sure, therefore, that your employee understands this mutual interest.

Try to get your employee to talk about her successes and failures. Listen attentively. Don't interrupt. But from time to time, attempt to summarize what your employee has said so that both of you understand what is developing from the conversation. Don't criticize or berate the employee for failure. Instead, view it as a problem that both of you need to discuss so that the two of you can find a solution. Be sure to give praise when it is deserved. And above all, be as factual and honest as you can in your answers to your employee's questions.

When you've discussed every angle, you and your employee should then develop a plan of action. This would be an agreement as to what you will do, as well as what your employee will do, to help her make progress towards achieving the agreed-upon objective. Be sure that you as the supervisor don't impose your will or thoughts on your employee. Make your discussion open, permissive, and mutual in its approach to analyzing the problem and determining what both of you will do to resolve it.

WHAT BENEFITS CAN YOU EXPECT FROM MBO?

Many supervisors report the following benefits from using MBO:

1. When using MBO, your employees are more self-motivated.
2. With MBO, goals are more frequently met.
3. MBO makes for better employee cooperation, thereby enabling you to more easily direct your employees' efforts.
4. MBO improves communication between you and your employees.
5. MBO gives you a tool for more effective supervision.
6. MBO gives your employees an incentive for improving their job performance.
7. MBO gives your employees a clear picture of what is expected of them.
8. MBO channels employee activity towards corporate goals.
9. MBO forces you to make plans—if you haven't made any. It also helps you formulate plans and overall goals.
10. MBO makes for a more effective utilization of your resources—both employees and facilities.
11. MBO reduces costs and enhances profits.
12. MBO helps minimize employee misunderstandings and conflicts.

DOES MBO HAVE ANY DRAWBACKS?

You'll find the following drawbacks in some MBO applications:

1. The supervisor uses MBO to pressure his employee to produce. Mutual agreement on goals and growth is ignored.
2. Depending on the installation, you may have an excessive amount of paper work to do.

3. Measuring performance is difficult in such areas as personnel development, interpersonal relations, etc.

4. Rapid technological changes and organizational instability increase the problems of implementing MBO.

5. Failure to update changes, complete forms, and process information results in employee dissatisfaction and disillusionment.

6. Some employees dislike, and therefore hesitate, to formally commit themselves to any specific goal. When they do so, under these conditions it is not done enthusiastically.

7. Poor supervisory administration and interviews result in lack of accurate feedback to employees.

8. Unless MBO is carefully discussed and administered, there can be a lack of awareness on the supervisor's as well as the employee's part as to the philosophy behind and value of MBO, thereby causing ineffectiveness.

9. Mutual goal setting may degenerate into a unilateral approach—the supervisor tells and the employee listens.

10. Goals may be established poorly, due to lack of understanding by the employee and supervisor as to how the goals should be set.

ARE THERE ANY PITFALLS TO WATCH FOR?

Organizational climate is critical for establishing an MBO program. In fact, experience has shown that MBO is most effective in those applications in which the supervisors and employees believe in and support the program. If these two ingredients are lacking, you should be on guard. In fact, if the supervisor and employees have in any way expressed lack of support, MBO is practically doomed to failure.

On the other hand, the more positive the attitudes toward MBO, the more effective the program will be, and the more enthusiastic will be the support.

MBO is most easily applied and is most typically effective where productivity can be easily seen and measured. On the other hand, when you have to use value judgments to measure an employee's accomplishments, this opens the door for disagreements and disputes. If, for example, you are trying to evaluate a research scientist's efforts, how do you do it? It probably would not be fair to say that the scientist didn't produce any measurable results. Or, if you said that the scientist's efforts were fair, good, excellent, or superior—what do these value judgments mean? It's like saying someone is beautiful. Beauty has a different meaning in everyone's mind. And, likewise, value judgments vary from individual to individual. What one person would call excellent work might be labeled as good by another individual. The moral to all this is, Be wary of applying MBO where goals or objectives cannot be easily discerned and measured.

1. What is MBO? Explain.
2. Why does MBO work? Explain.
3. With MBO, are work goals ever changed? Why?
4. Can MBO be easily applied? How?
5. Does MBO take more time than it is worth? Why or why not?
6. Why do you find resistance to MBO?
7. Explain the importance of an employee's performance review.
8. How should you conduct a performance review?
9. What are the important parts to an employee's objective?
10. What benefits can you expect from using MBO? What problems?
11. When and where is it unwise to apply MBO? Explain.

A Case Study
YOUR OWN MBO

Write an outline on how you would proceed to incorporate MBO into an organization you are familiar with. This organization can be a civic club, the place where you work, or a group to which you belong—social, religious, or school.

Show how MBO could probably help the organization improve its ability to achieve its objectives. Be specific.

Read your outline to your group or class and ask for ways in which your approach could be improved.

A Case Study
BRANDIS WHOLESALE GROCERY

Brandis Wholesale Grocery celebrated its first 50 years of business in 1980. It is a well-established firm, with sales exceeding two million dollars annually.

The company operates in its own five-story building strategically located in the downtown area of Austin. In general, wholesale grocers are engaged in supplying retail grocers with non-perishable items such as canned goods, brooms, notebooks, pencils, and the like. This is the type of activity that Brandis is concerned with, and in performing this service, the company engages in the following physical activities.

Salesmen call on retail outlets, write up their requirements on order blanks, and, when they return to the plant each afternoon, give the orders to the warehouse foreman. The foreman distributes the orders among the "pickers," who "pick" or gather the material called for on the order. This is accomplished by pulling a platform truck around one of the floors and placing the required material on it. Then the truck with the material is taken to the next floor by an elevator, where additional material is gathered and placed on the truck. In similar fashion, the picker proceeds from floor to floor, pulling the platform truck and placing the material desired by the customer on it. If a customer's order cannot be contained on one platform truck, as is frequently the case, the picker takes the loaded truck down to the first floor shipping area, empties it, and returns with the empty truck to complete the selection process. When the picker has gathered the material for a customer, he takes it from the truck and places it on the floor in the shipping area. Later it is checked by the foreman, and the goods are loaded into trucks for delivery to the customer.

When material is received from a manufacturer to replenish the warehouse stock, it is carried to its appropriate location using the platform handtrucks and elevators as described.

About 24 employees are engaged in the picking process, and there are frequent delays because of cluttered aisle space and waiting for elevator service.

Recently the founder and president of the company retired because of ill health, and his position was taken over by his son. At the son's request, the company's accountant made up a profit analysis. This analysis showed that profits expressed as a percent of sales dollars had been decreasing even though sales had shown positive increases during the past three years. Upon investigating the cause, the president's son found that, in part, it was due to the fact that they had not increased wholesale prices in line with the increases in their costs of goods. He was convinced, however, that a major part of the cause stemmed from poor labor utilization, and suggested that MBO might be just the thing for the company.

1. Do you agree with the founder's son that MBO might be the answer to their problems? Why?
2. How would you go about installing MBO in the Brandis Wholesale Grocery Company?

A Personal Case Problem

Visit one of your local businesses such as a grocery store, supermarket, etc., and talk with the manager about how his or her employees' work performance is evaluated. Also, find out if any employee's pay is a function of how much is produced rather than the number of hours the employee works. Get permission from the manager to talk with the employees about what they are doing. Analyze the situation and see whether the work is suitable for the establishment of MBO. Report the problem to the class and get their opinions as to whether MBO could be installed and how they would go about installing and utilizing it.

Using your class's suggestions, develop a report covering an MBO installation that would be suitable for the concern. If the manager expressed an interest in seeing your final report, give him a copy and get his reactions. Report the final outcome to the class.

PART FOUR
GETTING THE JOB DONE

15

HOW ORGANIZATION HELPS YOU SUPERVISE

This chapter explains—

- How a typical company is organized
- What authority is and where it comes from
- How to make delegation work

If you stop to think about it, most of your life is spent in organizations like clubs, churches, schools, governments, and business firms. You work with all these organizations for only two reasons: (1) you can accomplish some objective through them that you could not accomplish as easily or as effectively by yourself, or (2) you can accomplish things in organizations that you could never do alone. The United States, for example, put a man on the moon through organized endeavor. California built the Golden Gate Bridge through organized endeavor. And, likewise, you can accomplish tasks more easily when you are organized because organization gives direction, coordination, and authority to human endeavor.

The company where you work, and how it is organized, is obviously important to you. You earn a living there and you typically spend 50% of your waking hours there. However, despite your involvement with this firm, you may not understand how it is organized, what its formal hierarchy is, and how all the parts fit into a working whole. Let's take a look, therefore, at (1) how a typical company is organized, (2) who its officers and managers are, and (3) how its jobs and departments are coordinated to produce the goods or services it sells.

First, let's look at the major corporate officers and managers.

IS A BOARD OF DIRECTORS NECESSARY?

A board of directors is not only necessary, it's required by law and represents the stockholders of the firm. As such, the board is the "supreme commander" in a modern corporation.

What Does the Board Do?   A board of directors appoints various corporate officers and fixes their wages. For example, the board usually appoints the president, vice-president, secretary, and treasurer. The board also establishes company policies. The board for a shirt manufacturing firm, for example, might decide that the company should make a shirt that is the finest in the world—even though it would cost the buyer $45.00. Or it might make a policy that the company should make the best shirt it can that would retail for less than $15.00.

board structure

The board sets general objectives for the firm, like aiming for a 10% return on investment or expanding operations to every one of the 50 states. After these policies and objectives are set by the board, it is up to management to carry them out. The board also reviews and approves or rejects plans and actions of the corporate officers. The president, for example, might propose building a new plant in Arizona. The board would either approve or disapprove of the president's proposal.

Who Makes Up the Board?   The board members may come from within the company, in which case it is known as an *inside board.* If the board members are not working for the company but are executives of other corporations, it is known as an *outside board.*

An inside board has the advantage of having members on it who know the workings of the firm and the technical aspects of its operations—individuals who are familiar with its problems. Its major drawback is that the members are all insiders and they don't bring outside, fresh points of view to bear on problems and policies of the firm.

Outside boards are considered to be more effective than inside boards because they bring a wide range of experience and ability to a company. However, a mixed board, consisting of both insiders and outsiders, is probably the best type of board because you get the best features of both. Most of the nation's leading companies have mixed boards with from 20 to 60% of the members coming from outside the company.

WHO ARE THE CORPORATE OFFICERS?

The president is the top boss, the overall manager of the company. He is supposed to operate the firm profitably (if it is a profit-making firm), within the guidelines and policies set by the board. Because of the comprehensive aspects of his job, he is given broad powers and authority by the board.

Some firms have a vice-president or executive vice-president who is second in command. He does whatever the president directs him to do, but his duties are usually similar to those of the president. Many times the responsibilities are divided between these two by having the president responsible for the long-range aspects of operating the firm, and the vice-president responsible for the short-range aspects.

"Does the treasurer keep
the company's money?"

A *secretary*'s duty is to transmit the policies and recommendations of the board to the company's corporate officers. To do this, the secretary attends all meetings of the board, keeps minutes of the meetings, maintains the corporate books, and handles all the board's correspondence. The secretary also has the job of issuing and transferring all stocks, bonds, and securities for the company.

Appointed by the board, the *treasurer* is responsible to the president for all financial activities of the corporation. He has the job of getting credit or borrowing money and then using it appropriately to finance the operation of the company. Because of his responsible position with money, the treasurer must be a person of proven financial and business ability. In large companies, he hires credit managers, cashiers, controllers, and security managers to help him in his work.

WHAT IS THE CONTROLLER'S FUNCTION?

The controller is the chief accountant, in a sense. He reports to the treasurer and is responsible for such activities as accounting, cost control, payroll, and financial analysis. To help him with his job, he usually hires accountants, auditors, and budgetary directors.

WHAT DO ACCOUNTANTS DO?

Management needs financial facts on which to make decisions, and *accountants* typically keep the records and supply management with the necessary facts. To get this information, the accounting organization works closely with production supervisors to gather labor cost figures, with the purchasing agents to get material cost figures, and with the sales organization to gather figures on sales revenues and costs.

In addition to getting these figures for management, accounting is also responsible for preparing figures for people outside the firm—figures such as reports to stockholders, reports for bankers and other creditors, and reports to the government for tax purposes.

ARE THERE OTHER TYPICAL MANAGERS?

As you will see in Chapter 16, the personnel director is charged with securing, training, and maintaining an adequate work force for the whole company. In single-plant firms, the personnel director usually reports to the plant manager. The purchasing agent is another manager you will often see. His job is to procure the necessary parts, tools, materials, and supplies from outside vendors. Like the personnel director, the purchasing agent (or director of purchasing) reports to the plant manager. An industrial engineer, also reporting to the plant manager, develops economical ways to do work. His job is not to get people to work faster, but to devise better ways to perform work using the same or less effort. He looks for better, easier ways to work and, in doing this, studies the motions an employee uses, the tools employed, the layout of the work area, the materials used, and the work process. The industrial engineer may also be called the methods engineer, motion and time study engineer, methods analyst, or methods and standards analyst. The production control manager, reporting to the plant superintendent, acts as the brain and nervous system of a firm and coordinates the work of engineering, purchasing, production, and sales. To do this, production control plans the work that needs to be done, determines when and where it should be done, and issues manufacturing orders to get the work accomplished. Production control also follows up on these plans, and where manufacturing is not proceeding according to plans, production control will make the adjustment necessary to get production back on the beam. Because of its broad coordinating responsibilities, production control is in close contact with practically every department and activity in a plant.

WHERE DOES THE SUPERVISOR FIT INTO THE ORGANIZATION?

First-line supervisors are individuals who are frequently caught between the proverbial "rock and a hard place." They are the middlemen who work with both labor and management. To the employees, they are "management." To the top managers, they are the low men on the managerial totem pole. They are, however, the key men in the organizational structure.

On their shoulders rests the responsibility for correctly and tactfully interpreting management's wishes to the workers. Because they work so closely with the employees, they are almost one of them, and, in some cases, they were one of them before their promotions. This may at times give them real problems with their loyalty. But because of this closeness, they are in the best position to correctly interpret the workers' feelings to top management. Being in this strategic position, first-line supervisors are the key persons in knitting both management and workers into a coordinated organization that works effectively and harmoniously to achieve its objectives.

*first-level
management*

DO YOU NEED AN ORGANIZATION CHART TO "SEE" AN ORGANIZATION?

An organization chart is the best way to clearly depict the structure we have just discussed. It is an attempt to "photograph" or picture how people are grouped, to tell who reports to whom, and to show the lines of authority and responsibility. It shows how the dynamic activities of enterprise are held together and are coordinated into a properly working unit.

Drawn correctly, an organization chart shows each person's assignment and its relation to other jobs. As a result, it helps avoid confusion and conflict that might arise because of an overlapping or haphazard arrangement of duties. When you try to depict a company's organizational structure on paper, you might see inconsistencies or problems and thus be able to solve them. The chart might, for example, point out an illogical grouping of personnel and marketing activities which, when recognized, can be corrected. Sometimes a chart points up the omission of an activity or function, thus allowing management to put it in the organization before serious problems result.

Although a chart doesn't make a firm have a good organization, companies that keep up-to-date charts generally have the best organizations. The reason for this, of course, is that the charts serve to keep the managers aware of the company's structure and thus afford them the opportunity of making changes and divisions when they appear needed.

An organization chart is a good way to help get a new employee oriented with the formal organizational structure of the company.

ARE THERE RULES FOR MAKING AN ORGANIZATION CHART?

Constructing an organization chart is not hard once management has determined what the general structure of the firm should be. Figure 15–1 illustrates the way most line and staff organizations are shown by a chart. Some good rules to follow in drawing an organization chart are:[1]

1. The vertical arrangement of functions, departments, and persons should be according to the grade or position in the company.
2. A rectangle should be used to indicate a unit or a person on a chart. Use straight vertical and horizontal lines to show the flow of authority.
3. Heavy black lines may be used to show the flow of line authority between any two positions.
4. Light lines may be used to show functional supervision.
5. Broken lines may be used to show the sources of advice and service.
6. Make the rectangles on the same level of equal size.
7. Place all rectangles for positions on the same authority level on the same horizontal line.
8. Normally, lines of authority enter each rectangle at the top center and leave at the bottom center. Lines of authority do not run through a rectangle.

[1] These rules are from Claude S. George, Jr., *Management for Business and Industry* (Englewood Cliffs, N.J.: Prentice-Hall, Inc., 1970), p. 36. Reprinted by permission of Prentice-Hall, Inc.

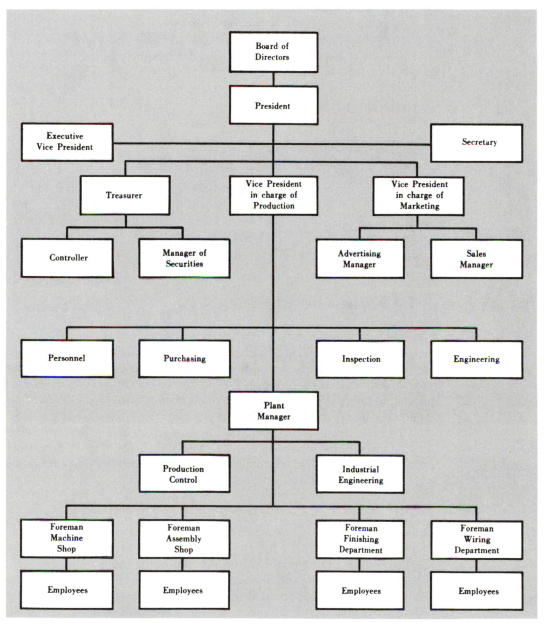

FIGURE 15–1
Organization chart illustrating a typical line and staff organization.

9. Rectangles for personnel are normally placed under the individual or unit that they serve, but above the line units in such a manner that they do not interrupt the lines of authority to line units.

10. If the chart centers around a person or unit, make the rectangle representing this person or unit the largest one on the chart. The rectangles above and below the key figure should be a smaller size. Rectangles on each lower level may be one size smaller.

11. On any individual chart, show at least one level above and two levels below the primary organization or person being charted.

WHAT IS A LINE ORGANIZATION?

definitions

A line organization is the oldest and simplest type of organization. It's the kind of organization you would find in a small manufacturing plant, such as that shown in Figure 15–2. This organization is easy to understand, there is no problem about who is the boss, and decisions can be made quickly. Its drawbacks are twofold: if the leader leaves or dies, usually no one is prepared to move in, and the business suffers; and, because the leader has no assistants, he is frequently overworked and places undue reliance on his subordinates. In many cases, this results in jobs being poorly done.

WHAT IS A LINE AND STAFF ORGANIZATION?

A line and staff organization is essentially a line organization to which staff assistants have been added. If our small manufacturing plant grew in size, the owner might need to add accountants to keep his books, a personnel supervisor to look after his employees, a production control person, and an industrial engineer. When he adds the new *staff* people, his organization would look like that in Figure 15–3.

The line organization is indicated by heavy lines and is much the same as it was, except that more people have been added. The staff organization, however, is new. The owner has hired the staff people to give expert advice and help to himself as well as to his supervisors.

WHAT'S THE DIFFERENCE BETWEEN LINE AND STAFF?

line vs. staff

The line organization *directly* aids in accomplishing the goals of the firm. The staff aids *indirectly*. Staff is usually advisory in nature, helping other people know what should be done and how to do it. Staff has no command authority over the line; it only recommends. The staff's purpose is to be on tap for advice, but not on top authoritatively.

Production and sales departments are most commonly thought of as

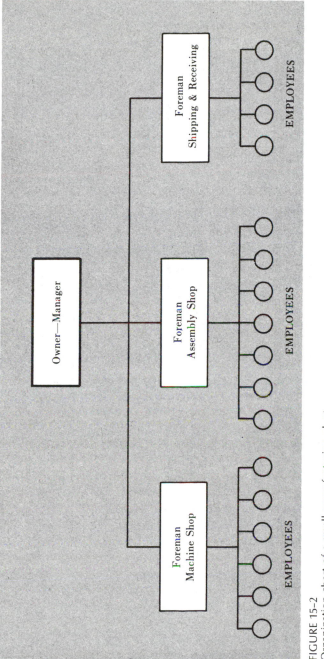

FIGURE 15-2
Organization chart of a small manufacturing plant.

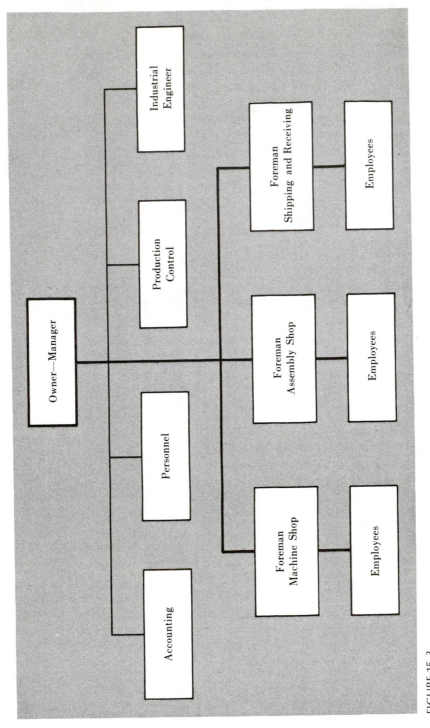

FIGURE 15–3
Organization chart of a small manufacturing plant that has grown.

line organizations, whereas such activities as engineering, accounting, personnel, and maintenance are usually thought of as staff activities.

DOES STAFF HAVE MORE AUTHORITY THAN LINE?

It might look as if staff members have more authority than line members, but they actually don't. When staff people are present, however, the problem usually arises as to how much authority these staff people should have over the shop foreman. For example, does the foreman control the work of his employee, or does production control tell the employee what to do? Remember the staff's job is to advise and help, but not to command—and production control is staff. The line supervisor is the one who has the authority to act and to command. The line supervisor, therefore, runs his department. The staff person has no authority over him or his employees.

the line commands

CAN STAFF TELL THE LINE WHAT TO DO?

Staff cannot tell the line what to do; it only gives advice. When you listen carefully, you'll find the staff isn't giving commands to the line. Instead, the staff person is saying, "This is what I think you should do," or, "You'd better do this if you want to improve the quality of your work." When the staff gives this type of advice, you as a supervisor would probably take it and make the changes. But you don't have to. You could refuse to do what the staff suggests. You should, however, be aware of the authority behind the advice given by the staff. Most of the time the staff person is an expert in the field, and knowing this, most supervisors are not prone to argue with him or her. Likewise, when you go to a doctor who tells you that you need to have your appendix out, you don't argue the case. You could if you wanted to. In fact, you could even refuse to have your appendix removed. You would, of course, have to suffer the consequences. In like manner, you could refuse to follow the advice of the staff, but in doing so you may have to suffer the consequences.

giving advice

ARE AUTHORITY AND RESPONSIBILITY ALIKE?

Authority is the right to command or act and is the power you have over others. If you have authority, you can cause a person to do something that you want done. Every supervisor is vested with the authority necessary to secure the cooperation of his employees. He might get this cooperation through his dynamic leadership, through coercion and persuasion, or by promise of some economic gain or loss.

Responsibility, on the other hand, is the obligation that an employee

difference between authority and responsibility

has to his boss to do a job or task that has been assigned to him. The key idea here is one of *obligation*. You are hired to do a certain job; therefore, you have an obligation or responsibility to your boss to do the job he hired you to do.

It wouldn't be fair to hold a person responsible for doing a job without first giving him or her the authority necessary to get it done. Thus, although authority and responsibility are different, they should go together. Where you have authority delegated, it should be coupled with responsibility.

WHERE DOES AUTHORITY COME FROM?

There are two ideas about where authority comes from. The first idea, or *classical theory*, says that authority is delegated from above. If you have authority to hire and fire, you were given this authority by your boss. Suppose you were delegated the authority by your boss to hire no more than thirty people. You could hire any number up to thirty, but you couldn't exceed thirty without additional authority from the boss. Thus, you get authority from your boss, who gets authority from his or her boss, and so on up the line.

The other theory of authority is called the *acceptance theory*. The idea here is that the authority you have over your employees is only the authority that your employees give you. In other words, they give you the authority to tell them what to do. In similar fashion, the only authority your boss has over you is what you give him, and the only authority that teachers have over students is the authority that the students give the teachers. Suppose you tell your employees that starting tomorrow, everyone must wear red uniforms and yellow shoes to work. Will they do it? If you have authority over them, they should do it. But they probably won't come to work with red uniforms and yellow shoes—which means you don't have authority over them. Suppose a teacher assigns 115 math problems as homework. Does the teacher have the authority to make you do it? Not unless you give him or her the authority. Of course your boss or teacher can withhold pay or grades if you don't do what they say, but neither of them can make you do it unless you give them the authority to command you to do so.

sources of authority

There's some truth in both of these theories. The authority to hire thirty employees comes from your boss—not from your employees. But the authority to force an employee to do a job a certain way comes from the employee and not from your boss. Thus, part of every supervisor's authority, the right to command, comes from his boss, and part comes from his employees.

WHY IS DELEGATION OF AUTHORITY IMPORTANT?

Delegation of authority is the key to organization. If you don't delegate, you won't have any organization—only one-man operations. No one expects a supervisor to personally tell every employee what to do, or to inspect every product, or to prepare shipping papers on everything that goes out. But he may well be responsible for seeing that all this is done, and the only way he can get it done is to delegate authority to his employees. Since the job of a supervisor is to see that his department operates smoothly through the efforts of his employees, he must, therefore, delegate authority to the appropriate employees in order to get the work done.

Another reason for delegating is that it gives your employees a sense of participating—of being somewhat in control. Being in control, or having authority to make decisions, is a great source of job enrichment for your employees and enhances their job potential. It is, in effect, a good way to educate and train your employee on the job. In addition, letting your employees make decisions is a great motivating influence. It makes them feel that they belong, that they are not just cogs in a wheel.

Delegating will also give you time to look ahead—time to do some long-range planning. You won't be troubled by today's problems.

Finally, delegation frees you from details and gives you enough time to be sure that (1) your department is operating smoothly, (2) its production is integrated and synchronized, and (3) you are meeting the goals your boss has set in a manner that is both acceptable and commendable.

TO WHOM SHOULD YOU DELEGATE?

Delegate authority only to people who have both the *knowledge* and the *competence* to make a decision. If these people have information about the job but are not competent to make a decision, they should not be given authority to make the decision. Likewise, if they have competence to make the decision but do not have sufficient information, they should not be delegated authority or be required to make the decision. If you delegate authority to people who lack both competence and knowledge (information), you can expect them to make bad decisions.

WATCH OUT FOR DELEGATION TO THE LAZY EMPLOYEE

Once you delegate authority to your employees to do a job, be sure that those who are lazy don't shift their job responsibilities back to you. Their ways can be subtle and sometimes devious, and you have to be alert to them. They may, for example, ask your help in developing a better way to do their job. When this happens, they are giving the job to you—not doing what you have given them the authority to do. Or, if some particular operation (or machine) is not working well in the employee's opinion, you may be asked to see what is wrong. You promise to think about it and be back in touch. Through this simple maneuver, the employee has very subtly shifted the job back onto your shoulders. You are now responsible for evaluating it and then telling the employee what to do.

Situations like these can add up, and when they do, you will find yourself involved in solving your employees' problems and doing their work instead of running your department by getting things done through others. What should you do when an employee approaches you for help? Be courteous, listen to the employee's problem, and then help the employee *who really needs your help.* You will have to be the judge. For those employees who are trying (perhaps unconsciously) to get you to solve their problem, tell them that they know the job better than you and that you have every confidence in them and their ability to analyze the process and improve the work situation. Let them know that it is their job and that you are confident that they will come up with an excellent solution. Later, check with these employees to see what they have done, offer suggestions if you wish, and give praise where praise is due. Remember that the reason you delegate authority to your employees is to give you time to run your department—not to run a job.

don't solve employees' problems

WHAT HAPPENS IF YOU DON'T DELEGATE?

You won't keep your job long if you don't delegate. You'll be the supervisor who is always pushing carts around the floor, cleaning a machine, relieving an operator, and doing a thousand other jobs, rather than doing your own job of supervising. You'll be constantly interrupted by your employees to give them help. You'll be called on by your secretary to tell her how to spell a word. In short, you'll be so busy doing odd jobs—work that isn't yours—that your own work will suffer. Your desk will be overflowing, and your employees will be in a state of confusion because you haven't organized things properly.

poor organization

If the above sounds like your situation, then your basic problem is that you don't understand what delegation is, how it makes for good supervision, and how it can be a sanity saver for you. Perhaps you don't trust your employees to do their jobs. Whatever your reason is for not delegating, remember that if you don't delegate, you aren't supervising. Your job is *to get things done through others.* You can't do it all yourself. You have to let someone else do something. You must, therefore, give the authority to your employees to make decisions and to do things where they have the competence and information necessary to get the work done. Only through wise delegation can you get on with your job of supervising the work and workers in your department.

Don't forget that *the job of a supervisor is to get things done through others.*

HOW SHOULD YOU DELEGATE AUTHORITY?

1. Call in the employee to whom you are delegating the authority, and indicate what authority you are delegating to him or her. Give the employee the whole picture and scope of the job. Indicate clearly

what the task is, how far to go, and how much you will check on him or her. Tell the employee the relative importance of the job and how it fits into the scheme of work. Remember that you understand the total situation, that you can see the whole picture, but that an employee does not have your vantage point. When an employee comes to a crossroads and has to make a decision, you want the right road to be chosen, but unless the employee can see the whole picture, he or she will not be in a position to make the right choice. Be sure, therefore, that you give the individual the whole story, all the facts. When an employee says, "But you didn't tell me that," you've done a poor job of delegating.

rules that help

2. It is a good idea to take the employee around to be introduced to all the people who will be concerned with his or her new authority, and explain the employee's job to them.

3. When you tell your employee about the new responsibility, be sure to mention why you picked him or her for the job. In other words, prepare the employee psychologically. Explain your confidence in his or her ability to do the job. Don't let the employee leave wondering, "Why did the boss pick on me to do another job when I already have more than I can do?" If you do, he or she may embarrass you by doing a poor job.

4. Be sure you delegate only those things that you should delegate. Don't push off a "hot potato" on an employee. Don't ask him or her to do an unpleasant job or one that you wouldn't do. And don't give the employee the job of discipline. That is a supervisor's job and should never be given to someone else.

HOW DO YOU KNOW WHEN TO DELEGATE?

A lot of red flags will signal that you need to delegate. Consider the following:

1. Do you do work that an employee could do just as well?
2. Do you think that you are the only one who actually knows how the job should be done?
3. Do you leave work each day loaded down with details to take care of at home?
4. Do you frequently stay after hours catching up when your peers don't?
5. Do you seem never to get through?
6. Are you a perfectionist?
7. Do you tell your employees how to solve problems?

If you answered yes to many of these, you need to delegate.

First, be sure that you delegate to a competent employee. Before you delegate, consider your employee's skills, experience, motivation, etc., with respect to the new job. In other words, don't delegate more than your employee's capabilities and experience justify.

Don't dump work on employees, tell them to straighten it out, and then walk away. Be clear in your instructions. Don't specify how to do the job, but do tell them the results you expect. Then stand behind your employees who are doing the work. Give guidance if needed, but don't oversupervise or criticize.

Delegate, don't abdicate. With delegation, you keep control through feedback. Therefore, get periodic reports, and then offer suggestions or advice if warranted.

Don't overdo it. Don't pile so much on your employees that they get overburdened and bogged down.

These, and similar common-sense rules, will take you a long way toward making delegation of work successful.

WHAT'S THE PRIME RULE OF ORGANIZATION?

The reason you organize is to help you achieve goals. The first rule of organization, therefore, is always to remember your objective before you organize to do it. Your goal, what you are trying to accomplish, should determine to a large degree what your organizational plan looks like. A lot of people forget this and develop an organization that works, but doesn't work well, because it was not developed with the particular job or goal in mind.

If you were called on to organize some people to build a reviewing stand for a parade, you wouldn't try to appoint a board of directors, a president, a sales manager, and so on, because that is not the kind of organization you need to get the stand built. Instead, you would probably hire a couple of carpenters and tell them the size of stand you want and where to get the materials. This is a temporary organization that will end as soon as the stand is built, and it does not have to be elaborate.

know your objective

Contrast this hastily developed organization with one that would be needed to operate a bank. In a bank, you would want permanence, safety for depositors, compliance with state and federal banking laws, etc. In this instance, your objectives are different, and the organizational structure will be different. You will need a board, a president, a controller, and a loan officer—lots of people you didn't need for the organization to build the reviewing stand.

Even though you can easily see the different needs of these two organizations, a lot of people overlook this rule when they begin to organize. They often get carried away with the development of an organization and forget *why* the organization is being formed. Then they wind up with an eight-cylinder organization to do a two-cylinder job.

The rules, then, are:

1. First get clearly in mind what you want to accomplish.
2. Then build an organization to achieve what you want done.

IS UNITY OF COMMAND IMPORTANT?

Unity of command is a situation in which every person in an organization has only one immediate superior who is his or her boss. In other words, only one person should give orders to an employee. Some companies are organized in such a way that sometimes two or more supervisors boss one person. This is poor organization for several reasons. If a receptionist, for example, has two or more bosses and she is conscientiously trying to work for all of them, she will probably reach the point where she gives up because of excess work (no boss knows how much work she has to do), frustration (she gets conflicting orders from different bosses), and maybe ulcers from worry.

"Having two or more bosses
is poor organization."

Having two or more bosses for one employee is poor from a supervisor's point of view because it provides an employee a good place to goldbrick or goof off. Neither boss knows exactly what the other one has given the employee to do. As a consequence, the employee can loaf pretty much as he pleases. Or it might end up as a situation where the "squeaking wheel

have only one
boss

gets the grease," that is, the boss who yells the loudest at the employee and beats the desk the hardest is the one whose work gets done. The other bosses take whatever time the employee has left.

For all these reasons, having two or more bosses should be avoided. It helps nothing and presents all sorts of possibilities for conflicts.

WHAT IS AN INFORMAL ORGANIZATION?

Every organization has two systems in operation: the *formal* and the *informal* system. The *formal* system is composed of the recognized and formalized lines of authority, communication, and control. This is the system we see "pictured" in the typical organization chart of a company.

The *informal* system is much more difficult to see and to understand. In any group of employees, some informal leader always emerges. This person sets the pace, and the others give him or her the authority to lead them. The individual, though not the leader designated by management, winds up with authority just as surely as the supervisor does. For example, in a sewing operation where a team of women work to produce certain parts of garments, one woman might emerge as the leader and spokeswoman for the group. The group does whatever she tells them to do. If she tells the group to sew slower, they do it. If she says she thinks the group should complain to their supervisor about the quality of the material they are sewing, they will complain. Thus, she is the informal leader of a group of employees who have organized themselves informally. This is not a formal organizational

organization developed by employees

structure set up by management. A supervisor can rescind or change a formal organization, but he cannot rescind or change an informal organization. The employees are the ones who set up the informal organization, and they are the ones who have the power to change it.

Some informal organizations are made up of employees who get together to get work done without the benefit of formal direction or authority. In a great many companies, these are the ones who actually make things go, who work with the sticky problems, and who give aid to the formal organization. However, they can also be just the opposite by being the ones who cause all the problems. It depends on their leadership and the direction their efforts take.

WHAT SHOULD SUPERVISORS DO ABOUT INFORMAL ORGANIZATIONS?

Every supervisor should recognize that informal organizations exist and that they are susceptible to human manipulation and opportunism because of their undefined structure. An informal organization might make trouble as well as give help. The alert supervisor, therefore, should try to develop a sensitivity to the presence of these informal organizations and should be alert to possible problems they may cause before the problems fester and erupt as full-blown complaints or grievances.

Inasmuch as informal organizations are going to exist whether the supervisor likes them or not, a wise course of action might be to view them as a positive force and use them to make the work of the department easier. This can be done by thinking of the informal leader not as a "ringleader," but as a person "in on things," whose talents can be used. By building good relations with the leader, the supervisor might get him or her to take charge in settling a knotty problem between two employees or to give the supervisor help in getting some concept accepted by the workers.

IS IT POOR PRACTICE TO COMMUNICATE OUT OF CHANNELS?

A channel is the official path through which orders and communications flow from management to workers and vice versa. On an organization chart, the lines that join various jobs show the path through which orders and communications flow from the top to the bottom in the organization.

Most companies set up these channels carefully and for good reasons. They are the highways for orders and communications to follow, and as such, they keep everyone aware of what is going on. They serve to coordinate and unify the organization into a whole unit instead of a series of parts. When you leave these channels and take a shortcut, you are apt to run into problems. If an employee takes his grievance straight to the president of his company instead of to his supervisor, he would be going out of channels. Most companies frown on going out of channels, so it is best to conform to the company's practices and wishes.

use of channels

Sometimes, of course, the normal channels of communication can delay work, and you might choose to take a shortcut and go around some individuals. If you do, be sure to tell those you bypassed, including your boss, what you have done and why. In this way, you will preserve the wholeness of the organization and keep your boss and others from thinking that you are doing things behind their backs.

WHAT IS SPAN OF MANAGEMENT?

Span of management is the number of people who report to a supervisor. If you have too many employees to look after, you will not be able to do a good job of supervising them. If you have too few, the company is not getting full value from you, and you may oversupervise and thereby destroy some of your employees' initiative. The problem is, How many employees can one supervisor effectively supervise? There is no magic answer, because the number that can be effectively supervised depends on a lot of factors. Let's look at some of them.

Factors Affecting Span of Management.　If all the people you supervise are in one room or area, you can supervise more employees than if they are scattered all over the plant. If all of them are doing the same thing, you can supervise more than if they are doing different things. With everybody doing the same job, you can tell them what to do in groups (like classes), thus saving time. Also, your work of planning, control, etc., will be easier because everyone is doing the same job. If their work is interdependent, that is, if what one person can do depends on what another employee does and so on, then you cannot supervise as many employees because you will have to plan and watch the work closely to be sure that there is no bottleneck. If the people you supervise are very intelligent, you can supervise more than if their level of intelligence is very low. Also, most of the time employees with good education catch on more quickly than those with poor education. They don't, therefore, need as much supervision.

effective span of management

Another factor, of course, is the supervisor's ability. Some people seem to have the capacity to keep eight or ten irons in the fire, whereas others have difficulty looking after two or three. The supervisor who can look after seven or eight things at once can supervise more employees than the supervisor who gets confused with only three or four items going.

Finally, factors like how exacting the quality standards are and how much time you have to get the work done have to be considered in trying to figure out the right number of employees for a supervisor to look after. As was stated earlier, there is no magic number. For one set of circumstances, the "right" number of employees for a supervisor might be twelve. In another case, it might be eighteen or twenty-two employees.

What you have to do is consider the types of things that affect your span of management, look at the situation you have, and come up with a reasonable number. Experience will show if your judgment is wrong, and you can make adjustments.

SHOULD A SUPERVISOR HAVE AN UNDERSTUDY?

As a supervisor, you will need someone you can call on to take over while you are out of the department. Even in the smallest departments, someone should be designated as an understudy. You never know when an emergecy will call you away or when the opportunity will present itself for you to attend a conference or educational session. Also, there are always vacation periods to be considered. And, of course, you may miss a promotion opportunity for yourself if no one has been groomed to take over your job. For these and other reasons that you can think of, every supervisor at one time or another will need a backstop. The problem is selecting the right person.

selecting and training an understudy

Selecting an Understudy.　When you select an understudy, look for a person to whom other employees seem to turn naturally for help and advice about their work, a person who has the respect of the other employees, and a person who is regarded by them as a leader. The understudy should be a levelheaded individual who is able to handle problems without getting excited. He or she should be the type who wants to learn, has an open mind, and is motivated to accept larger responsibilities. And finally, he or she should have demonstrated loyalty and dependability to you and to the organization. You may not see all of these in a worker right away, but when given the opportunity to prove him- or herself, you may find that the worker possesses many latent or hidden qualities that weren't readily apparent.

Training an Understudy.   Once you've decided on your understudy, it is not necessary to have a press conference to announce the decision. Instead, you can start giving the person small assignments for test purposes and to indicate your confidence in him or her. These will be signals to the other employees that it looks like, say, Sam Jones is learning your job. When you leave, of course, you should tell your department that Sam will be in charge until you get back.

There is no definite procedure that can be outlined for training every understudy. What will work in one case may not in another. You should, however, develop a plan to gradually bring Sam into focus on the details of how your department works, the reports issued, problem areas, and so on. If company policy allows it, you may also take Sam to supervisors' meetings, so he can meet other supervisors and get a larger picture of the company's problems. Finally, you can give Sam the responsibility for certain areas or activities in your department to let him try his wings. Using steps similar to these, you should be able to gradually get Sam into a position to take over your department. And then, just when you think you've got him trained, you have to start the process all over because he is transferred out of your department to be the supervisor in another! But you've done an important job for the company: you have identified and developed a person with managerial capacities. And you have given someone an opportunity to try to improve himself.

WHAT IS THE PERFECT ORGANIZATION?

Every supervisor should have in mind a plan for the perfect or ideal way his or her department should be organized. This would be the organizational structure that in the supervisor's mind would be most desirable and would best enable the department to achieve its objectives. The ideal organization might mean that old John, the strawboss, would not be in the picture. It might combine two or more jobs in a new operation. These things can't be achieved now, however, because John has four more years before retirement, and you don't want to change his job now. But having an ideal organization in mind is important to you because when the time comes that a change can be made, you will know what changes you want to make. When an employee suddenly leaves, for example, it might present an opportunity

*ideal
organization*

for you to make a change, *provided that you know what you want to do.* Your idea of what a perfect organization would be like also gives you a standard by which you can compare and evaluate your present organization, in addition to giving you a guide for making future changes when the opportunity presents itself.

WHAT ARE THE REWARDS OF GOOD ORGANIZATION?

An organization conceived and developed along the lines we have discussed will more than reward you for your efforts. Not only will you achieve your objectives more easily, you will also find that the physical operation of your department will be greatly enhanced. Everything will go more smoothly. This situation is achieved because a good organization typically:[2]

- Establishes responsibility and prevents "buck passing."
- Provides for easier communication.
- Eliminates jurisdictional disputes between individuals.
- Helps develop supervisory ability.
- Aids in measuring a person's performance against his charges and responsibilities.
- Aids in equitable distribution of work functions and/or personnel supervision.
- Permits expansion and contraction without seriously disrupting the structure.
- In times of change, affords movement in the direction of the "ideal" organization.
- Makes for closer cooperation and higher morale.
- Points out "dead-end" jobs.
- Delineates avenues of promotion.
- Prevents duplication of work.
- Makes growth possible with adequate control and without literally killing top executives through overwork.
- Aids in wage and salary administration through forced job analysis and description.

QUESTIONS FOR DISCUSSION AND REVIEW

1. Why do we organize ourselves instead of working alone? Give examples.

[2] The following points are from Claude S. George, Jr., *Management for Business and Industry* (Englewood Cliffs, N.J.: Prentice-Hall, Inc., 1970), p. 109. Reprinted by permission of Prentice-Hall, Inc.

2. Why is a board of directors necessary in a corporation? What does it do?

3. Who are the corporate officers? Explain their jobs.

4. What do accountants do in a firm?

5. What is production control's job?

6. Where does the supervisor fit in an organization?

7. What is an organization chart? Do you need it to show how a firm is organized? What are its uses?

8. What rules should you follow in constructing an organization chart?

9. Describe a line organization. What are its advantages and disadvantages?

10. Describe a line and staff organization. What are its advantages and disadvantages?

11. Explain the difference between line and staff.

12. Do staff members have more authority than line employees? Explain.

13. What's the difference between authority and responsibility?

14. Where does a supervisor's authority come from?

15. Why should you delegate authority? To whom should you delegate it?

16. How should you delegate authority?

17. How do you know when to delegate?

18. How do you make delegation work?

19. What is the prime rule of organization?

20. Explain what is meant by "unity of command."

21. What is an informal organization? What should a supervisor do about it?

22. Explain what is meant by "keeping in channels."

23. What is span of management? How does it affect supervision?

24. Does a supervisor need an understudy? Explain why.

25. What is an ideal organization?

26. What are the rewards of good organization?

A Case Study
EASTSIDE FLOUR MILL

In 1911 Sam Harris established the Harris Hickory Plant to manufacture and sell hickory handles for all types of hand tools and implements. Because of the quality of his work and the care with which he selected lumber, the company grew and prospered. By 1979 the organization of the company had developed into the seventeen-man structure illustrated in Figure 15–4.

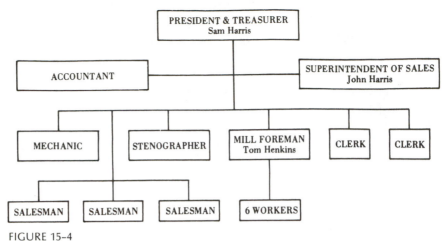

FIGURE 15–4
Organization chart of the Harris Hickory Plant.

Sam Harris was a strong-willed individual who had ruled and run his company with an iron hand. In a sense, he distrusted everyone and personally wanted to direct and supervise the efforts of all his employees. Insofar as possible, he did so, giving orders directly to his salesmen as well as to the plant workers. His "second in command" was Tom Jenkins, his mill foreman, who had been with the company for 52 years. Tom was well liked by the employees, was a capable worker, and was to a great degree responsible for the success of the firm. "T.J.," as everyone called him, had a "way" with people that made them like and respect him; he was the one who most often coordinated the overall efforts of the plant personnel after Mr. Harris had made a disturbing comment or observation.

Sales were under the direct supervision of Mr. Harris's youngest son, John, now 38 years of age. After receiving a college degree in chemistry, John Harris had been quite successful with one of the larger chemical companies. Five years ago his father had insisted that he return home to work in the family concern, and somewhat reluctantly, he returned. Although John did a respectable job, it was apparent to most of the employees that he did not have the drive of his father or the personality of Tom Jenkins. The accountant and the mechanic for the plant were both satisfactory in their respective areas, although neither was thought to possess the characteristics necessary for further advancement.

On January 18, 1979, Mr. Sam Harris died, and the business was sold to the Eastside Flour Mill. At the request of the new owners, the operation and name of the Harris Hickory Plant was to remain the same until some form of reorganization could be made.

The Eastside Flour Mill was located three miles from the Harris Hickory Plant and was a bustling concern. Originally, the company was founded to mill wheat and distribute flour and flour products. In 1936, however, lumber and mill work were added to the flour operations, and by 1950 the lumber operation (including the lumber milling work) had virtually taken over the Eastside Flour Mill, with only 4% of gross sales coming from flour operations. As a result, flour milling and flour products were dropped from the company's line in 1965, and attention was devoted exclusively to lumber and wood products. Figure 15–5 illustrates the current organizational structure of the company.

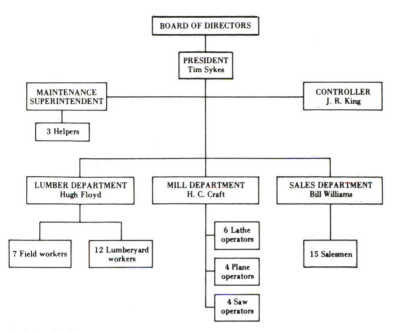

FIGURE 15–5
Organization chart of the Eastside Flour Mill.

The Eastside Flour Mill was a locally owned corporation, managed by Mr. Tim Sykes, president and largest stockholder. Mr. Sykes had an outgoing personality and was generally regarded as a "natural-born" salesman. Although 63 years old, he often traveled the territory with his salesmen, and invariably when he made the rounds with them, sales increased by 15 to 60%. The controller, J. R. King, was highly regarded by Mr. Sykes as a man of rare abilities. He was a good coordinator, well liked, levelheaded, and possessed a keen insight into sound financial management. Hugh Floyd, in charge of the lumber department, was a lumberjack type of employee who did a good job in keeping the company supplied with the needed lumber of the right kind and quality. In fact, he devoted his major attention to the field and cutting operations, often to the detriment of the lumberyard at the plant. H. C. Craft, head of the mill department, was recognized by all employees for his ability in mill and lumber work. Not only did he run his department efficiently, but he often found time to help Hugh Floyd in his lumberyard operations.

Sales were under the direction of Bill Williams, 42 years of age, who was quite competent as a salesman, but he had experienced some trouble in keeping his salesmen satisfied and enthusiastic about their work.

After acquiring the Harris Hickory Plant, the Board of Directors of the Eastside Flour Mill was faced with the problem of how to consolidate and effectively organize the operations of the two plants.

1. If you were called in to give advice to the Board, what organizational structure would you suggest for the consolidated firm?

A Case Study
THE CASE OF THE OVERWORKED SUPERVISOR

The Amos Construction Company was one of the largest and most successful building contracting firms in the state. By and large, its business consisted of erecting public buildings such as schools, city halls, auditoriums, dormitories, etc., and private buildings for factories, offices, and the like.

Joe Thompson was one of its best project foremen. The project foreman's work consisted of completely supervising all work performed on the site from the ground breaking to the final ribbon cutting. On a normal project, this involved the supervision of over 80 people, and on the larger projects the number frequently exceeded 200. The project foreman was responsible for hiring his crew, keeping records of their work, making up payrolls, paying the crew, maintaining various social security records, etc. In addition to these activities, he was completely responsible for planning what should be done, how it should be done, and giving instructions to the crew to do the work. By interview and questions, he determined each person's best qualifications and used him accordingly.

As the building progressed, the project foreman had to contact the suppliers and have them deliver certain quantities of material as needed. For example, the home office would place an order for all bricks necessary for a building and would tell the project foreman with whom they had placed the order. The project foreman would then contact the brickyard and make arrangements for them to deliver certain quantities and types of bricks on specified dates as demanded by the progress of the building. The same sort of thing held true for steel-fabricated parts, ready-mixed concrete, and the like.

As the building developed, the project foreman also had to make arrangements to have bricklayers, carpenters, and other workmen available when needed, as well as to tell them what he wanted done and supervise their work. In addition, he usually worked closely with the architect, and frequent conferences were often necessary to "iron out" certain points of disagreement.

Accurate time records had to be kept for cost and payroll purposes, and receipts for all material delivered to the job had to be verified and sent to the home office for payment. As material was delivered to the job, the project foreman had to decide where it should be placed to be most convenient for use without blocking access to other material that would be required.

In other words, the project foreman was the "plant manager" of a construction job. Everything that happened on the job was his responsibility, and it was his job to see that the work was completed according to specifications in minimum time.

Despite the fact that Joe Thompson was one of the company's best foremen, he apparently did not have the capacity to handle a big job. His work was superior on small jobs where he could personally supervise every operation and attend to each detail. On the major projects, however, the very quantity of things to be done weighed him down. The company, however, needed Joe for the big jobs—they wanted the advantage of his superior knowledge and construction know-how—but they couldn't decide how to break Joe into a big job. They first tried giving him a medium-size job and sending him an assistant. In six weeks, however, the assistant reported that he was wasting the company's money because he had nothing to do. At the completion of his job, however, Joe Thompson had to take a two-month sick leave to regain his health. The extra work of the larger project had caused him to overwork, and his physician recommended complete rest.

1. Construct an organization chart of how you think Joe Thompson ran the project.
2. If you were the owner of Amos Construction Company, what steps would you take to get Joe on the road to handling the larger, more complex jobs? Construct an organization chart showing your recommendations.

A Case Study
STAFF VERSUS LINE

The discussion was calm at first, but then it grew heated between John Lancing, head of Organization Planning, and Pete Bogs, the supervisor of the Purchasing Department. Pete claimed that John was trying to reorganize his department (Purchasing) out of existence, whereas John claimed that he was only trying to place the Purchasing Department in proper perspective within the company.

Basically, John's plan was this. The Purchasing Department was a staff activity in his mind and, as such, should be organized along those lines. Inasmuch as it was a staff department, he thought that it should report to the VP of Staff Services, Harry Council. This would mean that Harry would have Transportation, Purchasing, Personnel, Legal Relations, and Accounting reporting to him.

Pete claimed that this was not the logical place for Purchasing to be located. Purchasing, he argued, was not a staff activity. It was, instead, a line operation and should continue to be a part of Bill Marston's Manufacturing Department. Purchasing, he continued, was a necessary and vital part of Manufacturing. Without purchasing activities, Manufacturing would have no raw material to work with, no parts to assemble, and nothing for its employees to do (according to Pete). In addition, Pete claimed that Purchasing was vital to producing products at a minimum cost through control of inventory and the inflow of materials. Without question, in his mind Purchasing aided directly in accomplishing the objective of the company and, as such, should remain an important part of the basic line function of Manufacturing.

John Lancing couldn't see Pete's side of the question at all. To him, Purchasing was a pure and simple staff function. It served not only production, but all components of the company as well. Like the Personnel Department, it served all components of the firm by going into the marketplace and buying requisitioned materials at the best price and delivery available. In John's mind, it didn't matter whether a requisitioned part was to be used on a typewriter, a milling machine, or the cafeteria stove—the Purchasing Department served all equally. As a result, John reasoned, it was a service function that should not be placed under the control of Manufacturing. In Marston's organization, he argued, it would be subject to pressure to get Manufacturing's parts first, to serve Manufacturing first, and to give only whatever time was left to the procurement of materials for other parts of the company.

In addition to these arguments, John indicated that he thought that leaving Purchasing under Manufacturing would stretch the unity of command principle. He explained this by saying that instead of having one boss, Pete would, in effect, be responsible to the supervisors of Manufacturing, Transportation, Personnel, Finance, Accounting, and so on—all the departments that had him buy material for their use. If the Purchasing Department were located under the VP of Staff Services, however, he reasoned that it would have only one boss, Harry Council, to report to.

1. Do you think that John Lancing's arguments were sound? Why?
2. Where do you think that the Purchasing Department should be located? Why?
3. Is Purchasing a line or a staff activity? As such, where would you normally expect it to be located in a typical manufacturing organization?

A Personal Case Problem

Visit the owner/manager of a local concern (hospital, manufacturing firm, school, nursing home, etc.) and talk with him or her about how the firm is organized. Learn as much as you can about the company. Report to the class what you learned about the company's organization and what ideas the manager and employees had about delegation of authority, responsibility, span of control, line organization, staff, etc.

1. What do you think about the way the company is organized? Why?
2. If you were the manager, what changes would you make? Why? Draw an organization chart illustrating your ideas.

16

HOW YOUR PERSONNEL DEPARTMENT HELPS

This chapter explains—

- What the function of the personnel department is
- How the personnel department can help you

In every business, regardless of size, someone has to recruit and hire people to work for the company. In small firms, this work is frequently done by the owner–manager who hires, promotes, and discharges workers in accordance with their capacities and the needs of the firm. He or she plans for, recruits, and trains the employees. In fact, the owner–manager performs all the functions we normally think of as necessary to securing and maintaining an adequate work force.

As the business grows and he or she hires more and more employees, however, the owner–manager reaches a point where there is not enough time to make sure that the firm complies with all federal, state, and local laws pertaining to employees, or enough time to keep track of such personnel records as application blanks, letters of recommendation, records of jobs held in the company by each employee, records of promotion, accounts of disciplinary action, changes in pay grade, and so on. As a result, personnel work in larger firms is usually done by a separate department called the Personnel Department or the Industrial Relations Department. Its job is to secure and keep on hand an adequate, healthy work force.

WHAT DOES THE PERSONNEL DEPARTMENT DO?

The personnel department tries to help supervisors with their personnel work in every way that it can, by providing service, advice, and coordination among departments. Specifically, the personnel department's job is to help the company reach its objective by assisting you as a supervisor with the management of the persons employed by the company and working in your department. In lending this assistance, the personnel department recruits, hires, trains, places, and maintains an effective work force. However, although the personnel department helps you as a supervisor to do a better job, it cannot do everything for you. The responsibility for managing personnel does not belong to the personnel department alone. On the contrary, the responsibility for good personnel administration rests on you and on every other supervisor working for the firm. It is a *total, cooperative endeavor* that comes from a common feeling of responsibility and cooperation. All that the personnel department can do to bring this about is to offer every supervisor every ounce of help that it can in recruiting and training employees, to offer any suggestions it can about how personnel matters should be handled, and to offer any service it can—such as record keeping. Thus, the personnel department is essentially a service department in nature. It aids in the performance of personnel services for the entire company.

effective work force

WHAT ARE PERSONNEL POLICIES?

A personnel policy is a set of rules, usually written, that guides the personnel department and the company in its personnel relations. It tells how things are to be done, like recipes in a cookbook. Thus, it helps the personnel department and supervisors get their jobs done by providing directions. Personnel policies are usually made up by management in consultation with the personnel department. In large firms, these policies can get complex. One of the personnel department's jobs, therefore, is to keep up with these policies and interpret and explain them to supervisors. Personnel policies cover a lot of different topics and discuss items such as:

interpreting personnel policies

1. Hiring employees.
2. Employee absences.
3. Physical examinations.
4. Conditions of employment.
5. Employee dismissal.
6. Safety practices.
7. The employee suggestion system.
8. The grievance procedure.
9. Improving the employees' education with company help.
10. Promotions and transfers.
11. Conditions for financial aid.
12. Separation (resignation) of employees.

Although the responsibility for deciding what the company policy should be on these and similar matters rests with top management, it is the personnel department's responsibility to see that all such policies are applied uniformly throughout the company. As a result, the personnel department can be a big help to line supervisors, who are often so busy with the problems of their departments that they frequently do not have time to keep up with all the details of how something should be done. They can, therefore, turn to the personnel department for information, advice, or help regarding any personnel action that they need to take.

WHAT ARE THE PERSONNEL DEPARTMENT'S DUTIES?

The duties of the personnel department vary with the size and type of company, but its first duty, regardless of company size, is to keep enough workers on hand at all times to get the job done. To do this, personnel departments typically:

1. Estimate the labor requirements for the future.
2. Set up job descriptions.
3. Set up job specifications.
4. Establish sources of labor and recruit workers.
5. Interview, select, and place employees.
6. Develop educational and training programs for workers.

7. Coordinate and process promotions and transfers within the company.

8. Conduct separation procedures for all employees.

9. Set up and keep adequate records on all of the above.

Let's examine these activities briefly to see how they help supervisors do their jobs more effectively.

How Do You Estimate Labor Requirements?   In a lot of companies, labor requirements are not estimated. Instead, a new person is hired whenever an old one quits or retires. If the company operates on a regular basis and the number of workers it needs is constant, this might work all right. In most companies, however, this approach does not work well because waiting until an employee quits to hire another might make for a poor selection. Or even worse, applicants with the necessary qualifications might not be available at the time the job is open. Thus, instead of waiting for an opening before hiring someone, plans need to be made ahead of time for future personnel requirements.

adequate supply of workers

With fluctuations in business activity such as we have in this country, someone needs to plan how many employees will be needed to work in a company and when they will be required. For example, if a company's customers require 10,000 units each month for the next two months, 6000 units monthly for the next three months, and 22,000 units monthly for the balance of the year, someone has to give some thought to determining how many employees will be required to produce the units the customers need. Individual supervisors, of course, could do this for their own departments, but in a large company it might happen that one supervisor in a certain department would be reducing the number of employees by *discharging* them, while another supervisor in another department would be *hiring* new employees. Obviously, this is both bad for morale and uneconomical, because the employees are not being transferred from the departments where they are surplus to the departments where they are needed. This won't happen, however, if you use the personnel department to estimate the labor requirements for the whole company. With the personnel department in charge, the needs of every department can be coordinated so that surplus workers in one department can be transferred to open jobs in other departments.

figuring labor requirements

The best way to estimate labor requirements is:

1. Find out what has to be produced in the future—next week, next month, next quarter, or next year—as far ahead as you can. You can usually get this information from sales forecasts. Suppose, for example, that you do this and find that you will need to produce 12,800 units per week for the next six months.

2. Next, calculate how many man-hours of certain skills you will need to produce the 12,800 units per week. You do this by multiplying the number of units you need to produce per week by the man-hours it

takes of each skill to manufacture each unit of product. You can usually get this figure from the time-study department, or you might have to use your best estimate. You might find, for example, that to produce one unit you will need 30 minutes of work by a skilled carpenter. Thus, if you are producing 12,800 units per week, you will need 6400 hours of work per week by skilled carpenters.

3. Now you can determine the number of workers that you will need by dividing the number of man-hours you will need per week for each skill (which you figured in step 2 above) by the number of work hours in a week. This would be 6400 hours divided by 40 hours, giving an answer of 160 carpenters needed to produce 12,800 units per week.

4. If you think you need to, you can now throw in a factor for sickness and other absences. For example, if each of your carpenters averages about ½ hour of absences per week, then you will multiply the number of carpenters (160) by ½ hour to get the number of extra hours of work you will need per week to cover these absences. Thus, 160 men times ½ hour of absences per week equals 80 hours absent per week for these 160 men. This means that you might want to hire a couple of extra carpenters to cover the absences each week for the 160 carpenters.

5. Finally, add any other personnel (such as maintenance workers, cafeteria workers, material handlers, clean-up crew, secretarial help, and so on) that you think you will require. Don't forget to throw in an absence factor (discussed in step 4 above) for these service personnel if you think it will apply.

As you can see, estimating labor requirements for any specific future period is not hard to do if you translate sales forecasts into manpower requirements for each skill and then follow the steps indicated above.

What Are Job Descriptions?   After the personnel department determines the number and kind of employees needed for each department, the next step is to find out what the work of each job is. Thus, you'll want to know what the duties and responsibilities are for every individual job in the department. This is called a *job description*. It describes the job—not the person doing the job. The personnel department can be called on to do this work, or it can assist the supervisor in doing it. Inasmuch as the supervisor is in charge of each job in his department, he should know what makes up each job better than anyone else. He should therefore work with the personnel department to get the information necessary to write the job description, with the actual preparation of the job description under the control of the personnel department.

Job descriptions are needed in order to better match individual employees with appropriate job openings. A job description for a clerk typist, for example, might show that the employee performing the job has to operate an electric typewriter, with special type in the preparation of reports.

One of the employee qualifications for the job, therefore, would be that the employee be able to type.

Job descriptions should be reviewed periodically to be sure that they actually show what the job consists of. Jobs change over time, and job descriptions, therefore, get out of date unless they are periodically reviewed and changed. The personnel department can be of help in keeping these up to date.

Once the contents of jobs have been determined, the next requirement is for the supervisor to specify the knowledge and skills that employees should have in order to qualify for these jobs. This is called a *job specification*.

Why Do You Need Job Specifications? In a very small company, the personnel department might not have any problem knowing the skills that a new employee should have. In a large company, however, there are so many different jobs and people that some sort of written specification is needed by the personnel department in order for it to know what type of person is required. You can't say, "I need an electrician's helper." Instead, you have to spell out what an electrician's helper should be able to do. You might want the helper to be able to read blueprints, follow wiring diagrams, understand the local wiring code, and so on. Therefore, a job specification is set up for an electrician's helper showing what the job consists of and what abilities you would want a new employee to have. A job specification, sometimes called a *man specification* or *employee specification*, is therefore a written record of what qualities you need in a person to fill a particular job. It indicates such things as job knowledge, skill, experience, aptitudes, speaking or writing ability, and physical strength. These job specifications are short and list only the *minimum* capabilities that you expect a person to have.

The personnel department is responsible for developing the job specifications and keeping them up to date, and all supervisors should take care that their job specifications are not set too high. If they are set too high, the supervisors might not be able to find employees who can qualify, or if they do, the employees may be too costly. Also, if the supervisors specify an overly qualified employee for a routine job, the employee is likely to have capacities far in excess of the job requirements and therefore may become bored. The reverse is also true. You don't want to have a mediocre employee in a job calling for an expert because such an employee couldn't do the job, wouldn't be satisfactory, and would have to be fired. The supervisor, therefore, should carefully analyze what each job consists of and then, with equal care, specify the knowledge and skills required of a person to fill the job.

job descriptions and specifications

Job descriptions and job specifications should be maintained by the personnel department, with copies furnished to the supervisors. In this way, whenever supervisors need an employee to fill a certain job, they can notify the personnel department that the job is open, and the personnel depart-

"Job specifications list only the minimum capabilities you expect any employee to have."

ACTUALLY MR. SMITH, WE'RE NOT CERTAIN YOU MEET OUR NUMBER ONE JOB REQUIREMENT....

REQUIREMENTS:
1. WARM BODY
2. SO
3.

ment, by using the job description and job specification, can set the machinery in motion to recruit a qualified employee. After screening out the applicants who do not have the necessary qualifications, the personnel department typically sends the remaining applicants to the supervisor for interview and acceptance or rejection, as the case may be.

How Do You Establish Sources of Labor and Recruit Workers?   Once you determine the type of employee you need, the next problem is finding such employees. A good practice that many personnel departments follow is to fill a vacancy from within the company. "Inside" employees already know the company and its rules and apparently want to work there. Also, when workers are given a chance for a new job in the company, it improves their morale because you are showing an interest in them—giving them an opportunity to improve themselves. Another advantage of promotions from within is that when you promote one worker, several more are often upgraded, and then an unskilled person can be hired at the bottom. Job specifications are a big help to the personnel department in making such transfers and filling vacancies from within the company.

Other sources used by the personnel department to get new employees include former workers (if their records with the company were good), employment agencies, high schools, technical schools, and colleges. Handicapped workers also make good employees. Once an employee has been re-

finding and selecting employees

cruited, a lot of care has to be used by the personnel department in placing him or her in a proper job in the company. Placing the right person in the right job is good for morale and costs less. To do the best job it can, the personnel department uses application blanks, interviews, tests, references, and physical exams to select and place employees.

How Are Employees Selected and Placed?   The method used by most personnel departments to screen and select job applicants is the *application blank.* This is typically a simple blank that asks only for information such as name, address, physical characteristics, education, experience, necessary personal information, and references. Application blanks are used to screen out applicants who don't meet some requirement, such as education. They are not, however, used to hire a person. Instead, a person should be *interviewed* by you, the supervisor, in order for you to learn about the applicant and for him or her to learn about the company. This interview is the place where you can determine whether or not you think the applicant would make a good employee. If the job requires some special skill, typing for example, a *test* might be given by the personnel department. Also, most personnel departments *contact previous employers* to find out what kind of worker the applicant was and why he or she left the previous job. Finally, applicants should be given *physical examinations* to determine any physical defects that would cause them to be unsuited for the job.

hiring new workers

If the applicant passes all the tests and you tell the personnel department to put the applicant on the payroll, the next thing needed is *to introduce the new employee to the job.* This is a very important step that some personnel departments omit. Instead, they expect new employees to "find their way around" by talking with other employees. This is not a good practice. New employees are valuable people, and the personnel department should carefully introduce them to the company and to their jobs. They should be told something about the company's history, what products are made, employee benefits and activities, the way the company is organized, where they fit in the organizational structure, company rules and regulations, and any special duties and responsibilities involved in the job. A good deal of time and money have been spent up to this point to hire a new employee, and a haphazard, poor introduction to the job can do much to dampen spirits, lower morale, and get the employee off to a bad start. By contrast, a good introduction to the job may make an employee enthusiastic about learning the new work as well as give him or her a good opinion of the company.

Why Develop Training and Education Programs?   After people have been hired, the personnel department's next job is to provide the opportunity for the new employees to improve themselves and their skills so as to prepare themselves for advancement and further responsibility. Some training is basic to the job and is done while the employee is working. It is called *on-the-job training.* In this type of training, the employee is put on a new job and told what to do. Frequently, a skilled worker serves as coach and gives tips on how to get the job done. At other times, an employee is trained in a special area or room on a machine that has been set up for the employee to learn on. This is usually similar to a school with a skilled instructor to teach the workers correct work procedures. This will be discussed in more detail in Chapter 17.

In addition to these job-related skills, many companies today are helping to train their employees for larger responsibilities through educational courses given by the company in the evenings. Courses are offered in such things as letter writing, stenography, mathematics, blueprint reading, supervision, drafting, selling, speech, and so on. If technical institutes or evening colleges are in the community, many companies pay tuition for their employees to attend these night courses.

All of this is an attempt by the company to make the employee a healthier and happier worker. Training and general education exert a positive influence on the employee and may result in an improvement in morale and a decrease in turnover, absenteeism, accidents, and so on. Educational activities are expensive, but their worth is well recognized in growing concerns.

Who Coordinates Promotions and Transfers? In small companies, employees can be transferred between departments because vacancies are generally known by supervisors and transfers can be arranged. Not so in the large, complex firms. They may be so big that their size makes informal communication about job openings impossible. In large companies, therefore, the personnel department is typically responsible for notifying all persons qualified for the job and their supervisors that an opening exists. As we all know, such inside promotions and transfers can do much for employee morale. In fact, even when a new job is on the same pay level as an old one, it might be considered a promotion because of a change in shifts or a move from a hot, undesirable location to a cooler, cleaner part of the plant.

Are Exit Interviews Necessary? Whenever a person quits his job and leaves the company, you should know why and under what conditions. This is determined by what is called an *exit interview*. Conducting this interview is the responsibility of the personnel department because it can give an unbiased judgment as to why employees leave. Also, employees may not mind telling a disinterested personnel employee why they quit their job, but they would hesitate to tell their supervisor why they quit. When employees leave the company on their own accord, this interview gives the company the chance to find out why they are dissatisfied and perhaps take action to prevent this from happening in the future. When employees are fired, the interview gives them the opportunity to vent their feelings before leaving and also provides the company the opportunity to correct any misunderstandings that the employees might have. The interviewer might even find out that an employee has been unfairly discharged, and corrections can be

*training
employees*

*other duties of
the personnel
department*

made. Finally, from a legal point of view, the separation interview is a must. Employees leaving the company may institute union proceedings to be reinstated with back pay, and accurate records of the separation may be invaluable before a mediator or the National Labor Relations Board (NLRB).

Who Is Responsible for Keeping Records?   The personnel department has the big job of keeping straight all of the countless records and details relating to every employee and his employment, including complete and accurate records pertaining to his hiring, performance evaluations by his supervisor, promotions, transfers, merit increases, educational advances, grievances, suspensions, and so on. In union cases, these records are essential to determining what should be done under the terms of the union agreement.

In addition to records about individual employees, the personnel department also keeps general records of such things as labor turnover, absenteeism, number of people applying for jobs, average level of pay, and so on. Along with other varied and time-consuming activities, keeping records is an important part of the personnel department's job. The purpose of keeping records, as with all the other duties of the personnel department, is to help the supervisor do a better job of supervising and managing his employees.

WHAT ELSE DOES THE PERSONNEL DEPARTMENT DO?

Up to this point we've talked about the typical or average duties that personnel departments perform in order to help supervisors. A lot of personnel departments, however, are helping supervisors in other, special ways. For example, they are making sure that equal opportunity laws are being followed and that women and minority groups are represented in the right ratio on the work staff.

Many personnel departments are also adding electronic data processing of personnel records to their list of duties. Instead of the typical folder containing 8½ × 11″ information sheets on each employee, their records are on magnetic tape in a data bank of a computer. Application data, performance ratings, job histories, test results, promotions, payroll data, and the like are now on the computer and are maintained by the personnel department. With the information thus recorded, the personnel department can prepare and distribute to supervisors all types of reports showing employment trends, types of employees hired, absences classified by type of employee, and so on. All of these things can be helpful in estimating future employee requirements, as discussed on pages 300 and 301.

*records and
reports*

More and more personnel departments are making employee attitude surveys, rather than having outside firms do the work. Computerizing these surveys enables the personnel department to prepare different kinds of reports showing employees' feelings and opinions. Supervisors use these reports, of course, to learn more about their employees' ideas and feelings so that changes can be made and supervision can be improved.

There is almost no end to the ways in which a personnel department can help you as a supervisor do a better job. The factor that limits how much it does is the cost of doing the work versus its usefulness to you.

With all of this, however, there is one fact that you as a supervisor should not forget: staffing is a fundamental managerial activity for which you are responsible. And staffing includes such areas as recruiting, hiring, training, evaluating, testing, promoting, and compensating employees. Because of the time and complexity involved in doing a good job in each of these, however, you should feel free to turn to the personnel department for substantial help and guidance in any of these areas. This does not relieve you of the responsibility: it simply gives you help when and where you need it.

QUESTIONS FOR DISCUSSION AND REVIEW

1. Why are personnel departments needed?
2. What is the function of the personnel department in a large firm?
3. What are personnel policies? Give several examples.
4. Why are personnel policies needed?
5. What are the duties of a personnel department?
6. Why does the personnel department estimate labor requirements?
7. How are labor requirements estimated?
8. What is a job description? Why do companies need job descriptions?
9. What is a job specification? How does it differ from a job description? Why is a job specification needed?
10. Give examples of sources of labor. How are workers recruited?
11. Explain how a new employee for a company is selected and placed.
12. Why are education programs needed in a company?
13. What are exit interviews? Why are they necessary?
14. Who should keep employee records? Why?
15. What additional jobs are personnel departments frequently called on to perform?

A Case Study
JACK NELSON'S PROBLEM

As a new member of the board of directors for a local savings and loan association, Jack Nelson was being introduced to all the employees in the home office. When he was introduced to Ruth, he was curious about her work and asked her what her machine did. Ruth replied that she really did not know what the machine was called or what it did. She explained that she had only been working there for two months. She did, however, know precisely how to operate the machine, and according to her supervisor, she was an excellent employee.

At one of the branch offices, the supervisor in charge spoke to Mr. Nelson quite confidentially, telling him that "something was wrong," but he didn't know what. For one thing, the supervisor explained, employee turnover was too high, and no sooner had one person been put on the job, when another one resigned. With customers to see and loans to be made, he explained that he had little time to work with the new employees as they came and went.

Each branch supervisor hired his or her own employees, with no communications with the home office or other branches. When an opening developed, the branch supervisor did the best he or she could to find a suitable employee to replace the worker who quit.

After touring the twenty-two branches and finding similar problems in many of them, Mr. Nelson wondered what the home office should do or what action he should take. The savings and loan firm was generally regarded as a well-run institution that had grown from 27 to 191 employees during the past eight years. The more he thought about the matter, the more puzzled Mr. Nelson became. He couldn't quite put his finger on the problem, and he didn't know whether or not to report his findings to the president.

1. What do you think was causing some of the problems in the savings and loan home office and branches?
2. What do you think should be done to help solve the problem?

A Case Study
ADVANCE MANUFACTURING

It was one of those rush jobs. Sid Thompson, maintenance foreman for the Advance Manufacturing Company, called the Personnel Department and requested that they get him a painter right away. One of his painting crew, he explained, was moving to another state, and he needed a replacement as quickly as possible.

With a rush request like this, the Personnel Department got on the phone right away and started making contacts. Within three days they found a man who was a painter and sent him around to see Sid. After talking for a few minutes, Sid hired the man and put him to work that afternoon.

Within two weeks, Sid was back at the Personnel Department again, asking for a painter—explaining that the last man they sent him didn't know which end of a brush to dip in the paint, so he let him go. Personnel again tried to get someone for Sid, and within a week located an experienced painter. Sid quickly hired him and put him on the job. But again, within a few days, Sid was back in the Personnel Department asking for another painter. This time, he explained, the man didn't understand colors, color coordination, and how to mix tints and shades to match existing paint. With that, Jim Boles, the supervisor of Personnel, threw up his hands in despair, asking, "What do you want in a painter, Sid? A Michelangelo? We've sent you two good painters within a month and you let both of them go. What's the problem? What did the men have to say for themselves? What do you expect us to do? We aren't mind readers. We don't know precisely what kind of painter you want. We'll try again, but for gosh sakes, use some judgment in hiring and keeping another painter—if we can find one."

1. What do you see lacking in the operation of the Personnel Department?
2. What normal or typical practices appear to be violated?
3. What changes would you instigate if you were Jim Boles?

A Case Study
THE ADMINISTRATIVE ASSISTANT'S JOB

This was the last interview of the day, and Sally Lunsford, Chief Interviewer in the Personnel Department of the County Hospital, was glad. The applicant for the administrative assistant's job was Jeanette Rigsbee. It was an important and responsible job, with access to restricted information. Typing and the ability to write brief reports were required skills.

Jeanette seemed to be a pleasant person, well groomed, and articulate. Sally explained the position to her and answered Jeanette's questions. Sally finished explaining the job to her, and when she asked if Jeanette were interested, Jeanette replied, "You bet I am! This is the type of job I've always dreamed of and I know I can do it. I'm a good organizer, know my way around an office, and can get others to work with me."

The two women talked at length. Finally, Jeanette asked about sick leave, rules regarding absences, and retirement benefits.

The next day Sally was going over Jeanette's application and noted that she had attended the local community college. Upon checking with the college, Sally found that Jeanette had attended for only 16 months and had not finished her course of study. Her grades were about average, but she had made "D's" in English and typing.

A routine check of her references turned up nothing positive or negative. Her previous employer was fairly noncommittal, but did indicate that she was absent perhaps a little more than normal.

1. Would you hire Jeanette Rigsbee? Why?
2. Do you think Sally Lunsford had adequate records on Jeanette to hire her? Why?
3. If you had been interviewing Jeanette, what would you have done differently?

A Personal Case Problem

Assume that as the personnel manager of a large company, you have received a request to fill a vacancy. (You decide what the vacancy or job opening is. It could be a store clerk, a landscape manager, file clerk, machine operator, nurse, etc.) Let one of your classmates "apply" for the job. Interview the "applicant" in front of the class, and at the close of the interview tell the class whether or not you would have hired the applicant and why. Get a critical review from the class on how well you conducted the interview, whether or not you covered all the points you should have, etc.

17

INTERVIEWING, ORIENTING, AND TRAINING EMPLOYEES

This chapter explains—

- How you should conduct an interview
- Why you should orient new employees
- The most effective types of training to use

No one wants to hire employees without talking with them first. Likewise, most employees wouldn't take a job until they had first talked with a representative of the firm. The employment interview satisfies both of these needs: the employer can size up the employee, and the employee can find out about the job and the company.

Job interviews, therefore, are the most universally used method of employee selection. Some firms even use three interviews:

1. A preliminary interview to weed out those applicants obviously disqualified.
2. A main employment office interview to select several candidates for the job.
3. A final interview by the prospective supervisor who will make the decision about who will get the job.

WHAT DOES AN INTERVIEWER LOOK FOR?

Whether you are a personnel director of a first-line supervisor, you should look at a lot of things in interviewing and sizing up a job applicant. You should try to assess the applicant's emotional stability, maturity, interests, motivation, judgment, attitudes, and ability to communicate. In addition, you should look for such attributes as self-confidence, personal appearance, and openness. By the way the applicants answer questions, you should probably be able to tell how well they will fit into both the work and the social situation existing in the area in which you have a job opening. In fact, through well-directed interviews, you can even learn a lot about the applicant's home and family background, previous work experience, education, hobbies, and the like.

a satisfactory employee

The major purpose of the employment interview is to determine whether or not, say, applicant Ruth Jones's education and experience will make her a satisfactory employee in a particular job. In addition to work skills, you will want to find out whether Ruth's personal attributes would make her happy working with the people in your department. For example, does she have hobbies and interests that would make her congenial with the other workers? If she likes to talk art and antiques and doesn't care about bowling and fishing, while everyone else likes bowling and fishing, she might get bored and find little in common with the others. As a consequence, she probably would not be happy working with the group for a long period of time.

Does she have any special capacities or achievements that will make her a better employee? Is this job a complete switch from her previous work? For example, if she has always worked in outside maintenance, why does she now want to switch to assembly operator?

To summarize, you should try to find out everything you can in a tactful way that will help you decide whether or not the applicant would make a good employee and would be happy working with you and your company.

WHAT SHOULD YOU TELL APPLICANTS ABOUT THE JOB?

All applicants are interested in the job, or else they would not be there. So tell them everything about the job, covering such points as:

1. Duties and responsibilities of the job.
2. Activities involved in doing the job—like standing, walking, or sitting.
3. Job title and relationship with other jobs.
4. Promotion possibilities.
5. What kind of equipment and materials will be handled.
6. The environment or working conditions where the job will be performed.
7. Pay and all related factors.

You should be as honest and factual as you can. If the job is a dirty one performed in a hot room, you should say so. Don't paint a dark picture that will scare them off, but be sure they know what to expect.

job information

Applicants are also interested in the company in general, so tell them about the company as an employer. Cover such things as fringe benefits, free health examinations, opportunities to learn new jobs, and the like.

HOW SHOULD YOU HANDLE THE INTERVIEW?

First of all, don't be formal or stuffy in an interview. Put the person seeking the job at ease. Talk about some appropriate current topic. In other words, start a conversation. Don't start an interview.

After prospective employees have relaxed somewhat, you might ask them questions about their previous employment. Questions dealing with their work, such as the things they did and what their responsibilities were, are good ones to use. Such questions cover things they are familiar with and should encourage them to express themselves. Whenever you want to get the other person talking—whether it is for a job interview or over a card game—remember to ask questions that demand more than a yes or no reply. In other words, keep your questions open-ended. Wide-open questions that cause us to talk are usually those that start with *what, how, when, why,* and *who.*

take time, listen,
use open-ended
questions

If, for example, you ask a person, "Do you like to garden?" she may say either yes or no—depending on her likes. But if you ask her, "How do you always manage to grow such beautiful roses?" she'll probably get involved in a longer response. In a similar way, when you are talking about the job the person is seeking, you might ask questions like "How did you learn about this job?" "What was the biggest problem you had with your old job?" After you ask such questions, however, be sure to give the applicant enough time to think and make an adequate response. Remember that not everyone is as quick to respond as you are.

Always give the person you are interviewing your complete attention. This is an important step for both of you. You want to find out if the person will be a good employee, and the applicant wants to know if you'll be a good boss. So talk *to the applicant*—not to the ceiling or the floor. And *listen* to what is being said. Ask questions if needed.

Don't clutter up an interview with distractions such as shuffling papers, jotting down ideas, or taking telephone calls. These will serve to disrupt a trend of thought, as well as tell employees that you don't think they're important enough for you to give them your undivided attention. When they feel this, they'll shut up and you'll fail to get the information you need. Don't give your true feelings away by scowls, frowns, or grunts. If you do, the prospect will get the message and you won't get the full picture.

Don't drum your fingers on the table or tap your pencil or tap your foot. Such things tell him you are impatient and want to get the interview over with. Instead, keep quiet, be pleasant, and let the applicant talk. Remember, you can't learn about a prospect while you are talking. Let the applicant talk—and listen to what is being said to you.

Always be as honest and factual as you can when you answer questions.

Don't either oversell or undersell the company or the job. An oversell may mean a dissatisfied employee within a few days. An undersell may mean that you will lose a potentially excellent employee. Above all, make sure that the employee fits the job. Don't put a Cadillac man on a Chevette job. If you aren't thoroughly familiar with the job, look for and use the job specification and job description that have been prepared.

Don't let just one negative trait influence your judgment on all other traits. For example, if an applicant won't look you in the eye, but always looks down or away when talking to you (and you don't like this trait), don't let it influence you negatively in evaluating the applicant's other traits. Or if the applicant wears a hat and you are against those who wear hats, don't let this influence you negatively. Instead, try to determine whether or not the quality or trait will have any effect on the employee's future job performance. Don't jump to the conclusion that the prospect has a hot temper because he has red hair, or that he smokes pot because he has long hair, or that her short fingernails mean that she is stupid. These and similar prejudices are completely lacking any valid foundation and can easily hamper your sound judgment. Be on guard to avoid them.

"Don't let just one negative trait
of the applicant influence your judgment
on all other traits."

YES, THAT'S QUITE FUNNY MS. CARBUNKLE, I'M SURE A SENSE OF HUMOR IS AN ADMIRABLE TRAIT.

HOW SHOULD YOU CLOSE AN INTERVIEW?

Believe it or not, you have to make careful plans about how you should close an interview. Don't close the interview by saying to the applicant, "I'm sorry, sir, but your negative attitude (or general unreliability, or poor personality) makes you unqualified for this job." Such frankness may offend the applicant and leave a bad taste in his or her mouth concerning the company and its employees.

Instead, the interview should be concluded in a friendly manner, avoiding any generalizations or evaluations that might be open to question and perhaps develop into a long and fruitless discussion. Say something like "I appreciate your interest in our company and in this job. As you know, we will be interviewing several other applicants before making a decision. Thank you again for your interest. We'll let you know our decision within a couple of days." If the applicant doesn't get the job, the least you can do is see that he or she gets a courteous letter explaining that another person with more experience was chosen to fill the position.

If the applicant makes no move to leave after you have finished your closing speech, then the best thing to do is stand up, open the door, and say, "Thank you again for your interest in us. As soon as we make a decision, you'll be notified." Most people will get the hint and will rise and leave with you.

a friendly manner

Indeed there are legal requirements pertaining to interviewing! In fact, you frequently hear it said that about all you can safely say to an applicant is, "Hello. When can you come to work?" This is an exaggeration, of course, but there is a grain of truth in it.

As we learned in Chapter 8, Title VII of the Civil Rights Act of 1964 (which applies to any company employing 15 or more people) prohibits "discrimination because of race, color, religion, sex, or national origin in all employment practices." This means that the employment interview is included. What can you legally ask an applicant? The answer is unclear and is still being developed in the courts. We can, however, see some fairly clear guidelines developing.

Any question you ask that is based on a sound analysis of the job to be performed should not be discriminatory. The problem, however, is that if you are sued, you will have to *prove to the court* that your standards for selection are valid, that they apply directly to the job, and that in establishing the standards you did not require of the applicant any more than the job itself requires. Thus, you have to be certain that any question you ask doesn't inadvertently favor a particular class or group. If it does, you could be charged with discrimination.

Although there are no foolproof guides that you can use in developing questions, the guides used by some companies in framing questions adhere to the following suggestions:

1. Ask only job-related questions.
2. Do not treat women or minorities differently in any significant way from the way you treat others.

questions you can ask

3. Ask the same legitimate questions of men and women, and minority and nonminority applicants.
4. Don't ask questions of one group that you don't ask of all the others.
5. Avoid questions or statements that might imply or subtly indicate that you are biased for or against a particular group.
6. Don't state or imply that some particular jobs have been traditionally held by women or men, or blacks or whites.
7. Standardize the forms you use during an interview to record questions and answers. This will help you keep an unbiased record.

Using these guides, let's explore some typical questions and see whether they are legal. Should you ask a question about height, weight, etc.? No. If this is a requirement for the job, you would be wise to give the applicant an appropriate performance test. Asking about race, religion, etc., would not violate Title VII, but you would have to show that this information is needed and is job related. You would be wise to virtually never ask a question about an applicant's marital status, number of children, etc.

According to the courts, these facts almost never relate to job performance, and you would have difficulty proving that they did if you were sued. After the applicant has been employed, of course, you can ask the necessary information for withholding tax, social security, etc.

Questions asking about an applicant's membership in social groups, organizations, clubs, etc., should be omitted. However, if you think this information is needed, rephrase the question so that you ask the applicant to list the clubs, social organizations, unions, etc., that he belongs to which in his opinion have some bearing on his ability to perform the job. You should not ask about an applicant's arrest and conviction record. This has been ruled by the courts to be an unlawful basis for refusing to hire a person. The courts reason that an arrest is no indication of guilt and that conviction may not be used as the only reason not to employ a person. If you can absolutely prove that this information is necessary for the safe and efficient operation of your business, you might get by with this question. The courts, however, are very narrow in their interpretation of what constitutes the safe and efficient operation of your business.

In addition to the questions mentioned above, be careful of observations or statements that might indicate prejudice. For example, don't say things like "I guess people like you have problems moving about," or "We have two other minorities represented in our company." Applicants could infer discrimination if they are not hired, and the statements could be used against you in court. The best way to avoid this is to follow a carefully worded uniform script for each applicant.

Perhaps you now find yourself thinking that this is a free country and that as an employer you should be able to ask applicants any question you want to. Actually, you can. The catch, however, is that if you don't hire the applicant, he or she may sue you. If so, past court records indicate that you would probably lose.

We've touched on only a few sample questions in this discussion. Questions pertaining to relatives working for the company, age, Sunday work, credit rating, etc., are likewise touchy. So don't try to interview without getting legal help and advice on what the federal, state, and local laws allow in your location. It's better to be safe than sorry; therefore, get legal help. Play it safe.

WHAT DOES IT TAKE TO BE A GOOD INTERVIEWER?

Just because you are a supervisor doesn't mean that you automatically possess the knowledge and skills necessary to be a successful interviewer. Competence in the area of interviewing comes from practice, experience, and sound training in conducting interviews.

To be a good interviewer, you will need to have a good understanding about your company and the relationships that exist between departments and divisions. You'll also need to know how jobs in your division relate to each other, the route and opportunities for promotion from one job to the next, and what is required to be qualified for the particular job that is open. You'll need to be able to size up from long experience or formal study an applicant's abilities, personality traits, motivations, frustrations, attitudes, and individual differences. You must be objective in sizing up people. You can't let your personal biases or prejudices influence you if these have no bearing on the matter.

You must be a good listener. Don't take advantage of your captive audience by expounding at length about the virtues of the company, the advantages of the job, and your personal experiences while working for the company.

You'll need to be alert and perceptive to anything that applicants do that might throw a new light on how they feel. Such things as a change in their tone of voice, a shift in their expression, a pause or hesitation at a critical point, and any show of emotion about certain topics might give away applicants' true feelings.

Give encouragement and support to the applicant by nodding your head, by a reassuring gesture, or by saying such things as "That's interesting," or "Tell me more," or "Oh, I see." Remember when we talked about empathy in Chapter 6? Well here is a place to use it. Empathize with the applicant. Try to see what the applicant is trying to say from his or her point of view. Many applicants have difficulty in expressing their ideas. You can help them by restating their ideas in better organized, simpler ways. Ask questions like "Did you mean to say that you hated your boss, or that you disliked the job you were doing?" This will give applicants a chance to reflect and clarify the true meaning of what they were saying.

In addition to the above, you'll find it helpful to keep the following points in mind:

1. Set a friendly tone to the interview. Promote confidence and trust.

2. Use a structured set of questions for the interview. This gives you a record of what to ask each applicant.

3. Be sure you know and understand what the job consists of and the type of person needed to fill the job.

4. Make brief notes during the interview. Don't leave this to chance. Flesh out your notes later.

5. You learn about the applicant only when you are listening. Therefore, encourage the applicant to do most of the talking.

6. Don't make a decision during the interview. Wait until afterwards, when you can review your notes and consider all of the applicant's attributes.

7. Present a fair picture of the company and the job.

8. Don't forget Title VII of the Civil Rights Act!

Not all of us are capable of being good interviewers. It is an art more than a science. Yet it can be learned through reading, educational courses, role playing, and experience. You can also benefit by working with and observing experienced interviewers, learning from them how to develop your perceptiveness and skills.

WHICH ONE DO YOU HIRE?

Hiring is always a problem. You interview six or eight applicants, each of which has good points and some weaknesses. But which one do you hire? How do you know who is best? There's no sure way to tell in advance, but you will increase your chances of hiring the best one if you do the following:

1. Have clearly in mind the qualifications an employee should have in order to perform the job. Reviewing the employee specifications before the interview will help here.
2. Immediately after the interview, write down the strong and weak points that you could discern in the applicant.
3. Interview the applicant a second time (or have someone else interview the prospect) if you have any questions or doubts.
4. Follow up the applicant's prior work experiences. Call previous employers to establish work records and progress.
5. Try to visualize how the applicant would fit in with your other employees, with the job, and with your company's way of doing business.
6. Check the applicant's personal references carefully for problems.
7. Put all the data from these six steps together and, based on what you come up with, make your final choice. You'll probably pick the best applicant.

WHY BOTHER TO ORIENT THE NEW EMPLOYEE?

When new employees have been hired, the next step is to introduce them to their new jobs. In some companies, the personnel officer is responsible for introducing the employee to the company and its rules and regulations. In other companies, this responsibility falls on the supervisor in whose department the new employee will work. As a supervisor introducing new employees to the job, you should fully inform them about all aspects of their jobs and start them out on the right foot. A haphazard, ineffective introduction of new workers to their jobs, associates, and work facilities is both wasteful and inexcusable. However, despite the importance of a good introduction, probably no supervisory skill is more poorly handled than introducing the new employee. A good deal of money and effort has been spent up to this point in locating and hiring these individuals, and though first impressions are not always lasting ones, they can do much to make employees

introducing the employee to the job

enthusiastic in their approach to their new jobs as well as prepare them to react positively to future conditions. Remember that the employee is the most important possession that your company has and should be treated as such. A good job introduction serves as an excellent starting place to sell the company to new employees and engender confidence in them.

LASTLY, ONE IMPORTANT SAFETY RULE. DON'T HAND-FEED THE PULVERIZING MACHINE. YOU SEE I DID...

"One of the most important first steps is to properly introduce a new employee to the job."

Proper job orientation also reduces employee dissatisfaction and turnover because it gives you, the supervisor, the opportunity to explain the employee's job in relation to other parts of the company before the employee can be misinformed by rumor. While the employee is new and impressionable, you can carefully explain company rules and regulations, thereby minimizing subsequent disciplinary action, misunderstandings, and possible dismissal because the employee did not understand and follow company rules and regulations. And perhaps one of the biggest pluses of all is that a job orientation will serve to brush away the fear of the unknown that all employees have in going to a new place of employment. As you know from experience, the first few days in new surroundings are always disturbing and anxious ones for most new employees.

WHAT SHOULD A NEW EMPLOYEE BE TOLD?

It's a good idea for you as the supervisor to sit down with the new employee in some quiet place and talk with him or her about the department, the job, company regulations, and so on. Among many other things, you should be sure to cover such topics as:

1. *Pay*—how and when the employee is paid, pay rates, deductions, the first day the new employee will be paid, shift premium pay, savings opportunities, pay for overtime, and so on.

2. *Hours of work*—when to come to work, breaks, lunch period, wash-up time, quitting time, and what to do if the employee is late.

3. *Time clocks*—when to punch in and out, where clocks and time cards are located, what to do if the employee has to leave early, etc.

4. *Sickness*—when and where to call in, how to report to the company doctor, the location of first-aid and nursing facilities, how to report injuries, and so on.

5. *Everything about the work*—where and with whom the new employee will be working; what tools, equipment, and supplies will be used; layout of the department and plant so that the new employee will know the way around; where the cafeteria is; where the washroom and rest facilities are; safety precautions; use of special clothing; fire regulations; housekeeping; and so on.

It is basically up to you as a supervisor to choose what method you will use or how you will do the job. What you do and how you do it, however, are critical. If you convey the idea that you are interested in new employees and want to make their transition to a new job a smooth one, this will help minimize the employees' fears and make them receptive to suggestions and instructions. You should also assure the employees that you will work with them during the coming weeks to explain the details of their jobs and company policies, and will answer any questions that might arise.

WHY DO YOU NEED TO TRAIN EMPLOYEES?

Training employees makes good sense for many reasons. For one thing, it reduces the length of time it takes to reach an acceptable level of performance. Good instructions in carefully controlled learning situations can save a lot of money by shortening the learning periods. For example, prior to World War II, one machine tool company usually taught new employees a certain skill by having them work as an apprentice with an old hand for four years. During the war, however, a rapid expansion of operations forced such companies to try a formal classroom approach to speed up the learning process. Using this new approach, they found that new workers were able to reach acceptable performance levels within a year or less.

In addition to preparing employees for new jobs, training frequently improves job performance of employees in old jobs, through such things as cutting down on waste, reducing accidents, minimizing customer complaints, and the like.

Training frequently gives you an unexpected bonus by making employees feel that you are concerned about them and their welfare. As a result, their attitudes and feelings about the company may improve. As this happens, tardiness, absenteeism, and turnover are also reduced. Thus, when you train an employee to do a better job, you may also get unexpected bonuses in the way of improved morale and reduced turnover.

motivation, morale, and skill

When a firm moves into a town, it may not find workers who are skilled in jobs that it requires. Employee training in this case enables the company to fill its manpower needs. Thus, the company recruits unskilled, "green" employees and trains them to perform the work that the company requires. For example, one North Carolina firm manufacturing women's sleepwear maintains a constant training program teaching new employees how to operate special sewing machines that stitch light and lacy material.

Another important reason to train employees is that it helps them personally. They develop new skills, new abilities, and new concepts that upgrade their earning ability. They are more valuable to the company, frequently have more opportunities for jobs with other firms, and as a consequence find themselves more secure in their jobs because of these increased job opportunities.

Finally, training is not for new employees only. It is also used to upgrade supervisory personnel in such areas as human relations, grievance handling, and leadership. Training supervisors along these and other lines makes them better supervisors, thereby eliminating the causes of many employee complaints and grievances.

HOW CAN EMPLOYEES BE TRAINED?

There are a lot of ways in which employees can be trained. The choice of method depends a great deal on how much time is available, the type of training needed, the number of people to be trained, the cost, the amount of training required, and so on. Most business firms, however, use one of three major methods to train people: (1) on-the-job, (2) vestibule, and (3) classroom training.

types of training

1. *On-the-job* training is by far the most frequently used method, and as the name implies, the training is done at the work place. In this type of training, you as a supervisor are responsible, and either you or an employee appointed by you do the training. Teaching another person how to perform a job is not easy, and the instructor needs to know how to break the job down, how to teach it step by step, and how to guide and encourage the trainee as he learns the job. On-the-job training is most appropriately used to teach knowledge and skills that can be learned in a relatively short time—no more than, say, two or three weeks—and where only a few employees are involved. Sales jobs, clerical skills, and simple machine operations are examples of skills that can be learned on the job.

2. *Vestibule* training takes place in a classroom (or vestibule) that is used to train employees in clerical and semiskilled jobs. An attempt is made

in the class to duplicate work conditions, with machines and other equipment set up if needed. A common example of vestibule training found outside of industry is the typical classroom found in high schools and technical schools where people are taught to use the typewriter. The emphasis in vestibule training is on learning rather than speed. And usually the instructors are much better qualified than those in on-the-job training programs. You'll find vestibule training used most frequently where a large number of employees need to be trained as machine operators, typists, office clerks, bank tellers, inspectors, and so on.

3. *Classroom* training is most frequently used where mental abilities such as problem solving, theories, and new concepts are emphasized rather than manual skills. Some portions of orientation programs may take place in classrooms, but most frequently we think of classroom training in connection with in-depth knowledge of a field in which a person needs to be well grounded in principles and theory.

The classroom lends itself to all sorts of teaching and learning techniques. The typical lecture or formal talk by the instructor to the students can be boring and dull and can lull the student rather than excite his interest. As a result, most experienced teachers combine lectures with other techniques, such as case study and role playing. Case study involves the use of a realistic case or problem that makes the material come alive and shows why and how it is used. In your study of multiplication and division, for example, you were probably given short cases or problems to solve rather than tables to fill out. In this way, you could see how multiplication and division could be used and why you needed to learn them. It made the subject seem alive and useful. Thus, when using cases, you learn by doing rather than by reading about it. Cases are good learning devices for problems in such areas as organization, human relations, labor negotiations, policy, business ethics, law, and personnel management.

Role playing is typically used along with the lecture method in classes. In role playing, two or more employees are given roles to play before the group. There are no lines to memorize, but the employees must act out a situation that has been described to them. For example, one employee might act as the supervisor and the other as a worker who has a grievance. How the "worker" presents the grievance to the "supervisor" and how the "supervisor" handles the "worker's" grievance are observed and criticized by the other employees. They learn from watching, and the role players learn from doing and from class criticism. Role playing is a good learning technique because it allows you to put into practice what you have learned from texts and lectures.

Role playing is particularly useful in making us more sensitive to how others feel and how our behavior affects others. The best use of role playing, therefore, is in such situations as a salesman selling a

lectures, cases, role playing

product to a customer, a foreman interviewing an applicant for a job, a supervisor conducting an exit interview, or a union representative negotiating with a management team for a new union contract. Many times, the participants are asked to swap roles and play the scene again. In this way, employees are taught to see and understand the other person's point of view. In role playing, you know immediately whether or not you were successful by how you feel as well as by the criticism that others give you. Involvement, interest, even excitement are high, and learning, as a result, is usually fast.

Other methods of classroom instruction, of course, are used by various instructors. Some teach by demonstrating how to do something. Simulation is another teaching technique in which actual conditions are duplicated as nearly as possible, with employees performing a task under these conditions. For example, your driving reflexes and skill can be tested by a machine simulating driving conditions. The machine is a realistic model of an actual automobile that you "drive" by watching a moving picture of traffic ahead. How you react to traffic is recorded, and your degree of driving skill is computed after you have finished the "drive."

The use of business games is another example of classroom simulation. Here, actual market conditions are simulated on a computer, with employees operating a business and making decisions about such things as how much to buy, what the selling price should be, and how much to spend on advertising. As in role playing and cases, interest is typically high in simulation exercises because the actions tend to closely duplicate real-world conditions.

HOW CAN YOU MAKE A JOB EASIER TO LEARN?

A job that you do regularly may seem simple to you but difficult to someone just learning it. Therefore, you can do a better job of teaching and the other fellow can learn faster if you will remember just two things.

1. Break the job down into simple, easy-to-understand steps. The steps in frying an egg, for example, might be: (a) turn on stove and place pan on gas jet; (b) pour grease in pan; (c) put egg into pan; and so on until you have the egg on your plate. You've broken the job down into simple steps.
2. Give the learner some key points that will enable him to get the knack of doing the step correctly.

learning aids

In the first step of frying the egg, for example, the key point might be "Don't leave the pan on the stove without grease in it." In the second step, the key point might be "Use about one tablespoon of oil or grease per egg to be fried, and never fry more than four eggs at one time." In the third step, the key point might be "As soon as the oil begins to sizzle, reduce the heat by turning the knob one-half way down; then break the egg in a bowl and pour it gently into the pan, taking care not to let hot grease pop up on you." These key points speed the learning process. Figure 17–1 illustrates the steps you would follow to make a drinking cup, with key points shown opposite each step. See if you can make a cup by following the steps.

HOW CAN YOU MAKE TRAINING MORE EFFECTIVE?

The secret to effective training is motivation. Make your employees want to learn. Show them how it will pay off in greater skill and more pay, in opportunities for advancement, or in job security. Tell them *why* something is done the way it is. Employees who only know what to do and how to do it have just part of the picture. If they also know why they should do it the prescribed way, they will be better motivated.

If you are training new employees, don't expect perfection in a short time. Most people have some kind of learning problem; some catch on to some things quickly, whereas others need more time and practice. Praise employees for what they learn quickly, and give them encouragement on the steps they are having trouble with. Show them again how to do it. Tell them that others, too, have had trouble learning this part of the job, but they will get the knack after a while. If the job is a difficult one, go through the cycle with the employees, letting them do the easy steps with you doing the hard ones. Then gradually work the employees into doing the harder steps. (See Figure 17–2.) Remember to tell them what to do, how to do it, and why they should do it that way. Heap on the praise and encouragement.

In training employees, be on guard against several common mistakes:

- *Don't present the training as a bag of tricks and gimmicks.* Any training you might attempt on the basis of this approach will serve to hurt the organization and to destroy or damage the employee's concept of the company and its programs.
- *Don't stress the development by the employee of efficiency or productivity.* This will come later. Stressing it too early will make the learner apprehensive and will impede learning ability.
- *Don't have one of the top bosses do the training.* This will serve to silence the trainees; it will make them nervous and will delay the training process.
- *Don't feed them too much at one time.* Give the learners just a "bite" at a time. Don't heap the facts on so fast that they can't assimilate them. Keep the pace slow and in line with the employees' ability to grasp and understand the steps.

motivating employees to learn

STEPS IN THE OPERATION	KEY POINTS
Step: A logical segment of the operation in which something is done to advance the work.	Key point: Any directions or bits of information that help to perform the step correctly, safely, and easily.
 Place 8" x 10½" sheet of paper in front of you on flat surface.	1. Be sure surface is flat—free of interfering objects.
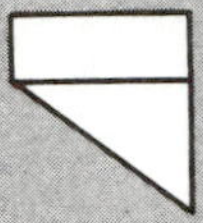 Fold lower left hand corner up.	2a. Line up the right hand edges. b. Make a sharp crease.
 Turn paper over.	3a. Pick up lower right hand corner with right hand and place it at the top. b. Folded flap should not be underneath.
 Fold excess lower edge up.	4a. Line up right hand edges. b. Fold should line up with bottom edge. c. Make sharp crease.
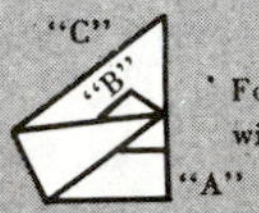 Fold lower left hand corner flush with edge "A."	5a. Keep edges "B" and "C" parallel. b. Hold bottom edge in the center with finger while making fold.
 Fold upper corner to point "D."	6a. Hold cup firmly with left hand. b. Bring upper corner down with right hand.
 Separate lower right hand corner and fold back.	7a. Hold cup with left hand. b. Fold back with right hand. c. Make sharp creases.
 Turn cup over and fold remaining flap back.	8. Make sharp creases.
 Check cup to be sure it will hold water.	9. Open cup and look inside.

FIGURE 17–1
Breakdown of an operation for purposes of training. (*Courtesy of U.S. Air Force Department*) From James E. Morgan, Jr., *Principles of Administrative and Supervisory Management* (Englewood Cliffs, N.J.: Prentice-Hall, Inc., 1973), pp. 206–7. Reprinted by permission of Prentice-Hall, Inc.

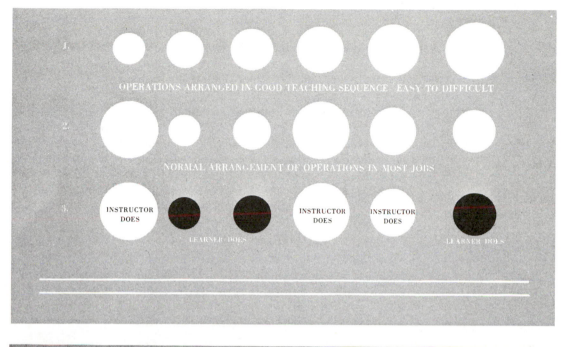

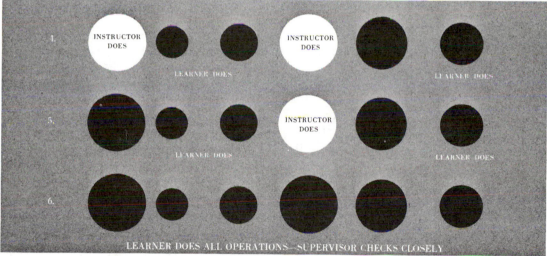

FIGURE 17-2

Sequence for instructing the complex job. (*Courtesy of U.S. Air Force Department*) If a job can be taught by proceeding from the easy steps to the difficult, teaching becomes easier. Few jobs, however, have their working sequence arranged in order of increasing difficulty, as does the first row of the chart. Instead, the difficult parts of the job are usually mixed in with the easy ones, as in the second line of the chart. These steps have to be done on the job in the correct order, and therefore they should be learned in that order. What can the supervisor–instructor do? He or she can keep the job in sequence and still teach the easier parts first by setting up the teaching plan as shown by the dark spots in each row of the chart. The instructor does the difficult or white spots while the worker does the easy or black spots, thus maintaining a learning sequence even in a difficult or long operation.

- *Don't talk without showing.* An illustration or a demonstration is worth a thousand words. Have you ever tried to *tell* a person how to tie a four-in-hand tie? Try it! Then *show* the person how. Which is better? Easier? Faster? Follow this same example in training employees. *Show* them how as you explain how and why.
- *Don't be impatient.* Not everyone can learn as fast as you can. You must, therefore, give the beginner time to assimilate facts. Being an impatient instructor is one of the best ways to destroy a person's confidence and motivation—as well as to slow down the learning process. So be patient. Explain, explain, and explain again until everyone understands.
- *Don't make the employee tense.* This is the other side of the coin of patience. Tension breeds confusion, inhibits clear thinking, and virtually stops the learning process. Remember that new employees have enough to be tense about without your adding even more tension. Their minds are already confused by all they have been told in the Personnel Department, and they need to be relaxed and clear-headed to assimilate the steps in the job. You should, therefore, put them at ease.

IS TRAINING WORTH THE EFFORT?

Without question, training is worth the effort. In fact, business thinks that training is so worthwhile that it spends over $2 billion yearly to train employees. Numerous surveys have been made showing the impact that such training has had on various parts of a business enterprise. One survey, for example, showed that after a training program was completed, customer complaints dropped 24% and production rose 23%. Other areas, such as safety, employee absence, and turnover also showed improvements ranging from 6% to 45% after training programs had been conducted.

However, when top management approaches you as a supervisor and says, "Show me the value of your proposed training program and I'll give you the money for it," what do you say? What is your response?

It is hard to prove that a dollar spent on training returns more than a dollar in savings. Here are a few ways, however, that you can try to evaluate the effect of training programs.

One way is to get the opinions of employees who participate in the program. Get their opinions by interviews, or use questionnaires. Another approach is to measure the skill of employees before the program and then after the program. This can be done by giving them the same examination *evaluating a* before and after. Of course, if the program is to teach a skill such as using a *training program* typewriter, a before-and-after test would readily show the improvement. Many times, however, the purpose of training is to change an employee's attitude and behavior on the job, and this type of change can't really be measured. Tests might show that the employee has learned something, and the employee might say he liked the course, but he may not bring this new knowledge to the job.

Another way to evaluate training is to compare an employee's work performance before and after training. For example, the amount and quality of work for salesmen, stenographers, production workers, and similar employees can be measured both before and after training to evaluate the effectiveness of the program. This is not a truly scientific way to evaluate a program, however, because we cannot be sure that an increase in output is due to the training program. It may instead be due to changes in economic conditions, better supervision, better production planning, and so on. If a salesman sells more after a program than before, is this because of the program or because economic conditions are better and customers have more money to spend? Or if he sells less after the program, is this because the training is no good?

The best way to make these comparisons is to compare the output of a group of employees who did not take the program with the output of another group of employees who did take the training program. This might show, for example, that while an employee who took the course sold 10% less after the course, the sales of employees who did not take the course had declined 24%. This would show that the course had real value.

Other before-and-after information may be obtained from records of quality defects, employee turnover, grievances, cost, incentive earnings, absenteeism, and morale surveys. Most companies keep records of these factors, and comparisons before and after may give a strong indication of the value or the direction of a trend. The value of this measure, of course, depends on the adequacy of the records and the type of training provided.

QUESTIONS FOR DISCUSSION AND REVIEW

1. Why is an interview important before hiring and placing an employee?
2. What should you tell an applicant in an interview?
3. How should you interview an applicant?
4. What should you avoid in an interview? Why?
5. What legal requirements should you be aware of in interviewing?
6. How should you close an interview?
7. What makes a good interviewer?
8. How can you decide which applicant to hire?
9. How should you introduce a new employee to his job?
10. What should a new employee be told?
11. Why bother to train employees?
12. Explain the three methods most frequently used to train employees.

13. Explain the difference between role playing and using the case study method as a learning device.

14. How can jobs be made easier to learn?

15. How can you make training more effective?

16. Is employee training worth all the time and effort put into it?

A Case Study
THE SOUR WHISKEY

Bertie Lloyd answered the advertisement for a part-time waitress in the Sirloin Steak House. According to the advertisement, the job was a Tuesday–Thursday–Saturday job with hours from 4:00 P.M. to 10:00 P.M. This suited Bertie fine and allowed her to continue her schooling at the Monroe County Community College.

As she walked into the Steak House, she was impressed. "It was a first-class restaurant," she told her roommate, "and everything was so pretty and attractive." The manager asked her to fill out a brief application blank and then asked her if she had ever been a waitress before. When she replied that she hadn't, he told her not to worry. It was a simple job, he indicated, consisting of carrying food from the kitchen area to the customer. Tables were cleared and cleaned by bus boys, so the waitress's primary job was to wait on the customers.

Bertie asked about pay, and the manager told her it was $2.80 per hour plus the tips she earned. He hinted that some of the girls made an average of $6.00 per hour in tips and that he believed Bertie could also. When he offered her the job, she took it and was told to report at 3:15 P.M. to be issued a uniform and be ready for work at 4:00 P.M.

Bertie was excited about her new job but wondered what kind of firm the Sirloin Steak House was. The manager had seemed friendly, but the interview was so brief. After reporting for work at 3:15 P.M. to get her uniform, one of the other girls took her to the employees' washroom and showed her where she could change clothes. When Bertie asked her for some advice on how to wait on tables, she replied, "There's nothing to it, Honey. Just smile, wink at the men, and wiggle when you walk."

Bertie wasn't sure where she was supposed to work, but one of the girls told her that she was responsible for tables eight through twelve. Bertie's first customer was a businessman who ordered a whiskey sour, a rare steak with french fries, a tossed salad, and coffee. When Bertie asked the cook for a "sour whiskey," he replied, "You're off your rocker? I don't cook sour whiskey!" When Bertie told the customer they didn't have any sour whiskey, he frowned at her and said in a loud voice, "What kind of a dame are you? I don't want sour whiskey! I want a whiskey sour!"

Hurt and confused, Bertie ran to the washroom in tears.

1. What changes would you suggest that the manager of the Steak House make in interviewing new employees for a job?

2. Do you think Bertie's orientation and training were adequate? What changes would you suggest?

A Case Study
MIDWEST OIL COMPANY

The Midwest Oil Company, with home offices in Dallas, operates in 32 of the 50 states. It is a progressive company and its management plans to have outlets in all states except Alaska within eight years.

Mr. B. C. Vawn is in charge of the company's retail outlets (service stations) in its midwest territory of Iowa, Missouri, Illinois, Indiana, and Ohio. In general, the company tries to locate a service station in every town of 15,000 or more population, but location also depends on competition, suitable site, potential for development, and the like.

Each of Midwest's service stations is leased or rented to a local manager. These units are somewhat autonomous and operate with minimum direct supervision. Indeed, each service station manager develops his business as he sees fit. Every station, of course, is required to sell Midwest's oil, gasoline, tires, batteries, and related products. However, additional products can be sold, and many stations carry a line of small home appliances such as toasters, mixers, electric ice cream freezers, etc. At company encouragement, most stations operate a service center where all types of minor automotive repairs are available. Most of these centers, for example, are prepared to give motor tune-ups, correct electrical troubles, reline brakes, balance and align wheels, grind valves, and install rings. Body repair and paint work, however, are not performed.

The manager of the company's station in Vancetown has notified Mr. Vawn that he will be leaving at the end of next month to accept a job as director of maintenance in a local manufacturing concern. The Vancetown station, located in an area with 88,000 population, is one of Midwest's most profitable and best stations. Situated at the intersection of two main highways, the station attracts a great deal of transient as well as local trade.

In terms of physical facilities, the station has eight islands (the raised concrete portion of a service station drive where gasoline pumps, oil, water facilities, etc., are situated), with four gasoline pumps on each island. In addition, the Vancetown station operates two wash pits, two grease racks, and one of the largest service centers, employing four full-time mechanics. With the exception of the service center, the station operates on a 24-hour basis. The Vancetown station is one of the company's largest and oldest retail outlets. Annual sales for the last ten years have climbed steadily and last year exceeded $780,000.

Finding the right person to replace the station manager has been difficult, but Mr. Vawn is encouraged by the background and record of one applicant, a Mr. Ralph Lewis. Lewis is a first-rate automotive mechanic who has been employed for the past twelve years with a local trucking firm. He has a good record with the company and at the present time is in charge of a fleet of twelve trucks, keeping them in tip-top running order. During his twelve years with the trucking firm, he has been the transmission mechanic, the tune-up specialist, and the front-end man.

1. If you were interviewing Ralph Lewis, what types of questions would you ask him? What facts would you need to know to make a decision about hiring him?
2. Do you think Mr. Vawn should employ Ralph Lewis as a manager? Why?
3. If he employed Lewis, what recommendations would you have for Mr. Vawn?

A Case Study
KENDALL'S DEPARTMENT STORE

Kendall's Department Store was organized in 1903. Originally a piece goods and shoe outlet, it soon branched into other merchandise, and by 1908 it could be called a full-line department store. Living up to its motto of "Satisfaction Guaranteed or Double Your Money Back," Kendall's prospered through the years.

In 1921 a new Kendall's was opened in a nearby town, and during the next nine years, seven additional stores were opened in other communities. By 1970 Kendall's represented a chain of 318 stores covering four states, with each store employing an average of 38 supervisors.

One of the problems experienced in this growth pattern was that of finding and hiring adequately trained individuals to be store managers and department managers. Up until the present time, Kendall's policy has been to hire individuals with prior managerial experience in department stores. However, the current president of the chain, Mr. B. J. Kendall, Jr., son of the founder, has questioned this practice for some time. He feels that the practice has been costly in that Kendall's has had to pay more to lure a good employee from another store, and in addition, the employee has had to be retrained in Kendall's methods—an additional expense.

In January 1984, Mr. Kendall hired Dr. John K. Pointfield, a businessman–educator, and placed him in charge of employee training. Dr. Pointfield's first priority was to develop a training program for prospective and newly promoted store managers, with the major emphasis on the supervisory aspect.

1. What method of employee training would you suggest for Kendall's training program? Why do you think your choice is the best?
2. Develop an outline for a training program for prospective or newly appointed store managers that you think Dr. Pointfield would find satisfactory.
3. Indicate the amount of time that you would allocate to each topic in your outline. How did you arrive at these times?

A Personal Case Problem

Train someone in your class *who doesn't know how to tie a four-in-hand tie* to tie one. Do this by first writing out the instructions on the board or on a piece of paper. Let the person read your instructions and attempt to tie the tie. If it isn't sufficiently clear to the learner how to do it, read the instructions aloud and demonstrate each step after you read it. Let the learner try again. If the learner still can't tie the tie correctly, let the learner tie a tie step by step as you tie a tie. Keep instructing the learner until he or she has mastered the simple job of tying a tie.

1. What steps do you think are most important in training an employee to perform a job? Why?
2. How can you improve on the above sequence of training a person to tie a tie?

18

HOW TO USE PERFORMANCE EVALUATION

This chapter explains—

- How and when performance evaluation should be used
- How to conduct evaluation interviews
- How evaluation can help you with promotions

All of us continuously size up things in our daily lives. We are always forming opinions about people, products, advertisements, and so on. Many times we do this unconsciously. We know that we "like" a product or a person without having gone through any systematic evaluation procedure. However, if we are selecting someone to build a house or take out our appendix, we usually exercise a little more care in our judgment.

Like it or not, as a supervisor you will be called on constantly to evaluate your employees for various reasons. It may be for a possible transfer, for a promotion, for enrollment in a training school, or for a pay increase. How should you make the evaluation? By intuition? Hunch? Spur-of-the-moment reactions? Hopefully, you will do it by using some systematic, carefully thought-out process in which the employee will be given a fair shake.

When you use some formalized system of evaluation, you are showing an interest in an employee's potential for training and development. Using a formal approach, you observe the worker's behavior and skill and record these observations as well as the employee's potential on a sheet of paper that is placed in the employee's personnel folder. This, along with other evidence, is used to determine an employee's potential for future promotions, for pay increases, and the like. So important is this careful evaluation of employees that about half of the major companies today have some formal system of employee performance evaluation.

WHAT IS PERFORMANCE EVALUATION?

rating an employee's performance

Performance evaluation consists of a systematic appraisal of the employee's performance and of his or her potential for development and training. The evaluation is usually done by the employee's immediate supervisor and is then reviewed by the supervisor's superior. Such evaluations are used to determine an employee's level of performance on the job. Supervisors usually go over the evaluation with the employee, pointing out strengths and indicating areas that need improvement. In areas where the employee needs improvement, the supervisor can suggest training programs or formal courses in which the employee can enroll. Performance evaluations are usually made on an annual basis and are used to help make decisions about transfers, promotions, salary increases, and even layoffs.

WHAT METHODS OF EVALUATION ARE COMMONLY USED?

Many performance evaluation methods have been developed and used over the years. The best known and most commonly used are rating scales, employee comparison, and essay. Inasmuch as these methods are the ones typically found in business, let's take a closer look at each of them.

AFTER STUDYING YOUR LATEST PERFORMANCE EVALUATION AND BREAKAGE RECORD, WE'VE DECIDED TO MOVE YOU FROM GLASSWARE TO AGRICULTURAL MACHINERY.

"Supervisors are called on constantly to evaluate employees."

evaluation techniques

Rating-Scale Method. In the rating-scale method, the supervisors are given a printed form for each person with the characteristics or traits to be rated listed on the form. Such things as quality and quantity of work, knowledge of the job, dependability, cooperativeness, industriousness, and initiative are listed on a scale on a form such as the one shown in Figure 18–1. The supervisor places a check on the scale at the point best describing the employee's abilities. For example, if you think the quality of your employee's work is almost (but not quite) superior, you would probably check the form under quality of work at a point between 10 and 15. The rating-scale method is easy to understand and use, and with numerical values assigned to the scale, employees are easy to compare by their numerical scores.

Comparison Method. With the employee comparison method, the supervisor ranks all employees on the basis of their overall job performance and value. Starting at the top, the supervisor lists the best employee, then the second best, and so on until the last person on the list is the worst employee. Using this method, someone must be chosen as the best and someone as the poorest employee. This method does have some disadvantages because it's difficult to compare every individual with every other individual. Therefore, in some ranking methods, employees are ranked as being in the top third, middle third, and lowest third instead of being ranked individually. Thus, the supervisor can say that Florence ranks in the top third of all employees (she is among the best employees), whereas Hank is in the middle third. Using this approach, no attempt is made to rank a person as "the best" or "the second best" and so on.

Essay Method. The essay method of evaluation uses no scales or ranking of employees. Instead, supervisors simply write down their impressions of

EMPLOYEE EVALUATION

Name _____

Department _____ Section _____

Supervisor _____ Date _____

Please rate each employee in your section on the traits or qualities listed below. Following each trait is a line with points along it to serve as a rating scale. The phrases beneath the line indicate the number of points that will be awarded to the trait rated. Rate your employee by checking at any point on the line the position that best evaluates your employee.

JOB KNOWLEDGE

0	5	10	15	20
Gaps in knowledge of a critical nature	Understands only routine aspects of job	Is well informed on all aspects of job	Has better than average knowledge of all aspects of job	Superior understanding of job; well informed

QUALITY OF WORK

0	5	10	15	20
Quality is unsatisfactory	Quality not quite up to standard	Quite satisfactory	Quality superior to typical employee	Quality exceptionally high

QUANTITY OF WORK

FIGURE 18–1
A portion of an employee evaluation form used in the rating-scale method.

each employee on a sheet of paper. Their comments can be general in nature or grouped under such headings as cooperativeness, job knowledge, performance, etc. This method requires a lot of thought and care on the part of the supervisor and is quite time consuming. Some people can write better and more convincingly than others. Therefore, if supervisors are not good writers, their employees may suffer by comparison with those rated by a supervisor who is an excellent writer.

WHAT FLAWS SHOULD BE WATCHED FOR IN EVALUATING EMPLOYEES?

No matter how much care the supervisor gives to evaluating employees, the results frequently reflect the supervisor's biases and weaknesses. The *halo effect*, for example, appears when a supervisor lets the rating assigned one characteristic affect the rating given the employee's other characteristics. The supervisor may say the employee is average in his job skill, for example, and then have a tendency to rate everything else about the employee as average.

Also, watch for a tendency to be either too *lenient* or too *strict*. Some supervisors are easy raters. Others are tough. It's difficult to decide on which of two employees to promote when each of them has been rated by a different supervisor, one tough and one lenient in his or her appraisal.

Because some supervisors don't know their employees well enough, they don't want to go out on a limb and rate anyone as either superior or poor. Therefore, they *rank everyone as average.* Supervisors who do this may reason that they're not hurting anyone—but they're not helping the deserving ones either.

evaluation flaws

Watch for *personal bias.* A supervisor sometimes unconsciously rates an employee according to whether or not he personally likes him. This is particularly true for exmployees in jobs where performance is difficult to measure and evaluate. An example would be an employee who matches colors in a textile mill.

The *end use* of appraisals also materially affects the way supervisors rate average employees. If the supervisor knows the appraisals are to be used for wage increases, the ratings will tend to be higher than normal so that the employee will get a pay increase. If they are to be used to determine whether or not the employee needs training in an area, they are apt to be a little on the low side.

HOW CAN YOU MAKE AN EVALUATION OBJECTIVE?

Insofar as possible, every effort should be made by you as a supervisor to base every evaluation on the context of the employee's overall job and on the employee's total job performance. Basing a rating on only one aspect of an employee's performance or on the way he or she performed on a particular job would not be fair. Instead, your appraisal should be based on the total record of what the employee has done, how well the job has been performed, the employee's total reliability, overall skill, resourcefulness, and so on. We all recognize that evaluations aren't perfect, but with some thought and work on your part, they can be fairly objective and can serve useful ends in rewarding and motivating employees.

HOW SHOULD YOU CONDUCT THE EVALUATION INTERVIEW?

After the performance evaluation has been made, the second step is to review the rating with your employee. This is perhaps the toughest problem a supervisor faces in the appraisal process. When poorly handled, these interviews can be difficult and can lead to misunderstandings and hostility. It takes planning, skill, and practice to develop the sensitivity needed to tell an employee, say, John Smith, how well he is doing on his job. As a supervisor, therefore, you should take every opportunity to prepare for this type of interview through classroom study and practice.

The interview itself should be held fairly soon after the evaluation takes place. The supervisor should assure the employee that the purpose of the appraisal is *not* to criticize the employee, but to help him improve himself so that he will be in a position to be upgraded, thus helping himself and the organization. Prior to the interview, some supervisors even hand the employee a rating form and ask him to rate himself. This gives the employee a feeling for the difficulty one experiences in rating individuals and also gives the supervisor an insight as to how the employee feels about his own ability. Usually the employee will rate himself lower than the supervisor does, which makes the interview easier.

reviewing the employee appraisal

The thrust of the interview should be for you to review the progress the employee has made since he was last evaluated. Areas in which the employee has made real improvement should be pointed out, and the employee should be complimented. In areas where progress has not been shown, you should make constructive suggestions for improvement. These should be specific suggestions such as courses to enroll in, where they are taught, when and how to enroll, and so on.

One common mistake that some supervisors make is to take a salesmanship approach as though trying to sell an employee on his need for improvement. The employee is in a precarious position and can't very well argue with the supervisor's rating and the suggestions for improvement. He may outwardly agree to the "sale," but inwardly the employee may have no thought of changing his behavior.

An interview is almost always doomed to failure when the supervisor saves up a list of shortcomings and unloads them on the employee during the interview. A whole list of shortcomings presented at one time overwhelms an employee and puts him on the defensive. Instead of focusing on failures, the best approach is for you to focus on goals, with a mutual agreement on the goals to be reached during the next rating period.

During the interview you should stress the fact that an evaluation was made of every employee, using the same standards of performance, and that no one employee was singled out for special study—that no one was treated any differently from the others. If the employee shows any interest, you should show him how his rating was developed, what factors were considered, and how each one was related to the actual job demands. This is important for the employee who doesn't get a high rating and wants to know why. It is likewise important for the employee who gets a good rating, so that he can understand and appreciate the care with which his good work was appraised.

The evaluation interview should give the employee an opportunity to discuss his job problems and aspirations with you, his supervisor, as well as give you the opportunity to help the employee become a better worker. Questions should be answered truthfully, fully, and tactfully. Each employee's reactions and questions will be different, of course, and you will have to be a practiced and skillful interviewer to accomplish your mission with skill and sensitivity.

Finally, you should make sure that the employee clearly understands his rating and that there are no unanswered questions. Both you and the employee should agree on some mutually established goals that will help the employee become a more useful individual. Given the proper encouragement, most employees will emerge from an evaluation interview with renewed vigor and determination to do a better job.

ARE THERE GUIDES FOR HANDLING A PERFORMANCE DISCUSSION?

Discussing job performance with an employee is an important part of supervision. It is a difficult job, however, and a great many supervisors handle it poorly. If you want to improve your techniques, then keep the following points in mind:

1. Keep good records. You'll need all the evidence you can find to convince some employees that their performance is not up to standard. Be sure to have records on attendance, lateness, job rejects, missed deadlines, and the like.

2. Let the employee do a lot of talking. Ask questions that can't be answered with a yes or no—questions like "What do you think you can do about this?"

3. Emphasize that you are not evaluating the employee as a person, but that you are evaluating the employee's performance—how well he has mastered and is performing his job.

4. Establish performance objectives that the employee can understand and agree to. This will give the employee something to work towards and will give you something to measure the employee by as well as talk over with him at the next performance discussion.

5. Conduct a performance discussion with each employee at least twice a year; three or four times a year might be better for some employees. This keeps you and your employee on your toes, and you can easily relate performance to goals.

6. Give your employees the option of having performance discussions with you as frequently as they wish. One employee might like to discuss performance six or eight times a year, while twice a year might be sufficient for another.

7. Always focus your performance discussion on what the employee can do. Emphasize growth on the employee's part. Discuss ways in which the employee can learn and apply new skills and concepts.

8. Give the employee an opportunity to discuss your performance as a supervisor. You'll get a lot of tips that can help you improve your job performance!

IS PERFORMANCE EVALUATION USEFUL WHEN YOU FIRE EMPLOYEES?

There was a time when a fired employee was the only one who suffered financial damage. Today it is different. No longer can you fire employees as Mr. Dithers in the comics fires Dagwood. Dismissed employees are suing former employers and are getting their jobs back, winning back pay, and even getting damages for emotional injury. The moral here is that as a supervisor you had better have an airtight case with clear evidence before an employee is fired. And this is where performance evaluation can be of tremendous help by documenting the employee's performance over a period of time.

*useful in
contested
situations*

All firings, of course, should follow a policy of consistency with respect to documentation. Be sure that your company publications such as personnel handbooks and bulletins clearly indicate the terms on which applicants are employed and the conditions under which they are fired. The "last hired, first fired" rule is simple to apply when you want to reduce your work force, but you'll run into problems when you start trying to fire on the basis of merit. Without adequate records, companies are finding in such instances that the courts are making awards of $100,000 or more. In fact, a two-year analysis of forty California jury verdicts shows that former employees won 75% of their cases and received a median award of $548,000.[1]

All this means that you've got to be sure about the legality of the way you hire, evaluate, discipline, and dismiss employees. In fact, state courts are now establishing new limits on firing that cover about 60 million nonunion employees. As a consequence, some companies are warning applicants both in handbooks and application blanks that an employee can be fired at any time without reason. Court actions and awards now demand

[1] For an excellent article on this subject, see Joann S. Lublin's "Firing Line" in the *Wall Street Journal*, September 13, 1983, pp. 1 and 16.

that supervisors make tougher, clearer, more accurate performance evaluations. They have caused companies to shore up and strengthen grievance procedures for nonunion employees and have brought home the need for honest, well-documented performance evaluations. You will find that they can be invaluable in contested situations.

WHAT ARE THE BENEFITS OF AN EVALUATION PROGRAM?

Several advantages can be realized from using an employee evaluation program:

need for
evaluation

1. You have a permanent written record of the relative strengths and weaknesses of your employees, which can be used for salary changes, promotions, transfers, demotions, court evidence, etc.
2. It forces you to evaluate an employee's performance and potential—forces you as a supervisor to analyze the strengths and weaknesses of each of your employees. Thus, you know them better, thereby putting you in a position to do a better job as a supervisor.
3. In case of contention over promotion, dismissal, pay, and the like, you have a record and a sound basis for your decision.
4. Once an employee comes to recognize some personal weaknesses, he or she will be stimulated to set goals for self-improvement.
5. Areas in which training is needed become more obvious, and training courses can be set up.
6. An individual employee's talents are more apt to be recognized and used where they are most needed in the organization.
7. The evaluation helps to eliminate poor placement or misplacement of employees.

WHAT ARE SOME TIPS ON EMPLOYEE EVALUATIONS?

1. Never let employees evaluate or rate each other. This is management's job and should be done only by a member of the supervisory staff.
2. Never discuss one employee's rating with another employee.
3. Evaluate the employee's performance at least once a year. Twice a year is better. If you wait too long, you forget. If you rate too often, you see day-to-day occurrences instead of the overall picture.
4. Measure an employee's skill against what the job requires, not what you think he can do. An employee may be an excellent typist but a very poor file clerk. If his job is to type only, measure his skills against the typing job only.

5. Take plenty of time for the evaluation interview. Tell the employee how well (or how poorly) you think she is doing; then give her plenty of time to ask questions about your opinions and tell you what she thinks.

6. Don't terminate an interview until you have cleared up all misunderstandings about the present rating, future goals, and what the employee can expect.

7. Be honest and candid in your appraisal. If an employee's work has been bad, say so. Then help him see where and how it can be improved.

8. Soften your criticism by saying something positive. You might, for example, say, "Max, you are one of our best typists and I appreciate all of your efforts. However, you tend to neglect your filing and sometimes misfile items. Do you think you can do something to improve yourself there? If you get to the point where you can file as well as you can type, you'll be headed for a top secretarial job!"

9. Follow up interviews by checking with your employees on how they are performing, the progress they are making, and what their problems are. This show of interest on your part can serve as a stimulus for the employees to strive for improvement.

10. Don't confuse longevity with job performance. Just because an employee has been with the company a long time doesn't guarantee excellence in performing a job.

DO YOU NEED PERFORMANCE EVALUATIONS WHEN MOVING EMPLOYEES TO NEW JOBS?

Every time you change an employee from one job to another, you should be able to back up your action by a well-executed employee evaluation. Let's see why this is true.

Supervisors frequently make decisions that affect the pay of their employees as well as their placement, promotion, demotion, or discharge. Which is better—that all of these critical personnel actions be based on spur-of-the-moment decisions, or that they be based on carefully thought-out judgments formulated in a systematic way? The answer is obvious. If you wish to be fair, equitable, and just—and if the company wishes to protect its employees from arbitrary decisions—then such changes should be based on a well-executed performance evaluation.

Inasmuch as you will make such decisions, decisions that vitally affect your employees' jobs, the question is not *whether* you need to evaluate your employees' performances, but *how* you will do it. The overwhelming vote by most supervisors is for some formalized system incorporating either rating scales, employee comparisons, or essay evaluations. These systems, they have found, provide the most accurate estimate of an employee's capacity

for justice and fairness

and value and, at the same time, provide the employee with the greatest protection against arbitrary decisions. By using performance evaluation, therefore, you can move or promote employees from one job to another with greater assurance that the moves are fair and just for the employees as well as for the company.

WHY DOES AN EMPLOYEE NEED TO BE MOVED TO A NEW JOB?

Employees need to be moved for any of several reasons:

1. You may need to move employees to new jobs either because you made an error in judgment in placing them in their original jobs or because you want to promote them.
2. Regardless of the care you exercised in selecting and hiring employees, you may have made a mistake. Maybe the selection process was faulty; or perhaps a tight labor market made you accept an employee who would otherwise be rejected.
3. The job itself may not prove to be as challenging as the employee originally thought.
4. There may be personality clashes.
5. An opportunity for a promotion to a better job may open up.

These are just a few of the reasons that employees are moved from one job to another within a company. Whatever the reasons, you should be certain that you select the right employee for the promotion or move.

SHOULD YOU PROMOTE FROM WITHIN?

Promotion of an employee who has been with the company for several years is a great morale booster and provides a strong incentive for employees to perform better and upgrade themselves. Needless to say, such promotions should be based on the employee's performance evaluation.

As you know, a promotion is the reassignment of an employee to a job of higher rank and higher pay. Most enlightened companies today follow the practice of promoting their own employees to better jobs rather than hiring outsiders to fill these vacancies. When companies don't promote from within, their employees suspect the better jobs will be reserved for outsiders, and as a consequence there is little motivation for them to work harder to develop themselves and to improve their job skills.

For the company, promotion from within means having an old hand on the payroll who knows the company and its regulations and obviously wants to work for it, instead of some new employee who may not work out well. Promotion from within also means a better selection and placement

a morale booster

process because management knows more about an old employee than it could ever learn about a new applicant. Promoting its own employees is important to the company because it means that in the new position, the employee can render a greater, more valuable service to the company. And finally, promoting from within lets the employee know that the company recognizes ability and rewards successful accomplishment. This spurs employee interest in training programs and in self-development in preparation for an eventual promotion.

WHO SHOULD GET A PROMOTION?

Some employees don't want to be promoted. They are happy where they are and don't want to disturb their routine by learning a new job. These employees place greater value on their leisure and freedom from pressure than they do on the status and added income of a bigger job. Other employees refuse to be promoted to a supervisory status either because they find they cannot be responsible for what others do, because they are unwilling to give up the security of the union and being in a bargaining unit, or because they know their limitations and recognize that they would probably fail on a more demanding job.

performance vs. seniority

However, for those employees who want promotions, we like to think that the person with the highest performance evaluation gets the job. But this is not always true. Sometimes workers who can do the job adequately and who have the longest service with the company get promoted. They may not be the best qualified of all employees, but they can do the job, so the decision is made on the basis of seniority. Unions usually press for seniority as a basis for promotions because they feel that employees who have invested the most time should have the opportunity for the better jobs.

WHY USE SENIORITY AS A BASIS FOR PROMOTION?

Promotion on the basis of seniority offers several advantages:

1. Seniority rights provide an employee with a greater sense of security. As he progresses in years, he is more comfortable with the knowledge that his job rights pertaining to promotion opportunities as well as to layoffs will be in accordance with seniority.
2. When a supervisor knows that promotions will be made on the basis of seniority, he will probably take more thought and care in initially selecting and hiring a new employee, thus getting a better one to begin with.
3. Knowing that the employee will probably stay with the company and be promoted, the supervisor will take greater efforts to provide training opportunities and suggest training programs that will better equip

the employee so that, when chosen for a promotion on the basis of seniority, the employee *is* truly the best qualified for the job.

4. Promotions based on seniority serve to reward long and faithful service to the company and therefore encourage good employees to stay rather than "job-hop."

5. Promotions on the basis of seniority eliminate virtually all the grounds for dissension and resentment. Supervisors cannot be accused of favoritism or discrimination.

ARE THERE PROBLEMS WITH PROMOTIONS BASED ON SENIORITY?

Problems can arise from promotions based on seniority:

1. Employees who are less competent, or even incompetent, may be pushed into a position because of seniority. Training under these conditions is undertaken in a perfunctory way, and the worker stays in the new job despite his poor performance.

2. Supervisors are reluctant to discharge or demote the senior person, arguing that his lack of capacity should have been noted long ago and that he should have been fired *then*, not *now*.

3. Most employees feel that they have a "right" to a new job based on seniority, and a discharge or demotion would be a blow to the morale and confidence of the other employees. Thus the marginal employee is kept in the job, and the company is not getting its money's worth.

4. Well-qualified, aggressive employees with high performance evaluations may leave the company or may have their morale seriously harmed by seeing the marginal employee get pushed ahead for no reason except seniority.

morale and seniority

5. When qualified employees leave, the organization may find itself composed of largely marginal employees of questionable competence.

6. Promotions based on seniority may destroy incentives for study, self-improvement, and excellent performance. "Why bother to excel," employees say, "when all you have to do is stick around and eventually move up?"

SHOULD PROMOTIONS BE BASED ON ABILITY OR SENIORITY?

As a supervisor, you have the responsibility to staff each position with the best available person if you expect to run your department in the most effective manner possible. Thus, many people think that when an employee extends his abilities through self-study and experience and thereby becomes best qualified for the job, he should be rewarded by being moved to the higher ranking job. This is not to say that seniority should be entirely disregarded in the move. What is being said is that you should use seniority only to give the edge to the employee who has substantially the same qualifications for the job as another employee who has less service. Promoting the marginal employee strictly on seniority is an open invitation to possible stagnation, regression, even failure.

Sometimes the supervisor's hands are tied by a union contract that stipulates promotion should be on the basis of seniority. Most contracts, however, specify that it doesn't have to be *the* senior employee who gets promoted, but the senior employee who *has the capacity* to do the job. The problem is proving lack of capacity. Careful employee appraisals and adequate records that prove abilities and skills are a big help to the supervisor who wants to promote the more qualified junior employee to a better job. If the differences between two employees are minimal, or if the differences cannot be documented, the supervisor has little choice under most union contracts other than to give the nod to the senior employee.

*the best
qualified*

WHAT ARE OTHER CHANGES IN EMPLOYEE STATUS?

An employee's status may be changed for any one of several reasons. Depressed economic conditions, for example, may cause a shift in an employee's status. Building repairs, new machinery, and similar things may also make changes in an employee's status necessary. Of course, when an employee is incompetent or undisciplined, a change in his status is likely. Whatever the reason for the change, a performance evaluation will be of real value to the supervisor who must make such changes in an employee's work status and who wants to be as equitable and fair as possible. Most shifts in work status (other than promotions) can be classified as either demotions, layoffs, or discharges. Let's take a look at each.

Demotions. A demotion is a reassignment to a lower paying, less difficult job with lower status. In most instances, demotions are caused by factors beyond an employee's control. Recessions may cause some layoffs, with consolidations and demotions occurring among the remaining employees.

Supervisors should virtually never demote a person for disciplinary reasons. If, say, employee Dick Jones comes to work drunk, if he is absent a lot, or if he is insubordinate, demoting him will not change his ways. It may, in fact, make him more antagonistic and will emphasize his negative qualities. Discipline, as you know, should be used to train and correct. An employee demoted for disciplinary reasons would have to learn the new job, correct his negative habits, and make a psychological adjustment caused by his lower status and pay. It is highly improbable that an employee could or would accommodate himself to all three such adjustments.

shifts in status

Many companies today depend on government contracts for their business. When such sources of funds run out, the number of employees on the payroll may have to be drastically reduced, causing otherwise well-qualified employees to be lost. In order to salvage as many such employees as possible, some companies give an employee the option of either termination or accepting a demotion with the understanding that he will be promoted when a suitable position opens up. In other companies, the process of "bumping" is common, where an employee who is to be terminated is given the option of "bumping" the next lower-level employee and taking a demotion to his job. The "bumped" employee has the same option, with the end result being that the lower-level employees with least seniority are usually the ones to be terminated.

Where demotion may prove embarrassing to the company and inappropriate for the employee, the employee may be "kicked upstairs"—that is, he is demoted by being given a "promotion." This type of "promotion," however, is usually in title only, with little or no change in pay, and typically occurs when an employee's job has outgrown his capacity to handle it. Because of his long and loyal service, however, the company may be unwilling to demote or discharge him, so he is eased out by being given a new title and stripped of his authority. Performance evaluations are of real assistance to supervisors in these situations.

Layoffs. Layoffs are indefinite separations from the company due to reasons beyond the employee's control. At the time of the layoff, no one knows how long it will last. It may be a permanent layoff if business doesn't pick up, or it may be for only a few weeks until an increase in business warrants calling the employee back. In nonunionized companies, employees are usually selected for layoffs by considering their job performance, ability, and length of service. In some instances, financial hardship might also be considered.

temporary vs. permanent separation

In companies with unions, the union contracts are usually quite specific about the sequence in which employees will be laid off. Temporary and probationary employees are typically the first to go, with other employees laid off on the basis of seniority. Some contracts state that "seniority shall prevail provided the employee is capable of doing the work." Here again, adequate appraisal records are of a tremendous help to the supervisor.

Discharges. A discharge is a permanent separation from the company as a result of incapacity to do the job or some offense by the employee. Most discharges for lack of capacity occur during an employee's probationary period—the period of time during which the employee is on trial.

In unionized companies, it is virtually impossible to discharge an employee after his probationary period except for some clear infraction of company rules. However, whether the employees are unionized or not, most supervisors take pride in treating their employees fairly, in preserving their job security, and in demonstrating that they will not be arbitrarily fired. Thus, where employees have to be discharged, most supervisors take care to ensure that they have "airtight" cases that can be documented. Employee evaluation records are virtually a necessity in these instances.

QUESTIONS FOR DISCUSSION AND REVIEW

1. Describe and explain a performance evaluation. What is it used for?
2. What methods of performance evaluation are commonly used? Explain the difference between them.
3. What flaws should a supervisor watch for in evaluating employees? How can the supervisor be objective?
4. How should you conduct an evaluation interview?
5. What benefits can you expect from an employee evaluation program?
6. Explain five tips (practices) that you should follow in employee evaluations.
7. How do performance evaluations aid the supervisor in job changes, dismissals, etc.?
8. Why do employees change jobs?
9. Is promotion from within the company a good practice? Why?
10. Who usually gets promoted to a better job?
11. What advantages come from promoting on the basis of seniority?
12. What problems arise from promoting on the basis of seniority?
13. Which do you think is best: (a) promotion on ability, or (b) promotion on seniority? Why?
14. Explain the differences between and uses of demotions, layoffs, and discharges.

A Case Study
THE CASE OF THE PROBLEM EVALUATION

Don Reaton sat at his desk pondering what he should do. Yesterday he had completed the semi-annual evaluation form on June Andrews, his secretary, and had "slept on" his comments overnight. As he reread the evaluation today, he was convinced that he had been fair and honest in his appraisal of her work, but he was worried about how she would take his comments during the thirty-minute review session scheduled later in the day.

He had rated June as follows:

Knowledge of job	good
Neatness in work	good
Ability	good
Dependability	excellent

Accuracy	excellent
Speed and productivity	fair
Ability to get along with others	good
Enthusiasm for work	good
Overall attitude toward job	good

As he recalled, June had protested vigorously during his last evaluation interview because she had not been rated "excellent" on her knowledge of what the job was, on her ability to do the work, and on her attitude toward her work. She had insisted that she knew the job inside and out, possessed all the necessary skills to do the job, and liked her work and looked forward to it each day. She implied, however, that "low ratings" like those he had given her could certainly cause her to change her mind about her work.

During the six months since that interview, Don couldn't see that she had changed very much. In his mind, she was a solid, loyal, good employee but not an exceptional or excellent one. He didn't want to lose her, and yet he felt he had to be honest with her in his appraisal. She was not speedy, but then her work didn't require speed as much as reliability and accuracy. He knew what her reaction to his rating would be, and he didn't look forward to fighting or arguing with her about it. He felt he was fair and honest, and he refused to change the ratings to make her feel good.

1. How should Don conduct his interview with June?
2. What points should be stressed? Why?
3. Should he change his ratings if she threatens to leave? Why?

A Case Study
TILLEY'S DEPARTMENT STORE

For some time now, Jane Tilley had been mentally debating the wisdom of trying to establish some formal system of rating the performances of the employees in her store. Jane's small department store employing 31 people was one of the leading stores in Torrence. Her employees were friendly, seemingly loyal, and in general did good or average work for her. Jane's problem was how she could be certain that raises and promotions were given where deserved.

What Jane had tried to do in the past was to hire employees at the going rate in the community and then give raises annually based on (1) the quality of their work and (2) the increases that had occurred in the cost of living. Figures showing changes in the cost of living weren't difficult to obtain, and Jane systematically applied them to each employee's salary, thus compensating for inflation. Increases based on the quality of the employee's work, however, were more difficult to arrive at. In fact, the best she could do was to make estimates; and estimates, in her mind, were not very dependable.

At a regular employee meeting last week, several employees had suggested that she have conferences with each one and tell them how they were performing, indicating what was good and what was bad about their work, how they measured up with other employees, and what the employees needed to do to improve their performance.

When Jane thought about all this, it made sense to her and sounded good. But she didn't know what should be done first, or how to start.

1. If you were called in as a consultant, what advice would you give Jane as to whether or not she needs an evaluation program?
2. What type of evaluation program would you suggest?
3. How should the evaluation program be started? How should it be introduced to the employees? How should it be conducted?

A Case Study
THE EVALUATION CONFERENCE

In his small savings and loan establishment, Harry Bridges was the uncontested chief. He was the picture of what a savings and loan president should be: neat, well groomed, conservative, pleasant, and articulate. As you would expect, Harry wanted his employees to fit somewhat in the same mold. He wasn't always successful, however, but he used every opportunity to try to get the message across.

In his annual evaluation conference with Ed Regan, for example, he brought up the subject of how a savings and loan employee should act and look. The conversation went somewhat as follows:

Bridges: Come in, Ed, and let's get this show on the road.
Regan: Sorry I'm late Mr. Bridges, but a customer wanted to change an account.
Bridges: I'm glad you brought up changes, Ed, because I'd like to see you change some. Your looks don't say "you can trust me" to a customer.
Regan: I'm afraid I don't understand, Sir.
Bridges: Well, take that stubby beard you wear. Our customers don't like to deal with employees who wear beards and loud ties. You do both.
Regan: I've never had a complaint and . . .
Bridges: And another thing, your clothes are too flashy. Bright colors are for the golf club, not a savings and loan. You ought to wear grays, blues, and browns in plain patterns. And you should never wear a striped shirt with a striped tie, like the one you have on now.
Regan: Mr. Bridges, I've been working for you for seven years and I've never had a customer refuse to see me. To the contrary, I have a good many who wait for me. In fact, insofar as I can tell, my beard and my dress have never interfered with services to our customers. I think you are wrong about . . .
Bridges: This review session is for you to find out what I think—not for me to find out what you think. I think you present the wrong image, and I hope you will work on changing it—starting with a shave.
Regan: What about my job performance, Mr. Bridges. Is my work satisfactory?
Bridges: No real complaint in that department, Regan. You ought to know your job by now. Oh, one thing, I noticed that you took a loan application last week that

was totally outside the criteria we use. You've placed the company and the customer in an embarrassing situation. You'd better watch that.

Regan: Mr. Bridges, I remember the case you are referring to. As a matter of fact, I knew it was marginal, but with the emphasis on equal treatment, I thought we ought to look at it. In fact, if you consider that the husband's father is willing to co-sign the note, it meets our criteria.

Bridges: H-m-m. Yes, well, that about wraps up the evaluation for this year, Ed. Send Sam Stevenson in, will you? He's next.

1. What mistakes did Mr. Bridges make in this evaluation?
2. If a particular image is desired in a concern, how should it be promoted?
3. How would you rate this evaluation conference? Why? How would you have handled it?

A Personal Case Problem

You have just been called by the office superintendent to come to the conference room to discuss the method you use in evaluating your employees. After discussing the subject in a general way, it appears clear to you that the superintendent is not too enthusiastic about the method of evaluation you use.

1. What, if anything, would you tell him about performance evaluation in general? Why?
2. What approach would you use to convince your superintendent that your method of performance evaluation is sound, fair, and advantageous to the employee as well as the company?
3. Would you ask the superintendent what method he wants you to use? Why?

19

HOW TO SIMPLIFY WORK AND INCREASE PRODUCTION

This chapter explains—

- How to go about making a motion study
- Which jobs are best to study
- How to make and use process charts, flow diagrams, and operations charts

As a supervisor you should always be interested in finding easier, simpler, and more effective ways to perform work. Why? If you can find a way to make a product cheaper and thus reduce production costs, then your company can be more competitive in the marketplace and can make more sales. More sales mean more business, and more business means more jobs and more profits. All of this is desirable from management's point of view.

When it comes right down to your own personal job, you can improve the way you work in lots of ways. Sometimes you may suddenly get an idea that really makes your job easier, and you wonder why it hadn't occurred to you before. Or maybe a neighbor makes a suggestion. Or something you see or read triggers your mind. Although all of these ways may occasionally work, they are unsystematic, and if you do improve your job, it is inspirational or accidental and not because you have made a study of what you are doing and how to improve it. The best and surest way to improve your job is through a systematic study of what you are doing, using a process called *methods improvement.* Whether it is called work study, motion study, methods improvement, or work simplification, it all means the same thing: a systematic attempt to eliminate unnecessary work and to make what remains easier to do.

"The idea in work simplification
is to work smarter, not harder."

There is nothing new in this, of course. People have always searched for ways to make their work easier. When humans substituted the sail for oars and added wheels to their sleds, they were working "smarter," not harder. We are doing the same thing today when we try to find an easier, better way to perform a task. As a supervisor, you want your employees to do their jobs in the simplest, easiest, most effective way. This makes your department more efficient and lowers your operating costs. The best way to approach this is through methods improvement.

WHAT IS METHODS IMPROVEMENT?

Methods improvement is the name given to the process of trying to improve the way you do a job. You would be making a methods study, for instance, if you tried to figure out a better and easier way to set a table or wash a car. To do this, you would study each part of the job to see whether you could eliminate it, improve it, or in some way make the work easier.

working more easily

The steps you use in making a methods improvement study are:

1. Select a job to be improved.
2. Break the job down into steps and record these on a piece of paper.
3. Analyze the steps, questioning the necessity for each one. If the step can't be eliminated, see what you can do to make it easier to do.
4. Develop a new method of doing the job using the improved steps you have designed.

Process charts and flow diagrams are frequently used in methods improvement. Let's look at what these are and how you use them.

WHAT IS A PROCESS CHART?

A process chart is nothing but a piece of paper on which you record the parts or steps in a process. When you write down the steps in a process, you place them in the right sequence. Then you can study the whole process without forgetting a step or getting it in the wrong place.

Once the whole job is recorded, you then sit down and look at each step, asking such questions as "Is this step actually necessary in order to get the job done?" "Can it be eliminated?" "Can it be simplified or made easier?" By asking questions like these about each step, you will frequently find that the job can be simplified or reorganized so that it can be done more easily and in less time than before.

How Can a Process Be Described?   Every process or job can be described by breaking it down into some combination of the following five steps.

1. An *operation* in a process consists of doing something, like painting a table, washing a plate, putting the top on a jar, or typing a letter.

2. A *transportation* occurs in a process when something is moved from one place to another. Moving a letter from the file cabinet to your desk, moving raw materials from the stockroom to the assembly area, and moving a dish from the cabinet to the table are examples of transportation.

3. A *delay* occurs in a process when something stops or delays what is taking place. If you were moving raw materials from storage to the shop floor and had to wait for the elevator, this would be a delay in the transportation of the material.

understanding the job

4. A *storage* describes storing a part or product to prevent unauthorized use. Dishes in a cabinet are in storage, as are materials in a stockroom. A storage is not a delay but is a regular part of the process.

5. An *inspection* is what the word says. A clerk checking the weight of a bag of potatoes and an inspector checking the hardness of a piece of steel are examples of inspections.

By using these five steps, any process can be broken down quickly and easily into its basic parts. To save time in writing, the following symbols are frequently used in constructing process charts:

$\bigcirc$ = Operation
$\Rightarrow$ = Transportation
D = Delay
∇ = Storage
$\square$ = Inspection

A further explanation of these symbols is shown in Figure 19–1.

Where Can a Process Chart Be Used?   You can use a process chart anywhere in order to study and improve what is being done. You could make a process chart of getting out of bed and dressing in the morning. Everything that you do would be classified under one of the five steps. Or you could make a process chart of what happens to a soft drink in a bottling plant. Everything that happens to the bottle would be classified under one of the five steps and would be recorded on the chart.

making and using a process chart

How Do You Construct a Process Chart?   You can make a process chart on a sheet of paper or on a form similar to the one shown in Figure 19–2. To construct the chart, you first follow the person about his or her work, noting and classifying on the chart everything the employee does. For example, if a typist carried a letter to her supervisor, you would draw an arrow because this is a transportation, note how far she walked (say 35 feet), and describe what she did as "Carried letter to supervisor." If she waited for the super-

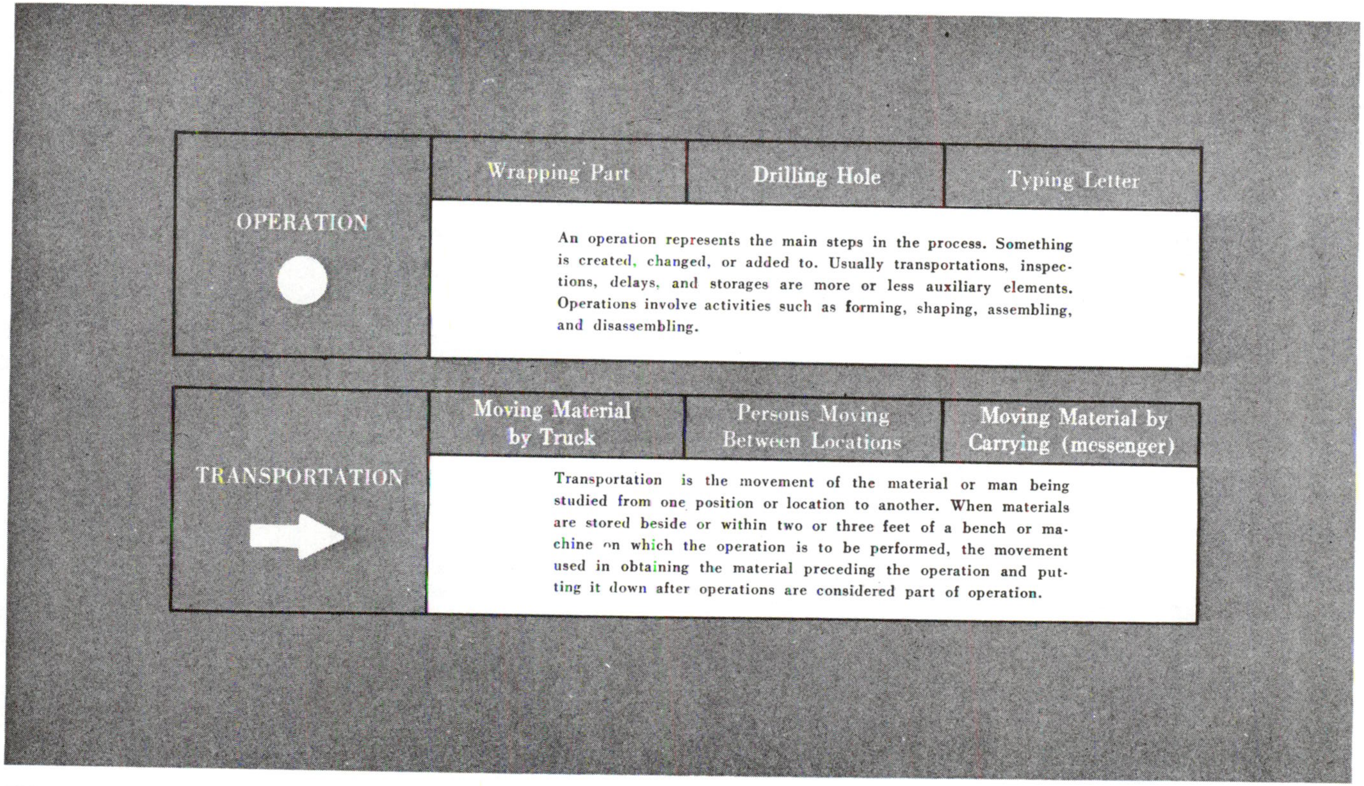

| OPERATION ● | Wrapping Part | Drilling Hole | Typing Letter |

An operation represents the main steps in the process. Something is created, changed, or added to. Usually transportations, inspections, delays, and storages are more or less auxiliary elements. Operations involve activities such as forming, shaping, assembling, and disassembling.

| TRANSPORTATION ⬆ | Moving Material by Truck | Persons Moving Between Locations | Moving Material by Carrying (messenger) |

Transportation is the movement of the material or man being studied from one position or location to another. When materials are stored beside or within two or three feet of a bench or machine on which the operation is to be performed, the movement used in obtaining the material preceding the operation and putting it down after operations are considered part of operation.

FIGURE 19–1

Flow process chart symbols. From James E. Morgan, Jr., *Principles of Administrative and Supervisory Management* (Englewood Cliffs, N.J.: Prentice-Hall, Inc., 1973), p. 336. Reprinted by permission of Prentice-Hall, Inc.

357

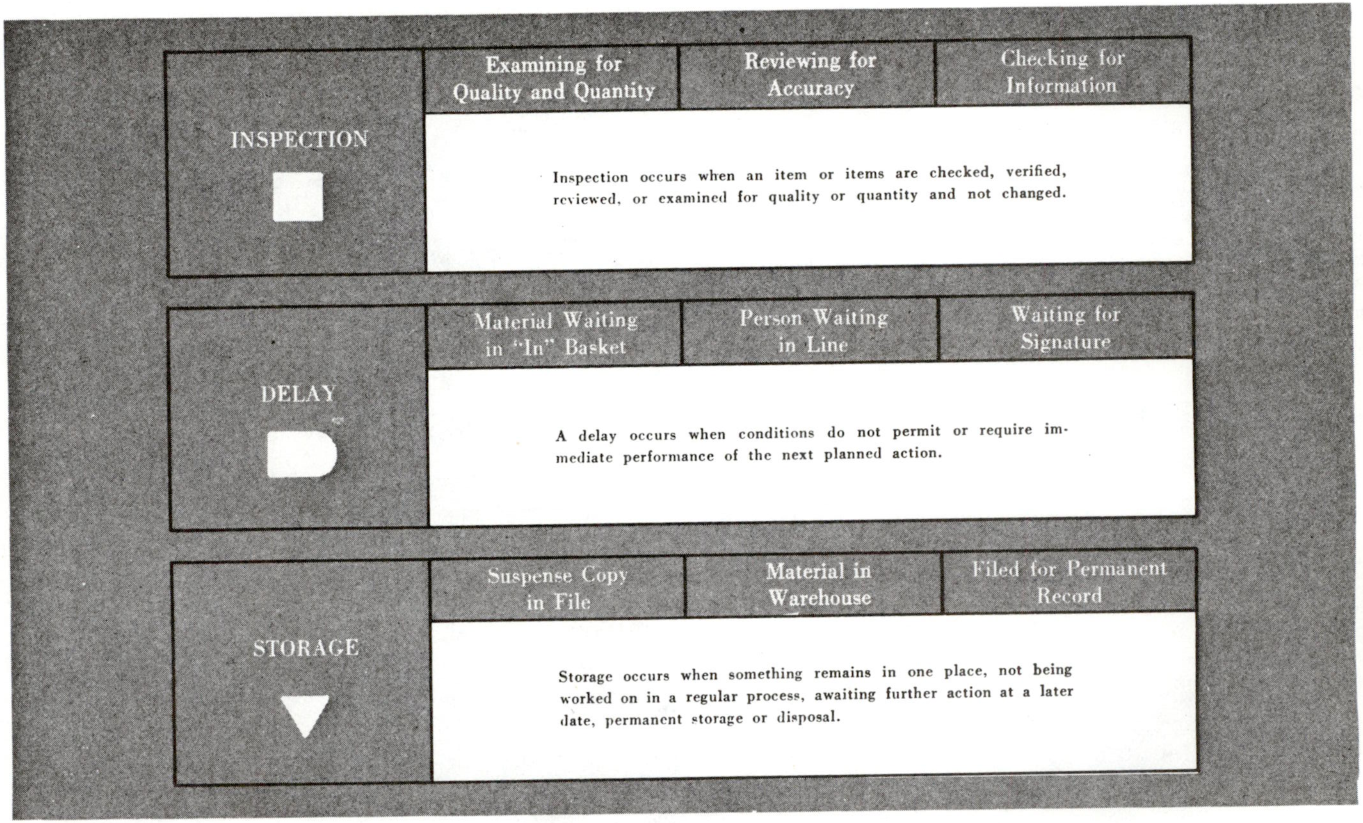

INSPECTION ■	Examining for Quality and Quantity	Reviewing for Accuracy	Checking for Information
	Inspection occurs when an item or items are checked, verified, reviewed, or examined for quality or quantity and not changed.		

DELAY	Material Waiting in "In" Basket	Person Waiting in Line	Waiting for Signature
	A delay occurs when conditions do not permit or require immediate performance of the next planned action.		

STORAGE ▶	Suspense Copy in File	Material in Warehouse	Filed for Permanent Record
	Storage occurs when something remains in one place, not being worked on in a regular process, awaiting further action at a later date, permanent storage or disposal.		

FIGURE 19-1 (continued)

358

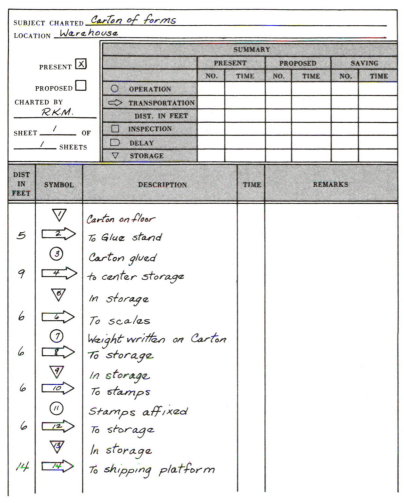

FIGURE 19–2
Process chart of the old method of shipping cartons of printed forms.

visor to read and sign the letter, you would draw a "D" (for delay) and note by it, "Waited for supervisor to read and sign letter." In this way, every step in a process is recorded so that it can be studied later. Figure 19–2 is a process chart of the old way of shipping cartons of printed forms.

How Do You Analyze a Process Chart?   Once you have made the process chart, your next job is to question and study each step in the procedure, using the following questions:[1]

[1] From Claude S. George, Jr., *Management for Business and Industry* (Englewood Cliffs, N.J.: Prentice-Hall, Inc., 1970), pp. 398–99. Reprinted by permission of Prentice-Hall, Inc.

Questions about each step

1. What is being done? Is it necessary? Why?

2. Who is doing it? Can someone else do it better or more easily? Why?

3. Why is it being done? Can it be eliminated or perhaps shortened in duration or reduced in scope?

4. When is it done? Can it be performed at a better time in the sequence? Why not?

5. Where is it done? Can it be done more easily at another location? Why?

6. How is it being done? Can it be done more easily? Can it be combined with another step?

In addition to the above general questions, you should ask specific questions similar to the following about each component.

Operations

1. Have conditions changed, making this operation unnecessary? Can it be eliminated?

2. Can it be performed more easily at another place in the process— perhaps during the idle time of another operator?

3. Can it be performed more easily at a different work place—perhaps on a table, conveyor, or rack?

4. Can it be performed more easily and quickly by another operator or person?

5. Can material be purchased that would eliminate or reduce the effort involved in this operation?

Transportations

1. Can the previous operation and the succeeding operation be combined or eliminated, thereby making this transportation unnecessary?

questions to ask

2. Can work areas be rearranged to eliminate or shorten this transportation?

3. Can some materials-handling device (conveyor, cart, etc.) make it easier to move materials and shorten the time required to make the move?

4. Can gravity conveyors, chutes, etc., be employed to shorten distance or time?

5. Can special equipment be relocated to eliminate or to shorten the transportation?

6. Can a new layout be developed for the area that would eliminate or materially reduce the transportations involved?

361

HOW TO SIMPLIFY
WORK AND
INCREASE
PRODUCTION

Inspections

1. Is inspection necessary? Can it be completely eliminated?
2. Is the inspection necessary at this point for completion of the productive process? Can it be performed more easily at a later time?
3. Can any of the inspection requirements be eliminated or reduced to shorten the inspection time or to eliminate it?
4. Can inspection be performed in combination with another step? During an operator's idle time?
5. Can a mechanical or electronic inspection device be employed, thus eliminating the operator's time and effort?

Storages

1. Does the storage aid in the overall productive process (such as aging tobacco or wine)? If not, can it be eliminated?
2. Do subsequent operations bottleneck the material, thus making storage necessary? If so, can the bottleneck be eliminated?
3. Can the storage time be reduced or eliminated by better planning and a better balance of the subsequent operations?
4. Can the steps immediately preceding and following the storage be eliminated, thus obviating the necessity for the storage?

Delays

1. Does the delay occur with any degree of regularity? If so, can the cause be controlled to prevent recurrence?
2. Can mechanical controls, electric signals, or other apparatus be effectively used to eliminate the delay?

By asking questions like these, you can usually simplify jobs, making them easier and quicker to perform.

ARE FLOW DIAGRAMS USED WITH PROCESS CHARTS?

Flow diagrams and process charts are often used together. A flow diagram is a picture of the *movement* or *flow* of products (or people) that you described on the process chart. It is a map of the work area on which you show where the various operations, delays, transportations, etc., take place.

Figure 19–3 is a flow diagram of the work described in the process

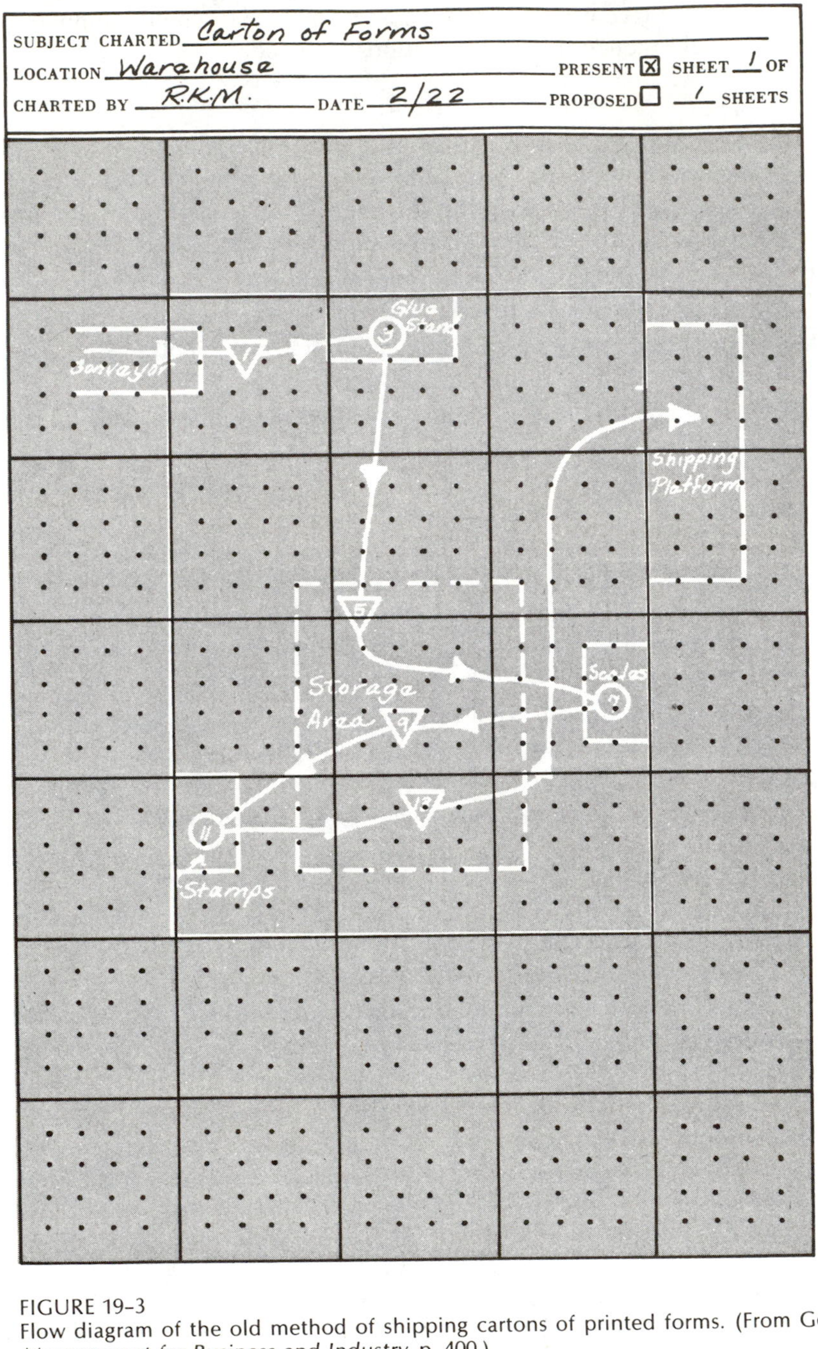

FIGURE 19-3
Flow diagram of the old method of shipping cartons of printed forms. (From George, *Management for Business and Industry*, p. 400.)

chart on p. 359. Note that the symbol for a step in the process is placed on the flow diagram at the place where it occurred. For example, the third step in the process chart (the operation of gluing the carton) is shown on the flow diagram by a circle (the symbol for an operation) at the exact spot where the gluing operation took place. Numbers corresponding to the step numbers on the process chart are placed inside these symbols for easy reference and identification.

map showing movement

HOW DO PROCESS CHARTS AND FLOW DIAGRAMS HELP MAKE WORK EASIER?

Process charts and flow diagrams make work easier because with them, you can better understand and study the whole job. For example, after analyzing the process chart and flow diagram shown in Figures 19–2 and 19–3, respectively, and then questioning each step in accordance with the foregoing checklist of questions, a company developed a new method for shipping material. A process chart and flow diagram of the new method are shown in Figures 19–4 and 19–5, respectively. Note the savings in the summary

SUBJECT CHARTED *Carton of forms*

LOCATION *Warehouse*

PRESENT ☐   PROPOSED ☒

CHARTED BY *R.K.M.*

SHEET *1* OF *1* SHEETS

SUMMARY						
	PRESENT		PROPOSED		SAVING	
	NO.	TIME	NO.	TIME	NO.	TIME
◯ OPERATION	3		3		0	
⇨ TRANSPORTATION	7		3		4	
DIST. IN FEET	52		12		40	
☐ INSPECTION	0		0		0	
▭ DELAY	0		0		0	
▽ STORAGE	4		0		4	

DIST IN FEET	SYMBOL	DESCRIPTION	TIME	REMARKS
3	⇨ 1	To Glue stand		
	◯ 2	Carton glued		
3	⇨ 3	To scales		
	◯ 4	Weighed		
	◯ 5	Stamps Affixed		
6	⇨ 6	To Shipping Platform		

FIGURE 19–4
Process chart of proposed new method of shipping cartons of printed forms. (From George, *Management for Business and Industry*, pp. 401–2.)

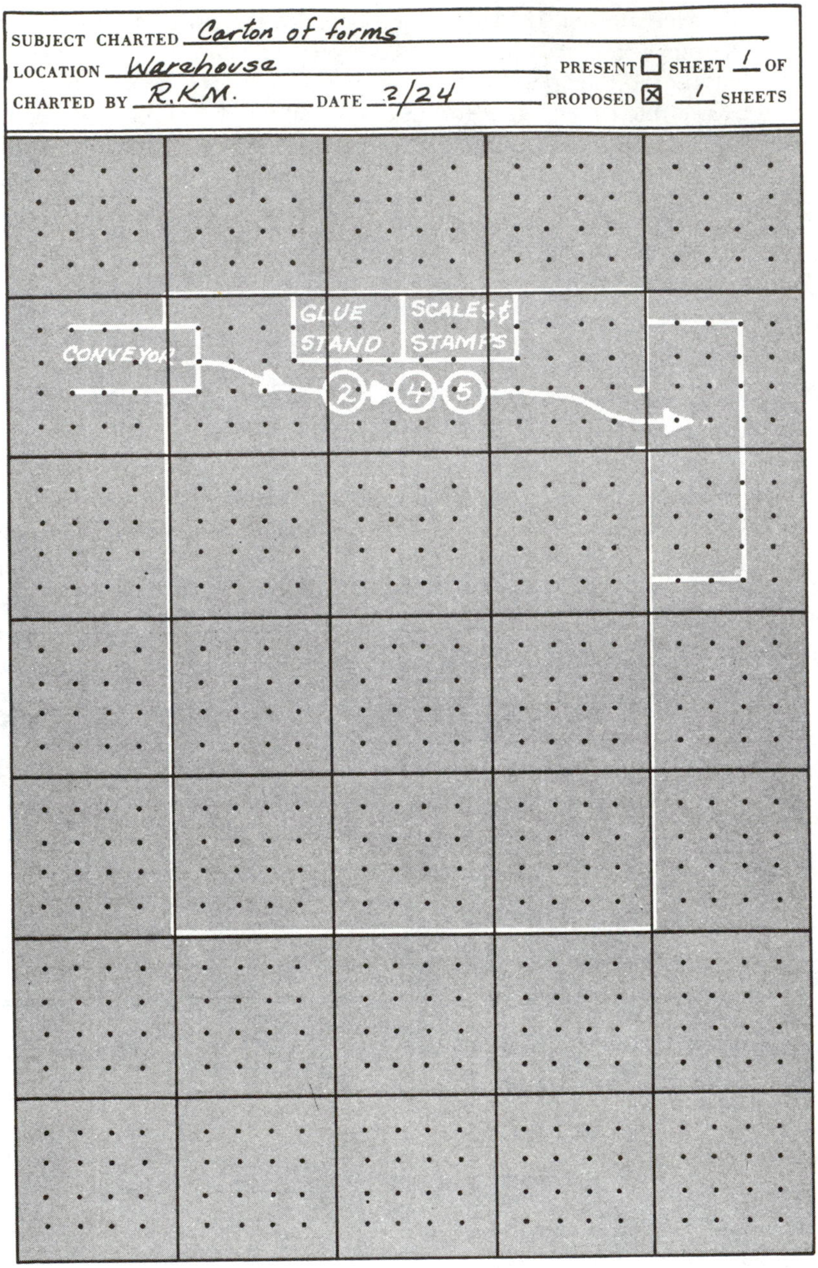

SUBJECT CHARTED _Carton of forms_
LOCATION _Warehouse_ PRESENT ☐ SHEET _1_ OF
CHARTED BY _R.K.M._ DATE _2/24_ PROPOSED ☒ _1_ SHEETS

CONVEYOR   GLUE STAND   SCALES & STAMPS

FIGURE 19-5
Flow diagram of proposed new method of shipping cartons of printed forms. (From George, *Management for Business and Industry*, pp. 401–2.)

shown in Figure 19–4 that you would realize if you used the new method. By analyzing this shipping room function using a process chart and flow diagram, this company was able to reduce the work force in the shipping room, thereby saving $12,670 annually.

365

HOW TO SIMPLIFY
WORK AND
INCREASE
PRODUCTION

*use in studying
work*

Process charts and flow diagrams are very simple, yet effective, tools of analysis. Both are of value in establishing the overall sequence of operations and in determining the best layout for an economical, efficient flow of materials. They present a clear picture of a process and are very powerful tools for studying and improving a complex job. Both process charts and flow diagrams are particularly useful in the following ways:[2]

1. Effectively locating work areas.
2. Establishing the best sequence of operations.
3. Eliminating unnecessary work.
4. Pointing out idle times and delays.
5. Establishing a better layout for an efficient flow of material.
6. Suggesting means of eliminating ill-directed effort.
7. Reducing the number of steps in a process.
8. Making the remaining steps as economical as possible.
9. Reducing materials handling.
10. Decreasing the distance material is moved.

WHAT IS THE BEST WAY TO STUDY A PROCESS?

The easiest way for you to study a process is as follows:[3]

1. Choose a definite starting and stopping point for the process studied.
2. Make a process chart of the work as it is currently being performed. Be sure that no steps are omitted.
3. Construct a flow diagram of the process, showing the steps and path of movement of materials or persons and indicating relationships.
4. Analyze the process chart and flow diagram. Question each step. Determine the validity of each step in the process. Devise a better method of performing the work.
5. Construct a process chart and flow diagram of the proposed way of performing the work, establishing proper relationships between departments and steps. Take particular care to find the shortest, easiest route.

[2] From George, *Management for Business and Industry*, pp. 401–3.
[3] Adapted with permission from George, *Management for Business and Industry*, p. 403.

6. Test the new method to assure its effectiveness.

7. Instruct the operators and others concerned, and put the new method into effect.

"The study of body motions is called motion analysis."

WHAT IS MOTION ANALYSIS?

Up to this point, we've been talking about improving a process by looking at each step. In motion analysis, you try to improve whatever a *person* is doing.

Most work is performed with the hands. If you watch what a worker's hands are doing instead of the product being worked on, you can usually spot many wasted or nonproductive movements. This study of body motions is called *motion analysis*. To help improve work motions, you should apply the rules of motion economy as noted in the next section.

WHAT ARE SOME OF THE RULES OF MOTION ECONOMY?

Most untrained workers use one hand first and then the other to perform work. For example, if your job called for you to pick up four different items and put them in a box to be shipped as spare parts for a product, you would probably use one hand exclusively to pick up the parts, or you would use first one hand and then the other. According to the rules of motion economy, neither of these methods would be a good way to do the job.

The first rule of motion economy is that *the work should be distributed between the hands so that both are working simultaneously.* To better balance the work of the two hands, the second rule adds that *the two hands should follow opposite and symmetrical motion patterns.* You can "feel" the logic of this rule when you move your hands through opposite and symmetrical motion patterns. For example, place your left hand on your left shoulder and your right hand on your right shoulder. Now move both hands straight up above your head, now back to your shoulders. Now extend them straight out on each side, now back to your shoulders. Now extend them straight out in front of you, then back to your shoulders, and so on. This is a routine exercise. Now try moving one hand up and the other out. Notice how "unbalanced" and "unnatural" this feels.

Another rule of motion economy is that *tools and materials should be located for easy accessibility and in a way that will employ the best possible sequence of motions.* Figure 19–6 illustrates the areas where materials and tools are most easily accessible.

Apply these rules to your job of picking up four different items and putting them in a box. The best layout and sequence would probably be to arrange the four parts in a semicircle in front of you, as shown in the diagram below. Now reach for part #1 with your left hand, and at the same time reach for part #4 with your right hand. Pick up the parts *at the same time*, bring both parts back to the box *at the same time*, and drop them in the box *at the same time*. Now repeat the process picking up parts #2 and #3, and put them in the box.

367

HOW TO SIMPLIFY
WORK AND
INCREASE
PRODUCTION

*making work
easier*

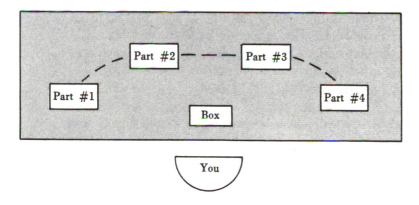

To prove how these principles of motion economy have helped, go through the actual motions of picking up four items one at a time, placing them in a box one at a time. Time yourself using the second hand on a watch. Now do the job the improved way using both hands. You'll probably cut your time in half!

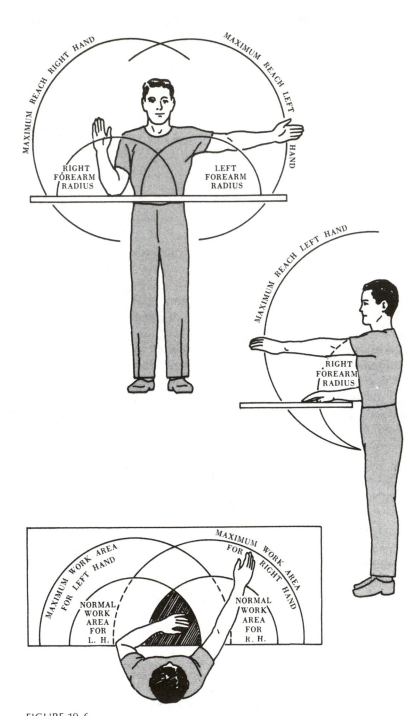

FIGURE 19-6
Normal and maximum work areas in horizontal and vertical planes. (From George, *Management for Business and Industry*, p. 409.)

Some other rules of motion economy are:

1. Study any hesitation to see whether its cause can be eliminated.

2. Make hand motions as simple as possible, so they are easier and faster. Hand motions classified from fastest to slowest are:
   a. Finger motions only
   b. Finger and wrist motions
   c. Motions involving the fingers, wrist, and forearm.
   d. Motions involving the fingers, wrist, forearm, and upper arm.
   e. Motions involving the fingers, wrist, forearm, upper arm, and body.

3. Locate tools and materials within the normal work areas and as close to the operator as possible.

4. It is usually quicker to slide, roll, or shove a small part rather than pick it up and carry it.

5. Motions that require sudden changes in directions are slower and more tiring than smooth, continuous, curving motions.

6. Arrange the parts of a job so that they are as simple, automatic, and rhythmical as possible.

7. Have a place for all tools and materials, and have all tools and materials in their place. This will eliminate the necessity of having to fumble and look for parts and tools.

SHOULD YOU STUDY A JOB MORE THAN ONCE?

You should study a job a number of times. You'll never reach perfection, and you'll never find the one best way of doing a job. The loom, for example, is in many ways the same today as it was 100 years ago. Yet at this very moment, people are studying looms and their operators in textile plants across the nation, trying to find still a better way to get the job done.

This doesn't mean that you should study a job, then turn around and study it again. You should first study jobs that haven't been studied or jobs where the possibility of striking "pay dirt" is greater.

WHICH JOBS SHOULD YOU STUDY FIRST?

Your common sense will probably be a good guide. You should study jobs first that are causing you trouble. Improving these will probably do the most good. After that, maybe the following will give you some hints on where the payoff will be.

1. Look for jobs that involve a large expenditure of man-hours, machine hours, and dollars. These usually afford good hunting.

2. Study the main process that the company is involved in. If the company bottles soft drinks, study this operation before you do the clerical operations.

3. Study jobs whose probable life will be long. If a job is only going to last a couple of weeks, it may not be worth studying.

4. Study bottlenecks, jobs where performance requirements are not being met, or jobs where a lot of overtime is worked.

5. Look for jobs involving a lot of people doing the same thing.

6. Study jobs that are short in duration and repetitive. Short-cycled, highly repetitive jobs involving a lot of people usually offer good opportunities to make a little improvement amount to a great deal.

7. Try to improve work that requires a great deal of physical activity along with frequent rest periods.

8. Look for jobs where excess material is wasted.

9. Try to improve jobs that are dangerous, where the accident rate is high, or where it is undesirable to work because of such things as noise, extreme temperature, fumes, and so on.

10. See if you can simplify the job being performed by highly skilled employees so that less skilled workers can do the job.

11. Look for jobs where quality or quantity standards are not being maintained.

WHICH PARTS OF A JOB SHOULD YOU STUDY FIRST?

Some parts of a job offer a better opportunity to make improvements than do other parts. Think of every task as being divided into three parts:

Part 1, you *get ready* to do the job. This means getting tools, supplies, parts—everything you'll need. Before you ice a cake, for example, you have to get out the cake, icing mix, milk, etc. Before you mow your lawn, you have to get your mower, shears, etc., in preparation.

Part 2, you *do the work*. This is the part that counts. This is the part that adds value to the product. You push or ride a mower around. You trim the edges. Your home looks better and is more valuable with a well-trimmed lawn versus an overgrown mass of weeds two feet high. Or you ice a cake in a bakery, and it adds value to the dry layers.

Part 3, you *put away* the tools. This involves everything that has to be undone, unloaded, washed, cleaned up, and put away. Cleaning the pots and pans and returning the icing to the refrigerator are part of "put away." Cleaning your lawn mower and storing it and your shears in the tool shed are parts of this step.

The part to study and try to improve is part 2, the "do" part. The reason is simple. If you can simplify or eliminate the "do" altogether, you will also eliminate or change the "make ready" and "put away" parts. After you have done everything you can to improve the "do" part, then move to the "make ready" and "put away" steps to study and improve them.

WHAT IS AN OPERATIONS CHART?

An operations chart is simply a "picture" of the simultaneous work that the right and left hands are doing. Sometimes we call it a left-hand/right-hand chart. The operations chart shown in Figure 19–7 shows what an employee is doing to assemble a pipe clamp. Note that you use the same symbols that you used in the process charts.

By studying Figure 19–7, you can see that the work of the two hands is not balanced. One is working and the other is either idle or merely holding a part. Applying the rules of motion economy and using a jig instead of the left hand to hold the parts, an improved procedure was developed, as illustrated in Figure 19–8. Note that the two hands are now productively employed in a balanced manner and that output has been doubled with no increase in the number of steps in the job.

making and using operations charts

CAN SUPERVISORS MAKE METHODS IMPROVEMENT STUDIES?

With a little practice, you can do methods improvement studies. However, there are specialists in motion study who are called *industrial engineers*. They use the same techniques we have discussed so far. In addition, they also use micromotion analysis. To do the most refined work in this field, you need to have some formal training in order to know how to do film analyses, multiple-activity analyses, and so on. However, anyone can do the type of motion study we have been talking about. Some supervisors are good at it. And the employees themselves who are doing the jobs can frequently figure out better ways to do the work than anyone else can.

anyone can improve jobs

DO EMPLOYEES FEAR METHODS IMPROVEMENT?

Employees sometimes distrust and suspect methods improvement because it involves changing their jobs so that work can be done more easily and in less time. This in turn makes them think that fewer employees will be needed and that they might lose their jobs. You have to assure them that this will not be true. You have to explain what methods improvement is and assure your employees that their jobs will not be eliminated—that they will not be fired, that their pay will not be decreased, and that they will not have to work harder. And be sure you mean what you are saying, and abide by it. If you don't, you're in trouble before you start.

Explain to your employees what methods improvement is. Try to get their cooperation in improving their own jobs. Consider offering rewards for the most improvement made. If you have a union, get the steward to ex-

explain the need for job study

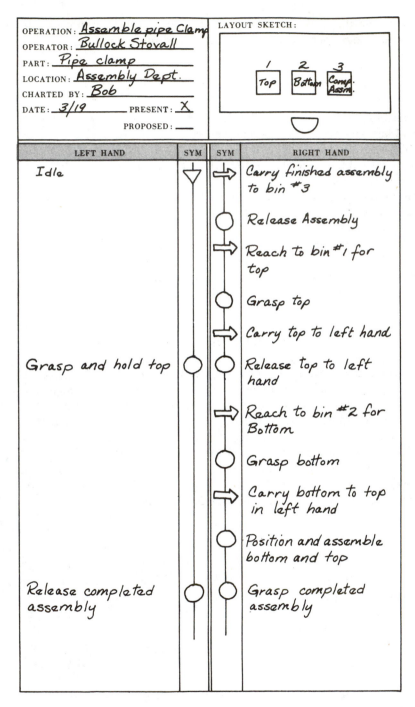

OPERATION: *Assemble pipe Clamp*			LAYOUT SKETCH:
OPERATOR: *Bullock Stovall*			
PART: *Pipe clamp*			
LOCATION: *Assembly Dept.*			
CHARTED BY: *Bob*			
DATE: *3/19* PRESENT: X			
PROPOSED: ___			

LEFT HAND	SYM	SYM	RIGHT HAND
Idle	▽	⇨	Carry finished assembly to bin #3
		◯	Release Assembly
		⇨	Reach to bin #1 for top
		◯	Grasp top
		⇨	Carry top to left hand
Grasp and hold top	◯	◯	Release top to left hand
		⇨	Reach to bin #2 for Bottom
		◯	Grasp bottom
		⇨	Carry bottom to top in left hand
		◯	Position and assemble bottom and top
Release completed assembly	◯	◯	Grasp completed assembly

FIGURE 19–7
Operations chart of the original method of assembling pipe clamps. (From George, *Management for Business and Industry*, p. 422.)

| | OPERATION: Assemble Pipe Clamp. |
| OPERATOR: Bullock Stovall |
| PART: Pipe Clamp |
| LOCATION: Assembly Dept. |
| CHARTED BY: Bob |
| DATE: 3/19 PRESENT: |
| PROPOSED: X |

LAYOUT SKETCH:

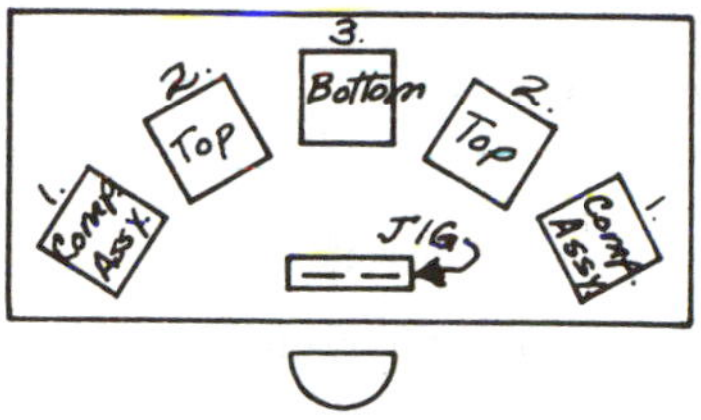

LEFT HAND	SYM	SYM	RIGHT HAND
Carry finished assembly to bin #1	⇨	⇨	Carry finished assembly to bin #1
Release assembly	○	○	Release assembly
Reach to bin 2 for top	⇨	⇨	Reach to bin 2 for top
Grasp top	○	○	Grasp top
Carry Top to jig	⇨	⇨	Carry top to jig
Position top in jig	○	○	Position top in jig
Reach to bin 3 for bottom	⇨	⇨	Reach to bin 3 for bottom
Grasp bottom	○	○	Grasp bottom
Carry bottom to jig	⇨	⇨	Carry bottom to jig
Position and assemble bottom to top	○	○	Position and assemble bottom to top
Grasp completed assembly	○	○	Grasp completed assembly

FIGURE 19–8
Operations chart of proposed new method of assembling pipe clamps. (From George, *Management for Business and Industry*, p. 423.)

plain what the company is trying to do, and assure the employees that they will not be penalized. We all fear the unknown, but if we know what is being done, and if we ourselves are applying the principles of methods improvement, then one of the greatest obstacles has been overcome.

HOW CAN METHODS IMPROVEMENT HELP THE SUPERVISOR?

Your job as a supervisor is to produce more and better products at less cost. One of the best and easiest ways you can do this is to apply methods improvement to the work done in your department. When work is thus improved, it means that your department is typically out front in terms of efficiency, costs, and job performance. As a result, you will have fewer problems getting what you ask for in terms of equipment, overtime, and working conditions. Inasmuch as you are running a good department, you will usually get what you want from management.

advantages of study

Methods improvement also makes supervision easier because the supervisor's employees are working "smarter," not harder—they are doing their jobs in a more efficient manner. When employees know what their jobs are and how to do them in the simplest and easiest way, they are typically happier with their work. And the satisfied and happy employee is usually the productive employee.

Finally, methods improvement helps you personally, because it puts your supervisory abilities in a favorable light when raises and promotions are up for consideration. Good work methods, productive employees, and a smoothly running department—all resulting from methods improvement—call attention to your good supervision.

QUESTIONS FOR DISCUSSION AND REVIEW

1. What is methods improvement? Motion study? Work simplification?
2. What is a process chart? How is it used?
3. Give examples of five steps in a process.
4. Where can process charts be used?
5. How do you make a process chart?
6. How do you analyze a process chart? Why do you do it?
7. What is a flow diagram? How is it used?
8. How can process charts and flow diagrams make work easier?
9. What is the best way to study a process?
10. What is motion analysis?
11. Explain and illustrate five rules of motion economy.
12. How many times should you study a job?
13. Which jobs should you study first?
14. Explain the use of an operations chart.

15. Why do employees fear methods improvement?

16. How can methods improvement help the supervisor?

A Case Study
GREYSTONE MANUFACTURING

The employees in the office of Greystone Manufacturing were preparing for the annual sales convention to be held in Miami. Some were cutting stencils, some were checking addresses and accommodations, and others were assembling packages of material. Over 700 salesmen were expected to be present, and preparing for them was no small task.

Mary Littleton and Nancy Hester probably had the two most monotonous jobs. Mary's job consisted of picking up and placing in a folder four sheets of paper, which outlined the tentative program for the convention. The program sheets, standard 8½" × 11", were picked up and placed in a standard manila file folder. Mary's work place is illustrated in Figure 19–9. She assembled the

Mary's Work Place

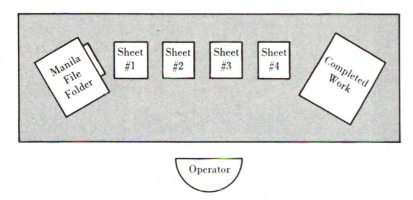

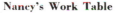

Nancy's Work Table

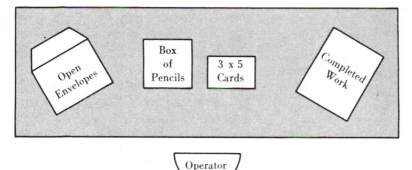

FIGURE 19–9
Layout of Mary's and Nancy's work places. (From George, *Management in Industry,* p. 392.)

sheets as follows. She picked up sheet #1 with her right hand and placed the sheet in her left hand. Her left hand then held the sheet while the right hand picked up sheet #2 and placed it in her left hand along with sheet #1. In similar fashion, she picked up sheets #3 and #4. Using her right hand, she got a manila folder from the stack on her left, opened the folder, placed the four sheets in the folder with her left hand, and placed the folder on the completed pile on her right hand.

Nancy's work, on the other hand, consisted of placing a 3″ × 5″ card and a pencil in a standard envelope. She was situated at a table as shown in Figure 19–9. In performing her job, Nancy picked up an open envelope with her left hand. Then, holding the envelope in her left hand, she picked up and placed a pencil in the envelope with her right hand. Still holding the envelope in her left hand, she placed a 3″ × 5″ card in it, transferred the envelope to her right hand, and disposed of it on her right.

The women had hardly completed 50 units when they saw that it was going to be a long, tiring task.

1. Construct an operations chart of each job.
2. Using the charts and the principles of motion study, devise a better and easier way for Mary and Nancy to do their work.
3. Illustrate your improvements by constructing operations charts of the new methods.

A Case Study
BURLINGTON MACHINE WORKS

The Burlington Machine Works was organized in 1970 to fabricate and manufacture metal parts and subassemblies for other manufacturing concerns. The plant makes a variety of products, but the major portion of its business consists of (1) fabricating a bracket assembly, (2) assembling a small gear train in a housing, and (3) fabricating a control lever for a vending machine. These three items are relatively easy to handle, are about the same size, and are manufactured in approximately the same quantities.

During the manufacturing process, the three items must go through the following departments in the sequence indicated:

Bracket Assembly	Gear Train	Vending Machine Lever
Storeroom	Storeroom	Storeroom
Machine Shop	Plating Shop	Machine Shop
Assembly Shop	Assembly Shop	Plating Department
Paint Shop	Paint Shop	Inspection Department
Packing & Shipping	Packing & Shipping	Machine Shop
		Assembly Shop
		Inspection Department
		Plating Department
		Paint Shop
		Inspection Department
		Packing & Shipping

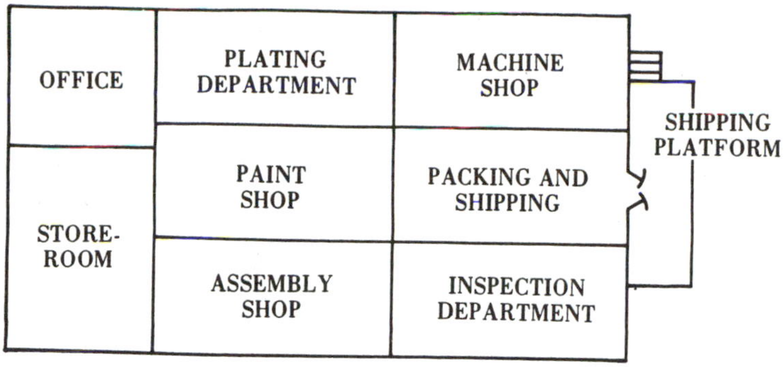

OFFICE	PLATING DEPARTMENT	MACHINE SHOP	
STORE-ROOM	PAINT SHOP	PACKING AND SHIPPING	SHIPPING PLATFORM
	ASSEMBLY SHOP	INSPECTION DEPARTMENT	

FIGURE 19–10
Layout of Burlington Machine Works Plant.

The layout of the paint, shown in Figure 19–10, was developed by Mr. Kingsley, the owner, without too much thought or study. With the three items taking up a major percentage of his shop's productive capacity, however, he is very much aware of the extra handling of material caused by poor layout and is trying to rearrange his plant so as to have a minimum movement of items and thus a smooth flow of material.

To accomplish this objective, Mr. Kingsley is willing to swap or move the departments about in any fashion. For example, if it would improve the flow of items through the plant, he would move the assembly department to the area now occupied by the plating shop, or put the paint shop where the machine shop is, etc. However, Mr. Kingsley doesn't want to move the packing and shipping department because he feels that it should remain at the rear of the building, where the exit doors and the shipping platform are located.

1. Considering the three products manufactured, what layout would you recommend for Mr. Kingsley?
2. Construct flow diagrams for each of the items as now manufactured.
3. Construct flow diagrams for each item in your improved layout.
4. Why is your layout superior to Mr. Kingsley's?

A Case Study
DEALING CARDS

Prepare an operations chart of the way you would typically deal two decks of 52 cards each into eight piles. Use Figure 19–7 as a guide for preparing the form. With it, show what the right hand and the left hand are doing simultaneously.

After completing the operations chart, ask yourself how both of your hands could be better used to achieve the same end result, i.e., two decks of cards divided into eight equal piles. Your objective here is not to use the cards to play a game, but to perform the job of dealing the cards into eight equal piles, one card at a time. The sequence in which the cards are dealt is immaterial. After you have devised a new way to deal the cards, make an operations chart showing how you have made the job more effective.

1. Do you find your new way of dealing 104 cards into eight piles less tiring than the old way?
2. Do you find your improved way easier? Does it take less time? Why?
3. Did the operations chart offer you substantial help in devising your new system? How?

A Personal Case Problem

One of the new employees in your restaurant has just told you that you expect her to set up tables too quickly—that you don't allow enough time. Setting up a table in your restaurant consists of placing a plate, a cup and saucer, a knife, a fork, a spoon, and a napkin at each of four places on the table. After watching the new waitress set up a table, you note that her method is slow and time consuming.

Prepare an operations chart of the way you want the waitress to set up a table, show the chart to the class, and then demonstrate the method using a card table (or a similar table). Start your demonstration with the four plates, four cups, four saucers, silver, and napkins stacked in the center of the table.

Can the class improve on your method? How?

20

HOW TO MEASURE WORK

This chapter explains—

- Why you need time standards
- How you can develop time standards
- What to tell your employees about time standards

Have you ever stopped to think that we buy coffee by the pound, coal by the ton, and gasoline by the gallon—yet when we buy an hour's worth of work from an employee, we don't know what we are buying? Workers have different capacities, and although they may be making the same amount of money per hour, the amount of work they turn out varies widely. In fact, in some plants it is not unusual for the output of employees doing the same job to vary by as much as 100%; that is, the best employee produces twice the amount of the poorest employee. The reason for this difference might be that one employee is more skilled than the other, that one employee works faster than the other, or that one employee knows and uses a better and shorter way to do the job. To help even out these situations, and to instruct your employees as to how they should do a job, you as a supervisor will need to know the best way to do a piece of work and *how long* it should take the average employee to do it. In other words, *you need to know the standard time.*

WHAT IS STANDARD TIME?

allowed time

Standard time is the time that is allowed to do a specified quantity and quality of work. It is the time that is allowed for an average employee, working at average pace, to do a job day after day without ill effects. You might find, for example, that you should allow 1.80 minutes for an employee to sew a seam in a garment. To sew 100 seams, therefore, you would allow the employee $100 \times 1.80 = 180$ minutes, or three hours.

Standard time includes:

1. How long it should actually take an average employee to do the work while working at a normal pace.
2. An allowance for work interruptions, fatigue, and personal time.

WHY DO YOU NEED TIME STANDARDS?

Once you know how long it should take an average employee to a job, then you can figure out how much work an average employee *should* turn out in an hour or a day. Or you can figure out what would constitute a fair day's work.

Other reasons for knowing how long it should take an employee to perform a task are:

1. As a supervisor, you can assign jobs more equally and fairly since you know how much work is involved in them.
2. You can plan and schedule your department's work load better.

3. Your employees can be paid fairly and equitably according to the quality and quantity of work they do.
4. The costs in your department can be calculated more easily.
5. The relative efficiency of an employee, a group of employees, or the entire department can be easily calculated by comparing how much work they actually completed to how much they should have done. For example, if they should have turned out 100 pieces and only did 80, then their efficiency would be 80% (80 ÷ 100 = 80%). If they turned out 120 pieces, their efficiency would be 120% (120 ÷ 100 = 120%).

*how much time
to allow*

WHAT EQUIPMENT IS USED TO DEVELOP A STANDARD TIME?

In many situations, you can time a job by using an ordinary wristwatch with a second hand. At other times, however, you'll need to measure time in shorter intervals than seconds and minutes. For these shorter intervals, use a stopwatch that measures times in hundredths of a minute.

HOW DO YOU DEVELOP A STANDARD TIME?

First of all, you *select an operator* who knows how to do the work using the right equipment and method. Select a good, average worker, not a speed demon, because most employees think that if you study a fast worker, the time allowed will be less than if you study a normal worker. This is not true, and as we will see later in our discussion of performance rating, the end result is the same regardless of the operator you choose. You should not, however, select an unskilled employee or one who is nervous and prefers not to be observed.

Second, *be sure that the working conditions are standard*—that is, that the raw materials, tools, layout, lighting, etc., are the same for each employee. It wouldn't be fair to time an operator using machines and raw materials different from those used by the other workers.

Third, *break the job down into steps or elements* of short duration. A step or element has an easily identifiable beginning and ending. For example, the elements in the job of testing a lock in a lock manufacturing plant might be:

*steps in
developing a
standard*

1. Get key from box and insert in lock.
2. Turn lock twice to be sure bolt works freely.
3. Remove key from lock and return to box.

These three elements make up one cycle of work.

You need to break the job down into elements, rather than time the whole job, because some elements in a job do not occur during each cycle.

For example, an operator might have to make slight changes in the machine every few cycles. If you timed the whole job for several cycles, you would get different times for each cycle, which you could not explain. These differences in times would be caused by the operator's making adjustments in the machine every few cycles. The cycle in which the employee made the adjustment would be longer than the other cycles. You wouldn't be able to explain these time differences unless you had broken the job down into steps or elements and thus became aware of the adjustment step. Also, you get the best description of the job and how it is performed when you break it down into its basic elements.

Fourth, *record the elements* on a piece of paper in the sequence in which they are performed.

Fifth, *time the work*. Time enough cycles so that you have a good sample of what the operator is doing.

Sixth, *determine the selected time*. The selected time is the time you select from your observations as being representative of each element. You might select the time that appears most frequently, or you could simply average the times to get the selected time. For example, assume that the times for the lock-testing cycle are:

| Element | Time in Minutes | | | | | |
	Cycle 1	Cycle 2	Cycle 3	Cycle 4	Cycle 5	Cycle 6
1. Get key from box and insert in lock	.25	.26	.24	.25	.23	.27
2. Turn lock twice	.50	.50	.48	.52	.51	.49
3. Remove key and return to box	.25	.23	.28	.25	.25	.24

The time appearing most frequently for element #1 (get key and insert in lock) is .25, which you could use as your selected time for element #1. Or you could average the times required to perform element #1. If you average the times required to perform each element and use this average as your selected time per element, you get the following:

1. Get key from box and insert in lock	.25 minute—selected time for element #1
2. Turn lock twice	.50 minute—selected time for element #2
3. Remove key and return to box	.25 minute—selected time for element #3
Selected time per cycle (all three elements) =	1.00 minute

Seventh, *determine a performance rating*. Not all operators work at the same pace. Therefore, it would not be fair for you to set a work standard based on the time required by either a fast or a slow operator to do the job. Some allowance for speed, therefore, should be made in the time you select as being representative. If the operator you timed worked faster than the average employee, you would need to add some time to the time you observed in order to get a fair time. If the operator you timed worked slower than an average employee, you would need to subtract from the time you observed.

Time study experts are trained to evaluate an operator's speed and thus rate the operator's performance. With this training as a background, the expert watches an employee work and rates or compares the operator's speed or pace with his or her concept of a normal pace. If the time study expert determines that the operator is working 10% faster than normal, he or she would rate the operator at 110%. If the expert determines that the operator is working 20% slower than normal, he or she would rate the operator at 80%. The expert would rate the operator at 100% if he or she determines that the operator is working at a normal pace.

Eighth, *apply the performance rating.* Assume you rated the operator in the key-lock example at 120%. The time required by an average employee working at average pace would be the time you selected for the cycle (1.00) multiplied by 120% (or 1.20). This would give 1.00 min. × 1.20 = 1.20 minutes. Since you rated the operator as working 20% faster than normal, the time that an average employee would take to do the job working at normal pace would be 20% longer than 1.00 minute, or 1.20 minutes. This is called the *normal time.*

Ninth, *add allowances.* To determine a standard time, you need to make some allowances for:

1. Normal work interruption. (The boss speaks to the employee or the employee drops a part on the floor.)
2. Fatigue. (As the employee works longer, he or she becomes tired and works slower.)
3. Personal needs such as cleaning one's glasses, going to the washroom, etc.

In a normal work environment, we commonly find 10 to 15% added for these allowances. If you use 10%, this would be the equivalent of allowing 48 minutes per eight-hour day to cover allowances.

Using our same example, you take the normal time of 1.20 minutes and add 10% of it for allowances. This would give you 1.20 minutes + .10 (1.20 minutes) = 1.32 minutes. This means that you would allow an operator 1.32 minutes to test each lock. Or you would expect the employee to test 45.45 locks per hour (60 minutes ÷ 1.32 minutes = 45.45). Stating it otherwise, the standard time per lock is 1.32 minutes.

Figure 20–1 illustrates a time study of the job of assembling electric coils. Note that under each element are columns headed R and T. R is the reading from a watch, and T is the time it took to do the element. For element 1, the reading was .06, for element 2 it was .16, for element 3 it was

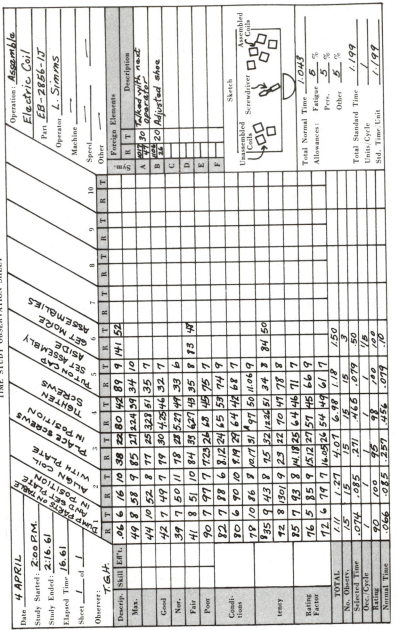

FIGURE 20-1

Time study of assembling electric coils (From George, *Management for Business and Industry*, p. 441).

.38, and so on. You determine the actual time for each of these elements by getting the differences in these watch readings. Thus, it took .10 of a minute (the difference between .06 and .16) to perform element 2; for element 3, the actual time is .22 (the difference between .16 and .38), and so on. Note the rating, allowances, and standard time on this study.

DO TIME STUDIES MAKE FOR POOR QUALITY?

The idea behind a time study is to set a pace at which *average* workers can perform day in and day out with no detriment to health or well-being. This should not make for a decrease in work quality. However, a particular employee with more skill than the average employee can produce more and therefore earn more if he or she is working at piece rates. But the catch is that only production that passes inspection and meets the company's quality standard will count. Thus, an employee who tries to go too fast at a sacrifice in quality won't get paid for the extra production. In general, employees soon learn to pace themselves at a level of output that they can sustain and at which they can produce a product of acceptable quality.

*pay and work
quality*

HOW IS STANDARD TIME LINKED WITH INCENTIVE PAY?

At this point, you know that the standard time for the lock problem is 1.32 minutes with a standard output per hour of 45.45 locks. You can convert this to wage rates per unit (piece rates) as follows. If the going rate of pay in the community for this type of work is $6.82 per hour, then you would pay an operator at the rate of 15¢[1] per unit ($6.82 ÷ 45.45 = 15¢). If an employee worked faster than average, he or she could test more locks per hour, say, 60. This means that for one hour of work, the employee would receive $9.00 (60 × 15¢ = $9.00).

WHAT INCENTIVE PLAN IS MOST COMMONLY USED?

The 100% bonus plan, also known as the *hour-for-hour plan,* is the most commonly used plan. It is identical to straight piecework illustrated above, except that it has a guaranteed base and allowances are made in terms of time for each unit of output instead of money.

Using our same lock illustration of 45.45 units per hour as standard and a base rate of $6.82 per hour, an employee would be allowed 1.32 minutes per unit of output (60 minutes ÷ 45.45 = 1.32 minutes) instead of a piece rate of 15¢ per unit. Thus, an employee who produced only 40 units

[1] Actually, 15.0055¢.

per hour would have a daily wage of $54.55 since he or she would receive the guaranteed base of $6.82 per hour, but would not receive a bonus due to not having exceeded the standard of 45.45 units per hour.

allowances in time

If the employee's rate of output had been 60 units per hour, he or she would have received an allowance of 1.32 minutes per unit for the 480 units produced during the day. The employee would have earned, therefore, 633.6 minutes of pay (480 units × 1.32 minutes allowed per unit = 633.6 minutes), or 10.56 hours. This, multiplied by $6.82 per hour, equals $72.02, the employee's rate of pay for the day.

This plan is simple and easy to understand and has the added feature that piece rates do not have to be refigured every time the wage rate changes. It is the most universally suitable incentive plan that uses carefully set standards based on an accurate system of time studies. Wages can be easily calculated by the employee regardless of what his or her hourly rate is. And, finally, management likes the plan because efficiency can be figured for individual employees, groups, departments, or the whole plant using the formula.

$$\text{Efficiency} = \frac{\text{Standard hours earned}}{\text{Actual hours worked}}$$

Using this formula, you could calculate employee efficiency, for the above figures. Thus, for 60 units per hour for a day, an employee's efficiency would be

$$E = \frac{\text{Standard hours earned}}{\text{Actual hours worked}}$$

$$E = \frac{10.56}{8}$$

$$E = 1.32 \text{ or } 132\%$$

DO UNIONS APPROVE OF INCENTIVE SYSTEMS?

Labor is keenly interested in any plan affecting the wages of its members. Some unions, like those of the miners, textile workers, clothing workers, cigar makers, shoe makers, iron and steel workers, potters, and flint glass workers, either prefer incentive pay systems or accept them willingly. Of course, some unions vigorously oppose incentive pay for their members. Much of labor's opposition, however, can be blamed on the malpractices of unscrupulous management in the application of incentive systems. During recent years there are many signs that these unions are not as opposed to incentives as they were previously. This has been brought about mainly by better personnel policies, better labor relations, better worker education, and more enlightened management practices.

In fact, when morale is high, and when trust and good relations exist between labor an management, almost any wage incentive system can be made to work. Millions of workers are moderately satisfied with their wage incentive plans, and many more employees accept them as a result of their positive experiences.

DO YOU NEED A TIME STUDY TO GET A STANDARD TIME?

You do not need a time study to get a standard time—if standard data are available. If many time studies have been made of highly repetitive work, these time values (standard data) can be used instead of making new time studies. For example, a standard operation in a furniture factory is drilling the same diameter hole in a standard-size board. The only variation in the job is the depth of the hole, and over the years data have been recorded in chart form (Figure 20–2) showing the time needed to drill various depths of ¼-inch holes in white pine. Thus, to get a standard time for a new job of drilling a ¼-inch hole in a white pine board, all you need to do is look up the time values (derived from time studies over the years) for picking up a

standard data

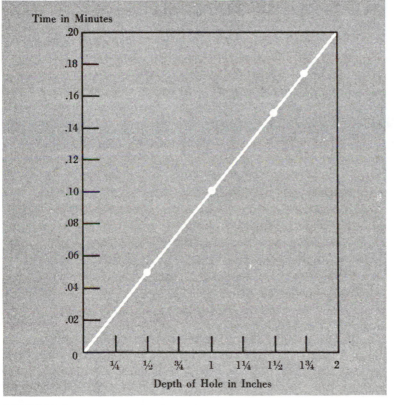

FIGURE 20–2
Leveled time for drilling ¼" hole in white pine board.

board and placing it on the drill press, drilling the hole, and removing the board from the press. This is a quick and reliable way to get a standard, and, inasmuch as the times have been used on hundreds of studies before, they are not apt to be contested by the workers.

WHAT IS A PREDETERMINED TIME STANDARD?

A predetermined time standard is a time standard that you can calculate by analyzing the movements (basic motions) required to do a job and assigning predetermined and fixed time values to these motions. For example, the motions required to pick up a pencil might be as follows: (1) *reach* to the pencil, (2) *grasp* the pencil, and (3) *move* the pencil to the required location. Time values for the *reach, grasp,* and *move* basic motions have been predetermined and recorded (see Figure 20–3) and can thus be assigned to these motions. Adding the three time values for each distance specification will give you a *normal time* per distance; that is, no allowances are included. From this normal time, you could calculate a time standard by adding the desired time for allowances.

Using predetermined time standards allows you to set time standards for jobs currently running in a plant, as well as calculate the time that will be required to perform a job *in advance of* its actual production. Using blueprints or other information, you can visualize the work that will need to be done, assign predetermined time values to this work, and thus calculate how long it will take to get the job done *in advance of* actually doing it.

Several basic types of predetermined time systems are used in industry—MTM (Methods–Time Measurement), Work Factor, and Basic Motion Time Study, to name a few.

Distance in Inches	Reach	Move
5	.01	.02
10	.02	.03
15	.03	.04
20	.04	.05
25	.05	.06
etc.		
Grasp: .01		

FIGURE 20–3
Leveled times for "reach," "grasp," and "move."

WHAT IS WORK SAMPLING?

Work sampling, or ratio-delay study as it is sometimes called, is another way to measure work. It is a statistical technique that you can use to get information about the work performance of an employee or a machine. For example, suppose you want to know how much time an employee spends oiling his machine. To get this information, you visit the machine at random intervals throughout the day for several days or weeks and record whether or not the operator is oiling his or her machine. Suppose that in 1,000 random observations you found the operator oiling the machine 150 times. This tells you that the operator spends 15% of his or her time oiling the machine. You could make the same sort of study on any other part of a job, but to ensure accuracy, the observations must be random and the number must be large.

Suppose, for example, that a certain machine needs an adjustment at *irregular* intervals. It would be quite time consuming to run a time study over the weeks or months necessary to find out how frequently this occurs. You could, however, make a ratio-delay or work sampling study as follows:

1. Set up a sheet of paper showing that the operator is either adjusting the machine or doing other required work.

2. Visit the machine at random intervals, and tally what the operator is doing. The visit must be random or the procedure won't work. You shouldn't, for example, observe what the operator is doing every hour on the hour because, of course, this is not random. One way to make it random would be to write down the times of the workday in five-minute intervals on individual pieces of paper. Thus, one piece of paper would have 8:00 A.M. on it. Another would have 8:05 A.M., another 8:10 A.M., and so on throughout the workday. Put all these pieces of paper in a hat, mix them up, and draw out, say, twenty-five pieces. You would observe the operator at the times shown on these twenty-five pieces of paper.

3. Make a large number of visits to ensure accuracy. Your study after two months might show:

Element	Number of Times Operator Was Performing This Element When Observed	Percent of Total
Adjusting machine	769	3
Doing other work	24,861	97
Total	25,630	100

This would indicate that your employee was spending 3% of his or her time adjusting the machine. Therefore, this amount of time should be added to the other time allowances to establish a standard time.

WHAT DO UNIONS THINK OF TIME STUDIES?

The stopwatch used to be a cause for war between unions and management. Today, however, the attitude has changed from hostility to acceptance because union officials and their members have a better understanding of what time studies are, how they are made, and how they can be fairly used. In many plants, unions even make their own time studies when grievances arise over a standard. Recognizing that they can protect their members from improper use of time studies, many unions today are more open-minded about the fairness, value, and reliability of time study procedures. Thus, although they aren't advocating them outright, neither are they actively fighting time study procedures.

WHAT ARE LOOSE STANDARDS? FAIR STANDARDS? TIGHT STANDARDS?

A loose standard allows an *average* employee, working at about normal pace, to easily produce many more units per hour than the standard calls for.

A fair standard allows the *best* workers to produce about 20 to 25% more than the standard calls for. If an *average* worker can also produce 20 to 25% more, then it is no longer a fair standard—it is a loose standard.

A tight standard is just the opposite: an average employee working at normal pace can't meet the production requirements, and even the best employees can't exceed it by more than, say, 5 to 10%.

ARE LOOSE STANDARDS A RESULT OF POOR TIME STUDIES?

Loose standards can be a result of poor time studies but probably aren't. In all reality, they probably developed gradually over time as the result of creeping changes. For example, suppose that in an original time study, a particular tool was used. Some employee, however, later finds that by changing the tool slightly, a unit can be produced in less time. Not a significant decrease in time, but about 1 or 2%. Then later, the specification for the raw material is changed, which also makes it quicker to make a part. It doesn't decrease the time much—about 2%. By themselves, these changes don't amount to much, but when they creep into the picture over time, they can be significant, changing the time standard by as much as 15 to 20%. This would make it a loose standard—easier to achieve.

evolved over time

The reverse could also be true: creeping changes could cause a tight standard. Employees, however, are more apt to complain about tight standards than loose ones. As a result, tight standards are more quickly corrected.

As a supervisor, you should be ever alert to any changes that would affect a time standard. You are obligated to your employees to protect them from tight standards that will cause a decrease in their pay. Likewise, you owe it to your employer to make sure the standards are fair and will not cause an increase in cost.

Most standards are put into effect for a trial period, say, 30 days. During this period, either the employee or management can suggest changes to make the standard a better one. If both sides agree that it is OK, then it goes into effect and cannot be changed unless there is a change in methods, tools, materials, or conditions of work.

When an employee complains that a standard is not right, listen to the complaint; it may be legitimate. Also, be sure the employee is following the prescribed method. If he or she isn't, this may be the problem. If the employee is following the prescribed method and still has problems, call the time study person to reexamine the study.

SHOULD YOU EXPLAIN TIME STUDIES TO EMPLOYEES?

By all means, explain time studies to your employees because these studies affect their jobs and their pay. Time studies are not secretive or underhanded, but failure to explain them will make the employees think they are. If your employees come to know the time study person and understand time study procedures, they will have more confidence in the fairness of the pro-

"By all means, explain time studies to your employees because these studies affect their jobs and their pay. Time studies are not secretive or underhanded, but failure to explain them will make employees think they are."

explain fully cedure. Knowing that you are not trying to hide something will build their confidence in you and will minimize gripes and complaints.

When you explain time study procedures, don't try to give your employees a "snow job." This will make them even more suspicious. Instead, use one of the jobs in your department and show precisely, step by step, how the study was made and how the time standard was set. Don't dodge issues like rating. Show how it is done, and explain that this keeps from setting a standard that is too high and not fair to the employee, or too low and not fair to the company. Be sure to explain how additional time is allowed for fatigue, personal needs, etc., to make the standard a just one.

If you have done a good job in explaining time study to your employees, they should be impressed with the fact that you want them to get everything that is coming to them, that you are looking out for them as well as for the company, and that neither one will be sacrificed for the other.

QUESTIONS FOR DISCUSSION AND REVIEW

1. What is standard time? What does it include?
2. Why do supervisors need to know standard times for jobs?
3. How do you develop a standard time? Explain each step.
4. How is standard time used in piece rates?
5. Do you need to make a time study to get time standards for a job? Why?
6. What is a predetermined time standard? How is it used?
7. Explain work sampling. Why is it used?
8. How do unions regard time study?
9. What are loose and tight standards?
10. What causes loose standards? Tight standards?
11. Do unions approve of standards systems?

A Case Study
LUCAMA PACKERS

One of the operations in the pickle plant of Lucama Packers consisted of packing small, party-type pickles in a glass jar by hand. The pickles had to be uniformly placed around the side of the jar to make an attractive appearance and to add sales appeal.

Until three years ago, the employees performing the work had been paid by the hour. Although most other jobs in the pickle plant were on an incentive basis, management felt that this job could not be placed on incentive because of the varying number of pickles per jar caused by the variation in shape and size of cucumbers. However, with the new sorting and grading operation recently installed, the pickles were much more uniform in size, and management believed that the job could be placed on incentive pay. Accordingly, one of the company's older and more experienced time study persons observed the operation and came back with the data shown below.

Element	Time in Minutes Per Cycle										Occurrences Per Cycle
1. Pick up 2 jars and place on fixture	.08	.07	.08	.08	.06	.07	.08	.10	.09	.08	1
2. Pick up 3 pickles from conveyor and pack parallel in jars	.12	.14	.12	.14	.14	.14	.13	.13	.12	.14	*
3. Place jars aside on rack	.08	.06	.07	.08	.06	.08	.08	.07	.08	.06	1

* The number of pickles per jar varied from 19 to 23.

In addition to these times, the time study person recommended that the operator's performance should be rated at 120% and that an allowance of 5% should be made for personal time, as well as 5% for fatigue.

1. Using these data, determine a time standard for packing a jar of pickles.
2. What would be the standard output of jars per hour?

A Case Study
BLACKWELL CLEANING

In 1980, Bob Johnson doubled the capacity of his cleaning plant and purchased all new equipment. New equipment meant that his employees would have to learn new techniques, new routines, and new work methods. With these changes, Bob decided that this would also be a good time to install some type of wage incentive plan. Therefore, after this new equipment had been in operation for about a week, Bob announced to his employees that he was going to give them a chance to get extra pay for extra work—that beginning the next week their pay would depend on the amount of work they produced.

The spotters (those who check the clothes and clean spots), the wet cleaners, and the dry cleaners worked as a team in Bob's plant; therefore he installed a group incentive plan for these employees. Theirs was the basic job of cleaning the clothes. The pressers and the ironers, however, were independent workers and were placed on individual piece rates with a guaranteed base equal to 75% of their old hourly rate. The markers and sorters were on the same type of individual incentive system, i.e., piecework with a guaranteed base.

Bob used previous production records to establish his standards, and inasmuch as the equipment was newer and easier to operate, he raised the standards and used the adjusted figures as production quotas. The employees seemed eager to earn more money and worked hard the first week. In fact, the total work produced increased; however, when the paychecks were handed out, there was considerable grumbling. Although none of the employees complained directly to Bob, remarks similar to the following could be heard: "I work twice as hard and get $1.50 more." "My bonus was only $3.25—but I don't know how he figured it." "I pressed more suits than she did—but she made more money!"

Output for the second week dropped slightly, and by the end of the first month, production had dropped below the old levels of output despite the new equipment and incentive system.

In an effort to make the system work, Bob decreased everyone's production quota by 10%. The decrease, however, had little effect on output the first week following its incorporation. According to Bob, the net effect at this point of his new equipment and the wage incentive system was to increase the cost of processing a garment—rather than decrease it, as he had planned. By the end of the first month following the 10% decrease in standards, however, the workers seemed to have settled down and output was back at its old level. Three weeks later the number of garments cleaned and pressed exceeded the old average by 22%, and the employees seemed happy with their increased pay and the new system.

At this point, the delivery drivers and the women who waited on the cash-and-carry customers began receiving complaints about clothes not being clean, items with two creases instead of one, soiled spots on dresses, and the like. If allowed to continue, this could have had a drastic effect on Bob's business. Recognizing this, Bob stated that his first objective was to clean and press clothes properly. Therefore, he called his employees together, told them of the customer complaints, and asked for suggestions. All of his workers indicated that the quality of their work had not decreased and they could not understand the reasons for the complaints. None of them made any suggestions as to how the condition could be corrected.

Bob disliked the idea of discarding his incentive system and was undecided as to what action he should take.

1. What do you think was wrong with Bob's installation?
2. What do you think is causing the poor quality of work?
3. What would you recommend that Bob do now? Why?

A Case Study
A FRIEND DEALING CARDS

Make a time study of a friend dealing two decks of cards (104 cards) into four equal piles (26 cards in each pile). Have your friend deal the cards in the way typically used in card games. Start the task with the two decks lying on the table.

By watching your friend deal the cards, break the job down into elements and time each element using the second hand on your watch. Establish a normal time for the job. Rate your friend's speed as best you can.

Using the principles of motion economy covered in Chapter 19, develop an improved way of dealing the 104 cards into four equal piles. Make a time study of your improved system. Assuming that your improved system is done by a worker for eight hours daily, establish a normal and a standard time for the job. Don't forget to rate as best you can your friend's speed in dealing the cards. Use 15% for allowances.

1. How do the normal times for the two methods compare?
2. Compare your new method and time standard with those of other members in your class. Is there considerable variation? Why?
3. Do you think your time standard is fair? Why?

A Personal Case Problem

Have a classmate set a table using the improved method of setting a table that you prepared in Chapter 19. Break the job down into elements, and time each element using a stopwatch or the second hand on your watch. Establish a normal time for the job. If the going wage for this type of work is $6.50 per hour, what rate per place setting would you pay an employee?

21

HOW TO CONVINCE MANAGEMENT TO BUY NEW EQUIPMENT

This chapter explains—

- Why you should consider replacing equipment
- How to assemble the cost figures you will need
- How you can prove to management that new equipment will pay for itself

Henry Ford once said that if you need a new machine and don't buy it, you pay for it without getting it. In other words, if you don't buy a new machine, the high costs of operating an old machine will pay for the new machine, and you will not be getting the benefits of the new machine.

Knowing *when* to replace a machine, however, is a difficult problem. A lot of people think a piece of equipment should be replaced only when it is worn out. However, just because a piece of equipment *is still running and hasn't fallen apart* is not reason enough to keep it if it has been superseded by newer machines that can do the job more effectively, in less time, and at a lower cost.

A lot of supervisors find themselves in this spot today. They are operating old machines that are expensive to run when they could be operating new machines at a lower cost. The problem they face is how to convince top management that a new machine should be purchased. This is not an easy job, but it is one that you can handle with a little study.

The first step, of course, is to single out a process or operation for study. It could be studying whether or not to switch work from a hand operation to a machine, or studying whether to change from an old machine to a newer model. For example, you might have a hand-cranked spirit duplicator and might be considering the wisdom of buying a new power-operated duplicator. Or you may be concerned with whether or not a new model delivery truck would be cheaper to operate than the old jalopy you are using.

Whatever you choose to study, you face the problem of proving to your boss that the proposed process or machine is economically justifiable—that it will save money and be cheaper to run. In most instances, the proof rests on determining whether or not total operating costs can be lowered enough to make the new machine a wise purchase.

WHY REPLACE MACHINES?

We need new equipment for one of four reasons:

no longer useful

1. *Deterioration.* When a machine wears out, it needs replacing. A 1927 typewriter may still be working, but in all probability it is so worn that you are losing money on labor costs, decreased production, poor quality of product, and increased maintenance. Your question is not *whether* to buy a new typewriter, but *which one* to buy.

2. *Obsolescence.* A new piece of equipment may be available on the market that is more efficient than the machine you currently use.

This chapter is adapted with permission from Claude S. George, Jr., *Management for Business and Industry*, Englewood Cliffs, N.J.: Prentice-Hall, Inc., 1970, pp. 288–97. Reprinted by permission of Prentice-Hall, Inc.

However, your present machine may be functioning well mechanically, and the need to buy a new one may be hard to prove. For example, a manual typewriter that is only two years old might be obsolete because it cannot do your required work as effectively and quickly as a new electric typewriter.

399

HOW TO
CONVINCE
MANAGEMENT TO
BUY NEW
EQUIPMENT

3. *Inadequacy.* New products may make old machines inadequate. Thus, a new form that is 14 inches wide that must be typed would make a typewriter with a standard carriage inadequate.

4. *Working conditions and morale.* Employee dissatisfaction, lack of safety, and low morale resulting from the unpleasantness or hazardous nature of a process might be reasons to consider new equipment.

"A lot of supervisors are running old machines that are expensive to run when they could be operating new machines at a lower cost."

YOUR COMPANY USES THAT?? I DIDN'T REALIZE THERE WERE ANY STEAM-OPERATED DRILL PRESSES LEFT...

HOW DO YOU DEFINE THE PROBLEM?

If deciding when to replace a piece of equipment were as simple as deciding when to replace a ball point pen, you would not have any problem. You'd get a new one when the old one gave out. Unfortunately, this is not the case. Like automobiles, most pieces of equipment require a series of maintenance expenditures, which often increase as the equipment ages. With age, most equipment deteriorates and, in addition, is subject to obsolescence as newer, better machinery is produced to perform the same job more effectively. In fact, today most supervisors find that their equipment is more often superseded technologically rather than worn out by deteriora-

displacement vs. replacement

tion. The problem that you as a supervisor will face, then, is one of equipment *dis*placement rather than *re*placement because improvements tend to *displace* a piece of equipment long before it is worn out. Few of us, for example, wear out a car. Instead, we *replace* it with an improved model.

The problem in business is to determine *when* you should purchase a new piece of equipment and *how* you can convince management that you are right. You can do this by following a systematic and logical approach to solving the problem.

WHAT TYPES OF COSTS ARE INVOLVED?

The costs involved in buying a new piece of equipment are of two types:

1. *Recurring costs* are those that continue year after year as the equipment is used and include such items as direct labor, material, taxes, insurance, and power. Although these costs may vary slightly from year to year, they are usually a relatively constant amount.
2. *Nonrecurring costs* are those that are incurred only once in the life of the equipment and include such items as the purchase price of the new machine, transportation costs involved in getting the new equipment to the plant, and the installation charges.

When a company decides to buy a new piece of equipment, it usually does so only after the best estimates indicate that the money invested in the new equipment will be recovered and a reasonable return will be forthcoming. This return is figured on the difference between the recurring operating costs for both the present and the proposed equipment and is known as the *cost savings.*

HOW DO YOU COMPUTE COST SAVINGS?

*steps in cost
computation*

You compute cost savings by listing the operating costs of the old equipment and the estimated operating costs of the proposed machine. In listing these operating costs, you consider only those costs that will be *different* from one machine to the other. For example, if a proposed machine will take less labor to run than the old machine, then this type of cost should be listed because the amount varies for the two machines. However, if a cost, such as heating, will stay the same whether or not you replace an old machine, then this cost should not be considered.

After you have listed the operating costs of the old and the proposed machines, you then compare the totals of each to determine whether or not the proposed equipment would be cheaper to own and operate. For example, suppose that you are considering the purchase of a new machine at an *installed* cost of $5000. You find that the *annual out-of-pocket operating costs* of the old and proposed machines are:

401

HOW TO
CONVINCE
MANAGEMENT TO
BUY NEW
EQUIPMENT

	Old Machine	Proposed Machine
Direct labor	$3,000	$2,000
Indirect labor	1,500	1,000
Maintenance	800	200
Power	200	800
Taxes and insurance	100	600
Total out-of-pocket expenses	$5,600	$4,600

In addition to these costs, you should also include such costs as fringe benefits, floor space, tools, set-up time, materials, and materials handling, if they apply.

As you can see, you would save $1000 per year if the proposed machine is purchased. However, these figures represent only the *out-of-pocket* costs, with no allowance made for interest and depreciation. Both interest and depreciation are expenses and should be considered.

WHY INCLUDE INTEREST CHARGES?

The new equipment mentioned in our illustration above will cost $5000. If this amount is borrowed, the costs involved in this transaction, such as interest, must be paid. If, instead of borrowing, the company has the funds necessary to purchase the equipment, you would still have an interest charge. The reasoning is as follows. If the $5000 available for purchase of the equipment were *not* used to buy the machine, it could be invested elsewhere, and a return could be realized on the money. It could, for example, be placed in a bank and earn interest at the rate of, say, 5% per year—a return of $250 per year. However, if the company uses the $5000 to purchase the new equipment, this interest return of $250 would not be received and should therefore be considered as a cost for the new equipment.

In all probability, the 5% interest rate used above is not a good figure. Instead of placing money in a bank, many firms invest it in their own or other companies with greater risks but yielding a higher rate of return than that normally paid by a bank. You should, therefore, determine what rate of return you could get from an investment of a similar risk and then use this rate of return to figure the interest charges, which you would add to the annual operating costs. For example, suppose that you find that from an investment of comparable risk, you can get an interest rate of 10%. This figure of 10%, then, would be used and would add an annual interest charge of $500 (10% of $5000) to the total out-of-pocket expenses of $4600. Although next year's interest charges on the new equipment would be $500, the interest for each succeeding year would, of course, be less, as the amount of money you have tied up in the machine decreases by depreciation. For the

an operating expense

purposes of replacement, however, this annual decrease in interest charges is not usually considered significant.

Next, you must determine what interest charge, if any, should be applied to the old equipment. The same reasoning as that used for the proposed equipment is applied to the old equipment. For example, if you can determine that the company is giving up a possible interest return on the money invested in the old equipment, then this loss of interest should also be charged as an annual operating cost against the old equipment. Determining how much money or capital the company has invested in the old equipment is simply a matter of determining the current market price of the old equipment. For example, suppose that the old piece of machinery could be sold for $1500. If it is sold, the $1500 could be invested at 10%, and a return of $150 per year would be realized. This $150, therefore, constitutes a charge because it is something the company gives up or "pays" when it keeps the old machine. If the old machine had no market value, then you would have no interest charges.

By listing the interest charge of $150 for the old machine and $500 for the proposed machine, you can now compare the two machines as follows:

	Old	Proposed
Total out-of-pocket expenses	$5,600	$4,600
Interest expense @ 10%	150	500
Total	$5,750	$5,100

The proposed equipment still shows a net annual savings of $650.

DO YOU NEED DEPRECIATION COSTS?

Depreciation is a decline in value of an asset. It is an accounting concept that is used to allocate the charges for a piece of equipment in some equitable fashion over the operating life of the equipment. In one sense, depreciation can be thought of as "rent" paid for use of the equipment during a period of time.

There are many ways in which depreciation can be figured, but for simplicity, use the straight-line method. You can figure it as follows. You know the proposed equipment will cost $5000. Assume it will have an operating life of four years, after which it can be sold for $1000. Subtracting the $1000 salvage value of the machine from its original cost leaves $4000 that must be charged as depreciation over the four-year life of the equipment. This $4000 divided by four years yields an annual depreciation charge of $1000. Thus, the equipment, like a resource, is being used up at the rate of $1000 per year. An annual charge of $1000, therefore, should be made in your analysis against the proposed machine in addition to those charges already listed.

The depreciation charge for the old equipment, however, is nothing but its loss in value from *this time on*. This loss-in-value figure has no connection with the depreciation estimates that were made by the accountants when the equipment was originally purchased.

403

HOW TO
CONVINCE
MANAGEMENT TO
BUY NEW
EQUIPMENT

To illustrate depreciation charges on the old equipment, suppose that the old machine will last two additional years and at the end of that time will have a salvage value of $500. You have already determined the current market value of the old equipment to be $1500. At the end of two years, therefore, it will be worth only $500, declining $1000 in market value during these two years. This $1000 decline in market value over a two-year period represents the depreciation on the old machine and is an annual equivalent of $500 ($1000 divided by two years). This $500 figure, then, is the annual amount you should charge off as depreciation against the old equipment. Obviously, if the old machine did not decline in value over this two-year period, or if it had no current market value, then no annual depreciation charges would be made against it.

decline in value of an asset

Your annual cost figures now read:

	Old	Proposed
Direct labor	$3,000	$2,000
Indirect labor	1,500	1,000
Maintenance	800	200
Power	200	800
Taxes and insurance	100	600
Interest expense @ 10%	150	500
Depreciation	500	1,000
Total	$6,250	$6,100

This leaves you an annual *cost saving* of $150 if the new machine is purchased. Is this sufficient to warrant investing $5000? Other factors are often considered before this final decision is reached. For example, the proposed equipment may increase the capacity of the plant in line with a sales forecast, or it may be more flexible equipment and make for ease in product variation. Both of these factors would also favor the replacement, not to mention the $150 annual cost saving. In addition to these factors, however, management is interested in how long it will take to get its investment back.

WHAT IS THE CAPITAL RECOVERY PERIOD?

Many companies establish a standard payoff period during which time any investment in new equipment must "pay for itself." For example, one large meat packer will not invest in any tool that will not pay for itself in one year or any piece of major equipment that will not pay for itself in five or fewer years. This capital recovery period is sometimes expressed as a *rate of return on investment.* Actually, both concepts are identical. If your company has a payoff period of two years, then the rate of return is 50%. A one-year recovery period would obviously be a 100% return, whereas a five-year recovery period would be the same as a 20% rate of return on investment.

rate of return

You can figure how quickly a proposed machine will pay for itself by dividing the annual saving plus depreciation on the new equipment into the investment necessary to realize the saving. For example, in our problem, the new machine costs $5000, but we could realize $1500 by selling the old machine. The net investment, therefore, would be $3500. To determine the recovery period, this $3500 is divided by the sum of the annual cost saving ($150) and the depreciation on the proposed machine ($1000), yielding a recovery period of 3.04 years ($3500 ÷ $1150/year = 3.04 years). The $1000 depreciation charge is added to the annual saving of $150 because in addition to the $150 saving realizable each year, $1000 will be set aside as a depreciation allowance that is also applied to recovering the $3500 net investment. Or you can look at it another way. If the total annual operating costs for the old and proposed equipment were the same, then the proposed equipment could still be "paid for" through the depreciation charge set up for the proposed machine. Thus, $1000 as a depreciation charge is available annually to help pay for the new machine, and, *in addition,* a total net saving of $150 is also available. Therefore, to figure the recovery period, $3500 is divided by $1150/year, yielding 3.04 years. This means that in approximately 3.04 years the net investment of $3500 in the new machine will have been recovered, and after that time the $1150 return will be "pure profit."

Deciding whether the payoff period will be two, four, or eight years is mostly a matter of "business judgment," or "sound business reasoning." In general, however, management seems to feel freer to invest money that will be recovered in two to five years rather than longer periods of, say, ten or twenty years. They indicate that beyond the relatively short range of two to five years, their estimate of future economic conditions is much more uncertain; therefore, they are hesitant to commit larger sums of money for longer periods, sums that might involve a loss.

CAN DEPRECIATION BE OMITTED FOR THE PROPOSED MACHINE?

Although the previous discussion of depreciation indicated that it would be included as a cost factor for the *proposed* piece of equipment, this is not actually necessary. Depreciation can be entirely omitted on the *proposed* machine with no difference in the final answer. This is true because the depreciation charges included in the operating costs were "taken out" and added to the annual savings, with the net effect that no numerical difference occurred in the final figure.

added to annual savings

To illustrate this fact, consider the depreciation charges for the proposed equipment in the problem previously discussed. By adding the $1000 depreciation charge to the annual saving of $150, you determined that the

405

HOW TO
CONVINCE
MANAGEMENT TO
BUY NEW
EQUIPMENT

total amount that would be available to help pay for the new equipment would be $1150. Look at what this figure would have been if you had not included depreciation. With the $1000 depreciation figure omitted from the proposed equipment, your total operating costs would have been $5100. Your annual saving would have been the difference between this figure and $6250, or $1150—the same as that calculated previously. Therefore, because depreciation on the new equipment has no net effect on the final figure, it is often omitted from replacement calculations.

HOW DO YOU TREAT THE UNDEPRECIATED BOOK VALUE OF THE OLD MACHINE?

The book value of a machine is the amount the accountants show on the company books as the undepreciated value of the machine. Some people feel that depreciation for the *old equipment* should be figured on the basis of this book value and not market value. They say, for example, that if a stamping machine that is expected to last ten years is purchased for $10,000, then annual depreciation would be $1000 if the machine is expected to have no scrap value. At the end of eight years, the book value of the machine would be $2000. Suppose, however, that at the end of eight years the stamping machine has a market value of $1000 and is expected to have a scrap value of $200 at the end of ten years. This means that the machine will lose $800 in market value during the ninth and tenth years, or depreciate at the rate of $400 per year. Which depreciation figure should be used for equipment replacement problems—the $1000 depreciation based on the book value as estimated by the accountants, or the $400 figure based on actual market value?

forget the book value

Because accountants most frequently use the $1000 figure in their various statements, and because the government accepts that figure for the purpose of income tax statements, some managers see no reason why they should not use the same figure in computations arising from equipment replacement analysis.

Replacement problems and accounting problems, however, are not the same. The accounting figure of $1000 was the best estimate of the stamping machine's decline in value *at the same time the machine was bought.* This figure is the result of actions taken in the past. Actually, it has no relevance to equipment replacement problems because no current decision can alter the figure. The current market value of the stamping machine is relevant, however, because the machine may be sold and the money applied toward the purchase of a new machine. Therefore, depreciation for the old stamping machine should consist of the annual decrease in market value that the business would actually experience if the old equipment were retained.

Looking at it another way, you could say that if the $1000 depreciation figure is used, you would actually be overcharging the old equipment's operating costs and thus tend to make the proposed machine more attractive. Conceivably, this could lead you to replace the machine prematurely. For example, if operating costs for the old stamping machine, including the $1000 book depreciation charge, totaled $5000, and if operating costs for the new machine were $4400, then you would probably say that you should buy the new machine because of the annual "saving" of $600. If, however, you use the true depreciation figure of $400, then total operating costs for the old stamping machine would be $4400, equal to those of the proposed equipment. With other things equal, replacement of the old machine obviously would not be made.

use current market value

IS THE BOOK VALUE OF THE OLD MACHINE A COST OF THE NEW MACHINE?

When a new machine is purchased, some people feel that the undepreciated book value of the old machine should be a part of the total cost of the new machine. This is incorrect. The book value of the old machine is a sunk cost. Nothing can be done about it. Regardless of whether or not you buy the new machine, the sunk cost of the old machine will be written off by your accountants.

To illustrate this fact, suppose that you have a machine with an annual depreciation of $1000, an undepreciated book value of $5000, and no scrap value. Suppose also that a proposed new machine will cost you $10,000. If you buy the new machine, do you need to recover $15,000 in order to cover the $10,000 cost of the new machine plus the $5000 book value of the old? Of course not!

sunk cost

Regardless of whether or not you buy the new machine, the undepreciated balance of $5000 for the old machine will be written off. Thus, if you keep the old machine, the $5000 balance will be written off in five years at the annual rate of $1000 per year. If you buy the new machine and discard the old, then this undepreciated book value will be written off as a loss. In either event—whether you buy the new machine or keep the old—you write off the undepreciated balance of the old machine, with the same ultimate effect on company profit. The undepreciated book value of the old machine, therefore, can be ignored and need not be treated as capital to be recovered through cost savings resulting from the purchase of a new machine. To do otherwise would place an undue burden on the proposed piece of equipment.

SHOULD YOU CONSIDER TAXES?

You can consider taxes as a factor in deciding whether you should purchase the new machine. It is possible that the proposed replacement would enhance profits and that annual federal taxes would be higher as a result. In fact, it is possible that because of the tax structure, a proposed investment in new equipment, though providing an "annual operating cost saving," could cost more to own and operate because of the increase in resulting taxes. Or it may be that from a tax standpoint, purchasing the new machine could save money.

easier to omit

Many companies, however, omit the question of income or property taxes from replacement decisions because they feel that the situation that offers the greatest saving (or increase in profits) before taxes will usually offer the greatest saving (or increase in profits) after taxes. For this reason, forget about the effect of taxes when you figure replacement problems.

WHAT IS THE TOTAL-LIFE AVERAGE METHOD?

The total-life average method is another approach to justify buying a new machine. Some companies figure replacement analysis by lumping *all* costs involved in owning and operating a machine into one total figure and dividing this total by the estimated life of the machine, thus giving them the average annual cost. It works as follows:

average cost per year

Old Machine		Proposed Machine
Given: $1,000 market value		$10,000 installed cost
no scrap value		$ 1,000 scrap value
2 years of life		9 years of life
$4,600 annual operating costs		$ 3,700 annual operating costs
excluding depreciation		excluding depreciation
10% interest		10% interest
Costs: $ 1,000	Depreciation	$ 9,000
9,200 (2 yr)	Operating costs	33,300 (9 yr)
150	Interest @ 10%	5,400
$10,350	Total-life cost	$47,700
$ 5,175	Average cost per year	$ 5,300

Interest is figured each year on the value of the equipment. For example, the old machine is worth $1000 today and will have no scrap value in two years. Therefore, it depreciates at the rate of $500 per year. Thus, interest for the first year would be $100 on the full $1000. For the second year, however, interest could be computed on only $500, the value of the machine at that time, and would amount to $50. The interest for the two years, therefore, would be $150. In like manner, interest for the new machine for the first year would be computed on $10,000, for the second year on $9000, and so on.

On the basis of this analysis using the total-life average method, and considering no other factors, the old machine would be cheaper to own and operate. The new machine, therefore, should not be purchased at this time.

Most of the time, if you can show through cold, hard facts that the purchase of a new piece of equipment will save money and pay for itself, then top management will go along with you. One of the best ways to demonstrate this is through a cost analysis of the old and the proposed equipment using the procedures covered here. It might look like hard work and a lot of figuring, but when the smooth operation of your department depends on it, the end result is well worth the time and effort you put into it.

QUESTIONS FOR DISCUSSION AND REVIEW

1. Explain what is meant by "paying for a piece of new equipment without getting it."
2. What are the reasons for replacing equipment?
3. What types of costs are involved in figuring operating costs?
4. How do you compute cost savings?
5. Should you include interest charges as a cost? Why?
6. How should you use depreciation charges in figuring costs?
7. What is the capital recovery period?
8. Can you omit depreciation charges on the proposed machine? Why? Explain.
9. How do you use the undepreciated book value of the old machine?
10. Why is the book value of the old machine not a cost of the new machine?
11. Explain the total-life average method.

A Case Study
TRAMWAY POWDER COMPANY

In 1978, the Tramway Powder Company installed a new packing machine to package poultry disinfectant; this machine replaced an old machine designed and built by the owner. The new machine cost $4800 to install and produced 800 units per eight-hour day. It ran an average of 2000 hours per year and consumed three kilowatts of electricity for each hour it ran. At the time of installation, the estimated life of the machine was ten years.

In 1984, a salesman called on Mr. Tramway and tried to interest him in buying a new multiple-unit machine for $9000, installed. He indicated, however, that he could not allow the company a trade-in allowance on the old machine because it had no market value. The salesman claimed that the new machine would produce the same number of units per hour as the old machine, but at a lower cost. For one thing, he showed that labor on the new machine would not have to be specialized, thus reducing hourly labor costs from $6.25 to $4.60. In addition, he pointed out that his machine consumed only two kilowatts of electricity per hour at the current rate of 6¢ per kilowatt-hour.

One of the salesman's strong points was that his new machine would not have to be set up each time the package size was changed, as was necessary on the machine the company then owned. In fact, he showed that the company changed the setup for its machine on an average of every 25,000 units at a cost of $100 per setup. These savings, coupled with an estimated life of fifteen years (no scrap value), would enable the machine to pay for itself in two years, he claimed.

The company averages 250 working days per year.

1. Using an interest rate of 10%, was the salesman correct?
2. If Tramway's policy was to buy only if a new machine would pay for itself in three years, should he buy?
3. Do you think the three-year policy is a good one? Why?

A Case Study
MARCIE McCAIN

Marcie McCain desperately wanted to get new electric typewriters for her typing pool employees. The manual ones currently used by all twenty employees had been requisitioned by the previous supervisor, Gloria Brown, who was firmly convinced that manual typewriters were superior to and more efficient than electric typewriters. As a consequence, Gloria had persuaded management two years ago to purchase the latest and best manual typewriters with an expected useful life of at least eight years.

Marcie, however, felt that the manual machines were inferior, were slower, cost more to own and operate, and had a definite impact on the overall morale of the department. Her problem was to convince her bosses that the new machines were desirable, were needed, would cost less to keep, and would be more efficient in the long run.

1. If you were called in to give Marcie help, what would you suggest that she do?
2. List the things that Marcie should consider in preparing a report showing the need for new typewriters.
3. How can you justify discarding typewriters that are in excellent operating condition?

A Case Study
BUYING A NEW CAR

If an auto salesman said you'd be smart to buy his new car because it would pay for itself in 5 years, would you believe him?

To check his figures, assume the following:

1. You drive an average of 15,000 miles per year.
2. Gasoline costs $1.50 per gallon.
3. Maintenance for your old car averages $680 per year; for the new one it should be about $75 per year.
4. You get an average of 15 miles per gallon on your old car. The new one should average 45 miles per gallon.
5. Taxes and insurance on the old car are $561; on the new car they will be $878.
6. Interest is 10%.
7. The market value of your old car is $725; the cost of the new auto is $8500.

1. Should you buy the new car? Why?
2. How long would it take the new car to pay for itself?
3. What other factors should you consider in purchasing a new auto?

GLOSSARY

Affirmative Action.   Actions that employers take to eliminate the present effects of past discrimination.

Agenda.   A memorandum or list of things to be done or discussed.

Authority.   The right to command. The power you have over others.

Brainstorming.   The development of ideas without evaluating them. Innovative thinking to generate new ideas without immediate regard to the feasibility of the ideas.

Capital Recovery Period.   The time period during which investment in new equipment must pay for itself.

Checkoff.   The collection of union dues by the employer, who then turns them over to the union.

Civil Rights Act of 1964–Title VII.   An act that, as amended by the 1972 Equal Employment Opportunity Act, prohibits discrimination with respect to race, color, age, sex, religion, and national origin.

Classroom Training.   Training that takes place in a classroom rather than at the work place.

Closed Shop. A shop in which an applicant has to join the union before he will be hired. (Now outlawed.)

Collective Bargaining. The activity involved when management and the union get together to bargain over and agree upon wages, hours of work, and working conditions.

Communication. The transfer of information and understanding from one person and/or machine to another.

Communication Feedback. An indication of understanding (or lack of understanding) of a face-to-face communication, usually taking the form of a nod, puzzled expression, smile, or some other indication of understanding or not understanding the message.

Computer. A programmable electronic device that can store, retrieve, and process data.

Controlling. Checking or regulating activities so that activities or events will conform to plans.

Counseling. Helping an employee get over a problem by listening, understanding, and giving helpful advice.

Craft Union. A union that accepts members only from a single trade or occupation, such as a carpenters union or a machinists union.

Depreciation. The loss or decline in the value of an asset.

Directing. Guiding, influencing, or telling another person what to do.

Discipline. Any action undertaken to get a person to comply with rules and regulations.

Diskettes. See Floppy Disk.

Empathy. Looking at a problem from the other person's point of view.

Equal Employment Opportunity Commission (EEOC). A commission set up by Title VII to enforce the laws pertaining to discrimination contained in the Civil Rights Act of 1964.

Equal Pay Act of 1963. An act that requires that men and women subject to the Fair Labor Standards Act must be given equal pay for equal work.

Esteem Needs. The need for recognition, status, achievement, or sense of accomplishment. Self-respect.

Exception Principle. Principle according to which one checks only those items that fall outside of predetermined limits.

Fair Labor Standards Act of 1938. (Wage–Hour Law). An act setting forth laws governing overtime pay, minimum wages, and hours of work for most employees.

Fair Standard. A standard that allows the best workers to produce about 20 to 25 percent more than the standard.

Feedback. See Communication Feedback.

Floppy Disk. Sometimes called diskettes, floppy disks are software instructions about the size of a 45 rpm record. They are flexible or floppy, therefore their name. The disks have a magnetic coating that stores information as does a magnetic tape.

Flow Diagram. A map of the movement or flow of a product or a person through a work process.

Forelady.   A female supervisor who directs the efforts of others.

Foreman.   A male supervisor who directs the efforts of others.

Formal Organization.   The recognized and formalized lines of communication, authority, and control.

Grievance.   A complaint that has been formally registered with an employee's supervisor or some other management official in accordance with the recognized grievance procedure.

Hardware.   Components of a computer that you can see and touch. Video screens and printers are examples of computer hardware.

Human Relations.   A mode of management that is concerned with getting employees to work together harmoniously, productively, and cooperatively to achieve economic as well as social goals.

Industrial Union.   A union that represents all workers in a particular company or industry regardless of what job the worker performs.

Informal Organization.   A hierarchy or organization set up by the employees but not agreed to or recognized by management.

Job Description.   A statement setting forth the duties and responsibilities of a job.

Job Evaluation.   A systematic way of determining the relative worth of each job in a company but not the wages that will be paid for doing the job.

Job Specification.   A written record of the qualities and capacities that an individual would need to fill a particular job. Sometimes called a man specification.

Labor–Management Relations Act of 1947 (Taft–Hartley).   An act which (1) attempts to reduce union power and equalize bargaining strength between labor and management; (2) identifies the rights of employees as union members; (3) recognizes the rights of employers; and (4) enables the President of the United States to delay a strike for up to 80 days where the strike would create a national emergency.

Labor–Management Reporting and Disclosure Act of 1959 (Landrum–Griffin).   An act that provides protection for union members from wrongdoings on the part of the workers union and sets forth what is known as the worker's "bill of rights."

Landrum–Griffin Act.   See Labor–Management Reporting and Disclosure Act of 1959.

Leader.   An individual who knows where he is going and can persuade others to join him.

Leader, Authoritarian.   A leader who exercises strong control over his employees.

Leader, Democratic.   A leader who solicits aid and advice from his employees, thus getting them involved in the solution to work problems.

Leader, Dictatorial.   A leader who holds the threat of punishment or discharge over his employees to get them to do his will.

Leader, Permissive.   A leader who holds virtually no power over his employees. A leader in name only.

Line Organization.   An organization that has the power to act or to command.

Line and Staff Organization. A line organization to which staff assistants have been added.

Loose Standard. A standard that allows an average employee working at a normal pace to easily produce more units per hour than the standard calls for.

Management. The formally designated supervisors or bosses in a company.

Management by Objectives (MBO). A managerial process in which employees and management agree on and set specific employee goals to be accomplished within a given period of time.

Manager. One who supervises and gets work done through the efforts of others.

Methods Improvement. The process involved in trying to improve the way a job is performed.

Morale. A person's state of mind—how he or she feels about things.

Morale Survey. An opinion poll or attitude survey that tries to measure or find out how employees feel about their jobs, their supervisors, the company, and so on.

Motion Analysis. The study of the body motions employed by an individual to perform a job.

Motivate. To make others want to perform an assigned task. To make an employee want to do his work.

National Labor Relations Act (Wagner Act). An act that gives workers the right to join a union, to bargain collectively, and to engage in concerted activities such as strikes. Prohibits certain unfair labor practices by employers.

Need Hierarchy. The rank assigned by psychologists to the five basic human needs.

Nonrecurring Costs. Those costs that are incurred only once in the life of a piece of equipment.

Obsolescence. The condition of a piece of equipment that functions well mechanically, but has been superseded by a newer, more efficient machine.

Occupational Safety and Health Act of 1970 (OSHA). An act that places on employers the responsibility to provide a safe place for employees to work.

On-the-job Training. Training that is carried on at the employee's work place.

100 Percent Bonus Plan. A piecework plan in which allowances are made for each unit of output in terms of time instead of money.

Operations Chart. A "picture" of the simultaneous work that the right and left hands are doing. Sometimes called a left-hand, right-hand chart.

Organizing. The process of coordinating the efforts of employees so that objectives can be achieved in the most efficient manner.

OSHA. See Occupational Safety and Health Act of 1970.

Pay-back Period. The time required for a piece of equipment to pay for itself.

Performance Evaluation. A formalized, systematic appraisal of an employee's performance and his or her potential for development and training.

Physical Needs. The basic necessities of life, such as food, shelter, clothing, etc.

Piecework Plan. A system of pay in which the employee receives a stipulated amount for each unit of product produced.

Planning. The process involved in deciding what you will need to do to accomplish your objective.

Predetermined Time Standard. A time standard that one can calculate by analyzing the movements required to do a job and then assigning predetermined time values to these movements.

Process Chart. A piece of paper on which the steps in a process are recorded.

Professional Worker. A worker with particular educational skills or training, such as a nurse or engineer.

Rating Scale Method of Performance Evaluation. A system of rating an employee's abilities by placing a check on a scale that best describes the employee's quality and quantity of work, job knowledge, dependability, cooperativeness, and other factors.

Ratio-delay Study. A statistical technique used to get information about the work performance of an employee or machine.

Recurring Costs. Those costs that continue year after year as a piece of equipment is used, as opposed to one-time or nonrecurring costs.

Rehabilitation Act of 1973. An act that requires employers to take affirmative action to hire the handicapped.

Responsibility. The obligation that an employee has to his boss to do a job that has been assigned to him.

Safety Need. The desire or need to protect yourself from danger, to be secure.

Self-realization Need. The need to feel that you have accomplished things to the best of your abilities and potentialities. The need to realize what you are capable of becoming.

Social Needs. The needs to belong, to be a part of a group, and to be accepted and respected by members of the group.

Software. Electrical instructions for a computer. Software tells the computer what to do.

Span of Management (or Control). The number of people an individual can effectively supervise.

Staff Organization. An organization that is advisory in nature, helping other people know what should be done and how to do it.

Staffing. All the activities involved in recruiting, hiring, and retaining employees on the job.

Standard Time (Time Standard). The time allowed to do a specified quantity and quality of work.

Straight Piecework. A pay plan in which the employee gets paid only for each acceptable unit of output. If the employee doesn't produce, he or she doesn't get paid.

Straight Piecework with a Guaranteed Base. The same as the straight piecework plan, except that an hourly base rate equal to the going rate for the job is guaranteed.

Supervisor. One who gets things accomplished through the efforts of others. An overseer. A boss.

Taft–Hartley Act. See Labor–Management Relations Act.

Theory X. A system of supervision in which the supervisor appeals to his employees through their lower-level needs.

Theory Y. A system of supervision in which the supervisor appeals to his employees through their higher-level needs.

Tight Standard. A standard that an average employee working at a normal pace cannot meet. Even the best employees cannot exceed a tight standard by more than 5 or 10%.

Time-Analysis Chart. An accurate account of what you do throughout a day, showing when you did something and how long it took. Usually made by listing vertically on a sheet of paper the hours of the day in fifteen-minute intervals.

Title VII. See Civil Rights Act of 1964.

Union. An organization of employees that seeks to improve its members' economic, social, and political interests through the process of collective bargaining.

Union Shop. A shop with an agreement whereby an employee must join the union within a given period of time after being hired, or lose his or her job.

Unity of Command. An authority relationship in which an employee in an organization has only one boss. Only one person gives orders to the employee.

Vestibule Training. Training that takes place in a classroom (vestibule) where an attempt is made to duplicate working conditions, with machines and other equipment set up.

Wage–Hour Law. See Fair Labor Standards Act of 1938.

Wagner Act. See National Labor Relations Act.

Work Sampling. A statistical technique used to get information about the work performance of an employee or a machine. Ratio-delay study.

Work Simplification. The process involved in trying to improve the way a job is performed.

INDEX

Affirmative action, 152–3
Age differences and supervision, 222–3
Allowances in time study, 383
Appraisals, employee, *see* Performance evaluation
Appraising and promoting employees, 334–48
Appraising employees, *see* Performance evaluation
Authoritarian leaders, 31
Authority, 279–81
    delegation of, 281–4
    source of, 280
Authority and responsibility, 271–81

Barriers to communications, 71–2
Board of directors, 270–1
    activities of, 270
    inside, 270–1
    makeup, 270–1
    outside, 271
Body language, 211–12
Brainstorming, 189
Breakdown of communications, 70–1
Breakeven charts, 245–7

Budgeting time, 47–9
Budgets, precise, 47–8

Capital recovery, 403–4
Cases
    A state of morale, 141–2
    Abe Salem and the union, 157–8
    Administrative assistant's job, the, 309
    Advance manufacturing, 308–9
    Allen Manufacturing Company, 253
    Allison Auto Parts, 139–40
    Beamon Plating Company, 253–4
    Ben Brown and his supervisory style, 104–5
    Bill Wilder's opportunity, 21–2
    Blackwell Cleaning, 393–4
    Brandis Wholesale Grocery, 265–6
    Bunnies Burgers, 38–9
    Burlington Machine Works, 376–7
    Buying a new car, 409–10
    Case of Marge Burns, the, 233–4
    Case of the oily rag, the, 37–8
    Case of the overworked supervisor, the 294–5

Cases (*Contd.*)
　　Case of the perfectionist supervisor, the 124–5
　　Case of the problem evaluation, the 348–9
　　Christmas party, the 85–6
　　Communication in the bank, 215–16
　　Dealing cards, 377–8
　　Decisions! Decisions! 195–6
　　Delway Vacuum Cleaner Company, 176–7
　　Departmental update, 254–5
　　Eastside Flour Mills, 291–3
　　Edith Gates' problem, 23
　　Electric Components Corporation, 215
　　Evaluation conference, the, 350–1
　　Friend dealing cards, 394–5
　　Gene Hubbard, 140–1
　　Geraldine's promotion, 235
　　Gracie's complaint, 84–5
　　Greystone Manufacturing, 375–6
　　Hazel Francisco's punishment, 175–6
　　Helen Goodman, Forelady, 40
　　Holding a meeting, 214
　　How do you spend your day?, 60
　　Jack Nelson's problem, 307–8
　　Janie Hennis, 60
　　Jeff Barnes' problem, 158–9
　　Joe Mann versus the union, 156–7
　　Kendall's Department Store, 332
　　Lazerbean's, 125–6
　　Lucama Packers, 392–3
　　Marcie McCain, 409
　　Matt Henshaw's problem, 59
　　Midwest Oil Company, 331
　　New London Furniture, 196–7
　　Planning a Meeting, 214
　　Retired watchman, the, 177–8
　　Rougemont Company, 105–6
　　Sour whiskey, the, 330
　　Staff versus line, 295–6
　　Supervisor Harris, 22–3
　　Surefit Hosiery Mills, 106–7
　　Tilley's Department Store, 349–50
　　Todd Richardson's group problem, 126–7
　　Tramway Powder Company, 408–9
　　Typing pool, 197
　　Unwritten letter, the, 87
　　Whitset Hosiery Mills, 234–5
　　Writing a letter, 86–7
　　Your own MBO, 265
Channels of communication, 68–70
　　formal, 68–9
　　informal, 69–70
Chart, organization, 273–6
Civil Rights Act, 152
Classroom training, 323–4
Climate for giving orders, 218
Coach or team leaders, 32–3
Collective bargaining
　　defined, 144
　　help by supervisor, 150–1
Communicating with employees, 64–84
Communications, 64–84
　　barriers, 71–2
　　breakdown of, 70–1
　　channels, 68–70
　　cultural differences, 73
　　defined, 64
　　effects of, 83–4
　　empathizing, 72
　　face-to-face, 71

Communications (*Contd.*)
　　feedback, 65–6
　　and leadership, 34
　　listening, 66–8
　　points to remember, 77
　　speaking, rules of, 210–11
　　supervisor's rule in, 73–5
　　talking, 65
　　two-way, 66
　　understanding, 65
　　upward, 75–6
　　word meaning, 65
　　written, 77–83
　　　　evaluation, 83
　　　　form to use, 81–2
　　　　length, 78
　　　　letters, 81–2
　　　　rules, 79–81
　　　　style, 78–9
Communications barriers, 71–2
　　age, 71
　　overcoming, 71–2
　　prejudice, 70–1
　　status, 70
Company organization, *see* Organization
Complaints, avoiding, 174–5; *see also* Grievances
Complaints, handling, 172–4
Computers, 54–7
　　help in making decisions, 55–6
　　help in saving time, 55–7
　　how supervisors use, 55–7
　　software, 54–5
　　hardware, 54
　　what they are, 54–5
　　where used, 56–7
Conceptual skills, 9
Conferences and meetings, *see* Meetings
Controller, 272
Controlling, 11
Cooperation, 92–104
　　employees as individuals, 97
　　formula for, 99
　　getting others to work, 94–5
　　important areas, 97–9
　　interesting work, 98
　　knowing what workers want, 95–6
　　need for opportunity for growth, 99
　　and participation, 98
　　praise, 97–8
　　supervisor who motivates best, 99–101
　　Theory X, 102
　　Theory Y, 102–3
Counseling employees, 229–32
Crisis decisions, 194

Decisions, decision-making, 182–95
　　analyzing problem, 185–6
　　barriers, 189–90
　　being alert for problems, 183–4
　　best solutions, 186–8
　　brainstorming, 189
　　communicating decisions, 192
　　computer use, 191
　　crisis decisions, 194
　　defining problem, 184–5
　　following up, 192–3
　　how to make, 183–8
　　implementing, 192–3
　　logical solutions, 186–7

Decisions, decision making (*Contd.*)
   poor decisions, 194–5
   postpone decisions, 190–1
   practical tips on, 193–4
   putting decisions into effect, 192–3
   quick decisions, 188–9
   routine decisions, 188
   snap decisions, 193
   solving problems, 186–7
   types of, 182–3
Delays, 356
Delegation of authority, 281–4
   to lazy employee, 281
Democratic leaders, 31
Demotions, 346
Dependent type leadership, 32
Depreciation costs, 402–3
Deterioration of equipment, 398
Dictatorial leaders, 31
Directing, 11
Discharging employees, 347–8
Disciplinary policy, 168–9
Discipline, 162–9
   appropriateness, 164
   climate for, 163
   defined, 162
   discharge, 168
   how to, 165–7
   and morale, 163
   need for, 163–4
   objectives, 164
   oral, 167
   policy, 168–9
   self-discipline, 165–7
   suspension, 167–8
   types of, 167–8
   written, 167
Discrimination in employment, 152–4
Diskettes, 55

EEOC, 152
Education, *see* Training
Effects of good communications, 83–4
Elements in a job, 381
Empathy, 115
Employee appraisals, *see* Performance
   evaluation
Employee attitudes, 113
Employee-centered leadership, 30
Employee differences, 110–12
Employee needs, 92–4
Employee promotions, *see* Promotions
Employee supervision
   age, 222–3
   biological makeup, 93–4
   communications, 66
   counseling employees, 229–32
   giving orders, 218–21
   motivating older employees, 223–4
   professional workers, 226–9
   white collar, 229
   women, 224–5, 229
Employees
   age and supervision, 222–3
   cooperation and teamwork, 98–9
   desires of, 95–6
   fear of methods improvement, 371–4
   important motivation areas, 97–9
   and time studies, 391

Employees (*Contd.*)
   and unions, 386–7, 389–90
   working groups, 118–19
Equal Employment Opportunity Commission, 152
Equipment, purchasing, *see* Equipment replacement
Equipment replacement, 398–408
   book value, 405–6
   capital recovery, 403–4
   convincing management to buy, 408
   costs involved, 400
   defining the problem, 399–400
   depreciation costs, 402–3, 404–5
   deterioration, 398
   figuring cost savings, 400–1
   inadequacy, 399
   interest charges, 401–2
   obsolescence, 398–9
   payback period, 403–4
   taxes, 406–7
   total-life average, 407
   undepreciated book value, 405–6
   why replace, 398–9
   working conditions and morale, 399
Essay method of appraisals, 335–7
Esteem needs, 92–3
Exception principle, 50

Fair Labor Standards Act, 151
Feedback, 65–6
Firing employees, use of performance evaluation, 340–1
Floppy disks, 55
Flow diagrams, 361–3
   defined, 361–3
   symbols, 361–3
   why used, 361–3
Flow process charts, *see* Flow diagrams
Forelady, 5
Formal channels of communication, 68–9

Giving orders, 218–21
   climate for, 218
   explaining why, 220
   reasonableness, 219
   right words, 220
   understanding of, 219–20
Glossary, 411–16
Grapevine, 69
Grievances, 169–75
   defined, 169–70
   nonunionized companies, 170–1
   unionized companies, 171–2
Group participation in meetings, 201
Groups
   attraction, 117
   formal, 117
   informal, 117
   quality circle, 118–19
   supervising, 118

Hardware, 54
Human relations, 110–23
   changing employees, 116
   defined, 110
   effects of, 122
   empathy, 115
   employee attitude, 113
   employee differences, 110–12
   and groups, 118–19

Human relations (*Contd.*)
    knowing your employees, 115–16
    practices, 121
    scale rating, 122–3
    understanding yourself, 113–14
    working with others, 112–13
Human skills, 8–9

Ideal organization, 289
Inadequacy of equipment, 399
Individual needs, 92–3
    esteem, 92–3
    physical, 92
    safety, 92
    self-realization, 93
    social, 92
Industrial engineer, 272–3
Industrial relations, *see* Personnel department
Informal channels of communication, 69
Informal organization, 286–7
Informational meetings, 201
Inside board, 270
Interviewing employees, 312–19
    closing interview, 315
    how to interview, 313–14
    legal requirements, 316–17
    need for, 312
    what to ask applicant, 312–13, 316–17
    what to avoid, 316–17
    what to look for, 312–13
    what to tell applicant, 313
Interviewing, orienting, and training employees, 312–29
Interviews
    appraisal, 338–9
    exit, 305–6

Job
    burnout, 95–6
    employer needs, 119–20
    fair pay, 119
    good leadership, 120
    group acceptance, 120
    interesting work, 120
    opportunity, 119–20
    recognition, 119
Job-centered leadership, 30
Job description
    defined, 301–2
    need for, 302–3
Job simplification, *see* Methods improvement
Job specifications, 302–3

Labor-Management Relations Act of 1947, 151
Labor-Management Reporting and Disclosure Act of
    1959, 151
Labor requirements, estimating 300–1
Labor sources, 303–4
Layoffs, 347
Leader, role in meetings and conferences, 202–3
Leaders
    authoritarian, 31
    best, 31–2
    born or made, 33–4
    common traits, 34–5
    communications, 34
    democratic, 31
    dictatorial, 31
    informal, 29–30
    intelligence, 34

Leaders (*Contd.*)
    permissive, 31
    poor, 28, 35–6
    qualities of, 27–8
    social activity, 34
    types of, 30–2
    understanding, 34
    in work groups, 29
Leadership, 26–7
    best type, 31–2
    employee centered, 30
    job centered, 30
    qualities needed for, 27–8
    and supervision, 28–9
    traits of poor, 28
    in work groups, 29
Leadership patterns, 32–3
    coach or team, 32–3
    commanding, 32
    dependent type, 32
    diplomatic, 32
    points to remember, 36–7
    and teamwork, 32–3
Leading conferences and meetings, 200–13
Leading others, art of, 26–37
Leading versus supervising, 28–9
Line and staff, 276
Line organization, 276
Listening, 66–8
    asking questions, 67
    biases, 67
    implied message, 67
    interest, 67
    rules for, 66–7
    skills, 67–8
Listening to complaints, 173

Making work easier, *see* Methods improve-
    ment
Man specification, 302–3
Management by objectives, 258–64
    benefits, 260, 263
    defined, 258
    drawbacks, 263–4
    ease of use, 259–60
    employee objectives, 259, 261–2
    objectives, 259
    performance review, 262–3
    resistance to, 261
    when not to use, 260
    where used, 259
Maslow, A. H., 92
McGregor, Douglas, 102
Measuring work, 380–92; *see also* Time study
    developing time standards, 381–5
    employee complaints, 391
    equipment used, 381
    explaining to employees, 391–2
    fair standards, 390
    loose standards, 390
    making a time study, 381–5
    need for time standards, 380–1
    piece rates and standard times, 385–6
    predetermined time standards, 388
    standard data, 387–8
    standard time, 380
    tight standards, 390
    union reactions, 386–7, 389–90
    work sampling, 388–9

Meetings, 200–13
    advantages of, 203–4
    agenda for, 206–7
    body language, 211–12
    compulsive talkers, 208
    digressions, 208–9
    employees who argue, 208
    evaluation of, 212–13
    group participation, 209
    how to hold, 204–6
    informational, 201
    leader's role in, 202–3
    need for vote, 209–10
    new ideas, 201
    non-talker, 208
    opinion-seeking, 201
    private discussions, 208
    problem-solving, 201
    questions to ask, 207
    speaking, rules of, 210–11
    time and place, 205
    types of, 201
    voting, 209–10
    weaknesses of, 204
    when to call, 210
    where to hold, 201–2
    why hold, 200–1
Methods improvement, 354–74
    contributions to supervision, 374
    defined, 355
    delay, 356
    employee fear of, 371–4
    flow diagrams, 361–3
    inspection, 356, 361
    motion analysis, 366–9
    operation, 356, 360
    operations charts, 371
    process charts, 355–61
    rules of motion economy, 367–9
    storage, 356, 361
    studying a process, 355, 365
    transportation, 356, 360
    where used, 356
    which job to study, 369–70
    who makes studies, 371
Morale, 130–9
    building, 138–9
    defined, 130
    factors affecting, 134–5
    importance, 130
    improving, 133–4
    influences on, 133
    low morale, 137–8
    measuring, 135–6
    and productivity, 135
    and supervision, 131–2
    surveys, 136–7
    variations in, 130–1
    and work climate, 132–3
Motion analysis, 366–9
    defined, 366
    rules of motion economy, 367–9
    which job to study, 369–70
Motion economy, *see* Motion analysis
Motion study, *see* Methods improvement
Motivating employees, 92–104
    best approach, 101–4
    cooperation and teamwork, 98–9
    employee needs, 92–4

Motivating employees (*Contd.*)
    employees as individuals, 97
    formula for, 99
    getting others to work, 94–5
    how to motivate, 99–101
    important motivation areas, 97–9
    individual needs, 92–3
    interesting work, 98
    knowing what workers want, 95–6
    need for opportunity for growth, 99
    participation, 98
    placement, 95
    praise, 97–8
    Theory X, 102
    Theory Y, 102–3
Motivation areas
    cooperation and teamwork, 98–9
    growth opportunities, 99
    interesting work, 98
    participation, 98
    praise, 97–8
    treating employees as individuals, 97

National Labor Relations Act, 151
Needs
    esteem, 192–3
    physical, 92
    safety, 92
    self-realization, 93
    social, 92
New employees
    interviewing, 313–14
    training, 321–4
    what to tell, 313

Obsolescence of equipment, 398–9
Older employees
    learning new jobs, 223–4
    motivating, 224
    and supervision, 223–4
On-the-job-training, 322
Operations, 356, 360
Operations charts, 371
Opinion-seeking meetings, 201
Oral reprimand, 167
Orders
    choice of words, 220
    climate for, 218
    and employee who disobeys, 221–2
    explaining reasons for, 220
    problems, 220–1
    reasonableness, 219
    understanding, 219–20
Organization, 270–90
    accountants, 272
    authority and responsibility, 279–81
    board of directors, 270–1
    channels of communication, 287
    chart, 273–6
    controller, 272
    corporate officers, 271–72
    delegation of authority, 281–4
    formal, 286
    how to delegate, 282–3
    ideal structure, 289
    industrial engineer, 272–3
    informal, 286–7
    inside board, 270
    line and staff, 276

Organization (*Contd.*)
   line organization, 276
   outside board, 271
   personnel director, 272
   president, 271
   prime rule of, 284–5
   production control, 273
   purchasing agent, 272
   rewards of good organization, 290
   secretary, 272
   source of authority, 280
   span of management, 287–8
   supervisor's place in, 273
   supervisor's understudy, 288–9
   treasurer, 272
   unity of command, 285–6
Organization charts, 273–6
   rules for making, 274–6
Organizing, 10–11
Organizing function, 10–11
Orienting new employees, 319–21
   need for, 319–20
   what to tell employee, 320–1
OSHA (Occupational Safety and Health Act), 154
Outside board, 271

Pay-back period, 403–4
Performance evaluation, 334–48
   benefits, 341
   comparison method, 335
   defined, 334
   essay method, 335–7
   flaws in, 337
   interview, 338–9
   methods used, 334–7
   need for, 342–3
   objectivity, 337–8
   rating scale, 335
   tips on, 339–40, 341
   use in firing, 340–1
Performance rating, 382–3
Permissive leaders, 31
Personnel department, 298–307
   activities, duties, 298–306
   employee selection and placement, 304
   estimating labor requirements, 300–1
   exit interviews, 305–6
   job descriptions, 301–2
   job specifications, 302–3
   man specifications, 302–3
   policies, 298–9
   promotions and transfers, 305
   record keeping, 306
   recruiting workers, 303–4
   training and education programs, 304–5
Personnel director, 272
PERT, 247–52
   critical path, 250–1
   network, 248–9
   slack time, 251–2
   steps in using, 248
   use, 247
Physical needs, 92
Piece rates and time studies, 385–6
Planning, 10, 238–52
   advantages, 241
   breakeven charts, 245–7
   defined, 238
   ease of, 238–9

Planning (*Contd.*)
   effects of, 241
   essentials of, 240–1
   for the future, 239–40
   GANTT charts, 244–5
   need for, 239, 241
   PERT, 247–52
   responsibility for, 239
   by supervisor, 241–4, 252
   tools, 244–52
Points to remember about communications, 77
Predetermined time standards, 388
President, 271
Problems and problem solving, 182–95
   analyzing, 185–6
   best solutions, 186–8
   brainstorming, 189
   defining, 184–5
   logical solutions, 186–7
   routine solutions, 188
   snap decisions, 193
   solving, 186–7
Problem-solving meetings, 201
Process, study of, 355–61, 365
Process charts, 355–61
   analysis of, 359–61
   construction of, 356–9
   steps in a process, 355–6
   symbols, 356
   where used, 356
   why used, 363–5
Productivity and morale, 135
Professional workers, supervision of, 226–9
Program Evaluation and Review Technique, *see* PERT
Promotions, 343–6
   ability and seniority, 344–6
   from within, 343–4
   how supervisors get, 20
   and seniority, 344–6
Public policy, 151–55
   affect of EEO on supervision, 155
   affirmative acton, 152–3
   defined, 151–2
   discrimination in employment, 152, 153–4
   EEOC, 152
   other laws to be aware of, 154–5
Puchasing new equipment, 398–408

Quality and time study, 385
Quality circles, 118–19

Rating scale appraisals, 335
Reasonableness of orders, 219
Reasons for orders, 220
Record keeping, 306
Recruiting workers, 303–4
Replacement analysis, *see* Equipment replacement
Rules for listening, 66–7
Rumor mill, 69–70

Secretary, 272
Selection and placement of employees, 304
Self-discipline, 165–7
Self-realization needs, 93
Seniority and ability, 344–6
Seniority and promotion, 344–6
Sexual harassment, 225–6
Simplifying work, 354–74; *see also* Methods improvement
Social activity in leadership, 34

Social needs, 92
Software, 54–5
Span of management, 287–8
Speaking, rules of, 210–11
Special employees, supervising, 218–33
Staffing, 11
Standard data, 387–8
Standard time, 380
Standard working conditions, 381
Steps in a job, 381
Supervising, 218–33
  age differences, 222–3
  answering problems, 222
  counseling employees, 229–32
  employee who refuses to work, 221–2
  giving orders, 218–21
  groups, 118
  older employees on new jobs, 223–4
  professional workers, 226–9
  sexual harassment, 225–6
  signals of poor job, 232–3
  special employees, 218–33
  white-collar employees, 229
  women, 224–5, 229
Supervising versus leading, 28–9
Supervision
  and affirmative action, 152–3
  best approach, 101–4
  and EEO, 152
  and leadership, 28–9
  and morale, 131–2
  opportunities in, 20
  Theory X, 102
  Theory Y, 102–3
Supervisor
  and affirmative action, 152–3
  budgeting time, 47–9
  duties of, 6–7
  effect of union on, 145–7
  employee centered, 30
  functions, 9–11
  getting promoted, 20
  job, 4–20
  job centered, 30
  kinds of plans, 243–4
  laws to be aware of, 152–5
  mental acts, 7
  need to plan, 239, 241
  physical acts, 7
  poor, 35–6
  qualities needed, 14–18
  development of, 19
  relationship between union steward and, 151
  responsibilities, 11–13
    to customers, 13
    to employees, 12–13
    to owners, 11–12
    to public and government, 13
  rights when union tries to organize, 147–9
  role in collective bargaining, 150–1
  time analysis chart, 46–7
  traits, 18–19
  types, 30–2
  understudy, 288–9
Supervisory levels, 5
  first-line supervisors, 5
  middle-level supervisors, 5
  pyramid of, Figure 1-1, 6
  top-level supervisors, 5

Supervisory skills, 7–9
  conceptual, 9
  human, 8–9
  technical, 7–8
Supervisory style, 45
Suspending employees, 167–8

Talking, 65
Taxes and equipment replacement, 406–7
Team leader, 32–3
Teamwork, 98–9
Teamwork and leadership, 32–3
Technical skills, 7–8
Theory X, 102
Theory Y, 102–3
Time, 41–58
  as a resource, 42
  budgeting, 47–9
  how wasted, 43–4
  planning use of, 44–5
  time analysis chart, 46–7
  use of computers, 54
  wise use of, 49–53
Time analysis chart, 46–7
Time study, *see also* Measuring work
  allowances, 383
  determining selected time, 382
  developing time standard, 381–5
  elements, 381
  employee complaints, 391
  equipment used, 381
  explaining to employee, 391–2
  fair standards, 390
  how made, 381–5
  loose standards, 390
  performance rating, 382–3
  and piece rates, 385–6
  and quality, 385
  rating the operator, 382–3
  selected time, 382
  selecting operator, 381
  and standard data, 387–8
  standard time, 380
  standard working conditions, 381
  steps in a job, 381
  tight standards, 390
  union reactions, 386–7, 389–90
  work sampling, 388–9
Title VII, 152
Total-life average method, 407
Training, 321–9
  classroom, 323–4
  common mistakes in, 325–8
  how to train, 322–4
  making jobs easier, 324–5
  making training more effective, 325–8
  need for, 321–2
  on-the-job, 322
  types of, 322–4
  vestibule, 322–3
  worth the effort, 328–9
Transportation, 356, 360
Treasurer, 272
Two-way communications, 66
Types of discipline, 167–8
Types of leaders, 30–2

Undepreciated book value, 405–6
Understanding in leadership, 34

Understanding orders, 219–20
Understanding yourself and employees,113–14
Understudy for supervisor, 288–9
Unions, 144–51
    collective bargaining, 149–50
    defined, 144
    effect on supervisor, 145–7
    relations between supervisor and union steward, 151
    supervisor and collective bargaining, 150–1
    supervisor's rights with union, 147–9
    and time study, 386–7, 389–90
    why workers join, 144–5
    why workers reject, 145
Unity of command, 285–6
Upward communications, 75–6
Using time wisely, 41–58

Vestibule training, 322–3
Voting in meetings, 209–10

What a supervisor does, 4–20
White-collar employees, supervision of, 229

Women, supervision of, 224–5, 229
Words
    choice of in communications, 65
    meaning, 65
    used in orders, 220
Work groups, 118
    leadership in, 29
    quality circles, 118–19
Work sampling, 388–9
Work simplification, *see* Methods improvement
Working with others, 112–13
Written communications, 77–8
    evaluation of, 83
    form to use, 81–2
    length, 78
    letters, 81–2
    rules, 79–81
    style, 78–9
Written discipline, 167